AMERICA ON THE WORLD STAGE

AMERICA
ON THE WORLD
STAGE

A GLOBAL APPROACH
TO U.S. HISTORY

THE ORGANIZATION OF
AMERICAN HISTORIANS

EDITED BY
GARY W. REICHARD
AND TED DICKSON

THE UNIVERSITY OF ILLINOIS PRESS
Urbana and Chicago

Library of Congress Cataloging-in-Publication Data
America on the world stage : a global approach to
U.S. history / The Organization of American Historians ;
edited by Gary Reichard and Ted Dickson.
p.   cm.
Includes bibliographical references and index.
ISBN-13: 978-0-252-03345-2 (cloth : alk. paper)
ISBN-10: 0-252-03345-0 (cloth : alk. paper)
ISBN-13: 978-0-252-07552-0 (pbk. : alk. paper)
ISBN-10: 0-252-07552-8 (pbk. : alk. paper)
1. United States—History—Study and teaching.
2. United States—Historiography.
I. Reichard, Gary W.
II. Dickson, Ted.
III. Organization of American Historians.
E175.8.A52   2008
973.007—dc22   2007052553

CONTENTS

PREFACE

GARY W. REICHARD, COEDITOR
AND JOINT ADVISORY BOARD CHAIR

TED DICKSON, COEDITOR

This volume represents the culmination of a collaborative project undertaken by the Organization of American Historians and the College Board's Advanced Placement Program in 2003. The prime movers of the collaboration were Lee W. Formwalt, executive director of the OAH; Michael Johanek, then of the College Board; and Uma Venkateswaran of the Educational Testing Service. The Joint Advisory Board they assembled represents a combination of secondary- and university-level historians with long experience in teaching the United States history survey. Several—but not all—of the historians on the advisory board have had substantial experience with the United States History Advanced Placement program. That experience has helped influence choices of themes and topics for coverage in the series, but the essays and teaching strategies contained in this volume are aimed at instructors of the basic United States history survey course at all levels.

Specifically, the essays in the "America on the World Stage" series, all of which first appeared in issues of the *OAH Magazine of History,* are designed to offer practical assistance to both secondary- and college-level instructors in the design and substance of the U.S. history course. The series was inspired by the recommendation of the OAH's *La Pietra Report* (2000) that the time had come for "rethinking American History in a global age." Such a reframing is necessary, as the authors of the *Report* argued, so that students "will better understand the emergence of the United States in the world and the significance of its power and presence." The United States history survey course, the authors note, "is properly a focal point for the creation of an international American history." In the years since the appearance of the *La*

Pietra Report, the need for such a reframing of the U.S. survey has become more compelling, as the impact of globalization is increasingly manifest in everyday American life. If we are to succeed in preparing today's young Americans for life as global citizens, it is important to help them understand how the United States has always been part of world history.

Internationalizing the U.S. history survey should provide a way for instructors to bring global perspectives to their courses by offering new contexts in which to approach fundamental issues in U.S. history. The essays in this volume each cover a specific chronological period, placing significant topics and events in United States history in international context. In treating their topics, the authors—all outstanding scholars in their areas of specialization—were asked to emphasize both the importance and distinctiveness of the American national experience in the context of world history. They were invited to treat their respective themes and subjects in either comparative or interactive context (that is, showing how events in the United States have been interrelated with events elsewhere). A number of the essays incorporate both of these approaches.

We have not attempted to constrain authors by insisting that they adhere to the traditional periodization of the survey course, although some essays—notably, those on the Declaration of Independence, the American Civil War and Reconstruction, and the civil rights movement will likely fit smoothly into most instructors' syllabi. Other essays provide information that instructors may be able to insert in more than one place in their courses. Some may even suggest ways to reorder and even re-periodize the survey course. Our objective in collecting these essays, however, was to provide survey instructors with ways to bring new perspectives to the survey course without necessitating a makeover of the course's structure.

Because these essays are intended for use by high school and college-level survey course instructors, we asked our authors to present their insights and ground their pieces in the most recent scholarship, while avoiding jargon and extensive historiographical discussion. For instructors who may wish to dig more deeply into some of the themes and concepts in each essay, authors have included annotated bibliographies or bibliographical essays that cite the most important and useful works on the subject. We hope that readers will agree that all essays are written in an accessible style, even while reflecting the authors' mastery of the most recent literature in their respective fields.

Although each of these essays has already appeared in the *OAH Magazine of History,* this volume represents more than a convenient collection of all essays. Appearing for the first time in print are teaching strategies—one for each of the fourteen essays in the series—that have been constructed by successful U.S. survey instructors at both the secondary and postsecondary levels. The authors of these strategies explore ways that the content of the essays can be presented to students and ways that these ideas have changed or will change their teaching. A number of these authors address most or all of the concepts found in the essays; others focus on just a few of the points made in the essays. These instructors explore a number of primary sources that can be used successfully to broaden the scope of the survey, including posters, cartoons, songs, and documents. Several of the authors discuss refocusing their surveys; others suggest contextualizing to alter the focus of what teachers are already including. Readers will find in these teaching strategies valuable suggestions for globalizing their survey courses without adding too much to their syllabi.

On behalf of the Joint OAH–Advanced Placement Advisory Board, and of the sponsoring organizations of this series, we want to acknowledge and thank the more than thirty outstanding historians who helped authors refine their essays by providing review and comment along the way. To ensure that each essay would reflect a global approach, we engaged one United States history scholar and one world history scholar to critique each one. These anonymous reviewers greatly strengthened the essays—and thus, this volume. The coeditors wish also to thank our colleagues on the Joint Advisory Board: Joyce Chaplin of Harvard University; Michael Grossberg of Indiana University; David Huehner of the University of Wisconsin; Michele Forman of Middlebury Union High School (Vermont); Michael Johanek, now of the University of Pennsylvania, who participated actively until he left the College Board in 2005; Lawrence Charap, who has participated on behalf of the College Board since 2005; Uma Venkateswaran; Kevin Byrne and Phillip M. Guerty, who have served on the board in their respective terms as editor of the *OAH Magazine of History* (the changing of the guard occurred in 2006); and Lee W. Formwalt and Michael Regoli, both of the OAH. For the first few essays in the series, Susanna Robbins, then assistant editor of the *OAH Magazine of History,* was also a constructive and helpful colleague in the project. OAH staff Amy Stark, Ashley Howdeshell, Zachary Vonnegut-Gabovitch, Phillip M. Guerty, Michael Regoli, Chad Parker, Jason Groth, and Keith Eberly assisted with copyediting the manuscript. We are also indebted to Eric Rothschild, who provided editorial help in connection with the teaching strategies in this volume.

We hope that readers will enjoy and learn from the contents of this volume, and that the essays and accompanying teaching strategies will make a positive contribution to the internationalizing of U.S. history as called for in the *La Pietra Report.*

INTRODUCTION
THE REVOLT AGAINST ENCLOSURE:
U.S. HISTORY OPENS OUT TO THE WORLD

THOMAS BENDER

There is ample evidence that U.S. history as taught and written is beginning to overflow the channel established by the national narrative. Though there is considerable variation in the positioning of the territorial nation, and boundaries are increasingly treated like borders rather than barriers, the national history is still what American historians are teaching and writing. It is, however, increasingly being written in a new key. U.S. history is being examined in a larger context, one that denies to the nation-state the privilege of being its own historical context. Such historiographical initiatives represent a fuller address to the study of American national history, an enlargement of the frame of analysis and an extension of the interpretive context.

This volume, which displays the historian's craft being exercised at a very high level of professional skill, offers a sampling of this new scholarship. In the following chapters new and significant perspectives tumble off the pages. Causal interpretations are enriched, novel findings are reported, issues are sharpened, and new variables are introduced in appraising significance. And the gross simplifications inherent in the notion of "American exceptionalism," a line of thinking common among historians and laypersons in the early cold war years and resurgent today, are exposed.

The United States is at once entangled in the larger world and distinct, even unique—as is every other nation. Instead of exceptionalism, which presumes the United States to be *here* and the world *over there,* the world becomes a diverse terrain of polities, all different, all interdependent. The greatest contribution of this more worldly approach to the American national narrative is the most obvious: the global connections so widely noticed today are not novel. We are, as the *New York Journal of Commerce* put it in 1898, "a part of abroad." The editorial writers were right, but they thought it was a novel condition—a product of the newly acquired overseas empire. In fact, from the point of the first European arrivals in the Western Hemisphere, this Hemisphere has been a participant in global history. Current historiography and this volume put U.S. history into that global history.

This book demonstrates that from the national beginning there was an intense awareness of the world of nations. The compelling article on the Declaration of Independence shows how the Declaration articulated the founders' desire to have the newly proclaimed United States take its place among those nations. We see too in that chapter the subsequent global circulation of the ideas and even some of the Declaration's precise language. This expansive context, including the reception of the Declaration at the time and by later generations, recovers the historical career of the document. In compact fashion the chapter reveals a common pattern of an ahistorical reading of it. We tend to deem phrases that became important in the age of the Civil War, such as the declaration of the equality of men, as central, when at the time the Declaration was written the most important passages were understood to be those claiming a place in the community of nations. It was that passage, as well, that appealed to anticolonial nationalists nearly two centuries later. If the Declaration of Independence, truly the founding document of the distinct polity that became the United States, is better understood in an international context, then surely other aspects of U.S. history must lend themselves to such analysis. And that is precisely what this book offers.

A sketch of the context out of which the current interest in transnational and global approaches to U.S. history has emerged may serve as a useful introduction to the essays in this volume.

That the nation-state is both self-contained and the natural carrier of history has been a foundational assumption, usually unstated and unexamined because it seems so obvious and natural. The reason for this blindness is historical. It is the legacy of the founding moment of academic disciplines in the nineteenth century, which was, after all, the age of nation making. The newly established academic discipline of history was a collaborator in that process. Our job as historians—whether in universities, secondary schools, or museums and historical societies—was to contribute to the formation of national citizens. The special work of a national history was to constitute a national common memory that would in turn create a national people as loyal citizens and sovereigns. To do that it was thought that the nation had to be presented as the fundamental and exclusive form of solidarity and identity.

Although among American historians this assumption was occasionally challenged, it persisted and was even strengthened—becoming a strong conception of American exceptionalism—during World War II and in the early years of the cold war.[1] In the past two decades, however, there has been a continuous and growing tendency to question such historiographical enclosure. Within the Organization of American Historians (OAH) there was a movement to "internationalize" the study of U.S. history. This meant more than looking beyond the nation's borders. It also hoped to bring foreign scholars into the conversation of U.S. history, both to learn more about their point of view and to help Americanists in the United States acquire a bit more perspective from outside the nation. A larger frame of reference was sought as a form of intellectual cosmopolitanism. The OAH presidencies of Joyce Appleby of UCLA and Linda Kerber of the University of Iowa in the 1990s particularly forwarded this agenda, as did the editorship of David Thelen at the *Journal of American History*. In 1996, the OAH and the International Center for Advanced Studies at New York University established a collaborative project that involved four summer meetings of scholars from the United States and every continent at La Pietra, an NYU villa in Florence, Italy. Participants sought to explore the issue of international cooperation among historians and to rethink the basic narrative of U.S. history in a way that would open both research and teaching to the world, placing U.S. history into its world context. The meetings produced two published results: The *La Pietra Report* (2000), which focuses especially on curriculum, and a collection of essays oriented to research issues, *Rethinking American History in a Global Age* (2002).[2] The essays in the latter volume revealed the substantial research that had emerged in recent years, plus much that had been rediscovered. They did much more than synthesize what had become available; they moved onto new and exciting transnational terrains in each of the fields covered.

What prompted this shift in the scholarly and teaching orientation of the profession? It is best explained by putting the discipline into a larger context. The phrases "globalization" and "multiculturalism" both entered public discourse in the 1980s, and by the 1990s they were penetrating the logic of the discipline. Multiculturalism was partly the result of the rise of social history with its attention to questions of class, race, gender, region, religion, and more. That work exposed the complexity of American society, particularly in the lives of those Americans on the margins who did not participate in the supposed consensus posited in 1950s scholarship. It became clear that the nation was constituted by a variety of histories smaller than the United States itself.[3] If social history and multiculturalism thus heightened awareness of subnational histories, the growing talk about globalization made historians take note of the permeability of national borders. Like historians always, their first question concerned novelty: Was this really so new? They already knew that multiculturalism had a deep history in American life. A quick survey revealed that so did global connections.

Although they always knew that the nation-state was a recent development, it was only in the 1990s that historians began to explore the implications of that fact. Of course, empirical evidence invited such inquiry. And the oddity of calling an event that occurred a thousand years ago in what is now the national territory of France "medieval French history" was evident. But larger intellectual trends were at work as well. What is sometimes called "postmodernism," a slogan celebrated by self-styled academic avant-gardists and bemoaned by traditionalists, both prompted a critical attitude toward inherited categories and understood them in historicist terms. This opened the nation-state to interrogation, making it a product of history, thus with a trajectory and a context beyond itself. Ironically, this "advance" in scholarly practice was a return to "thinking with history," the nineteenth-century tendency to historicize modernity.[4] In the nineteenth century, however, historicism solidified categories, while in the late twentieth century, historicism opened these categories to critical inspection: race, gender, and nation. The reemergence of historicist thinking freed the historical imagination, allowing—even encouraging—scholars to follow people, money, ideas, and things across national borders.

In the course of opening U.S. history to the world, historians found predecessors among the most distinguished historians of the 1890s. One could even argue that the new scholarly initiative that motivates this book is a return to professional origins; it is traditional. The 1890s were the first moment of modern or self-conscious globalization, and historians responded to these developments and the talk about it. People all over the world were intensely conscious of their interconnection. Direct foreign investment (as a percentage of total investment), a usual measure of globalization in our time, was greater in the 1890s than the 1990s. With our Internet we think we have initiated rapid communication, but a century ago they spoke of the instantaneous communication made possible by the telegraph and oceanic cables. Steamships, which are for us considered leisurely vacations, for them crossed oceans with lightning speed. They spoke constantly of the annihilation of space. W. E. B. Du Bois, whose Harvard dissertation on the suppression of the slave trade, published in 1896, was framed in a global context, clearly understood the modern world as small and interconnected. In a commencement address at Fisk University in 1898 he made that point:

> On our breakfast table lies each morning the toil of Europe, Asia, and Africa, and the isles of the sea; we sow and spin for unseen millions, and countless myriads weave and plant for us; we have made the earth smaller and life broader by annihilating distance, magnifying the human voice and the stars, binding nation to nation, until to-day, for the first time in history, there is one standard of human culture as well in New York as in London, in Cape Town as in Paris, in Bombay as in Berlin.[5]

A few years before Du Bois completed his dissertation, Henry Adams published his monumental history of the administrations of Thomas Jefferson and James Madison. Although it begins very locally, with accounts of the new nation's major cities appraising them as centers of civilization in comparison with Europe, the multivolume history encompasses the whole world and is based on archives of multiple nations.[6] In 1891, two years after Adams's opus was published and two years before his famous frontier essay appeared, Frederick Jackson Turner published an essay on the larger topic of "The Significance of History." Addressed to a group of Wisconsin teachers, Turner's piece urged upon them the importance of the interconnection of all national histories. Recognizing that national boundaries rein in neither people nor history, he explained that "in history . . . there are only artificial divisions." No country, he continued "can be understood without taking account of all the past; it is also true that we cannot select a stretch of land and say we will limit our study to this land; for local history can only be understood in the light of the history of the world." Invoking the same processes linking the world together that had impressed Du Bois, Turner drew a historiographical lesson: no nation can be studied alone as if it were self-contained.

> To know the history of contemporary Italy, we must know the history of contemporary France, of contemporary Germany. Each acts on each. Ideas, commodities even, refuse the bounds of a nation. All are inextricably connected, so that each is needed to explain the others. This is especially true in the modern world, with its complex commerce and means of intellectual communication.[7]

In 1912, J. Franklin Jameson, who did more than any other historian of his generation to give shape to the profession of history in the United States, made an even more radical suggestion in an article on "The Future Uses of History." "The Age of Nations," he wrote, "is approaching its end." This was an idea then circulating in Atlantic intellectual circles, and he recognized that it had implications for the way historians did their work. "The Nation is ceasing to be the leading form of the world's structure; organizations transcending national boundaries are becoming more numerous and effective." These developments suggested to him that "we are advancing into a new world which will be marked by cosmopolitan thought and sentiment."[8] The experience of this age would, presumably, encourage a view of history that would be attentive to the cosmopolitan aspects of the past.

World War I brought to an end the accelerating thinking of global interconnections, and such historical reflections largely disappeared. With the exception of Du Bois, who embraced Pan-Africanism and related U.S. history to it, American historians tended to respond to the nationalism of the interwar years with nation-bounded histories. But in 1933, Herbert E. Bolton, influenced by Turner as a student at the University of Wisconsin, called for a larger U.S. history of the sort Turner had envisioned nearly a half century earlier. In Bolton's presidential address to the American Historical Association (AHA), he sketched out what he called "The Epic of Greater America." The Berkeley historian of Latin America and of the North American borderlands took his colleagues to task for the tendency to study the "thirteen colonies and the United States in isolation," an approach, he declared, that "has obscured many of the larger factors in their development, and helped to raise up a nation of chauvinists." The justification for broadening this approach, he argued, was not only to shape better citizens, but also to achieve greater historical verisimilitude. In the spirit of his mentor, he urged his colleagues to recognize that "each local story will have clearer meaning when studied in the light of the others."[9]

During World War II the issue of a broader, international approach to the teaching of U.S. history reemerged. Both within the discipline and in the wider public there was a discussion about the role of history in respect to challenges presented by the war and of the issues of future world affairs. The prompt for the discussion was a survey of college students to determine their knowledge of U.S. history. On the basis of a survey of seven thousand students at thirty-four institutions of higher learning, the *New York Times* concluded that they knew scandalously little.

The *Times* made it a cause, and one of its leading reporters, Benjamin Fine, won a Pulitzer Prize for his series—written from a point of view but quite well informed and fair—on the state of American history in the schools. Columbia University historian Allan Nevins was also a major advocate—often on the pages of the *Times*. His point was quite direct: Without knowledge of U.S. history, how would our soldiers know what they were fighting for? He also insisted that the nation was the proper unit of historical narrative. Particularly in wartime, he explained, "national identity" must be emphasized, and nothing could produce such self-understanding but the historical study of national development.[10]

Historians agreed with Nevins on the importance of U.S. history and the need for better teaching.[11] But many were concerned by the prospect of a parochial or isolationist historiography. These historians were no less "one-worlders" than Wendell Willkie, whose book, *One World,* was published in 1943, or than Henry Luce, whose famous "American Century" article in *Life* magazine insisted that "our world . . . is one world, fundamentally indivisible."[12] Anti-isolationist historians were pressing for world history courses and U.S. history courses that located U.S. history in that context.

Two efforts were made to establish U.S. history guidelines for the schools that would better prepare students to be citizens ready for the new international responsibilities likely to be thrust upon the United States after the war. The first was initiated by the Division of Higher Education in the Federal Security Administration, which contacted the American Historical Association about the possibility of devising a report on "Adjustment of the College Curriculum to Wartime Conditions and Needs." In 1943, the AHA established a committee chaired by Professor Bessie L. Pierce of the University of Chicago, and the project was staffed entirely by members of the Chicago department. They thought that world history was a pertinent curriculum response to the circumstances of the world war—the growing power and responsibility of the United States. For that reason, the professors developed a world history syllabus, but they also developed a syllabus for a more worldly U.S. history course. In their report, they argued that "the college survey course in United States history, even when it is ably taught, does not give enough attention to the hemispheric and world setting of our history." U.S. history, according to the Pierce group, "must be wider in scope than United States history alone." The proposal was clearly driven by an anti-isolationist politics, a point especially pressed by Walter Johnson, a newly recruited assistant professor; putting the point negatively, they wrote that the survey course and curriculum generally "should serve as an antidote to our traditional isolationism and provincialism." More positively, they proposed that it "provide a worldwide frame of reference for our domestic as well as our foreign problems."[13] There were other syllabi and even courses taught at the University of North Carolina and Barnard; at the latter Eugene Byrne mounted a course titled "De-Isolationized U.S. History: World History from the American Standpoint, 1500–1942." There were experiments elsewhere, but the Pierce proposal was the most ambitious, and it was circulated to all American colleges and universities by the Federal Security Administration. But, as we shall see, it was displaced in public discussion by a more nationalist movement for U.S. history—pure, simple, essentialized—and a lot of it.

There was another large project prompted by the *Times* survey. With funding from the Rockefeller Foundation, the American Historical Association, the Mississippi Valley Historical Association (today's Organization of American Historians), and the National Council for the Social Studies collaborated on an examination of history teaching. Challenging the claims of Nevins, the *Times,* and many patriotic groups that not enough U.S. history was taught, they argued instead that enough was taught, but that too much of it was taught poorly. Chaired by Professor Edgar B. Wesley of the University of Minnesota, the Special Committee on the Teaching of American History proposed what might be called a critical understanding of history. They rejected memorization, stressing what we might today call analytical skills and historical thinking: The emphasis should be on important events and themes; the development of interpretive and synthesizing skills; the capacity to "distinguish between fact and opinion"; and skills in reading and interpreting maps, charts, and other forms of data presentation. Finally, the committee encouraged development of skills for group discussions of historical questions. They also argued that U.S. history should be written and taught toward producing in the minds of students a "keen consciousness of the world beyond the United States." The report pointed out that the United States has never been "isolated."[14] Students should be taught U.S. history with a "continuous awareness of the relations between the United States and the rest of the world."[15] There was substantial support within the profession for such an approach to U.S. history, including versions of the history of the Americas (following Herbert E. Bolton) and the Atlantic world.[16]

Nevins, who held to a strongly exceptionalist view of U.S. history, was sharply critical of anything that would dilute the amount of U.S. history taught or that would blend it into a larger history. While not explicitly anticosmopolitan, the position of Nevins and the *Times* undercut efforts to broaden U.S. history. Their efforts fueled a panic that not enough U.S. history was being taught, or that it was not even being taught at all. The one-worlder Willkie, apparently thinking that the crisis was the entire absence of U.S. history in the curriculum, was quoted by the *New York Times* as saying that "it is about time that United States history should be taken up in United States schools."[17] Two-thirds of college presidents felt the same way, as did the National Education Association, the National Association of Manufacturers, the General Society of Mayflower Descendants, and the Daughters of the American Revolution. And, of course, the omnipresent and always quotable President Nicholas Murray Butler of Columbia University weighed in on the subject of more U.S. history, pointing out that the national story of the United States is a model for the future of the world.[18]

The result of the debate that played on for months, not only in the *Times* but in newspapers across the country, was not de-provincialism but a deeper provincialism, marked by the flowering of American Civilization programs, all embedded in exceptionalist thinking. Many state legislatures and local school boards mandated U.S. history within this frame. In 1950, Edgar Wesley, who had chaired the committee that had insisted the problem was poor teaching and parochialism, not an insufficient number of courses, declared: "legislative fiat" had "sentenced American boys and girls of the atomic age to close their eyes to the rest of the world."[19] It was not that the Pierce and Wesley proposals were challenged directly, but they were simply swamped by a number of influential elites and a nervous public concerned about bolstering national identity (and nationalism) and more than ever committed to notions of American exceptionalism. In the circumstance, a cosmopolitan U.S. history seemed irrelevant at best and at worst downright dangerous.[20]

In the aftermath of the 1960s, American historical writing was transformed. Social history, responding in part to social movements and the rights revolution of the period, placed emphasis on conflict, difference, and inequality and thus subverted the exceptionalist "consensus" history of the early cold war years. Clearly, the American past was made up of many histories, some inflected by class, others by race or gender, and still others by region or religion. The nation as container was more complex than had been assumed. It was more difficult to generalize about U.S. history, resulting in a sometimes ungainly but more complex account of American diversity.[21] Other movements weakened the supposed solidity of national borders; reframing African-American U.S. history within the context of an African Diaspora had large implications for both boundaries and identity, as did the Chicano/a movement in the Southwest, speaking as it did of a porous borderland that connected the peoples of Mexico and the United States as much as it separated them.[22] Then, in the 1990s, globalization talk transformed the dimensions of these transnational discussions to the farthest extreme of the globe.

The scholarship and teaching that has resulted, including that in *America on the World Stage,* is various and thus best characterized as transnational, that being the least specific of possible descriptions. Not every transnational theme necessarily extends to fully global dimensions. The idea of borderlands is a regional concept, and so, in a sense, are the Atlantic world or the Pacific world, or the African and Asian diasporas. Yet one must keep open to the possibility of global connections, for the more one examines the past since 1500 the more one sees crucial connections that touch all continents. But just how often and how important is not a matter to decide before the necessary research is completed. And that will take time; this expansion of the domain of U.S. history is still very new, and there is much work to be done. But the immediate lesson is not to stop at the border unless the phenomenon you are explaining definitely stops there. If an idea, person, capital, or thing crosses borders, the inquiry ought to follow it or them into transnational space, even if the question at hand is a national one.

That said, the essays in this volume reveal that a remarkable amount of work has already been done. Some of it is new, as the publication dates in the bibliographies reveal. Yet here and there older works show up, revealing that there has always been an undercurrent of work, even at times when notions of national self-enclosure dominated the profession.

The essays that follow are so concise and so clear that there is no need for my summarizing their various contributions. But offering a few illustrative examples of the insights scattered through each of the essays may entice. Some, perhaps most, are formed out of historical information already known, but under the transnational lens their significance is better appraised and clarified. In addition, the essays and the teaching guides provide strategies for integrating the new insights into courses.

When the nation's founders congratulated themselves on claiming an "equal place among the nations," they were also, in effect, making a "declaration of interdependence." Many lectures on mercantilism—that national trade policy so concerned to hoard gold—are enriched by recognizing that trade was as much about serving a consumer economy as about hoarding specie—an economy global in its reach—including the Pacific, where two-thirds of the world's population lived. The specificity of slavery in the Western Hemisphere can only be understood historically by considering its variation over space, with slavery in the United States considered as one version of the manifold forms of unfree labor—still the dominant form of labor in the eighteenth century—scattered across the globe. American Christianity was at once integrated into the larger Christian world of ideas and piety, but awareness of that very commonality heightens the significance of its radical difference in the United States: the separation of church and state, something unprecedented at the time and perhaps the most radical accomplishment of the American Revolution. What we call the American West was so only from a particular perspective, that of an expanding nation that annihilated indigenous peoples. The United States moved from the country to the city in the late nineteenth century, but so did peoples on every continent. And the uprooting and transplanting of the peoples who moved to the cities was embedded in global systems of economic transformation. The stakes involved in saving the Union are clarified by a global perspective, because looking around the world forces a recognition that working republicanism was an exotic and rare thing in 1860, a local experiment understood by Lincoln and liberals around the world to have universal implications. The destruction of indigenous peoples in North America was part of a larger history of what historians call settler societies. Without taking into consideration the global context of industrial capitalism and urbanization, one cannot understand the emergence of social politics or the sources of the ideas upon which American progressives drew. Every nation resolved the challenge differently depending upon local political alignments and traditions, but the family resemblance is unmistakable.

Self-contained national histories give the impression that there were only two points on the map for immigrants, home and the United States. But in fact migration systems were global, and availability of land and kin, not particular national destinations, were the determinants of migration choices, often marked by multiple stops. One learns that Martin Luther King's powerful phrase, "We Shall Overcome," was quite mobile before and after he invoked it. Originally brought to America by enslaved Africans, it was sung by tobacco workers on strike in the 1940s and later by the supporters of the anti-Apartheid movement in South Africa. Nor was its deployment wholly in the English language. It was sung in Spanish by United Farm Workers and in Arabic by Palestinians. The American civil rights movement was deeply embedded in movements for decolonization. Both movements were part of the same quest for rights by peoples of color. But the U.S. government also linked civil rights to decolonization and sought the support of newly independent nations in Africa during the cold war. Segregation was a blot on America that had to be removed.

Despite what critics in the United States and abroad say, globalization is not Americanization; the transnational movement of culture is transformed in reception and globalization. Human rights movements no less than consumer items can escape the site of the origination and acquire a dynamic of their own. Finally, to understand America in the cold war, it is necessary to look beyond the division of Europe to a global framing. Though the cold war in Europe was cold, there were very hot and devastating wars in the third world, and that is why the European settlement in 1989 did not bring a peaceful new world order. Such and much more is what one learns about a global perspective in these essays.

The notion of autonomous nations was always a myth, but a useful myth in the work of nation making. It was not true to experience, however. The world since 1500 has been interconnected. The writing and teaching of history must accommodate that fact. To the extent we connect U.S. history to the history of the world in which we as a people and a nation are embedded, we advance a self and a national understanding that is more nearly adequate to living in the world as we experience it. It is possible to be both a proud national and a citizen of the world. For me and, I hope, for the readers of this book, it will be important in the coming years to sustain the cosmopolitan citizenship a more worldly U.S. history implies and the sense of human connection it promises to nourish.

Notes

1. Daniel Rodgers, "Exceptionalism," in Anthony Molho and Gordon S. Wood, eds., *Imagined Histories: American Historians Interpret the Past* (Princeton, N.J., 1998), 21–40.

2. The *La Pietra Report* was published in digital and pamphlet form. The digital form may be accessed through the OAH Web site (http://www.oah.org/activities/lapietra/index.html); Thomas Bender, ed., *Rethinking American History in a Global Age* (Berkeley, Calif., 2002)

3. See Herbert G. Gutman, "The Missing Synthesis: Whatever Happened to History," *The Nation* (Nov. 21, 1981), 521, 553–54; Eric Foner, "History in Crisis," *Commonweal* (Dec. 18, 1981), 723–26; Thomas Bender, "Making History Whole Again," *New York Times Book Review* (Oct. 6, 1984), 1, 42–43; Bender, "Wholes and Parts: The Need for Synthesis in American History," *Journal of American History,* 73 (1986), 120–36.

4. See Carl E. Schorske, *Thinking with History: Explorations in the Passage to Modernism* (Princeton, N.J., 1998), especially 3–34.

5. W. E. B. Du Bois, "Careers Open to College-Bred Negroes," in Nathan Huggins, ed., *Du Bois: Writings* (New York, 1986), 831. See his *The Suppression of the Atlantic Slave-Trade to the United States of America, 1638–1870* (New York, 1896).

6. Henry Adams, *The History of the United States of America* (1801–1817), (9 vols., New York, 1889–1891).

7. Frederick Jackson Turner, "The Significance of History," in *Frontier and Section: Selected Essays of Frederick Jackson Turner,* ed. Ray Allen Billington (Englewood Cliffs, N.J., 1961), 20–21.

8. Quoted in Ian Tyrrell, "Making Nations/Making States: American Historians in the Context of Empire," *Journal of American History,* 86 (1999), 1031. A recent article by Charles Maier suggests he and others of his time may not have been wholly off base with such a prediction, though nations and nationalism seem to have revived since Maier wrote. But still see his "Consigning the Twentieth Century to History: Alternative Narratives for the Modern Era," *American Historical Review,* 105 (2000),

807–31. On the more general tendency of intellectuals of the era to think this way, see Thomas Bender, "The Boundaries and Constituencies of History," *American Literary History,* 18 (2006), 273–74. See also Akira Iriye, *Global Community: The Role of International Organizations in the Making of the Contemporary World* (Berkeley, Calif., 2002), introduction and chapter 1.

9. Herbert E. Bolton, "The Epic of Greater America," *American Historical Review,* 38 (1933), 448–49.

10. Allan Nevins, "American History for Americans," *New York Times,* May 2, 1943. Making some of the same points but emphasizing the importance of history, not social studies, see his earlier article, "Why We Should Know Our History," *New York Times,* April 18, 1943. Interestingly, it was the Federal Security Administration, which had a higher-education division, that monitored and kept statistics on the amount of U.S. history being taught in the schools; Ian Tyrrell, *Historians in Public* (Chicago, 2005), 139.

11. Here there was a difference between many historians involved and the *Times*/Nevins position. The former wanted history taught better, Nevins and the *Times* wanted more of it.

12. Quoted in Iriye, *Global Community,* 41.

13. Quotes from Ian Tyrrell's excellent account in his "The Threat of De-Provincializing U.S. History in World War II: Allan Nevins and the *New York Times* to the Rescue," *Amerikastudien/American Studies,* 48 (2003), 42–43. The issue of de-parochializing U.S. history, at least making it part of hemispheric history, was the theme of Herbert E. Bolton's presidential address to the American Historical Association, "The Epic of Greater America," *American Historical Review,* 38 (1933), 448–74.

14. Quotes from Benjamin Fine, "Education in Review: Findings of the Special Committee on the Teaching of American History."

15. Benjamin Fine, "Reforms Prepared for History Study," *New York Times,* Dec. 13, 1943. The report also proposed some sequencing of teaching; college course content should not repeat high school, for instance. They proposed more specialized courses for college.

16. See Tyrrell, "Threat of De-Provincializing U.S. History," 48–50.

17. Quoted in ibid., 51.

18. Quoted in ibid.

19. Quoted in Tyrrell, *Historians in Public,* 139.

20. On the postwar embrace of exceptionalism, see Daniel Rodgers, "Exceptionalism," in *Imagined Histories,* 21–40.

21. See note 3, above.

22. Robin D. G. Kelley, "How the West Was One: The African Diaspora and the Re-Mapping of U.S. History," in Bender, ed. *Rethinking American History,* 123–47; "Rethinking History and the Nation-State: Mexico and the United States as a Case Study: A Special Issue," *Journal of American History,* 86, no. 2 (1999); "The Nation and Beyond: Transnational Perspectives on United States History: A Special Issue," *Journal of American History,* 86, no. 3 (1999).

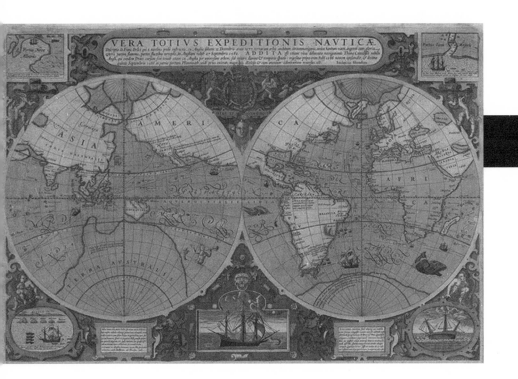

CHAPTER 1

An excerpt from *Vera Expeditionis Nauticae* by
Dutch cartographer Jodocus Hondius, which
records the first English circumnavigation of the
globe by Sir Francis Drake (1577–1580) as well as
by his countryman Thomas Cavendish a few years
later (1586–1588). (Geography and Map Division,
Library of Congress. See The American Treasures
Collection online at <http//www.loc.gov/exhibits/
treasures/trr059.html>.)

AMERICA, THE ATLANTIC, AND GLOBAL CONSUMER DEMAND, 1500–1800

CAROLE SHAMMAS

The Atlantic migration of Europeans and Africans to America and the commercial activities associated with it created an economy that for the first time in history could be called global. For many years, historians have relied upon the word *mercantilism* to capture this international world. Over the last decade, as research has focused more intently on ties between early modern consumers, producers, and distributors in America, Europe, and Africa, the concept of an Atlantic world economic community has eclipsed the mercantilism paradigm. More recently, scholars have cautioned against portraying the commerce of the Atlantic as a separate economic world unto itself and ignoring the true globalism of trade in the period. In discussing the evolving conceptualization of the early modern economy, it is important not only to recognize the commercial growth that occurred during the period, but also to take into account the demographic and environmental changes that were consequences of that growth.

The mercantilist explanation for what kept the early modern economy running is quite straightforward. The kingdoms of Spain, Portugal, Great Britain, and France as well as the Dutch Republic each sought to accumulate wealth through advantageous overseas trading arrangements and colonies, while thwarting the ambitions of their rivals to do the same. America played the role of colony. When I use the term *America* here, I do not just mean the thirteen colonies that bolted from the British Empire in 1776, but rather the entire Western Hemisphere. For nearly all of the period under consideration, the area that became the United States had no separate identity. The thirteen colonies were neither the only colonies nor the only British colonies, and in the view of the rest of the world, none of the thirteen was considered the most important in the New World. That honor would probably go to the sugar islands of the West Indies or, depending on the century, either the viceroyalty of Peru or New Spain, the main sites of silver mines. The scrappy, slave-trading, rum-running, smuggling-prone merchant communities that sprang up in towns like Boston, Newport, New York, Philadelphia, and Charleston might command center stage from the perspective of the national history of the United States, but they contained just a small proportion of the cast of thousands who developed new markets in America.

Though the mercantilist paradigm was a global one, the most common visualization of it in U.S. history textbooks featured a map of Atlantic commerce. This map illustrated the "Triangular Trade" whereby eastern American colonies furnished raw materials, western Africa provided the labor force to produce the raw materials, and the imperial center, often referred to as the Mother Country, shipped manufactured goods to both. Historians pointed to inequities in this system as an important cause of the American Revolution.

Today, this schema has not so much been repudiated as reinterpreted. The most salient economic characteristic of the period remains the growth in overseas commerce, but the term *mercantilism* is now used infrequently, and the marketplace desires of individuals—especially on the consumption side—receive much greater credit for effecting change. Students are encouraged to think less about European empires struggling for control of the major sea lanes and colonial bases to achieve favorable trading balances and more about the Atlantic as a meaningful economic entity where coastal inhabitants from all continents exchanged people and goods without always honoring imperial boundaries.[1]

To Atlantic scholars, it is not just a European or European transplant story. Transatlantic migrants were three times more likely to be from Africa than Europe during the period,[2] and as a result historians now have to take account of the strategies of African kingdoms and institutions in the making of the slave trade.[3] Indian nations are not only relevant as providers of furs and skins and consumers of manufactures and alcohol, but also—as the introducers of new agricultural commodities a prime source of labor and cultural identity in some regions of America. The persistence with which colonists fixed their gaze across the Atlantic, rather than across the American continent, may have had less to do with their attachment to Europe and more to do with the ability of Indian nations to contain colonial settlements to coastal areas, up until the latter eighteenth century.

The availability of land and natural resources in America enabled the collection or production of a wide variety of commodities—furs, lumber, cod, and wheat, for example. It was, however, the demand for two categories of goods that stands out as being most responsible for the continuing flow of capital, labor, and governmental military services across the Atlantic: groceries and silver.

Contemporaries called the tropical dietary items that acted as energizers and appetite appeasers for the population on either side of the Atlantic and in Asia *groceries*. They included tobacco, sugar, sugar byproducts such as molasses and rum, and caffeine drinks, namely tea, coffee, and cocoa. America became the prime site for growing all of these crops except for tea, and the enslaved migrants from Africa became the prime cultivators. Tobacco and the beans to make cocoa were indigenous to America while others—coffee and sugar—were transferred over to take advantage of the low cost of land and the bound labor force. Because many of these plantation commodities were thought of as luxuries—that is, not essential for human survival—their central role in the expansion of the world economy has been often overlooked.[4] That is a misconception, however. By the late seventeenth century, the Dutch and the English dominated the carrying trade over the Atlantic. Seventy-four percent of the value of imports coming into Amsterdam and more than 85 percent coming into London from colonies in America consisted of tobacco and sugar products.[5] At first, consumption spread throughout the aristocratic and more middling classes, who often displayed the paraphernalia—tea service, porcelain tea cups, sugar bowls, clay pipes, snuff boxes—associated with the consumption of these tropical groceries. By the eighteenth century, the laboring classes also used these groceries on a regular basis.[6]

Initially, western European governments gave little encouragement to the consumption of such commodities. In fact royal authorities often disparaged their production and use, considering them either harmful or trivial. Instead, support for the commodities came from transatlantic merchant-planter alliances along with consumers living in maritime communities and urban centers. Once the revenues from the import duties began pouring into the treasury, however, the royals changed their minds. These seemingly frivolous raw materials altered the dietary habits of the Atlantic community and ultimately the world. They were responsible for the spread of the plantation complex, a system of production that would become extremely controversial in the nineteenth-century United States.[7] Taking a specific commodity such as tobacco and tracing the diffusion of consumption and the transformation in production and distribution to meet demand has emerged as an important way to study Atlantic history in the early modern period.

Even the way historians portray the relationship between the commercial system and the American Revolution has been transformed by the Atlantic world approach. Americans reacted to the taxation of sugar products, tea, and British manufactured goods, it has been argued, as consumers. Colonists from disparate provinces with divergent interests could all relate to problems connected to the consumption of the empire's goods. Their mass consumption led to their mass mobilization: resisting the Sugar, Stamp, and Townshend Acts, boycotting tea, pledging nonimportation, and ultimately declaring independence.[8] Rather than viewing the American Revolution as the point at which the colonies threw off mercantilism and embraced economic liberalism, students are now encouraged to regard the market principles of demand and supply as representing the colonial status quo.[9] The colonists, in this telling of the story, mobilized in order to halt any heavy-handed imperial state meddling that would turn back the clock.

The Atlantic world concept has much to recommend it as a way to understand the global economy in which the United States came to be a dominant player. The Atlantic as the supplier of population for America cannot be denied. Migration from other parts of the globe during these years amounted to little more than a trickle. The dramatic transformation of Atlantic commerce is also obvious. For thousands of years prior to the mid-fifteenth century, existing evidence suggests that nothing ventured far out into the Atlantic aside from a few Viking expeditions and occasional fishing vessels, while in the next three hundred years global commerce came to be directed and conducted from nations and cities bordering that ocean. And so it remained until the later twentieth century when the emergence of the Pacific Rim, the European Union, and NAFTA suggest a realignment is now taking place.[10]

Where the Atlantic world paradigm falls short, in the view of some scholars, is in its poor integration of Asia, home to two-thirds of the world's population, into the early modern network of trade. They argue that western

Europe and even parts of the Americas and Africa had relationships with Asia that were as or more important than their relationships with one another.[11] The choice then is whether we should think in terms of two separate worlds operating in this period, the Asian world and the demographically much smaller Atlantic world of which America was a part, or whether we should consider the east-west connection significant enough to argue for a fully integrated global economy.

Those arguing the latter position would point out that capturing the East Indian and Chinese market loomed much larger in the minds of Europeans than anything having to do with America or Africa and that America owed its "discovery" to that preoccupation. Columbus's and his sponsors' stated purpose was not the discovery of a New World but a northwest passage to the "Indies," by which they meant East Asia. Just as the first Portuguese attempts to sail around Africa had been sparked by the hope to establish trade with India, about the only reason for undertaking voyages to the Americas, until Cortes defeated the Aztecs in 1519, was to find East Asia. Even after Cortes's conquest, which led to an influx of sword-wielding military adventurers seeking tribute, a northwest passage project proved much more attractive to merchant investors than any military expedition. The picture changed once again, however, with the discovery of rich silver mines in America. Silver is the other major product that most directly linked America with the global economy and, in terms of chronology, it came before the groceries associated with the plantation complex.

The old histories of mercantilism centered their story on the infusion of Spanish empire silver and gold, the rampant inflation in Europe it produced, and its role in the underdevelopment of Spain and its colonies. The new version of this story considers inflation less of a problem and concentrates on the enormity of Chinese demand for silver, which was needed both to expand its monetary system and to manufacture silver wares. Its willingness to offer advantageous terms of trade for those sought-after commodities created a global commercial network in which America and Africa supplied the bullion and foodstuffs to pay for Asian commodities distributed largely in European ships.[12]

It was the mining of precious metals that kept European kings and commoners interested in the Americas during that awkward half century or so between the last conquistadors and the first big boom in sugar and tobacco cultivation that ushered in the American plantation complex. Not until the discovery of silver at Potosi in the Peruvian vice-royalty during the 1540s did the Spanish Crown, as distinct from private adventurers and religious orders, make a commitment to govern America directly. Forcing Indians to extract the valuable ore, the Spaniards shipped more than fifty tons of silver abroad every year. They sent it across the Atlantic, where their European creditors used it in the Chinese trade, or they transported it across the Pacific to Manila, Spain's East Asian entrepôt. Why in the 1570s did Sir Francis Drake, the famous Elizabethan privateer, venture into the Pacific and circumnavigate the globe? Pure love of adventure? Or could the mines of Peru have had something to do with it? Without the lure of these Atlantic and Pacific fleets full of bullion, the majority of English, French, and Dutch exploration and colonization expeditions would never have materialized.

Western European nations granted monopolies to trading companies, the big businesses of the day, to compete for Asian commodities. Some were dietary products like Chinese tea and spices from what is now known as Indonesia, but others were manufactured goods such as Chinese porcelain and silk and Indian cotton cloth.[13] All of these goods became wildly popular in Europe and America. In fact, in 1720 the British government forbade the importation of cotton cloth because it weakened demand for light woolens, their major industrial product. The Chinese refused to allow western European trading companies to establish permanent facilities in their port cities, so western Europeans, first the Portuguese and then a wider international community, built a commercial center at Macao on the west banks of the Pearl, the river that leads to the Chinese port of Canton. Not until later in the nineteenth century did Hong Kong, on the east side of the Pearl River, overtake Macao. Both cities remained under the control of western Europeans until the end of the twentieth century. Manila, the Spanish entrepôt, also spent most of its history as a colony. Originally, however, these outposts had been set up because it was the only way westerners could obtain Chinese products.

Consumer demand for East Indian commodities grew during the course of the eighteenth century. In an important departure from the past and one that foreshadowed nineteenth-century developments, Europeans learned how to mass-produce "knock-offs" of east and south Asian cloth, furniture, and pottery. It was the manufacturing of Indian-like cotton fabric in Britain that launched the Industrial Revolution. After independence, as the American merchant community regrouped, those on the Atlantic seaboard began competing with their former partners for the lucrative China trade and manufacturing "knock-offs" of their own. Using Hawaii as an entrepôt, the United States also expanded Pacific commerce.[14] By 1800 it was Britain's biggest competitor in the China trade and later in cotton cloth manufacturing.[15]

The three different approaches to understanding the place of pre-1800

America in the international economy each have their strengths and weaknesses. The mercantilism paradigm, emphasizing as it does imperial rivalries, is global in scope but relies almost exclusively on the machinations of European royal governments to explain commercial expansion and colonization. The proponents of the Atlantic world view assert that the use of said ocean as a highway for migrants, capital, and commodities represented the period's biggest change in world trade patterns and that consumer demand from the societies bordering the ocean had much to do with that change. Assuming, however, that a self-contained commercial system existed within the boundaries of that ocean, critics contend, means leaving out more than two-thirds of the earth's consumers, including those in China, India, and Southeast Asia, producers of some of the world's most sought-after commodities. Better integration of such important elements as the silver trade to China, the boom in Indian cotton textiles, and the commercial history of the settlements and islands of the Pacific is a task currently underway, even if the exact importance of each of these elements in the overall picture has yet to be ascertained.

Regardless of the approach, it seems clear that the economic order that took shape after the European discovery of America redistributed unprecedented numbers of people to satisfy a growing global demand for its resources and products that in turn kept more labor and capital flowing in to the so-called New World. Overseas trade has been identified as the leading sector in economic growth during this period. Even in well-established European nations, growth depended primarily on the expansion of the overseas trade sector.[16] A major impetus for the adoption of the U.S. Constitution was the belief that survival as a nation depended on overseas commerce and that its success required a strong central government.

If the origins of world economic growth are linked to this global commerce, other forms of growth that have been associated with the discovery of America appear to be more problematic. The sizable Atlantic migration proved disastrous for the indigenous population, primarily because of its susceptibility to new diseases brought by invaders or merchants who did no more than trade from their sailing vessels anchored offshore.[17] Despite the staggering losses of Indian life in the Americas, the demographic record suggests growth in global population from the time of discovery onward. At first the ascent was modest, with population growth numbers even suggesting a stall in the seventeenth century. Over the course of the eighteenth century, however, world population is estimated to have jumped by 50 percent, and continued to grow dramatically throughout the nineteenth and twentieth centuries.[18]

In the Americas, succeeding generations of Atlantic migrants and their descendants enjoyed high fertility rates in their new low-density environment. Concurrently, Europe's population, despite the out-migration, began to climb, as did China's. Some of this "Old World" growth has been attributed to the transfer of "New World" foodstuffs such as potatoes, sweet potatoes, peanuts, and corn (maize) as well as American sales of wheat and rice in European markets.[19] Although in North America the bounty in foodstuffs and the accompanying high fertility never produced a Malthusian reaction, in certain parts of nineteenth-century Europe and in China it eventually did. The denser population put greater pressure on natural resources. The environmental repercussions of the human species spreading into previously uninhabited parts of the globe is a fascinating subject that deserves a great deal more attention. Nowhere might the investigation be more worthwhile than in America during the period under consideration here.

Bibliographical Essay

Classic treatments of the emergence of global trade include J. H. Parry's beautifully succinct *The Establishment of the European Hegemony 1415–1715: Trade and Exploration in the Age of the Renaissance* (New York, 1961); Immanuel Wallerstein's three comprehensive volumes on the modern world-system, *The Modern World-System: Capitalist Agriculture and the Origins of the European World-Economy in the Sixteenth Century, The Modern World-System II: Mercantilism and the Consolidation of the European World-Economy, 1600–1750,* and *The Modern World-System III, The Second Era of Great Expansion of the Capitalist World-Economy, 1730–1840s* (New York, 1974–1989); and Fernand Braudel's magisterial *Civilization and Capitalism III: The Perspective of the World,* tr. Sian Reynolds (Berkeley, Calif., 1992, orig. pub. in French, 1979).

The *OAH Magazine of History,* 18 (April 2004) issue edited by Alison Games is an excellent guide to the ever-growing literature on the Atlantic world approach, particularly as it relates to the area that became the United States. The Atlantic Seminar at Harvard University maintains a Web site, <http://www.fas.harvard.edu/~atlantic/> that features recent research in the field and has links to other sites of interest. In addition to the Thornton book on the African Atlantic cited below, the existing ship manifests recording the African migration across the Atlantic are now available for study on CD: David Eltis et al., *The Transatlantic Slave Trade: A Database on CD-Rom* (New York, 1999). The most exhaustive examination of transatlantic commerce is for Spain in the sixteenth and seventeenth centuries, in Huguette Chaunu and Pierre Chaunu, *Seville et l'Atlantique* (1504–1640) (8 vols., Paris, 1955–1959). The phenomenal rise in consumer demand for groceries and the growth of the plantation complex is documented in Curtin, Mintz, Enthoven, Zahedieh, and Shammas, mentioned below. For those seeking a regional breakdown of Anglo-American trade, see John J. McCusker and Russell R. Menard, *The Economy of British America 1607–1789* (Chapel Hill, N.C., 2nd ed., 1991). Breen's book, below, relates the American Revolution to the Atlantic trade boom.

The need to take a global rather than an Atlantic world perspective, as expressed in Coclanis's essay cited below, comes largely from studying the work on monetary flows, Asian commerce, and the Pacific Rim. Dennis O. Flynn, in the article he co-authored below and in a series of other books and articles, has made the strongest case that the demand for silver in China created an integrated global economy both Atlantic and Pacific. In addition to the works on Chinese commerce and products by Dermigny and Wills cited below, a number of volumes have recently appeared confirming the size, allure, and sophistication of Chinese, Indian, and Southeast Asian production during the period 1500 to 1800. Coclanis's essay cites many of them. Kenneth Pomeranz and Steven Topik, *The World that Trade Created: Society, Culture, and the World Economy: 1400 to the Present* (Armonk, N.Y., 1999) is designed for a general audience that picks up on that theme, among others.

Colin McEvedy and Richard Jones, *Atlas of World Population History* (New York, 1978) remains the best source for world population figures. The USC–Huntington Library Institute for Early Modern Studies has a new Web site <http://college.usc.edu/emsi/> that offers a list of recent papers with a world perspective on specific topics. Finally, <http://www.h-net.org> is the Web address for H-Net, which features numerous networks for different fields in history, among them h-world and h-atlantic. These networks offer teaching resources, discussions, and reviews.

Notes

1. The April 2004 issue [volume 18, no. 3] of the *OAH Magazine of History*, entitled "The Atlantic World" and edited by Alison Games, takes this approach and focuses on three themes in the Atlantic: disease, commodities, and migration. The issue contains references to the many books and articles that have been written on early modern Atlantic communities in the past two decades.

2. James Horn and Philip D. Morgan, "Settlers and Slaves: European and African Migrations to Early Modern British America," in Elizabeth Mancke and Carole Shammas, eds., *Creation of the British Atlantic World* (Baltimore, forthcoming).

3. John Thornton, *Africa and Africans in the Making of the Atlantic World, 1400–1800*, 2nd ed. (New York, 1998).

4. Immanuel Wallerstein, *The Modern World System: Capitalist Agriculture and the Origins of the European World-Economy in the Sixteenth Century* (New York, 1974), 41–42.

5. Victor Enthoven, "An Assessment of Dutch Transatlantic Commerce, 1585–1817," in *Riches from Atlantic Commerce: Dutch Transatlantic Trade and Shipping, 1585–1817,*

ed. Johannes Postma and Victor Enthoven (Leiden, Neth., 2003), 438; Nuala Zahedieh, "Overseas Expansion and Trade in the Seventeenth Century," in *Oxford History of the British Empire: Origins of Empire,* ed. Nicholas Canny (Oxford, 1998), 410.

6. Carole Shammas, *The Preindustrial Consumer in England and America* (Oxford, 1990).

7. Philip D. Curtin, *The Rise and Fall of the Plantation Complex: Essays in Atlantic History,* rev. ed. (New York, 1998). Sidney Mintz recounts this process in *Sweetness and Power: The Place of Sugar in Modern History* (New York, 1985).

8. T. H. Breen, *The Marketplace of Revolution: How Consumer Politics Shaped American Independence* (New York, 2004).

9. Economic liberalism is used here in its nineteenth-century sense of belief in market forces of demand and supply rather than governmental policies directing production and consumption.

10. The later twentieth century witnessed a significant geographic shift of world trade toward the Pacific Rim.

11. Peter A. Coclanis, "Drang Nach Osten: Bernard Bailyn, the World-Island, and the Idea of Atlantic History," *Journal of World History,* 13 (2002): 169–82.

12. Dennis O. Flynn and Arturo Giraldez, "Cycles of Silver: Global Economic Unity through the Mid-Eighteenth Century," *Journal of World History,* 13 (2002): 391–428, and Enthoven, "Assessment of Dutch Transatlantic Commerce," 435–36 refer to the Dutch use of American silver for East Indies trade.

13. John E. Wills Jr., "European Consumption and Asian Production in the Seventeenth and Eighteenth Centuries," in *Consumption and the World of Goods,* ed. John Brewer and Roy Porter (London, 1993), 133–47.

14. David Igler, "Diseased Goods: Global Exchanges in the Eastern Pacific Basin, 1770–1850," *American Historical Review,* 109 (2004): 693–719.

15. See the statistics in Louis Dermigny, *La Chine et L'Occident: Le Commerce a Canton au XVIIIe Siecle 1719–1833 tome II* (Paris, 1964), 521–28, 532, 539, 735, and 744 that show the scope of America's entry into the tea trade from the 1780s on and also its supplying of silver and cotton.

16. Robert C. Allen, "Progress and Poverty in Early Modern Europe," *Economic History Review,* 56 (2003): 431; Kevin H. O'Rourke and Jeffrey G. Williamson, "After Columbus: Explaining Europe's Overseas Trade Boom, 1500–1800," *Journal of Economic History,* 62 (2002): 417–62. The latter article asks a number of good questions about the reasons for the boom in trade but lacks the evidence to prove its central contention that transport costs did not decline over the three-hundred-year period.

17. Igler, "Diseased Goods."

18. Colin McEvedy and Richard Jones, *Atlas of World Population History* (New York, 1978), 342.

19. Flynn and Giraldez, "Cycles of Silver," concerning the effects of the transfer of maize, sweet potatoes, and peanuts over the Pacific.

IMAGINING A WORLD WITHOUT TEA AND SUGAR:
TEACHING STRATEGIES FOR AMERICA, THE ATLANTIC, AND GLOBAL CONSUMER DEMAND, 1500–1800

JONATHAN CHU

The vast sweep of this subject requires the use of discrete, manageable topics to help students retain content knowledge while learning complex analytical skills. Issues of consumer demand join macroeconomic considerations—mercantilism, the Western Hemisphere's impact upon foodways, global trade—to individual economic decision making, and can explain how colonial discontent led to the American Revolution. Furthermore, framing large international and global developments in terms of individual economic behaviors resonates with students because it places consumer transactions and the accompanying indices of social and cultural behavior into more familiar patterns.[1]

Developing lectures based on my students' current knowledge is central to my teaching.[2] Classes begin with a question that leads to a collaborative lecture. In dealing with the American Revolution and its consequences, tea and sugar provide an effective thematic spine for addressing the causes and consequences of the conflict. This focus seeks to teach students about 1) the emergence of Americans' cultural identification with Great Britain, 2) the recognition of global consumer markets, and 3) an understanding of the continuities and discontinuities that transcended independence.

"Why," I ask students, "would small taxes on sugar and tea lead colonists to revolt against a nation with which a decade earlier they had so clearly identified?" Desperate for revenue after 1763, Parliament was deterred from further raising taxes and coincidentally faced the failure of the British East India Company to pay its annual dividend. It discovered a solution it thought was consistent with mercantile policies, beneficial to the company and the consumer of its tea, and more productive in the collection of taxes. Imagining a world without tea and sugar helps students see how this mundane process of governing the empire transformed colonial patriotism into resistance and rebellion. "What is the big deal about tea and sugar?" "What do you know about English tea ceremonies?" "Who can," I ask them to speculate, "'take tea?'" "Who knows who Josiah Wedgwood is, or what Wedgwood porcelain is?"

This discussion leads me to use visual images to stimulate a discussion about the place of tea in Anglo-American culture. Tea consumption reflected colonists' understandable desires to be thoroughly modern, fashionable, eighteenth-century Britons. The rise of tea drinking—or more accurately, taking tea—illustrates Americans' cultural identification with the mother country in the same way the architecture of Boston's Old State House, Williamsburg's Governor's Palace, and Philadelphia's Independence Hall illustrates the British Empire's hold on colonial government.[3] An image of Paul Revere's silver teapot illustrates social elites engaged in tea drinking. A Wedgwood teapot image represents more widespread tea drinking out of more modest, but still socially pretentious, chinaware.[4]

Discussing English tea ceremonies also leads students to the connection between sugar and tea and to the ways that the use of the two commodities denoted social class. Students invariably see tea as having analgesic effects, sugar as ameliorating its bitterness, and the household ceremony as being associated with women and the home.[5] Also, as in students' own lives, the aping of fashion by the less socially adept led to predictable and memorable faux pas committed by the conspicuous consumption of the nouveau riche. "One family," a New York woman reported, "boiled it in a pot and ate it like samp-porridge"; another told of someone who "spread tea leaves on his bread and butter."[6]

As taking tea became more fashionable, it contributed to American resistance to British tax policies after the Seven Years' War.[7] In 1766, the imported

Maidstone teapot celebrated the repeal of the Stamp duties and illustrated the joining of American protest over taxes and the attraction of British fashion. Manufactured in England for export to America, the pot illustrates the economic and cultural interdependence of colony and mother country.

The very pervasiveness of colonial customs represented both the colonists' identity with the empire and the lever Parliament used for its own immediate needs. The reduction in the sugar and tea taxes explains why Parliament thought it was acting judiciously and why colonists thought their liberties were endangered. Eliminating all the Townshend duties except those on tea focused attention upon a single commodity that symbolized both the need to increase tax revenues and seemingly arbitrary British policies. It also suggested ways for Parliament to respond to protests and the ways colonies could apply political and economic pressure. Connecting tea to sugar, Britain's first foray into increasing the tax revenues in North America—again with lower taxes on sugar in the American Revenue Act—reminded colonists about the length of the dispute, giving credence to conspiracy theories that the Crown was attempting to deprive them of their liberties.[8] By boycotting tea and sugar, the colonists challenged the legitimacy of Parliament's revenue authority. When the government decided to relieve the financial distress of the East India Company by allowing direct shipments to America, the colonists were convinced of the conspiracy to impose tyranny upon them. This fact was proven further by the imposition of the Intolerable or Coercive Acts.[9] Conversely, students are asked to consider why British politicians were confused by American protest. The Janus-like quality of the measures taken to deal with the Boston Tea Party can be portrayed as an act designed to coerce lawlessness into obedience or to impose an intolerable tyranny upon Bostonians.[10]

Tea and sugar also connect students to the consequences of independence. Students can examine the structural continuities that determined new trade patterns and the practical influences of the Constitution. The objectives of this discussion point out 1) the unanticipated consequences of the demise of British imperial regulatory mechanisms, 2) the uncertainties of the future American economy, 3) how existing structures defined future trade activities, and 4) the links between economic activity and the rise of constitutional government. Similar to the questions on sugar and tea, I ask students to use their knowledge as a bridge to future learning, to consider what would happen to residents of Massachusetts if the federal government disappeared. The question elicits a discussion on the adjustments that have to be made (how would one deliver a letter from Boston to New York, what money would we use?) or the impact upon patterns of consumption and behavior. A common theme raised is the value of the different currencies. Would the value of our assets in banks disappear, would we cease to denote their values in dollars? Clearly, student response would focus upon how the structures of the marketplace dictated continuities and practical changes that in turn illustrated post-Revolutionary commerce.

Closed out of the empire by the Navigation Acts, American trade developed in patterns consistent with an existing infrastructure and the new circumstances of independence. Smuggling and the West Indies' food trade created incentives for the construction of smaller, shallow-drafted ships designed to sail quickly with fewer sailors. The incentives to build small, quick ships were increased with the advent of privateering during the Revolution.[11] With ships ill suited for high-bulk cargoes, American vessels could not ship grain and tobacco, the prices of which had declined precipitously. Had it not been for the collapse of the Chinese ginseng market in 1784, the United States would have had no significant goods to trade. Ginseng, then furs and Hawaiian sandalwood, gave Americans the commodities that made America China's second largest Western trading partner within two years of commerce's initiation. American trade with China began in 1784 with the shipment of 60,000 pounds of ginseng yielding profits of nearly $38,000, approximately 31 percent. Modest by modern standards, the return was equal to approximately one-tenth the capitalization of the First Bank of the United States. Drawing participants from across state lines, the first voyage reoriented trade connections away from London and initiated national investment communities, confirming the need for a political structure to protect nascent commercial activities.[12]

Tea and sugar are not the only useful windows into the larger picture of the American Revolution; other commodities like wheat or textiles serve equally well when placed in proper contexts. Familiar material objects also have the advantage of being presented in specific ways: holding up a canister of tea or a china tea service, while theatrical, provides graphic images that facilitate thought, memory, and speculation on the part of students. All have the advantage of using student knowledge and curiosity to find the pervasiveness of the past in contemporary life—William Faulkner's dictum about the past not yet being past—and to demonstrate the ways in which the right habits of inquiry or analysis can use ordinary objects to lead to better understandings of historical events and broader perspectives on the present.

Notes

1. Using agricultural commodities also gives students a window into the economic history of the Revolution; a subject of controversy if not clarity can also introduce students to basic economic concepts and historiography. The most celebrated example of this is Charles Beard's *Economic Interpretation of the Constitution of the United States* (New York, 1913). For an excellent description of the Beard debates, see James Etienne Viator, "Give Me that Old-Time Historiography: Charles Beard and the Study of the Constitution," *Loyola Law Review*, 36 (1991) 988–1022.

2. This is akin to the Socratic Method used in law school instruction, but with greater attempts to sustain the topical and organizational focus in the traditional lecture.

3. Charlotte Miers, *Independence Hall in American Memory* (Philadelphia, 2002), 10–14.

4. For images of the Revere and Wedgwood teapots, please visit the Museum of Fine Arts, Boston's Web site: <http://www.mfa.org/collections/search_art.asp?coll _keywords=revere+teapot&submit.x=0&submit.y=0>.

5. Woodruff Smith, *Consumption and the Making of Respectability* (New York, 2002). Note too that the person who pours during tea is known as "mother."

6. Timothy H. Breen, *The Marketplace of the Revolution: How Consumer Politics Shaped American Independence* (New York, 2004), 171.

7. Sugar's by-products, molasses and rum, also provide useful windows into colonial smuggling, the tacit acceptance of smuggling, and the problematic nature of the assertion of greater imperial controls after the Seven Years' War. Fred Anderson, *Crucible of War: The Seven Years' War and the Fate of Empire in British North America, 1754–1766* (New York, 2000), 572–80.

8. Bernard Bailyn, *Ideological Origins of the American Revolution,* enlarged ed. (1967; Cambridge, Mass., 1992). On the Seven Years' War, see Anderson, *Crucible of War.*

9. Permitting the East India Company to ship its tea directly to the colonies reduced its costs to below that of smuggled tea. Colonists, particularly in New England, were more likely to buy legal tea and pay taxes. This allowed the company to sell off its inventories of tea and avert financial ruin for it, its stockholders, and the British economy. Benjamin Woods Labaree, *The Boston Tea Party* (London, 1968), 66–77.

10. *Ibid*, 256–64; Bailyn, *Ideological Origins of the American Revolution*, 128.

11. Richard Buel Jr., *In Irons: Britain's Naval Supremacy and the American Revolutionary Economy* (New Haven, Conn., 1998).

12. Jonathan M. Chu, "Reorienting Trade: American Commerce and the Origins of Sino-American Trade," *Proceedings of the 2002 Conference on Sino-American Communications* (Changchun, PRC, 2002). See also Robert A. McGuire, *To Form a More Perfect Union: A New Economic Interpretation of the United States Constitution* (New York, 2003), 65–93.

CHAPTER 2

La Destruction de la Statue royale a Nouvelle Yorck/Die Zerstorung der Koniglichen Bild Saule zu New Yorck. By Andre Basset. Paris: Chez Basset. Hand-colored engraving. (Library of Congress, Prints and Photographs Division, LC-USZ62-22023.)

THE DECLARATION OF INDEPENDENCE IN WORLD CONTEXT

DAVID ARMITAGE

Where better to begin internationalizing the history of the United States than at the beginning, with the Declaration of Independence? No document is as familiar to students or so deeply entwined with what it means to be an American. The "self-evident truths" it proclaimed to "life, liberty, and the pursuit of happiness" have guaranteed it a sacrosanct place as "American scripture," a testament to the special qualities of a chosen people. Little wonder, then, that it stands as a cornerstone of Americans' sense of their own uniqueness. If a document so indelibly American as the Declaration of Independence can be put successfully into a world context, then surely almost any subject in U.S. history can be internationalized. This can be done for the Declaration by showing that it was the product of a pressing international context in 1776, by examining the host of imitations it spawned and the many analogous documents that have been issued from 1790 to 1988, and by comparing the starkly different histories of its reception within and beyond the United States. Accordingly, this essay will deal with the immediate motivations that led to the Declaration in 1776, with the first fifty years of reactions to it, at home and abroad, and with the subsequent history of declaring independence across the world, from Venezuela to New Zealand. It will then conclude with some reflections on what the Declaration's afterlife can tell us about the broader modern history of rights, both individual and collective.

To ask just what the Declaration declared is to see that, first and foremost, it announced the entry of the United States into international history. The very term "United States of America" had not been used publicly before its appearance in the Declaration. As the opening paragraph stated, the representatives of the states were laying before "the opinions of mankind" the reasons "one people" had chosen "to assume among the powers of the earth, the separate and equal station to which the Laws of Nature and of Nature's God entitle them." Those "powers of the earth"—meaning other sovereign states—were the immediate international audience for the Declaration. The United States intended to join them on an equal footing "as Free and Independent States" that "have full Power to levy War, conclude Peace, contract Alliances, establish Commerce, and to do all other Acts and Things which independent States may of right do."[1] With that statement from the concluding paragraph of the Declaration, the United States announced that they had left the transnational community of the British Empire to join instead the international community of sovereign states.

The Declaration of Independence was therefore a declaration of interdependence. Its primary intention was to turn a civil war among Britons, and within the British Empire, into a legitimate war between states under the law of nations. In August 1775, George III had already turned the American colonists into rebels by proclaiming them to be outside his protection. To transform themselves from outlaws into legitimate belligerents, the colonists needed international recognition for their cause and foreign allies to support it. Thomas Paine's best-selling pamphlet *Common Sense* made this motivation clear. In February 1776, Paine argued in the closing pages of the first edition of *Common Sense* that the "custom of nations" demanded a declaration of American independence, if any European power were even to mediate a peace between the Americans and Great Britain. France and Spain in particular could not be expected to aid those they considered rebels against another monarch. Foreign courts needed to have American grievances laid before them persuasively in a "manifesto" that could also reassure them that the Americans would be reliable trading partners. Without a declaration, Paine concluded, "[t]he custom of all courts is against us, and will be so, until, by an independence, we take rank with other nations."[2]

The records of the Continental Congress confirm that the need for a declaration of independence was intimately linked with the demands of international relations. When on June 7, 1776, Richard Henry Lee tabled a resolution before the Continental Congress declaring the colonies independent, he also urged Congress to resolve "to take the most effectual measures for forming foreign Alliances" and to prepare a plan of confederation for the newly independent states. Congress formally adopted the resolution on July 2, 1776, but only after creating three overlapping committees to draft the Declaration, a model treaty, and the Articles of Confederation. The Declaration announced the states' entry into the international system; the model treaty was designed to establish amity and commerce with other states; and the Articles of Confederation, which established "a firm league" among the thirteen free and independent states, constituted an international agreement to set up central institutions for the conduct of vital domestic and foreign affairs. To grasp the original meaning of the Declaration, it should be read alongside the Franco-American treaty of 1778 and the Articles of Confederation as one of a trio of international documents produced in sequence by the Continental Congress.

The Declaration's primary meaning in 1776 was to affirm before world opinion the rights of a group of states to enter the international realm as equals with other such states. John Adams, writing in 1781, called the Declaration of Independence "that memorable Act, by which [the United States] assumed an equal Station among the Nations." John C. Calhoun concurred a generation later: "The act was, in fact, but a formal and solemn announcement to the world, that the colonies had ceased to be dependent communities, and had become free and independent States." For almost fifty years after 1776, the Declaration's meaning for Americans lay in its opening and closing paragraphs, not in the self-evident truths that "all men are created equal" with unalienable rights to life, liberty, and the pursuit of happiness. Even Abraham Lincoln saw those truths as strictly surplus to requirements in 1776: "The assertion that 'all men are created equal' was of no practical use in effecting our separation from Great Britain; and it was placed in the Declaration, not for that, but for future use."[3] The history of the responses to the Declaration, and the imitations of it, prove that Lincoln's point held true not only in the American context but also in a world context.

The rapid transmission and translation of the Declaration around the Atlantic world and across Europe indicated the systems of communication and the common arguments that bound together the late-eighteenth-century international community. It appeared in London newspapers in mid-August 1776, had reached Florence and Warsaw by mid-September, and a German translation appeared in Switzerland by October. The Spanish-American authorities actively banned its distribution, but other obstacles (not least that it was written in English) stood in the way of its circulation. The first copy of the Declaration sent to France—the most likely and sought-after ally for the new United States—went astray; a second copy arrived only in November 1776, when American independence was already old news throughout Europe. By that time, too, the British government of Lord North had commissioned an anonymous rebuttal of the Declaration by a young conservative pamphleteer and lawyer, John Lind, and his friend, the even younger philosopher, Jeremy Bentham. Bentham's blistering attack on the "contemptible and extravagant" "opinions of the Americans on Government" in his "Short Review of the Declaration" foreshadowed his later criticisms of the "nonsense upon stilts" he found in the French Declaration of the Rights of Man and the Citizen.[4] The Declaration thereby became a primary document in a larger international debate over the origins, the scope, and the limits of rights, both collective and individual.

The Franco-American Treaty was signed only in February 1778 but it helped ensure ultimate American victory over British forces. However, if the United States had been soundly defeated at the battle of Saratoga or Yorktown, the American rebellion might be only as famous today as the other failed independence movements of the late eighteenth century, in Corsica, Montenegro, Greece, or the Crimea, for example.[5] The Declaration of Independence might then be just another historical curiosity, known only to scholars and a dwindling band of hard-core nationalists keeping the flame of independence alive.

The recognition by Britain of the colonies' independence by the Peace of Paris in 1783 indisputably confirmed what the Declaration had contentiously affirmed: that the colonies were free and independent states, not just de facto but de jure, too. Its immediate purpose having been served, the opening and closing paragraphs of the Declaration fell into oblivion in the United States, except when they were recalled by southern proponents of states' rights like Calhoun. The second paragraph did not immediately rise to prominence in the first generation after American independence. Its claims to natural rights and a right of revolution sounded suspiciously like the "jacobinical" tenets of the French Revolution and were tainted with Jeffersonian republicanism in an age of partisan strife. Only in the aftermath of the War of 1812, once all suspicion had been removed that the Declaration was anti-British, pro-French, and an incitement to insurrection, could the second paragraph of the Declaration begin its progress toward becoming the presumed heart of the Declaration's true meaning in the United States.[6]

Yet if the assertion that the united colonies were "free and independent States" was not long remembered in the United States, it would frequently be recalled as the inspiration for other anti-imperial and anticolonial secession movements over the next two centuries. There have been three major periods of declaring independence: the years from 1776 to the revolutions of 1848 in Europe; the immediate aftermath of the First World War (and the break-up of the Ottoman, Romanov, and Austro-Hungarian Empires); and the decades from to 1945 to 1979, when seventy newly independent states emerged from the wreckage of the European colonial empires. During the first great age of declaring independence, other declarations generally alluded to the opening and closing paragraphs of the American Declaration, as did the earliest known imitation, which came from Flanders in 1790 when rebels in the Austrian Netherlands declared that their province "EST & a droit d'æTRE un *Etat libre & indépendant*" ("is, and of right ought to be, a Free and Independent State") in words taken directly from the American Declaration.[7] Two decades later, the Venezuelan Congress proclaimed on July 5, 1811, (having just missed the anniversary of the American Declaration) that the "United Provinces" of Venezuela now stood "among the sovereign nations of the earth the rank which the Supreme Being and nature has assigned us" as "Free, Sovereign and Independent States."[8] Likewise, the Texas Declaration of Independence (1836) affirmed the necessity of "severing our political connection with the Mexican people, and assuming an independent attitude among the nations of the earth."[9] In this early period, the Liberian Declaration of Independence (1847), composed by the Virginia-born African American Hilary Teague, alone enshrined the recognition of "certain inalienable rights; among these are life, liberty, and the right to acquire, possess, enjoy, and defend property"; it, too, began with a declaration that the Republic of Liberia was "a free, sovereign, and independent state."[10]

It was only in the mid-twentieth century that the second paragraph of the Declaration would be used in other declarations of independence. Two such examples, each of which heralded one of the later heydays of declaring independence, were the Declaration of Independence of the Czechoslovak Nation (1918) and the Vietnamese Declaration of Independence (1945). The Czechoslovak Declaration was drafted in Washington, D.C., by, among others, Gutzon Borglum, the sculptor of Mount Rushmore. It placed the American Declaration within a lineage stretching from the proto-Protestantism of Jan Hus in the fifteenth century all the way to the Wilsonian promise of self-determination in the early twentieth.[11] Likewise, Ho Chi Minh's Declaration opened with quotations from the second paragraph of the American Declaration and the French Declaration of the Rights of Man. Ho Chi Minh, long an admirer of George Washington, thereby placed the Vietnamese revolution into a longer revolutionary tradition while also making a shrewd, albeit unsuccessful, bid for American support for Vietnamese independence.[12] However, even these examples were not typical in their respect for the Declaration's "self-evident truths." More characteristic of the century before the Universal Declaration of Human Rights (1948) was the British foreign secretary Arthur Balfour's response at the Versailles conference in 1919 to a proposal that the covenant of the League of Nations include a racial equality clause "commencing with the proposition taken from the Declaration of Independence, that all men are created equal. Mr. Balfour said that was an eighteenth century proposition which he did not believe was true. He believed it was true in a certain sense that all men of a particular nation were created equal, but not that a man in Central Africa was created equal to a European."[13]

Active resistance of the rights to life, liberty, and the pursuit of happiness helped turn the Declaration of Independence into a blueprint for white settler revolt. Thus, the South Carolina Declaration of Secession (December 20, 1860) asserted that "South Carolina has resumed her position among the nations of the world, as a separate and independent State; with full power to levy war, conclude peace, contract alliances, establish commerce, and to do all the other acts and things which independent States may of right do."[14] Even more closely modeled on the form, and even the purpose, of the American Declaration was the Unilateral Declaration of Independence issued by the embattled white minority government of southern Rhodesia (November 11, 1965). In conscious imitation of the 1776 Declaration, it opened with the words, "Whereas in the course of human affairs history has shown that it may become necessary for a people to resolve the political affiliations which have connected them with another people and to assume among other nations the separate and equal status to which they are entitled." Two years earlier, in 1963, the British government had prepared military contingency plans against the possibility of just such a unilateral declaration: the ominous title of the secret file containing them was "Boston Tea Party."[15]

The great majority of the unilateral declarations of independence issued after 1776 made no direct reference to the American Declaration. For example, the Haitian Declaration of January 1, 1804, the first declaration of independence in the Western Hemisphere after 1776, ignored the American Declaration altogether, and with good reason in light of Thomas Jefferson's policy not to recognize the legitimacy of the Haitian Revolution. "To draw up the act of independence," wrote Louis Boisrond Tonnerre, the author of the Haitian declaration, "we need the skin of a white man for parchment, his skull for an inkwell, his blood for ink, and a bayonet for a pen!"[16] His declaration, unlike the American, marked a wholly new beginning for the first black republic in the Western Hemisphere and made no concessions to the former colonial masters. Many later declarations would be more pragmatic, even as others, like the declaration issued by the Palestinian National Council in November 1988, catalogued unresolved grievances and unfulfilled aspirations to statehood.[17]

This brief global history of the Declaration of Independence since 1776 should be contrasted with Gordon Wood's recent judgment that it "set forth a philosophy of human rights that could be applied not only to Americans, but also to peoples everywhere. It was essential in giving the American Revolution a universal appeal."[18] Rather, it is more the story of the rights of states than of individuals or groups. Indeed, the history of the Declaration of Independence in world context is above all an account of how our world of states emerged from an earlier world of multinational empires. The transition from one to the other did not necessarily benefit equally all those who had been the subjects of empires. Thus, declarations of independence by indigenous peoples are historically rare. The most notable instance—the "Declaration of the Independence of New Zealand" (1835)—is in fact a counterexample because it preceded the imposition of colonial authority, and made such authority possible by constituting the Maori chiefs as a sovereign body with which the British could then conclude the Treaty of Waitangi in 1840.[19] Successful examples of declarations of independence by ethnic minorities within independent nation-states are just as rare. It seems to be a historical rule that once states have established their right to external self-determination, they become resistant to further internal challenges to their autonomy or integrity.

The Declaration of Independence possessed meanings as varied for international audiences as it did for different American publics. Its status, however, as a charter of individual rights has never been as prominent on the world stage as it has been within the United States. To examine the Declaration's reception in world history since 1776 is to discover just how relatively recent and persistently fragile is the prominence of talk about the rights of non-state groups and individuals in international affairs. Perhaps the only self-evident lesson to be learned from this global history of the Declaration of Independence is that the protection of those rights demands constant vigilance against the powers of the earth, not least because the individual rights to "life, liberty, and the pursuit of happiness" have not always been easily reconciled with "all the other Acts and Things which independent States may of right do."

Bibliographical Essay

The international and global context for the American Revolution, and hence for the Declaration of Independence, has been variously chronicled in R. R. Palmer, *The Age of the Democratic Revolution* (2 vols., Princeton, N.J., 1959–1964); Franco Venturi, *The End of the Old Regime in Europe, 1776–1789,* trans. R. Burr Litchfield (2 vols., Princeton, N.J., 1991); and, most recently and most expansively, in C. A. Bayly, *The Birth of the Modern World, 1780–1914* (Malden, Mass., 2004), ch. 3, "Converging Revolutions, 1780–1820."

The various drafts of the American Declaration of Independence, along with Richard Henry Lee's resolution, are handsomely reproduced in Julian P. Boyd, *The Declaration of Independence: The Evolution of the Text,* rev. ed. (Washington, D.C., 1999). Some of the documents can also be found online in the Library of Congress exhibition, "Declaring Independence: Drafting the Documents": <http://lcweb.loc .gov/exhibits/declara/declara1.html>; and in the National Archives' exhibition of "The Charters of Freedom": <http://www.archives.gov/national_archives_experience/ charters.html>.

The debate around the drafting of the Declaration can be followed in Thomas Jefferson's "Notes of Proceedings in the Continental Congress" (June 7, 1776–Aug. 1, 1776), printed in Julian P. Boyd, ed., *The Papers of Thomas Jefferson, I: 1760–1776* (Princeton, N.J., 1950), 309–29. The best recent discussion of the drafting is Pauline Maier, *American Scripture: Making the Declaration of Independence* (New York, 1999).

There are many easily available paperback editions of Thomas Paine's *Common Sense,* most recently one edited by Gordon S. Wood (New York, 2003). The best scholarly edition is Eric Foner, ed., *Paine: Collected Writings* (New York, 1995), which prints a wide range of Paine's writings during the American Revolution and after.

Many of the "local" declarations of independence, issued by towns, states, and other groups can be found in Peter Force, ed., *American Archives: Fourth Series* (6 vols., Washington, D.C., 1833–1846). For discussion and an indispensable finding-list, see "The 'Other' Declarations of Independence" and "Appendix A" in Maier, *American Scripture,* 47–96, 217–23.

The Declaration of Independence was the culmination of a series of public documents— petitions, addresses, declarations, and speeches—issued by the Continental Congress. Many of these documents—for example, the "Declaration . . . Setting Forth the Causes and Necessity of Taking Up Arms" (6 July 1775) or "A Speech to the Six Confederate Nations . . . From the Twelve United Colonies" (Aug. 26–28, 1775), addressed to the Iroquois Confederacy—make illuminating comparisons with the form and argument of the Declaration of Independence. They are all collected in James H. Hutson, ed., *A Decent Respect to the Opinions of Mankind: Congressional State Papers, 1774–1776* (Washington, D.C., 1975). Mary A. Giunta and J. Dane Hartgrove, eds., *Documents of the Emerging Nation: U.S. Foreign Relations, 1775–1789* (Wilmington, Del., 1998), provides a generous selection of sources concerning the United States' entry into international affairs.

The international context of the Declaration and the subsequent responses to it are discussed in David Armitage, "The Declaration of Independence and International Law," *William and Mary Quarterly,*, 3rd ser., 59, 1 (Jan. 2002): 39–64, and in Armitage, *The Declaration of Independence: A Global History* (Cambridge, Mass., 2007), ch. 2.

Jeremy Bentham's attack on the Declaration is reprinted in Armitage, *Declaration of Independence*, 173–86. The only other extended contemporary reply to the Declaration, Thomas Hutchinson's *Strictures upon the Declaration of the Congress at Philadelphia* (1776), has also recently been reprinted, as an appendix to Hans L. Eicholz, *Harmonizing Sentiments: The Declaration of Independence and the Jeffersonian Idea of Self-Government* (New York, 2001), 177–99.

The various declarations of independence referred to here from Czechoslovakia, Flanders, Haiti, Liberia, New Zealand, Rhodesia, Texas, Venezuela, and Vietnam can be found in Armitage, *Declaration of Independence*, 187–245. A broader selection appears in Albert P. Blaustein, Jay Sigler, and Benjamin R. Breede, eds., *Independence Documents of the World* (2 vols., New York, 1977), and various Latin American declarations can be found in Javier Malagón, ed., *Las Actas de Independencia de América* (Washington, D.C., 1955). The 1988 Palestinian Declaration of Independence is available online at <http://en.wikipedia.org/wiki/Palestinian_Declaration_of_Independence>.

A wide range of documents relating to contemporary movements for independence, separation, and secession can be found online at <http://www.constitution.org/cs_separ.htm>.

Other declarations of independence produced in the United States have been collected in Philip S. Foner, ed., *We, the Other People: Alternative Declarations of Independence by Labor Groups, Farmers, Woman's Rights Advocates, Socialists, and Blacks, 1829–1975* (Urbana, Ill., 1976). The volume does not include the white Nativist "Declaration of Principles . . . of the Native American Convention" (July 4, 1845), extracts from which can be found in Stanley Feldstein and Lawrence Costello, eds., *The Ordeal of Assimilation: A Documentary History of the White Working Class* (Garden City, N.Y., 1974), 147–53.

Translations of the Declaration of Independence into languages from French and Spanish to Hebrew and Malay can be found in the online roundtable, "Interpreting the Declaration of Independence by Translation," <http://chnm.gmu.edu/declaration>, along with a set of illuminating interpretive essays also available in the *Journal of American History*, 85, 4 (March 1999): 1280–1460. For a useful overview of the findings of those essays, see David Thelen, "Reception of the Declaration of Independence," in *The Declaration of Independence: Origins and Impact,* ed. Scott Douglas Gerber (Washington, D.C., 2002), 191–212. An informative set of perspectives on the German reception can be found (in English) online at <http://www.dhm.de/magazine/unabhaengig/decl_index.htm>.

Notes

1. "The Declaration of Independence as Adopted by Congress" (July 4, 1776), in Julian P. Boyd, ed., *The Papers of Thomas Jefferson: I, 1760–1776* (Princeton, N.J., 1950), 429, 432.

2. Thomas Paine, *Common Sense* (Jan. 14, 1776), in Eric Foner, ed., *Paine: Collected Writings* (New York, 1995), 45–46.

3. [John Adams,] *A Collection of State-Papers, Relative to the Acknowledgement of the Sovereignity [sic] of the United States of America* (The Hague, 1782), 4; John C. Calhoun, *A Discourse on the Constitution and Government of the United States,* in Ross M. Lence, ed., *Union and Liberty: The Political Philosophy of John C. Calhoun* (Indianapolis, 1992), 90; Abraham Lincoln, "Speech at Springfield, Illinois" (June 26, 1857), in Roy P. Basler, ed., *The Collected Works of Abraham Lincoln* (9 vols., New Brunswick, N.J., 1953–1955), II, 406.

4. [Jeremy Bentham,] "Short Review of the Declaration," in [John Lind and Jeremy Bentham,] *An Answer to the Declaration of the American Congress* (London: T. Cadell, J. Walter and T. Sewell, 1776), 119–32; reprinted in David Armitage, *The Declaration of Independence: A Global History* (Cambridge, Mass., 2007), 173–86.

5. Franco Venturi, *The End of the Old Regime in Europe, 1768–1776: The First Crisis,* trans. R. Burr Litchfield (Princeton, N.J., 1989).

6. Philip F. Detweiler, "The Changing Reputation of the Declaration of Independence: The First Fifty Years," *William and Mary Quarterly,* 3d ser., 19 (1962): 557–74.

7. J. F. Rohaert, *Manifeste de la Province de Flandre* (Paris, 1790), 27–28; Armitage, *Declaration of Independence,* 189.

8. "Acta Solemne de Independencia" (July 5, 1811), in *Interesting Official Documents Relating to the United Provinces of Venezuela* (London, 1812), 2–21; Armitage, *Declaration of Independence,* 206.

9. "The Unanimous Declaration of Independence Made by the Delegates of the People of Texas" (March 2, 1836), in John H. Jenkins, gen. ed., *The Papers of the Texas Revolution, 1835–1836* (9 vols., Austin, Tex., 1973), IV, 493–97; Armitage, *Declaration of Independence,* 212.

10. "A Declaration of Independence by the Representatives of the People of the Commonwealth of Liberia in Convention Assembled" (July 26, 1847), in Alfonso K. Dormu, *The Constitution of the Republic of Liberia and the Declaration of Independence* (New York, 1970), 37–42; Armitage, *Declaration of Independence,* 217–18.

11. T. G. Masaryk, et al., "The Declaration of Independence of the Czechoslovak

Nation (Oct. 26, 1918), in George J. Kovtun, *The Czechoslovak Declaration of Independence: A History of the Document* (Washington, D.C., 1985), 53–55; Armitage, *Declaration of Independence,* 225–30.

12. Ho Chi Minh, "Declaration of Independence of the Democratic Republic of Vietnam" (Sept. 2, 1945), in Ho Chi Minh, *Selected Works,* (4 vols., Hanoi, 1960–1962), III, 17–21; Armitage, *Declaration of Independence,* 231–35.

13. David Hunter Miller, *The Drafting of the Covenant* (2 vols., New York, 1928), I, 183–84.

14. "Declaration of the Immediate Causes which Induce and Justify the Secession of South Carolina from the Federal Union" (Dec. 20, 1860), in *Journal of the Convention of the People of South Carolina, Held in 1860, 1861 and 1862* (Columbia, S.C., 1862), 461, 466.

15. [Government of Rhodesia,] "Proclamation" (Nov. 11, 1965), in Blaustein, Sigler and Breede, eds., *Independence Documents of the World,* II, 587; Armitage, *Declaration of Independence,* 243–45; National Archives (Kew, Eng.), Public Record Office, DO 183/253.

16. Thomas Madiou, *Histoire d'Haiti* (1847–1848) (8 vols., Port-au-Prince, 1989–1991), III, 145; Armitage, *Declaration of Independence,* 193–98.

17. Palestine National Council, "Declaration of Independence" (Nov. 15, 1988), in Walter Laqueur and Barry Rubin, eds., *The Israel-Arab Reader: A Documentary History of the Middle East Conflict,* 5th ed. (Harmondsworth, Eng., 1995), 542–46.

18. Gordon S. Wood, *The American Revolution: A History* (New York, 2002), 57.

19. "He W[h]akaputanga o te Rangatiratanga o Nu Tirene" (Declaration of the Independence of New Zealand) (Oct. 28, 1835), in *Fac-Similes of the Declaration of Independence and the Treaty of Waitangi* (Wellington, 1877), 4; Armitage, *Declaration of Independence,* 209–10.

STRATEGIES FOR TEACHING THE DECLARATION OF INDEPENDENCE IN A GLOBAL CONTEXT

TED DICKSON

I find teaching the Revolutionary War very challenging. I grew up in Boston and am passionate about teaching military history. As a result, I always wish I could spend at least a week of my survey course on the war itself. However, the time demands of the Advanced Placement course usually restrict me to one day on the Declaration of Independence and two days on the reasons the colonists won the war (including advantages, strategies, battles, leadership, and so forth).

David Armitage's essay has inspired me to rethink how I approach not just how I teach the Declaration of Independence but also my time allocation. Because of the success of my more global approach to the Declaration, I am convinced of the utility and necessity of globalizing my teaching of the fundamental issues in the U.S. history survey. Although I reallocated time from the war to the Declaration, I did not revamp everything. The challenge is to enhance my course at key points so that my students understand the interconnectedness of global events and increase their understanding of United States history, while preserving precious time.

In the past, I approached the Declaration by emphasizing its antecedents, especially John Locke and Thomas Paine. We discussed the background to the Declaration, including Whig ideology, republicanism, and contract theory, and then continued by analyzing Paine's arguments for independence by reading an excerpt from *Common Sense*. In response to recent scholarship, I briefly lectured on the question of whether the Declaration influenced or reflected public opinion. This lecture is based on Pauline Meier's work (summarized quite well in Ray Raphael's *Founding Myths*).[1] I then introduced the document itself by showing video produced by the Declaration of Independence Road Trip in which actors "perform" the Declaration.[2] Our analysis of the document was organized around traditional questions:

1. What was the purpose of the Declaration of Independence?
2. What were the various audiences the Continental Congress was trying to reach?
3. What was Jefferson's philosophy of government?
4. What are some of the specific British actions or laws to which Jefferson referred in his list of grievances against the King ("He has . . .").
5. According to the document, how did the colonists try to address these grievances? How did the king respond?
6. How does the document conclude?[3]

We also discussed the following clause, removed from the final draft of the Declaration:

he has waged cruel war against human nature itself, violating its most sacred rights of life & liberty in the persons of a distant people who never offended him, captivating & carrying them into slavery in another hemisphere, or to incur miserable death in their transportation thither. this piratical warfare, the opprobrium of *infidel* powers, is the warfare of the CHRISTIAN king of Great Britain. determined to keep open a market where MEN should be bought & sold, he has prostituted his negative for suppressing every legislative attempt to prohibit or to restrain this execrable commerce: and that this assemblage of horrors might want no fact of distinguished die, he is now exciting those very people to rise in arms among us, and to purchase that liberty of which *he* has deprived them, by murdering the people upon whom *he* also obtruded them; thus paying off former crimes committed against the *liberties* of one people, with crimes which he urges them to commit against the *lives* of another.[4]

After reading David Armitage's article, I changed my approach to the Declaration. By globalizing my approach, I not only use the discussion of the Declaration to place the war in a more global context, but also add a new kind of document analysis and introduce other topics of future study.

I now begin with a teacher-guided discussion to introduce the document. We still discuss *Common Sense* briefly (adding the international perspective found in Armitage's article), review the popular push for independence, and analyze the basic structure and philosophy of the document using copies of the Declaration itself, and the previously cited "slavery" clause. The discussion of that clause includes an emphasis on the concept "all men are created equal" and the question of whether this claim could have changed U.S. history if it had been included in the final draft. To save time, I now eliminate the video and give my own examples of specific references from Jefferson's list of grievances.

My next question to the students is: "What was the most important paragraph in the Declaration?" This question becomes the key transition to the global context. I then lead a discussion based on Armitage's article by concentrating on the following points:

- The Declaration transformed the Revolution from a civil war into a war between states (enabling France and Spain to enter the war);
- The committee to write the Declaration was one of three overlapping committees (the other two were working on the Articles of Confederation and the Treaty of Alliance with France);
- The Declaration was transmitted around the world quickly;
- The first generation after Independence was suspicious of the second paragraph (which sounded too much like the French Revolution, too pro-French and too anti-British).

At this point, I divide the class into small groups and give each group a different declaration of independence. Each group's task is as follows (I have the following questions posted for the entire class to see). In the interest of time, I encourage them to read the first few paragraphs, skim the middle of their document, and read the conclusion.

Scan your group's document. Read the first few paragraphs, look at the structure of the document, read the concluding paragraphs, and consider the following questions:

- What is the date?
- What country is declaring independence?

- How is this document similar to the American Declaration of Independence (look for similar language and structure)?
- How is it different? Is anything missing?

What I hope the students will find—in addition to a similar structure—are references to "free and independent states," "life, liberty, and property" and maybe "all men are created equal." One important point we discover in this project is that many of the declarations do refer to part of the second paragraph of the American Declaration, but not necessarily the phrase "all men are created equal."

We use declarations that are cited in Professor Armitage's article: Venezuela (1811), New Zealand (1835), Liberia (1847), Texas (1836), South Carolina (1860), Czechoslovakia (1918), and Vietnam (1945).[5] The Venezuelan document is in Spanish, so I have a group of advanced Spanish students look at it—this document does not work as well because of the language difficulty, but it is still instructive (translations of it have been published and are available—see Armitage's bibliography). It is no surprise that all of the documents mention the idea of an "independent state." Texas, Vietnam, and Liberia mention "life, liberty, and property" or "the pursuit of happiness." Only the Vietnam Declaration specifically quotes, "all men are created equal," although this is certainly implied in the Czechoslovakia Declaration. The New Zealand document is interesting and somewhat problematic as it was more of a step toward becoming a British colony (five years later) rather than the opposite. My students are also interested in the different ways that the various documents refer to God.

After we discuss the documents, we review Armitage's main points about the suspicion of the second paragraph and the greater acceptance of these ideas in the declarations of the twentieth century. We also discuss independence as an agency of white supremacy. Our concluding discussion centers on the legacy of the Declaration: a universal philosophy of human rights or the story of the rights of states? I then provide Armitage's concluding sentence for the students to read and react to: *Perhaps the only self-evident lesson to be learned from this global history of the Declaration of Independence is that protection of those rights demands constant vigilance against the powers of the earth, not the least because the individual rights to "Life, Liberty, and the Pursuit of Happiness" have not always been easily reconciled with "all other Acts and Things which Independent States may of right do."* After we discuss Armitage's meaning, I inform the students that his essay was published in 2004 and ask if there were any historical events in that year that might give that statement more resonance.

The discussions about these documents are interesting and enjoyable. In addition to introducing my students to a more global approach, I am able to introduce other topics that will help globalize the course later in the survey, including the history of Liberia, the drive for independence in Latin America, the independence of Texas, and the events immediately following both world wars. I revisit the South Carolina Declaration during our discussion on the causes of the Civil War. We are also able to connect the lesson to the present quite effectively. I also hope that the focus of this discussion will help my students remember the source of the phrase "all men are created equal."

This more global approach also changes my discussions of the war itself. I now teach the war primarily with a lecture and discussion. We begin with the students evaluating the advantages that each side enjoyed at the beginning of the war and then discuss a series of turning-point battles and events: Lexington and Concord, Bunker Hill, Trenton and Princeton (and *The Crisis*), Saratoga, Valley Forge, and Yorktown. I then ask the students to analyze why they think the rebels won. I include the Declaration of Independence in my discussion of the events of 1776—from the escape from Long Island to crossing the Delaware (based on David McCullough and David Hackett Fisher).[6] My discussion of French assistance and of the global nature of the war after 1778 makes more sense to my students. Because I emphasize the global significance of the Declaration, the examination of the war itself has more resonance. We even briefly compare the Revolutionary War to Vietnam and the war in Iraq. This deeper understanding continues into our study of the problems facing the country under the Articles of Confederation and the Constitution.

Although I achieve a number of my goals with this lesson, I do find myself pressed for time to complete the activity effectively. However, I have found that the benefits of this approach to the Declaration resonate throughout the year. As a result, I now spend two days on the Declaration. I assign the questions on the Declaration for homework prior to class to allow more time for discussion. I also show the Declaration video. The students then read their individual declarations for homework prior to group discussion on the second day. In smaller classes, I choose to leave out the New Zealand declaration.

In the future, I may also reword my questions on the Declaration to emphasize the structure of the document and to introduce more of my themes (such as the question, "What is the most important paragraph?"). If I were teaching a section of a U.S. survey at the college level, I would consider assigning Armitage's article as a reading prior to examining the documents in class.

After this lesson, my students are much more aware of the global context of the events we discuss. Our treatment of topics such as Toussaint L'Ouverture, the American Colonization Society, and the dispute over Texas is deeper. Globalizing the survey has not only made my lessons more interesting but also added depth to my students' understanding of both the past and the present.

Notes

1. Pauline Meier, *American Scripture: Making the Declaration of Independence* (New York, 1997) and Ray Raphael, *Founding Myths: Stories that Hide Our Patriotic Past* (New York, 2004), 107–24.

2. This video can be downloaded from the Web at <http://www.independenceroadtrip.org>.

3. These questions are inspired by the lesson in Roberta J. Leach and Augustine Caliguire, *Advanced Placement U.S. History 1: The Evolving American Nation-State 1607–1914* (Westlake, Ohio, 1997), 54.

4. Taken from "Jefferson's "original Rough draught" of the Declaration of Independence" at <http://www.princeton.edu/~tjpapers/declaration/declaration.html>.

5. I found all of these declarations on the Internet by using Google:

Liberia: <http://onliberia.org/con_index.htm>.

The Avalon Project at Yale Law School had two of them:

Texas: <http://www.yale.edu/lawweb/avalon/texdec.htm>;

South Carolina: <http://www.yale.edu/lawweb/avalon/csa/scarsec.htm>.

Paul Halsall's Modern History Sourcebook at Fordham University has Vietnam: <http://www.fordham.edu/halsall/mod/1945vietnam.html>.

Professor T. Mills Kelly's Web site at George Mason University has Czechoslovakia's: <http://www2.tltc.ttu.edu/kelly/Archive/CzSl/10–18–18.html>.

Venezuela's: <http://es.wikisource.org/wiki/Acta_de_Independencia_de_Venezuela>.

New Zealand's: <http://aotearoa.wellington.net.nz/imp/dec.htm>.

6. David McCullough, "What the Fog Wrought," reprinted in Robert Cowley, *What If's of American History* (New York, 2003), 43–54; David McCullough, *1776* (New York, 2005); David Hackett Fisher, *Washington's Crossing* (New York, 2004).

CHAPTER 3

This illustration—"In the Slave Market of Cairo"—appeared in *Egypt & Nubia: From Drawings Made on the Spot by David Roberts* (1846–1849) and demonstrates the long history of the slave trade in North Africa and the Middle East. (Library of Congress, Prints and Photographs Division, LC-USZC4-4043.)

ORIGINS OF AMERICAN SLAVERY

PHILIP D. MORGAN

Slavery is often termed "the peculiar institution," but it was hardly peculiar to the United States. Almost every society in the history of the world has experienced slavery at one time or another. The aborigines of Australia are about the only group that has so far not revealed a past mired in slavery— and perhaps the omission has more to do with the paucity of evidence than anything else. To explore American slavery in its full international context, then, is essentially to tell the history of the globe. That task is not possible in the available space, so this essay will explore some key antecedents of slavery in North America and attempt to show what is distinctive or unusual about its development. The aim is to strike a balance between identifying continuities in the institution of slavery over time, while also locating significant changes. The trick is to suggest preconditions, anticipations, and connections without implying that they were necessarily determinations.[1]

Significant precursors to American slavery can be found in antiquity, which produced two of only a handful of genuine slave societies in the history of the world. A slave society is one in which slaves played an important role and formed a significant proportion (say, over 20 percent) of the population. Classical Greece and Rome (or at least parts of those entities and for distinct periods of time) fit this definition and can be considered models for slavery's expansion in the New World. In Rome in particular, bondage went hand in hand with imperial expansion, as large influxes of slaves from outlying areas were funneled into large-scale agriculture, into the *latifundia,* the plantations of southern Italy and Sicily. American slaveholders could point to a classical tradition of reconciling slavery with reason and universal law; ancient Rome provided important legal formulas and justifications for modern slavery. Parallels between ancient and New World slavery abound: from the dehumanizing device of addressing male slaves of any age as "boy," the use of branding and head-shaving as modes of humiliation, the comic inventiveness in naming slaves (a practice American masters continued simply by using classical names), the notion that slaves could possess a *peculium* (a partial and temporary capacity to enjoy a range of goods), the common pattern of making fugitive slaves wear a metal collar, to clothing domestic slaves in special liveries or uniforms. The *Life of Aesop,* a fictional slave biography from Roman Egypt in the first century C.E., is revelatory of the anxieties and fears that pervade any slave society, and some of the sexual tensions so well displayed are redolent of later American slavery. Yet, of course, ancient slavery was fundamentally different from modern slavery in being an equal opportunity condition—all ethnicities could be slaves—and in seeing slaves as primarily a social, not an economic, category. Ancient cultural mores were also distinctive: Greeks enslaved abandoned infants; Romans routinely tortured slaves to secure testimony; and even though the Stoics were prepared to acknowledge the humanity of the slave, neither they nor anyone else in the ancient world ever seriously questioned the place of slavery in society. Aristotle, after all, thought that some people were "slaves by nature," that there were, in effect, *natural* slaves.[2]

Arabs and their Muslim allies were the first to make use of large numbers of sub-Saharan black Africans. They developed a long-distance slave trade, which began in the seventh century and lasted into the twentieth. It delivered many millions of Africans across the Sahara Desert, Red Sea, and Indian Ocean to North Africa, the Mediterranean, and the Persian Gulf. Although over a much longer period of time and comprising far more females, the number of Africans exported via these trans-Saharan or Indian Ocean slave trades probably equaled, or even outmatched, those of its transatlantic counterpart. The preexistence of these export trades facilitated Atlantic trade: systems of slave marketing were already in place. So numerous were black Africans at certain times and in certain places that they were able to launch massive slave revolts—in 869, for instance, in what is now southern Iraq, where the so-called *Zanj* (who came from the Swahili Coast and lands farther north) worked in large gangs draining marshlands. Although the Qur'an and Islamic Law were essentially color-blind, and Muslims enslaved many so-called "white" people, medieval Arabs came to associate the most degrading forms of labor with black slaves. The Arabic word for slave, *'abd,* came to mean a black slave. Many Arab writers had racial contempt for black people, and the racial stereotypes of the medieval Middle East were probably transmitted to the Iberian Peninsula.[3]

As the long-standing trans-Saharan slave trade reveals, slavery existed in sub-Saharan Africa long before the Atlantic slave trade. In some—perhaps most—places, slavery tended to be a minor institution, with the slave able to pass in time from alien to kin member; in others, most notably a number of Islamicized regimes, slavery was more central, with violence, economic exploitation, and lack of kinship rights more evident. In large part because Africa was underpopulated, a broad spectrum of dependent statuses, with slavery just one variant, existed and slaves played a wide range of roles from field workers to soldiers, from domestics to administrators. The ethnic fragmentation of sub-Saharan Africa meant that there were few states strong enough to prevent opportunistic African kings or merchants profiting from slave raiding. Those kingdoms that opposed exporting slaves did not have the means to stop the traffic. Lacking an overall religious or political unity, Africans could enslave other Africans because the concept of African-ness had no meaning. Accustomed to tropical climates, inured to agricultural labor, and reared in a harsh epidemiological environment, sub-Saharan Africans made productive slaves.[4]

As Europe's economy began to expand in the tenth and eleventh centuries, attention focused on the rich Mediterranean region. By the twelfth century, various Crusader states had been established at the eastern end of the Mediterranean Sea. Venetian and Genoese merchants pioneered the development of these conquered Arab sugar-producing regions and began supplying them with slaves. They first victimized the Slavic inhabitants of the Dalmatian Coast and then transported Circassians, Georgians, Armenians, and the like from the Black Sea region. At this time, the Latin word for people of Slavic descent, *sclavus,* became the origin of the word *slave* in English (and in French *esclave,* in Spanish *esclavo,* and in German *sklave*), and replaced the nonethnic Latin term *servus*. In Europe in the Middle Ages, then, the slave population was predominantly "white." Sugar production gradually spread from the eastern Mediterranean, through Cyprus and Sicily, to Catalonia in the west; and the white slave trade followed in its wake. This trade mirrored the later transatlantic version, with its complex organization, permanent forts, and long-distance shipment by sea to multinational markets. When in 1453 the Ottoman Turks captured Constantinople, Christian Europe was cut off from its major source of slaves. The only available alternative became sub-Saharan Africans.[5]

Two sources of African labor were then available. First, the Arab caravan trade across the Sahara, long in existence, gathered impetus to provide more black slaves to Libya and Tunisia and then to the western Mediterranean region. Second, Genoese capital and technology augmented Portuguese sea power, and from the 1440s onward the Portuguese began importing significant numbers of black African slaves into Lisbon via the Atlantic. Still, in the fifteenth and sixteenth centuries, North African and Muslim slaves exceeded black slaves in Iberia. Nevertheless, by the early seventeenth century black slaves numbered about 15,000, or 15 percent of Lisbon's population. This influx of African slaves into Iberia owed much to a transfer of personnel and knowledge from the Black Sea–Mediterranean slave nexus to that of an emerging Atlantic system.[6]

Sugar production meanwhile was making its way westward in search of fresh lands. Thus by the late fifteenth century the Iberians began colonizing the Atlantic islands off their coasts, first using as slaves Guanche natives of the Canary Islands. The Spanish and Portuguese enslavement of the Berber-like Canary Islanders is a prelude to the later fate of Caribbean, Mexican, Central American, and Brazilian Indians. Furthermore, the Atlantic islands of Madeira and São Tomé became forerunners for the spread of racial slavery and sugar plantations in the New World. Admittedly, Madeira's slave forces were limited, its properties often small, and small farmers and sharecroppers supplied much of its cane. Nevertheless, by the end of the fifteenth century it was Europe's largest producer, and its model would be the one later followed by Brazilians, who soon became the Atlantic world's major suppliers of sugar, and who drew directly on the expertise of Atlantic Islanders. From the late fifteenth century to the mid-sixteenth century, São Tomé—situated in the Gulf of Guinea—imported more African slaves than Europe, the Americas, or the other Atlantic islands combined. Particularly in the universality of slave labor, São Tomé was the nearest approximation to an American prototype.[7]

As slavery underwent a resurgence in southern Europe, it gradually disappeared from the northwestern part of the continent. Economic changes help to explain this development, but perhaps more important were cultural constraints. Over the course of the Middle Ages, Christians often committed atrocities on each other, but increasingly they avoided enslaving one another. Apparently, a sense of unity had emerged in Christian Europe that effectively barred the enslavement of those deemed fellow Europeans. Christianity's long struggle with Islam no doubt played a major role in this development. That from 1500 to 1800 Muslims enslaved well more than a million western Europeans, many of whom were subsequently ransomed and celebrated as symbols of freedom, was a major element in the growing sense that Europeans should never be slaves. Nevertheless, these so-called free-labor nations would develop some of the harshest slave regimes in the Americas. As David Brion Davis puts it, "it is an astonishing paradox that the first nations in the world to free themselves of chattel slavery—such nations as England, France, Holland, and even the Scandinavian states—became leaders during the seventeenth and eighteenth centuries in supporting plantation colonies based on African slave labor." He likens this divide to a primitive Mason-Dixon Line, "drawn somewhere in the Atlantic, separating free soil master-states from tainted slave soil dependencies."[8]

This paradox illumines the unpredictability of events in the Americas. No European nation embarked on New World ventures with the intention of enslaving anyone. They had no blueprint, but rather proceeded haphazardly and pragmatically. Their first resort was to forced Indian labor (the *encomienda,* or a semifeudal system of tributary labor), as the Tainos found to their cost on Hispaniola. To make up for the rapid decline of these earliest Indian laborers, over the course of the sixteenth century Spanish conquistadors first raided islands such as the Bahamas and then shipped more than fifty thousand Indian slaves from Central America to Panama, Peru, and the Caribbean. Similarly, from roughly the 1530s to the 1580s, the Portuguese in Brazil relied on Indian slave labor to produce sugar. Early South Carolina resorted to Indian slaves who, in the first decade of the eighteenth century, comprised one-third of the colony's slave labor force. From 1670 to 1715 an active Indian slave trade saw as many as fifty thousand Indians from the Carolinas and Florida sold to the West Indies and to the northern mainland colonies. There were basic problems, nevertheless, with using Indians as slaves. First, Indians regarded any kind of agriculture as work fit only for women. Second, European opinion was decidedly ambivalent about enslaving Indians, as the famous debate in Spain in 1548 between Juan Ginés Sepúlveda and Bartolomé de las Casas revealed. Most important, Indians were remarkably susceptible to Old World diseases. Indian slaves were not able to survive long enough to be profitable. Suffering catastrophic losses, Indian labor literally wasted away. On Hispaniola, the Taino Indians, numbering perhaps five hundred thousand precontact, were almost extinct a half century later; in central Mexico perhaps fifteen million Indians in 1500 fell to just 1.5 million a century later. The scale of the disaster is staggering.[9]

Consequently, Europeans faced a huge labor shortage. The Ottoman Turkish Empire blocked access to Black Sea or Baltic captives. European nations no longer enslaved Christian prisoners of war. Some dreamers talked of enslaving the poor, or other marginal groups, but the practical and principled problems of reviving European slavery were considerable. Another expedient was the transportation of convicts, but their numbers were never sufficient. Temporary bondage—indentured servitude—was the most obvious and most widely used other option, particularly in the early years. But servants, if they survived, eventually became free, and in any case the majority of servants would not travel to the areas where most labor was needed. Thus, almost by default, African slaves proved by far the best available labor supply. Consequently, from 1500 to 1820 almost nine million African slaves left for the New World, compared to fewer than three million whites. In terms of migration, the New World was more black than white.[10]

Slavery's center of gravity did not, however, immediately shift to the western shores of the Atlantic. Not until 1700 did Africa earn more from the export of its slaves than it did from precious metals and spices. In addition, not until the late seventeenth century did black slaves in the New World outnumber white slaves in the Old World (then located primarily in the Islamic Middle East, North Africa, and Russia). White slaves in the Maghrib became so numerous that they mounted serious rebellions—in 1763 in Algiers four thousand Christian slaves rose and killed their guards, making it "perhaps the largest slave revolt in the Atlantic and Mediterranean worlds between the end of the Roman Empire and St. Domingue rebellion."[11]

If the sheer availability of African slaves and the lack of available alternatives is the primary explanation for the development of racial slavery in the New World, did racism have nothing to do with it? Did antiblack racism or protoracism point particularly to African slaves to supply the immense labor demands of the New World? Or did racism intensify only after long-term interaction with black slaves had occurred? Was it there from the beginning or was it a consequence? This is a complicated subject and space will not permit a full accounting here. Ancient Greco-Roman art and writing offer caricatures of black Africans, although their relative scarcity is perhaps most telling. Medieval images of Africans ranged from the black magis to agents of the Devil. In various settings—in medieval Europe, where peasants were often depicted as "black" because of working in the sun and in close proximity to dirt, or in modern Russia, where noblemen even claimed that Russian serfs had black bones—blackness and debasement had a long connection. In Western culture the color black evokes a highly negative symbolism, conjuring up images of death and sin. Although these pejorative associations existed, European ambivalence toward sub-Saharan Africans seems the dominant response. Medieval Europeans did not, for example, automatically associate the biblical Ham with Africa; Asia was often identified with Ham, and his "Curse" was also used to justify European serfdom and the enslavement of Slavs. Nevertheless, however it happened, slavery became indelibly linked with people of African descent in the Western Hemisphere. The dishonor, humiliation, and bestialization that were universally associated with chattel slavery merged with blackness in the New World. The racial factor became one of the most distinctive features of slavery in the New World.[12]

New World slavery's other most distinctive aspect was its highly commercial character. Though it is true that plantations—that is, large agricultural enterprises, managed for profit, producing a crop for export, with a hierarchically stratified labor organization—existed outside the New World, they reached their apogee there. The economies of scale, the expansion in unit size, the almost exclusive use of black slaves, a highly regimented and commodified labor force, and a system of close management all raised profit levels significantly. Such a productive system placed enormous demands on its laborers. As early as the 1630s a visitor to a Jesuit-owned sugar plantation in Brazil vividly describes the unbearable horror of what had transpired: "People the color of the very night, working briskly and moaning at the same time without a moment of peace or rest, whoever sees all the confused and noisy machinery and apparatus of this Babylon, even if they have seen Mt. Etna and Vesuvius will say that this indeed is the image of Hell."[13]

Variations over time and space existed within New World slavery. Three stand out. First, although all New World regions imported more African men than women (thereby in part explaining the harshness of New World slavery because of the policing problems associated with large gangs of men), over time, the gender ratio among New World slaves became increasingly balanced. In that regard, the North American slave population is most notable because, as its number of slave women increased the most rapidly, it became one of the few self-reproducing slave populations in world history.

This early and rapid natural increase explains why North America received such a small percentage of the overall transatlantic slave trade—about 5 percent. Second, North America was also distinctive in being much less tolerant of racial intermixture than Latin America or the Caribbean. Once again demography— particularly the ratio of white men to white women (more balanced in North America than in Latin America and the Caribbean), and the availability of black women—was a crucial part of the explanation, but also important were the role of the church and cultural mores, based as much in Old World patterns of racial coexistence or segregation. The Spanish had mixed with Muslims for centuries; the English had created a Pale in their settlement of Ireland. Only in North America did the extremely arbitrary concept of "Negro"—denoting anyone with allegedly visible African ancestry—assume such a marked stigma. Third, the chances of gaining freedom varied from one society to the next. Except for the period surrounding the American Revolution, the North American colonies, and later the states, imposed the severest restrictions on the chances of a slave becoming free. Again, demography—the proportions of whites and blacks in the population—has some explanatory power, as do economic and cultural forces.[14]

North American slavery itself was hardly of a piece. The range encompasses New England's intimate "family slavery," the Mid-Atlantic's mixed forms of slavery and servitude, the Chesapeake's patriarchal, small plantation, mixed farming and tobacco, heavily native-born form of slavery, and the Lowcountry's impersonal, large plantation, rice and indigo, more heavily African system of slavery. In addition, various borderland forms existed: from a fluid world of interracial alliances in the Lower Mississippi Valley to a flexible one of fugitives and ex-slaves in Spanish Florida to one in which Indian slaves were transformed from symbols of alliance into commodities of exchange in French Canada.[15]

Racial slavery played an intrinsic and indispensable part in New World settlement. The institution was no abnormality, no aberration, no marginal feature; rather, its development is the grim and irrepressible theme governing the development of the Western Hemisphere. The truly distinctive features of North American (and to varying degrees, New World) slavery were its racial bedrock and its thoroughly commercial character. Increasingly, the stark polarity between freedom and bondage became glaringly evident, for the debasement of slaves liberated others to take control of their destiny and to dream of liberty and equality. This profound contradiction lay at the heart of the United States, a country conceived in freedom but based on slavery. The American dream always had its dark underside. Yet the dreamers would eventually try to rid themselves of the nightmare—with considerable prodding from the victims, it might be added. Unlike other previous forms of slavery, the New World version did not decline over a long period, but came to a rather abrupt end. The age of emancipation lasted a little more than one hundred years: beginning in 1776 with the first antislavery society in Philadelphia, through the monumental Haitian Revolution of 1792, and ending with Brazilian emancipation in 1888. An institution that had been accepted for thousands of years disappeared in about a century. One last watershed, therefore, is the unprecedented novelty and speed of the abolitionist moment.[16]

Bibliography

Blackburn, Robin. *The Making of New World Slavery: From the Baroque to the Modern, 1492–1800.* London, 1997. Covers all the European slave systems in the Americas and connects them to the advent of modernity.

Brooks, James F. *Captives & Cousins: Slavery, Kinship, and Community in the Southwest Borderlands.* Chapel Hill, N.C., 2002. Reveals the importance of slavery and slave-raiding to the intercultural exchange networks that emerged in the early American Southwest.

Carretta, Vincent, ed. *Unchained Voices: An Anthology of Black Authors in the English-Speaking World of the Eighteenth Century.* Lexington, Ky., 1996. Features such black voices as Briton Hammon, Phillis Wheatley, Ignatius Sancho, Olaudah Equiano, Benjamin Banneker, and Venture Smith.

Conrad, Robert Edgar, comp. *Children of God's Fire: A Documentary History of Black Slavery in Brazil.* Princeton, N.J., 1983. An excellent sourcebook for the American slave society that received the most Africans.

Davis, David Brion. *Challenging the Boundaries of Slavery.* Cambridge, Mass., 2003. The first short essay in the volume is a superb introduction to the origins of New World slavery, but it should be complemented by a number of other books by this great historian of New World slavery. I particularly recommend his *Inhuman Bondage: The Rise and Fall of New World Slavery.* New York, 2006.

Davis, Robert C. *Christian Slaves, Muslim Masters: White Slavery in the Mediterranean, the Barbary Coast, and Italy, 1500–1800.* Basingstoke, Eng., 2003. A useful reminder that slavery arose and flourished in the Mediterranean world at the same time as across the Atlantic. Explores the dimensions of white slavery and slave life.

Drescher, Seymour and Stanley L. Engerman, eds. *A Historical Guide to World Slavery.* New York, 1998. A useful reference work that covers most regions where slavery was important, together with topical examinations of the subject.

Eltis, David. *The Rise of African Slavery in the Americas.* Cambridge, Eng., 2000. A stimulating exploration of the paradox that the northern European countries most renowned for their commitment to individual freedom created the harshest systems of slavery in the New World.

———— et al., eds. *The Trans-Atlantic Slave Trade: A Database on CD-ROM.* Cambridge, Eng., 1999. Contains information on 27,233 transatlantic slaving expeditions. An expanded, online version (with information on 35,000 voyages) should be available by 2008.

Finklelman, Paul and Joseph C. Miller, eds. *Macmillan Encyclopedia of World Slavery.* 2 vols. New York, 1998. Another useful reference work that covers similar ground to the volume edited by Drescher and Engerman, but is more comprehensive in nature.

Finley, M. I. *Ancient Slavery and Modern Ideology.* Reprint. Harmondsworth, Eng., 1983, 1980. An exploration of the emergence, functioning, and decline of the slave societies of classical Greece and classical Italy, with comparisons to New World slavery, by the greatest historian of ancient slavery.

Fredrickson, George M. *Racism: A Short History.* Princeton, N.J., 2002. An authoritative introduction to the subject.

Handler, Jerome S. and Michael L. Tuite Jr. "The Atlantic Slave Trade and Slave Life in the Americas: A Visual Record," <http://hitchcock.itc.virginia.edu/Slavery>. Contains about one thousand pictorial images of slavery in Africa and the Americas, arranged thematically.

Kolchin, Peter. *American Slavery, 1619–1877.* New York, 1993. A good general account by a historian alert to comparative history.

Lewis, Bernard. *Race and Slavery in the Middle East: An Historical Enquiry.* New York, 1990. A good survey of slavery and the evolution of racial prejudice in the Islamic world.

Miers, Suzanne and Igor Kopytoff, eds. *Slavery in Africa: Historical and Anthropological Perspectives.* Madison, Wis., 1977. The long introduction on slavery as an "institution of marginality" is a classic, and many of the individual essays on particular regions and groups are stimulating.

Miller, Joseph. C., ed. *Slavery and Slaving in World History: A Bibliography, 1900–1996.* 2 vols. Armonk, N.Y., 1999. The most comprehensive work of its kind. Annual updates are available in the journal *Slavery & Abolition.* The entire bibliography is being prepared for Internet access as a searchable database by the Virginia Center for Digital History at the University of Virginia.

Morgan, Philip D. "African Americans," in Daniel Vickers, ed., *A Companion to Colonial America.* Malden, Mass., 2003, 138–71. A concise, up-to-date survey of the black experience in early America, with an extensive bibliography.

Patterson, Orlando. *Slavery and Social Death: A Comparative Study.* Cambridge, Mass., 1982. The best general survey of slave systems in sixty-six societies, written by a sociologist.

Phillips, William D., Jr. *Slavery from Roman Times to the Early Transatlantic Trade.* Minneapolis, 1985. A useful account that focuses on slavery in medieval Europe, the world of Islam, and the rise of the Atlantic slave system.

Thornton, John. *Africa and Africans in the Making of the Atlantic World, 1400–1800*. 2nd ed. Cambridge, Eng., 1998. A provocative account that emphasizes African agency in the development of slavery and the transatlantic slave trade.

Notes

1. The term "peculiar institution" became commonplace among southerners in the nineteenth-century United States: Kenneth M. Stampp, *The Peculiar Institution: Slavery in the Ante-bellum South* (New York, 1956).

2. Moses I. Finley, "Slavery," in *International Encyclopedia of the Social Sciences,* ed. David L. Sills and Robert King Merton (New York: Macmillan, 1968), 307–13; Finley, *Ancient Slavery and Modern Ideology,* reprint (Harmondsworth, Eng., 1983, 1980), 9, 96, 102, 111, 113–14; Keith Hopkins, *Conquerors and Slaves: Sociological Studies in Roman History* (vol. 1, Cambridge, Eng., 1978); Hopkins, "Novel Evidence for Roman Slavery," *Past & Present,* 138 (1993): 3–27; Keith Bradley, *Slavery and Society at Rome* (Cambridge, Eng., 1994), 12–13, 87; Peter Garnsey, *Ideas of Slavery from Aristotle to Augustine* (Cambridge, Eng., 1996); Keith Bradley, "Animalizing the Slave: The Truth of Fiction," *Journal of Roman Studies,* 90 (2000): 110–25. For studies that explore the classical legacy over a long sweep of time, see David Brion Davis, *The Problem of Slavery in Western Culture* (Ithaca, N.Y., 1966), especially 29–90, and William D. Phillips Jr., *Slavery from Roman Times to the Early Transatlantic Trade* (Minneapolis, 1985). In addition to the sanctions for slavery that the classical literature of antiquity provided and that assumed new force during the Renaissance, the religious undergirding for slavery evident in the Hebrew and Christian Bibles ideally should be explored.

3. Ralph A. Austen, "The Trans-Saharan Slave Trade: A Tentative Census," in *The Uncommon Market: Essays in the Economic History of Atlantic Slave Trade,* ed. Henry A. Gemery and Jan S. Hogendorn (New York, 1979), 23–76; Austen, "The Mediterranean Islamic Slave Trade out of Africa: A Tentative Census," *Slavery & Abolition,* 13 (1992): 214–48; and his most recent, "Slave Trade: The Sahara Desert and Red Sea Region," in *Encyclopedia of Africa South of the Sahara,* ed. John Middleton (New York, 1997), 4: 103; Pier Larson, "African Diasporas and the Atlantic" (unpublished paper, 2004); Ghada Hashem Talhami, "The Zanj Rebellion Reconsidered," *International Journal of African Historical Studies,* 10 (1977): 443–61; Alexandre Popovic, *The Revolt of African Slaves in Iraq in the IIIrd–IXth Century,* trans. Léon King (Princeton, N.J., 1998); Bernard Lewis, *Race and Slavery in the Middle East: An Historical Enquiry* (New York, 1990). For newer works on Ottoman and Islamic slavery, see Ehud R. Toledano, *Slavery and Abolition in the Ottoman Middle East* (Seattle, Wash., 1998); Shaun E. Marmon, ed., *Slavery in the Islamic Middle East* (Princeton, N.J., 1998); Minra Tora and John Edward Philips, eds., *Slave Elites in the Middle East and Africa: A Comparative Study* (London, 2000); John O. Hunwick and Eve Trout Powell, eds., *The African Diaspora in the Mediterranean Lands of Islam* (Princeton, N.J., 2001); and Paul Lovejoy, ed., *Slavery on the Frontiers of Islam* (Princeton, N.J., 2004).

4. Suzanne Miers and Igor Kopytoff, eds., *Slavery in Africa: Historical and Anthropological Perspectives* (Madison, Wis., 1977); Patrick Manning, *Slavery and African Life: Occidental, Oriental, and African Slave Trades* (Cambridge, Eng., 1990); John Thornton, *Africa and Africans in the Making of the Atlantic World, 1400–1680* (Cambridge, Eng., 1992); Paul E. Lovejoy, *Transformations in Slavery: A History of Slavery in Africa*, 2nd. ed. (Cambridge, Eng., 2000).

5. Charles Verlinden, "L'Origine de 'sclavus-esclave,'" *Archivum latinitatis medii aevi*, 17 (1943): 97–128; Verlinden, *L'Esclavage dans l'Europe médiévale*, Vol. 1: *Pénisule Ibérique—France* (Bruges, 1955); Vol. 2: *Italie, Colonies Italiennes du Levant, Levant Latin, Empire Byzantin* (Ghent, 1977); and Verlinden, *The Beginnings of Modern Colonization: Eleven Essays with an Introduction*, Yvonne Freccero, trans. (Ithaca, N.Y., 1970). For newer work on medieval slavery, see Ruth Mazo Karras, *Slavery and Society in Medieval Scandinavia* (New Haven, Conn., 1988); David A. E. Pelteret, *Slavery in Early Mediaeval England: From the Reign of Alfred Until the Twelfth Century* (Woodbridge, Eng., 1995); Steven Epstein, *Speaking of Slavery: Color, Ethnicity, and Human Bondage in Italy* (Ithaca, N.Y., 2001); and Sally McKee, "Inherited Status and Slavery in Late Medieval Italy and Venetian Crete," *Past & Present*, 182 (Feb. 2004): 31–53.

6. A. C. de C. M. Saunders, *A Social History of Black Slaves and Freedmen in Portugal, 1441–1555* (Cambridge, Eng., 1982); Hugh Thomas, *The Slave Trade: The Story of the Atlantic Slave Trade: 1440–1870* (New York, 1997), 21–24, 48–86.

7. Felipe Fernández-Armesto, *The Canary Islands after the Conquest: The Making of a Colonial Society in the Early Sixteenth Century* (Oxford, 1982); Stuart B. Schwartz, ed., *Tropical Babylons: Sugar and the Making of the Atlantic World, 1450–1680* (Chapel Hill, N.C., 2004), especially 1–26, 42–84, 201–36. For more on São Tomé, which requires more study, see Tony Hodges and Malyn Newitt, *São Tomé and Príncipe: From Plantation Colony to Microstate* (Boulder, Colo., 1988), and Robert Garfield, *A History of São Tomé Island, 1470–1655: The Key to Guinea* (San Francisco, 1992).

8. David Brion Davis, "Looking at Slavery from Broader Perspectives," *American Historical Review*, 105 (April 2000): 458, and his *Challenging the Boundaries of Slavery* (Cambridge, Mass., 2003), 14; Robert C. Davis, *Christian Slaves, Muslim Masters: White Slavery in the Mediterranean, the Barbary Coast, and Italy, 1500–1800* (Basingstoke, Eng., 2003). For more on the development of freedom and slavery, see David Eltis, *The Rise of African Slavery in the Americas* (Cambridge, Eng., 2000), and Sue Peabody, *There Are No Slaves in France: The Political Culture of Race and Slavery in the Ancien Régime* (New York, 1996).

9. Carl Ortwin Sauer, *The Early Spanish Main* (Berkeley, Calif., 1966); Irving Rouse, *The Tainos: Rise & Decline of the People who Greeted Columbus* (New Haven, Conn., 1992); William L. Sherman, *Forced Native Labor in Sixteenth-Century Central America* (Lincoln, Nebr., 1979); Stuart B. Schwartz, *Sugar Plantations in the Formation of Brazilian Society: Bahia, 1550–1835* (Cambridge, Eng., 1985); Alan Gallay, *The Indian Slave Trade: The Rise of the English Empire in the American South, 1670–1717* (New Haven, Conn., 2002); Joyce E. Chaplin, "Enslavement of Indians in Early America: Captivity

without the Narrative," in *The Creation of the British Atlantic World*, ed. Elizabeth Mancke and Carole Shammas (Baltimore, 2005), 75–121; for a recent discussion of Indian population decline, see David S. Jones, "Virgin Soils Revisited," *William and Mary Quarterly*, 3rd ser., 60 (Oct. 2003): 703–42.

10. David Galenson, *White Servitude in Colonial America: An Economic Analysis* (Cambridge, Eng., 1981); Timothy Coates, "Convict Labor in the Early Modern Era," in *The Cambridge World History of Slavery*, ed. David Eltis and Stanley L. Engerman (forthcoming); David Eltis, "The Volume and Structure of the Transatlantic Slave Trade: A Reassessment," *William and Mary Quarterly*, 3rd ser., 58 (Jan. 2001): 17–46. Two good microhistories of the transatlantic slave trade are: Robert Harms, *The Diligent: A Voyage through the Worlds of the Slave Trade* (New York, 2002) and Randy J. Sparks, *The Two Princes of Calabar: An Eighteenth-Century Atlantic Odyssey* (Cambridge, Mass., 2004).

11. David Eltis and William G. Clarence-Smith, "White Servitude," in Eltis and Engerman, eds., *The Cambridge World History of Slavery* (forthcoming). For slavery compared to other forms of coerced labor, see M. L. Bush, ed., *Serfdom and Slavery: Studies in Legal Bondage* (London, 1996); Stanley L. Engerman, ed., *Terms of Labor: Slavery, Serfdom, and Free Labor* (Stanford, Calif., 1999); and Bush, *Servitude in Modern Times* (Cambridge, Eng., 2000).

12. Frank M. Snowden Jr., *Blacks in Antiquity: Ethiopians in the Greco-Roman Experience* (Cambridge, Mass., 1970); Snowden, *Before Color Prejudice: The Ancient View of Blacks* (Cambridge, Mass., 1983); Benjamin Isaac, *The Invention of Racism in Classical Antiquity* (Princeton, N.J., 2004); Jean Devisse and Michel Mollat, eds., *The Image of the Black in Western Art*, Vol. 2: *From the Early Christian Era to the "Age of Discovery"* (Cambridge, Mass., 1979); Paul Freedman, *Images of the Medieval Peasant* (Stanford, Calif., 1999), 133–73, 300–303; Peter Kolchin, *Unfree Labor: American Slavery and Russian Serfdom* (Cambridge, Mass., 1987), 170–73; Winthrop D. Jordan, *White Over Black: American Attitudes toward the Negro, 1550–1812* (Chapel Hill, N.C., 1968); Ivan Hannaford, *Race: The History of an Idea in the West* (Washington, D.C., 1996); the essays in "Constructing Race: Differentiating Peoples in the Early Modern World," *William and Mary Quarterly*, 3rd ser., 54 (Jan. 1997): 3–252; David M. Goldenburg, *The Curse of Ham: Race and Slavery in Early Judaism, Christianity, and Islam* (Princeton, N.J., 2003); the best account is David Brion Davis, "The Origins of Anti-Black Racism in the New World," chapter 3 of *Inhuman Bondage: The Rise and Fall of New World Slavery* (New York, 2006).

13. Robert Fogel, *Without Consent or Contract: The Rise and Fall of American Slavery* (New York, 1989); Schwartz, ed., *Tropical Babylons*, 3.

14. Frank Tannenbaum, *Slave and Citizen: The Negro in the Americas* (New York, 1946); Carl N. Degler, *Neither Black Nor White: Slavery and Race Relations in Brazil and the United States* (New York, 1971).

15. For some examples, see William D. Piersen, *Black Yankees: The Development of an Afro-American Subculture in Eighteenth-Century New England* (Amherst, Mass.,

1988); Graham Russell Hodges, *Root and Branch: African Americans in New York and East Jersey, 1613–1863* (Chapel Hill, N.C., 1999); Philip D. Morgan, *Slave Counterpoint: Black Culture in the Eighteenth-Century Chesapeake and Lowcountry* (Chapel Hill, N.C., 1998); Daniel H. Usner, *Indians, Settlers, & Slaves in a Frontier Exchange Economy: The Lower Mississippi Valley before 1783* (Chapel Hill, N.C., 1992); Jane Landers, *Black Society in Spanish Florida* (Urbana, Ill., 1999); and Brett Rushforth, "'A Little Flesh We Offer You': The Origins of Indian Slavery in New France," *William and Mary Quarterly*, 3rd ser., 60 (Oct. 2003): 777–808. To this list might be added other forms of aboriginal slavery: see Theda Perdue, *Slavery and the Evolution of Cherokee Society, 1540–1866* (Knoxville, Tenn., 1979); William A. Starna and Ralph Watkins, "Northern Iroquoian Slavery," *Ethnohistory*, 38 (Winter 1991): 34–57; and Leland Donald, *Aboriginal Slavery on the Northwest Coast of North America* (Berkeley, Calif., 1997).

16. Slavery, however, continued in Africa until about the 1930s. There the abolitionist moment was rather prolonged and slavery underwent what has been termed a "slow death."

REFLECTIONS ON
"ORIGINS OF AMERICAN SLAVERY"

GLORIA SESSO

In the past, I taught the origin of slavery by asking students to identify the main elements developed in Peter Kolchin's "The Economic Origins of Slavery."[1] These elements include:

1. The key determinant of the labor system that emerged in the American colonies was the degree to which agriculture was geared to the market.
2. Slavery in the American mainland grew from the decline of indentured servitude, the decline of migration from England, and the need for a sustained and skilled labor force owing to the growing prosperity of the tobacco trade.
3. Slavery is rooted in economic production of a particular kind.

Next, I had the students contrast Kolchin's arguments with those presented by Edmund Morgan in "Slavery and Freedom: The American Paradox." Morgan argues that the aftermath of Bacon's Rebellion resulted in the necessity of resolving the class issues associated with indentured servants; the "race card" created a laboring class that could not threaten the hold of the planter system on the development of Virginia. Slavery as a codified system took root from the 1670s until 1701. We look at the progression of the slave codes resulting in the codified law of 1701.[2]

However, after reading Philip Morgan's essay "The Origins of American Slavery," I realized that a global perspective on the origin of slavery might help resolve the seeming paradox of a slave system built within a free society. Philip Morgan's essay concentrates on the importance of sugar and trade in the development of the transatlantic slave trade. Sugar and its concentration in the Caribbean accounted for the bulk of the slave trade in the Americas. The Atlantic coastline of the United States played only a small part in the origin of slavery. Using the global context developed in Philip Morgan's essay leads to an analysis of the justification for the slave trade and a more nuanced picture of the origin of slavery in the Americas.

With these points in mind, I now have my students concentrate on a set of documents associated with *The Diligent: A Voyage through the Worlds of the Slave Trade* by Robert Harms and other documents on the slave trade produced online by the Gilder Lehrman Center for the Study of Slavery and Resistance.[3]

I divide the class into four groups and ask each group to analyze a document that relates to the origin of slavery. They analyze the document using these categories:

1. Global context
2. National purpose
3. Economic gain
4. Point of view

GROUP ONE

FROM THE PERSPECTIVE OF THE KING OF WHYDAH [C. 1726]

"The tiny kingdom of Whydah functioned mainly as a terminus for trade routes that came from the interior. The slaves who were sold in Whydah did not come from Whydah itself. . . . The European slave traders played a central role in the coronation ceremony of King Huffon. Representatives of the European trading companies were present at the meeting at which Huffon was chosen King. After Huffon was installed as the King of Whydah, the

European trading firms competed for his favor. The English presented him with a crown. And the French countered by giving him the entire cargoes of two ships. The ornate Louis XIV style came later. . . . One reason the King allowed Whydah to be used as a major terminus of the slave trade routes was the revenue he received from the trade. He received a thousand cowrie shells for each slave that was sold in his kingdom and customs payments from European slave ships."[4]

1. Who is involved in the slave trade? Why?
2. How is the slave trade justified? Explain.

GROUP TWO

ON JUSTIFYING THE SLAVE TRADE

"The slave trade was absolutely necessary for the cultivation of sugar, tobacco, cotton, indigo, and other products that were exported from the Caribbean to France. The authority to carry on the slave trade came from the King of France himself and the slave trade would not have been authorized except for the indispensable need that we have for services in the colonies. . . . The slave traders were rescuing the slaves from error and idolatry to bring them to a place where they could be baptized and instructed in the Catholic religion. . . . In the land of Negritie, the people are so numerous that it would be difficult for them to maintain a substance were it not for the fact that each year the slave trade carries away a portion of the inhabitants. . . . These people, accustomed to make war on each other, would kill their prisoners of war were it not for the fact that they must spare their lives in order to sell or exchange them for the merchandise that we bring to our ships."[5] (Gerard Mellier [c. 1731])

1. How does Mellier justify the slave trade?
2. Explain the overriding principle in his reasoning. Why?

GROUP THREE

"DE MAJOREM DEI GLORIUM VIRGINIS Q MARIA"

(To the greater glory of God and the Virgin Mary) [The Journal of Robert Durand, c. 1731]
"With the help of God, we are undertaking to go from Vannes, whence we are now outfitted to the coast of Guinea in the ship *The Diligent* belonging to the brothers Billy and Mr. La Croix, our outfitters and thence to Martinique to sell our blacks and make our return to Vannes."[6]

1. According to Durand, what is the purpose of the slave trade?
2. Explain the connection between the "greater glory of God" and the explanation of where *The Diligent* is going.

GROUP FOUR

Study the two maps and answer the questions.

MAP ONE—THE SLAVE TRADE, FROM AFRICA TO THE AMERICAS 1650–1850

<http://www.slaveryinamerica.org/geography/slave_trade.htm>

1. Where were the slaves coming from? Where were they going?
2. Where were most of the slaves taken? Why?

MAP TWO—THE TRIANGULAR TRADE

<http://www.members.tripod.com/lylesj/trade/ytitade.html>

1. Describe the trade being represented in the map.
2. How are the two maps connected? Why?

After each group reports its findings, the students discuss the justifications of the slave trade and the implications of the slave trade in a global context. We focus on the specific states that played a major role in the slave trade and the economic and social power that came with controlling the trade. I also emphasize that the slave trade was a capitalistic venture.

The students then compare their analysis of the documents to the ideas that Philip Morgan presented in his essay. Many agree with his conclusion "that the sheer availability of African slaves and the lack of alternatives" was a primary factor in the development of slavery. Slavery's distinctive aspect was its "highly commercial character." The expansion of slavery is the product of an extensive plantation system.

The economic and nationalistic reasons for the expansion of slavery are clear from an analysis of the documents on which the groups report. At the same time, the local differentiations looked minor, to some students, in the face of the transatlantic trade system and its repercussions. Yet there are students who return to Edmund Morgan's essay ("Slavery and Freedom: The American Paradox") and point out the social reasons for the expansion of slavery in Virginia based on Bacon's Rebellion. After all, slavery was not codified until 1701 and its codification created an underclass that could not compete with the ruling class. According to many of the documents that are read in the groups, the slave trade focuses mainly on the Caribbean and South American countries in the production of sugar. Students often question the extent to which Virginia was an isolated, local development where the paradox of slavery being built on freedom persisted.

Philip Morgan's essay develops the global causes and consequences of slavery and its expansion and concludes that slavery "was no abnormality" or aberration. Slavery's origin was rooted in commercial and imperial ventures for gain, profit, and national power. Social and racial reasons take second place when the origin of slavery is analyzed in the global context.

Notes

1. Michael Perman, ed., *Perspectives of the American Past* (Lexington, Mass., 1996), 50:56–73.

2. David Harris, *Southern Slavery and the Law, 1619–1860* (Chapel Hill, N.C., 1996), 38–43.

3. For more information, visit <http:// www.yale.edu/glc/info/links.html>.

4. Robert Harms, *The Diligent: A Voyage Through the Worlds of the Slave Trade* (New York, 2002), 165–69; and the Letter From Bullfinch Lambe, see Slavery and Freedom in American History and Memory at <http://www.yale.edu/glc/aces/links .htm>.

5. Harms, *The Diligent,* 15; see also Gerard Mellier, "Report on the Commerce of Nantes and the Ways to Achieve It" in Harms, *The Diligent,* 118.

6. Harms, *The Diligent,* 4–5; *The Journal of Robert Durand* at Slavery and Freedom in American History and Memory, <http://www.yale.edu/glc/aces/links.htm>.

EVANGELISTS.

CHAPTER 4

NINETEENTH-CENTURY RELIGION IN WORLD CONTEXT

MARK A. NOLL

   Religious connections, influences, and exchanges between the United States and the rest of the world were probably at their low point in the period 1800 to 1870. For most of the major American religious denominations—like the Episcopalians and Methodists from England and the Presbyterians with their Scottish roots—the American Revolution not only led to national independence, but also set a course of independent religious development. An equally sharp break—this time, conceptual and cultural—was created by the First Amendment to the U.S. Constitution. By abandoning formal ties between church and state, the new United States set aside the standard European approach to religion that had prevailed for more than a millennium and so launched the American churches on an uncharted course of social and political, as well as religious, innovation.

   The dominant story in American religion through the period of the Civil War became the adjustment of the formerly British Protestant churches to the new nation's political and social landscape. This process involved a movement from hierarchy to democracy, from inherited structures to institutional creativity, from leadership by appointment to leadership by personal charisma, and from theology defined by elites to theology defined by popular common sense.[1] The break from European patterns was never complete, but it was substantial. It was also unusually successful. During an era of strong population growth (from 3.9 million U.S. residents in 1790 to 31.5 million in 1860), the rates of growth for church adherence, numbers of ministers, value of church property, and financial contributions to religious organizations advanced two or three times faster than the rate of population increase.[2]

The census of 1860 recorded the results of this successful adaptation. It counted almost 55,000 places of worship, of which fewer than 5 percent were Roman Catholic (2,550) and fewer than 0.2 percent were Jewish (seventy-seven). Of the remainder, more than 88 percent were Protestant of British origin (with about 75 percent representing the major British-origin churches: Methodist, Baptist, Presbyterian, and Congregational). That census counted no organized Eastern Orthodox, Muslim, Hindu, Theosophical, or Buddhist religious bodies.[3] The manifest internalization of American religion that has been evident with accelerating force from the 1870s to the present lay almost entirely in the future.

Nonetheless, the extent to which American religious life was connected to events, decisions, personalities, movements, and organizations outside the United States—even through this relatively insular period—is extraordinary. Immigration was a prime factor in opening American religion to the world, but far from the only one. Equally important was the enduring strength of British Protestant connections that, despite the rupture caused by the War for Independence, continued to link Americans to the world. As immigration and transnational Protestant connections grew stronger over the course of the nineteenth century, so too did American religion become even more strongly engaged with forces outside American borders.

MIGRATION, CATHOLICISM, AND THE REDIRECTION OF AMERICAN RELIGION

As so often before in human history, migration constructed international conduits through which personnel, programs, and practices flowed freely. And the movement was not all in one direction, as the interesting career of Lars Paul Esbjorn illustrates. In his native Sweden, Esbjorn was an ardent advocate of the evangelical emphases that were characteristic of the era's main American churches: revivalism, temperance societies, Sunday schools, attacks on slavery, and a willingness to adjust the Lutheran church's traditional Augsburg Confession for nineteenth-century citizens. Esbjorn's pietism effectively blocked his chances for advancement in Sweden's Lutheran state-church, and so in 1849 as a forty-one-year-old, he immigrated to the United States. In the New World, Esbjorn soon grew worried about what struck him as an excess of religious freedom and a loss of inherited church treasures. As a remedy, he worked to organize Lutheran churches and schools among Swedish immigrants in Illinois, Iowa, and South Dakota, and he began to argue for a strict application of the Lutherans' Augsburg Confession, the very doctrinal standard he had wanted to amend when he was in Sweden. Fourteen years provided Esbjorn with enough of the United States, and so in 1863 he returned to Sweden, where he accepted a position in the established Lutheran Church.[4] Yet through his labors, Lutheranism—a traditional, hierarchical, and confessional denomination—was being grounded in the United States among Scandinavian immigrants alongside the more democratized churches. The same process was even more advanced among the much larger communities of German Lutherans.

Catholic immigration meant even more for American religious history than the significant presence of continental Protestants. From the 1840s, a massive movement of peoples from Ireland and Germany transformed American Catholicism. From an exotic minority concentrated in only a few locales, mostly in Maryland and Kentucky, Catholicism burgeoned into a vigorous religious force active in many parts of the country. As of 1855, the number of immigrants from Ireland within the previous fifteen years equaled roughly 5 percent of the entire American population, and the number from Germany was only slightly smaller.[5] The majority of Irish and many of the Germans were Catholic; in the decade from 1850 to 1860, the number of Catholic churches doubled (from 1,227 to 2,550).[6] It was at that point an English-Irish-German-French church, with the French element surviving from the colonial period and being refreshed by significant immigration from Quebec. By 1890, at which time the number of churches had doubled twice more (to 10,258), Roman Catholicism was the nation's most numerous faith by all measures. To its earlier multiethnic character had now been added a tide of newcomers from Italy and Poland, as well as significant tributaries from central and southern Europe.[7]

International considerations were a simple given of American Catholic life. They ranged from the obvious (like the fact of bishops being appointed by Rome) to the subtle (like the wariness imparted by Catholic traditions toward principles of political liberalism). The appointment of bishops was one of the ways that the Vatican sought to balance ethnic influences in what historian Jay Dolan has expertly described as "the immigrant church."[8] The wariness toward liberalism was a consequence of what it meant for Catholic faithful to maintain allegiance to an ancient form of Christianity.

The internationalism brought about by the rising Catholic presence is illustrated by the interweaving of locales (including Quebec, Ireland, Illinois) and the interplay of issues (including immigration, temperance, and language) that marked one short stretch of the mid-nineteenth century. In 1851, Father Charles Chiniquy was sent from Quebec to central Illinois in order to tend French-speaking migrant parishes, but also to promote the cause of temperance. Chiniquy had become famous in Quebec for his ardent zeal on behalf of this reform more often associated with the era's Protestant voluntary societies.[9] That same year, Father Theobold Mathew was also touring in the United States, primarily in Irish Catholic parishes, where he too was promoting the temperance cause. A few years before, he had founded a temperance society in Cork, Ireland, which quickly exerted a broad influence in the Emerald Isle. Now with immigration sparked by the great Irish famine, Father Mathew was making the United States an outpost of his particular Irish reform.[10]

Charles Chiniquy's transnational story eventually became a great deal more complicated than Father Mathew's. In 1858, a series of conflicts with his Quebec superiors led Chiniquy to leave the Catholic Church; he then became briefly an American Presbyterian before joining the Canadian Presbyterian Church; and he entered into a second career as an anti-Catholic writer and speaker. Before returning to Quebec in 1875, he undertook ceaseless itinerations, mostly among Quebec immigrants in Illinois, where he crossed paths on several occasions with Abraham Lincoln, but also in Britain and on the European continent. His anti-Catholic writings became best sellers in the United States even as they circulated, through translations, in Europe.

Chiniquy's and Father Mathew's exertions occurred during an era when issues of immigration and international religion were prominent in American politics. For a brief period during the 1850s, nativist prejudices against immigrants in general, and Catholics in particular, threatened to displace disputes over slavery as the nation's central political controversy. In 1853, speeches by Alessandro Gavazzi, an ex-priest from Italy who denounced the Vatican, promoted Italian unification, and trumpeted the glories of American liberty, occasioned riots in both Canada and the United States that resulted in multiple fatalities and much property damage. More sporadic violence took place in the wake of activities of the Orange Order, a strongly Protestant fraternal organization that immigrants from the north of Ireland brought with them to America as a counterweight to the presence of Irish Catholics.[11] Such antagonisms led to the formation of the American (or "Know Nothing") Party, whose main goal was to restrict immigration and marginalize Catholics.

Throughout the nineteenth century, Catholics were among the Americans most attuned to European affairs. The struggles for *Risorgimento* (the effort to unify the Italian peninsula into a single state) pitted self-defined Italian liberals against a series of popes who defined themselves and their church as conservative. Americans who owed religious allegiance to Pope Gregory XVI (1831–1846), Pope Pius IX (1846–1878), and Pope Leo XIII (1878–1903) were often aware of papal doubts about the supposed virtues of democracy or church-state separation. Their response was usually not to reject these American values but to embrace them alongside the principles of authority informing the practice of their religion.[12]

For its part, the Vatican monitored developments in the United States with a reasonably charitable eye. During the Civil War, several American bishops wrote extensive reports on the conflict to Rome, from whence, in response, Vatican-connected periodicals wrote surprisingly sophisticated reports on the American conflict.[13] These reports displayed considerable sympathy for the American tragedy, but also suggested that the war was a direct outcome of strong Protestant individualism combined with the United States' excesses of democratic liberalism.[14]

Late in the nineteenth century, what has been called an "Americanist" crisis took place when the Vatican tried to ensure that the democratic and republican habits of the United States did not lead American Catholics astray.[15] The origin of this dispute was the growing belief among conservative European Catholics that leaders of the American church were going too far in approving the liberal principles that defined American freedoms. In 1895 Pope Leo XIII issued an encyclical, *Longinqua Oceani,* that praised Americans for their significant achievements but warned against setting up American standards of the separation of church and state as the universal norm. This document was followed in 1899 by an apostolic letter, *Testem Benevolentiae,* that condemned "Americanism" by name as the mistaken desire for the church to conform to American culture, especially by introducing greater personal liberty in ecclesiastical affairs.

The larger point that needs to be stressed is that by 1900, the most powerful religious organization in the United States defined itself to a considerable degree by its place in the world's largest international organization. Even as the church and its members adjusted to the American environment, and even as Catholics argued among themselves about how much and how rapidly to adjust, the vast majority remained self-consciously committed to the ethnic churches of their European origin, and many were also self-conscious about the international character of Catholicism itself.

In turn, Catholic engagement with core American values like "freedom" exerted an influence on the body politic.[16] By comparison with the United States' strongly Protestant traditions, Catholic faith brought a deeper commitment to inherited communities and less nervousness about joining religious organizations to public policies, and religious instincts pointed somewhat more to contemplation and mediation instead of action and intervention.

PROTESTANT "EMPIRES"

Despite the American Revolution, and despite the innovations pursued by the churches of the new United States, strong ideological and organizational bonds continued to join Protestants in the Old and New Worlds. An early instance illustrating the strength of those bonds was the rise of theological liberalism in the new United States, for it was an American development tied directly to British intellectual inspiration.

During the colonial period, theological liberalism had arisen in the colonies as a direct offshoot of influences from England and Scotland.[17] When in the 1790s Tom Paine published his proposals for radical democracy, *The Rights of Man,* and a two-part treatise entitled *The Age of Reason* that questioned traditional interpretations of the Bible, Paine became as important for the new nation's small cadre of deists, freethinkers, and theological liberals, which included Ethan Allen and Thomas Jefferson, as his *Common Sense* of 1776 had been for American patriots.[18] With his travels and radical connections in Britain, France, and the United States, Paine embodied the era's intellectual internationalism.

European connections were even more important for the main bodies of evangelical Protestants. The shape of American Protestantism owed much to the colonial Puritan heritage, but it was also greatly stimulated by a wide range of eighteenth-century influences, among which Moravian Pietism from Germany was the most important. The Moravians' activities in Georgia, the frontiers of Massachusetts and Pennsylvania, Ontario, the West Indies, and many other remote regions of the world established international networks through which flowed practices that would soon prevail widely in the United States: a stress on heart religion, the fervent singing of freshly written hymns, and attentive evangelism to racial minorities. After long neglect by historians, the extraordinary international sweep of Moravian activity—as well as the shaping impact of these German-speakers on the English-language world—is now beginning to receive serious historical attention.[19]

Much better known in historical literature is the evangelical impetus provided to Americans by the major British leaders of the colonial Great Awakening. The Anglican minister, George Whitefield, who made seven trips to the colonies and who died in Massachusetts in 1770, established many personal links between like-minded fellow-believers in England, Scotland, Wales, and America.[20]

Those links became immensely significant when Methodist immigrants from Britain brought their religion and its innovations to the New World: itinerating ministers, active evangelism outside the church, and small groups run by lay people. When the early American leader, Francis Asbury, arrived in America in 1771, there were four Methodist preachers caring for about three hundred people. By 1813, three years before his death, the official Methodist minutes listed 171,448 white and 42,850 African American members "in full society" served by 678 preachers and about seven thousand local class leaders.[21] As many as one million people (or about one out of eight Americans) were attending a Methodist camp meeting each year.[22] In 1860, the U.S. census recorded the presence of 19,833 Methodist churches, or more than one-third of all worship sites in the country.[23] A British import had remade American religion.

African American religion also witnessed significant internationalism in this same period. Christianity among African Americans had taken hold only when slaves and freed blacks responded to the revivalistic message of Whitefield and other British-inspired itinerants during the 1740s and 1750s. The first black churches were established by slaves in Georgia and South Carolina on the eve of the American Revolution. Their leaders, like the former slave David George, who helped found churches in Silver Bluff, South Carolina, and Savannah, Georgia, found better protection from British troops than from American patriots. As a result, when the British abandoned South Carolina, George went with them to Nova Scotia, where he established the first black churches in what became Canada. Then, in 1793, he took part in a migration of Loyalist Canadian blacks to Sierra Leone, where he not only set up Baptist churches but also established an African presence to which many Americans, black and white, would be drawn over the course of the nineteenth century and beyond.[24]

Similarly, another former slave from South Carolina, George Liele, immigrated to Jamaica, where in Kingston he founded a flourishing church that built on earlier labors of Moravian missionaries. Liele's substantial Jamaica congregation and his wide-ranging connections with Baptists in Nova Scotia and throughout the southern United States helped stabilize African American religion in the entire Atlantic region.[25]

The Atlantic highway was also an important clearinghouse for reform movements inspired by religion. In the early 1770s, John Wesley read one of the antislavery tracts of Philadelphia Quaker Anthony Benezet and was moved to renew his personal campaign against the slave trade, which he called "that execrable sum of all villainies."[26] Wesley thus added his influential voice to the growing sentiment against slavery that was leading a few British Quakers and evangelical Anglicans to struggle against the slave trade and for abolition. This British agitation encouraged the lonely voices of early American antislavery, such as the Rhode Island minister Samuel Hopkins and the Philadelphia physician Benjamin Rush. Eventually the British precedent inspired entire American organizations like the American Anti-Slavery Society (founded in 1833) to take up the battle.[27]

Interchange among far-flung networks that shared the British Protestant heritage continued unabated throughout the nineteenth century. American preachers were welcomed most readily among English Dissenters (Baptists, Congregationalists, Methodists), Scottish Presbyterians, and Irish Protestants, but many of them also succeeded in winning a favorable hearing among state-church Anglicans as well.[28] The pioneer was an eccentric exhorter from Connecticut who was loosely associated with the American Methodist Church. Lorenzo "Crazy" Dow (1777–1834) came to England first in 1805, but before he ended his extensive itinerations in Canada, Britain, the West Indies, and the United States, his compelling message of personal religious commitment had altered the life course of many on both sides of the Atlantic. Dow was followed by James Caughey (1810–1891), an Ulster-born immigrant to America who in 1841 returned as an unknown Methodist to Britain, but where in four tours over the next decade he created a sensation. Caughey was one of the prime influences in the religious awakenings of William and Catherine Booth, founders of the Salvation Army. Then came Charles Finney (1792–1875), whose book, *Lectures on Revival* (1835), had created an extensive audience for activistic, evangelical ultraism before he arrived for extensive British tours in 1849 and again in 1859. Finney was followed by Phoebe Palmer (1807–1874), who like Finney parlayed the renown of a book—in her case, *The Way of Holiness* (1843)—into wide British notice during a lengthy stay from 1859 to 1863. D. L. Moody (1837–1899) was probably the century's best-known American revivalist, but his noteworthy American career did not take off until an extended sojourn in England and Scotland (1873–1875) transformed him into a religious phenomenon whose British reputation paved the way for American prominence. A large part of Moody's appeal was his teamwork with a talented song-leader, Ira Sankey, whose performances and publications merged the products of British and American gospel music into a powerful statement of transatlantic musical evangelicalism.

For much of the regular practice of American religion, however, influence flowed the other way, from Britain to America. Throughout the nineteenth century, when American Protestants raised their voices in religious song, they usually did so with words supplied by British authors. Surveys undertaken of many American hymnals by historian Stephen Marini document the pattern: for American hymnbooks from 1736 to 1860, twenty out of the twenty-one most frequently reprinted hymns came from Britain; for the period 1861 to 1970, only two out of the twenty most frequently reprinted hymns were written by Americans; the rest were British.[29] Americans of all Protestant persuasions, and quite a few of the unchurched as well, could be moved deeply when they sang "All hail the power of Jesus' name," "Jesus lover of my soul," "Rock of ages cleft for me," "O for a thousand tongues to sing," and many more. As they did so, they testified to the international character of popular religion in the United States.

The voluntary society was another British institution that had an even greater American impact. Voluntary groups had been known in England from the late seventeenth century, but when the form was taken over by the Methodists, and seasoned by Moravian influences, it became an engine of nearly revolutionary power. In the early national period, Americans saw Britons organizing the Religious Tract Society (1799) and, supremely, the British and Foreign Bible Society (1804) that offered well-publicized examples of effective lay-led and interdenominational societies. A few small-scale voluntary societies had been formed in the United States before the turn of the nineteenth century, but as self-created vehicles for proclaiming the Christian message, distributing Christian literature, and bringing scattered Christian exertions together, the voluntary society came into its own only after about 1810. The most important societies represented interdenominational teams of evangelicals mobilizing for evangelical purposes. The best funded and most dynamic—the American Board of Commissioners for Foreign Missions (1810), the American Bible Society (1816), and the American Education Society (1816), which aimed especially at education for ministerial candidates—were rivaled only by the Methodists in their influence on the nation.[30] Voluntary organization, which meant so much for American religious life, and which showed the way for the political and economic voluntarism of American civil society, represented an ongoing bequest of Old World religion to the New.

The continuation of slavery in the United States was the chief impediment to even stronger ties between American Protestants and Protestants abroad. British antislavery advocates, who in 1833 had secured the liberation of slaves in the British West Indies, were aligned with the radical wing of American abolitionism, a group many American Protestants mistrusted as liberal extremists. This tension over slavery had institutional repercussions. When the first meeting of the international Evangelical Alliance convened in London in 1843, plans for a full-scale organization of worldwide Protestants collapsed over contrasting British and American proposals for dealing with slavery.[31]

Even after the Civil War brought an end to slavery, the American racial situation continued to divide a transatlantic Protestant world that otherwise shared so many natural connections. Still, during the last third of the century, connections among Protestants at home and abroad multiplied, with many ties related to issues of social reform.

In 1880 the Salvation Army, which had been organized by William and Catherine Booth after their encounters with American revivalists, "opened fire" (as the Army's own publicity put it) in the United States. Although the Salvationists were not as visible in the United States as in Canada, where they arrived in 1882, they nonetheless rapidly became the most effective Protestant response to the social problems of the new urban America.[32]

The Social Gospel movement, a home-grown parallel in response to the same urban and economic problems, drew broadly on European ideas rather than personnel. Thomas Chalmers, a Scottish preacher and urban reformer from the first half of the nineteenth century, was one of the sources used by Washington Gladden, a key figure in launching the Social Gospel.[33] In 1900 Charles Henderson of the University of Chicago issued an abridged edition of Chalmers's *The Christian and Civic Economy of Large Towns* and also published an essay on Chalmers in the *American Journal of Theology* that called this work "a classic" and commended it as an inspiration for the city missions then gathering force in the United States.[34]

Other leaders of the Social Gospel were even more directly inspired by Britain's ethical societies. The best-known leader, Walter Rauschenbusch of New York City and Rochester Theological Seminary, was typical for the movement in drawing inspiration from European Christian socialists, although somewhat atypical in finding such inspiration from German rather than British sources.[35]

By the end of the century, an even more consequential engagement with the world was expanding through the growing contribution of American Protestants to the missionary movement. In part a correlate to the rising commercial and military expansion of the United States government and in part direct product of religious motives, American missionary activity brought the world to the United States even as American missionaries took their version of Christianity to the world.[36]

The missionary interpretation of the world featured landmark publications and events. Books by and about the pioneering missionary to Burma, Adoniram Judson (1788–1850) and his three successive wives, communicated a great deal about the Far East as well as the multifaceted church work undertaken by the Judsons.[37] In 1900 a missionary conference in New York City enlisted former president Benjamin Harrison, sitting president William McKinley, and future president Theodore Roosevelt among the speakers.[38] Their presence testified to how significant missionary contact with the rest of the world had become for the United States as a whole.

In 1903, a thorough survey reported that more than one-fourth of the nearly 16,000 Protestants missionaries worldwide were from the United States.[39] Apart from the United States military in Cuba and the Philippines, this missionary force represented the largest contingent of U.S. citizens abroad, and the majority of missionaries were far more effective as brokers between American and foreign cultures than were military personnel.

Significantly, by the end of the century, leading figures of the African Methodist Episcopal Church, especially Henry McNeal Turner, had established exchanges with black churches in South Africa and elsewhere on the continent. These exchanges were little noticed by the majority population at the time, but they represented the beginnings of significant religious ties between Americans and Africans that have grown steadily since the 1890s.[40]

By 1900, Protestant Americans and Catholic Americans had not yet accepted each other as fully worthy citizens of the United States. As a result, the newer international connections that were multiplying so rapidly as a result of immigration were not coordinated with the continuing international connections that joined Protestants in the United States to Britain and, to a lesser extent, the European continent. Both connections, however, were strong and, as the century turned, primed to expand dramatically throughout the entire world.

Bibliographical Essay

General histories of American religion can be divided between those that stress the American story as an extension of European religious history and those that stress distinctly American features of the history. In the first camp are most of the early standards of the nineteenth century, of which Robert Baird's *Religion in America* (first published in Scotland in 1844) was the most informative. It is also the standpoint of James Bryce's *American Commonwealth* from the late nineteenth century, in which Bryce affirmed that "the churches of the United States are the churches of the British Isles, modified by recent immigration from the European continent" (3rd ed. [2 vols., New York, 1895], 2:706). The most compelling recent presentation of this view appears in Sydney Ahlstrom's still very valuable *Religious History of the American People* (New Haven, Conn., 1972; new ed. expanded by David D. Hall, New Haven, Conn., 2004).

The other perspective was given its definitive early expression by Alexis de Tocqueville. The character of the country he visited in the 1830s struck him as dissimilar from what he had known in Europe, not least because of its distinctive religious practices. Precisely those elements that featured large in the United States' definition of itself made American religion distinctive (*Democracy in America,* trans. Arthur Goldhammer [New York, 2004]). This view has been well represented in modern historiography, for example, by Winthrop S. Hudson, who focused on voluntarism and the separation of church and state as establishing what he called *The Great Tradition of the American Churches* (New York, 1953), and in the survey by Mark A. Noll, *The Old Religion in the New World: The History of North American Christianity* (Grand Rapids, Mich., 2002), which draws on the insights of Manfred Siebald of the Johannes Gutenberg University of Mainz.

For the nineteenth-century history of American religion, the path of wisdom lies between the two interpretive poles. A great deal of what was important in that century for religion and reform can be explained best by reference to American developments that made for a singular United States history. But much else remained in intimate relationship with Europe, and so represented the necessary background for understanding the intensive internationalizing that, since 1900, has made American religion so obviously a part of the religious history of the world.

Four excellent reference works provide outstanding material for understanding American religion in international perspective: Charles H. Lippy and Peter W. Williams, eds., *Encyclopedia of the American Religious Experience* (3 vols., New York, 1988); Daniel G. Reid et al., eds., *Dictionary of Christianity in America* (Downers Grove, Ill., 1990); *The New Catholic Encyclopedia,* 2nd ed. (Washington, D.C., 2003); and Edwin Scott Gaustad and Philip L. Barlow, *New Historical Atlas of Religion in America* (New York, 2001).

The best individual study to illuminate one facet of the interconnections of British and American religion during the nineteenth century is probably still Richard

Carwardine, *Transatlantic Revivalism: Popular Evangelicalism in Britain and America, 1790–1865* (Westport, Conn., 1978; new ed., Carlisle, Eng., 2005). James T. Kloppenberg, *Uncertain Victory: Social Democracy and Progressivism in European and American Thought, 1870–1920* (New York, 1986) is also outstanding on the transatlantic unity of its theme. David Paul Nord, *Faith in Reading: Religious Publishing and the Birth of Modern Publishing in America* (New York, 2004) documents the effect that British models had on the development of organized American voluntarism. On the role of missionaries in nineteenth-century American society, there is outstanding material in Dana L. Robert, *American Women in Mission: A Social History of their Thought and Practice* (Macon, Ga., 1996), and William R. Hutchison, *Errand to the World: American Protestant Thought and Foreign Missions* (Chicago, 1987). The ties linking nineteenth-century American Protestants to the world as a whole are well treated in David W. Bebbington, *The Dominance of Evangelicalism: The Age of Spurgeon and Moody* (Downers Grove, Ill., 2005), and John Wolffe, *The Expansion of Evangelicalism: The Age of Wilberforce, More, Chalmers and Finney* (Downers Grove, Ill., 2007). International connections among the same groups also figure large in Mark A. Noll, David W. Bebbington, and George A. Rawlyk, eds., *Evangelicalism: Comparative Studies of Popular Protestantism in North America, The British Isles, and Beyond, 1700–1990* (New York, 1994).

General histories of Catholicism in which American connections to the broader world are prominent include James Hennesey, *American Catholics: A History of the Roman Catholic Community in the United States* (New York, 1981), and Jay P. Dolan, *The American Catholic Experience: A History from Colonial Times to the Present* (New York, 1985). Hennesey leans to an interpretation that integrates American Catholics with the Catholic world, Dolan to one that stresses American distinctives.

Jay P. Dolan, *The Immigrant Church: New York's Irish and German Catholics, 1815–1865* (Baltimore, 1975), offers outstanding treatment of nineteenth-century Catholic organization as an American negotiation with European influences, while Patrick W. Carey, ed., *American Catholic Religious Thought* (Mahwah, N.J., 1987) provides the same for Catholic intellectual life. Two recent books offer the most compelling accounts of European connections for nineteenth-century American Catholics: Peter R. D'Agostino, *Rome in America: Transnational Catholic Ideology from the Risorgimento to Fascism* (Chapel Hill, N.C., 2004), which stresses American engagement with Italian cultural politics, and John T. McGreevy, *Catholicism and American Freedom* (New York, 2004), which treats its subject against the background of European influences. Also excellent is R. Scott Appleby, *"Church and Age Unite": The Modernist Impulse in American Catholicism* (Notre Dame, Ind., 1992).

General interpretations of American religion keyed to ethnic and immigrant experiences include pp. 752–54 in Ahlstrom's *A Religious History of the American People*; Martin E. Marty, "Ethnicity: The Skeleton of Religion in America," *Church History*, 41 (March 1972): 5–21; Harry S. Stout, "Ethnicity: The Vital Center of Religion in America," *Ethnicity*, 2 (June 1975): 204–24; Timothy L. Smith, "Religion and Ethnicity in America," *American Historical Review,* 83 (Dec. 1978): 1155–85; Jay P. Dolan, "The Immigrants and their Gods: A New Perspective in American Religious History," *Church History,* 57 (March 1988): 61–72; and Martin E. Marty, ed., *Ethnic and Non-Protestant Themes, Vol. 8: Modern American Protestantism and Its World* (New York, 1993).

Finally, a well-chosen collection that documents a wide range of ongoing American-European links is Milton B. Powell, ed. *The Voluntary Church: American Religious Life, 1740–1860, Seen Through the Eyes of European Visitors* (New York, 1967).

Notes

1. The best account of those adjustments is Nathan O. Hatch, *The Democratization of American Christianity* (New Haven, Conn., 1989).

2. See Roger Finke and Rodney Stark, "How the Upstart Sects Won America: 1776–1850," *Journal for the Scientific Study of Religion,* 28 (March 1989): 27–44; and Mark A. Noll, *America's God: From Jonathan Edwards to Abraham Lincoln* (New York, 2002), 165–70.

3. *Statistics of the United States . . . in 1860; Compiled from the Original Returns . . . of the Eighth Census* (Washington, D.C., 1866), 497–501.

4. George M. Stephenson, *The Religious Aspects of Swedish Immigration* (New York, 1969; orig. 1932), 147–77.

5. *Historical Statistics of the United States: Colonial Times to 1957* (Washington, D.C., 1960), 56–59.

6. *Statistics of the United States . . . in 1860,* 500; *Statistical View of the United States . . . Being a Compendium of the Seventh Census* (Washington, D.C., 1854), 133.

7. Edwin Scott Gaustad and Philip L. Barlow, *New Historical Atlas of Religion in America* (New York, 2001), 155–62.

8. Jay P. Dolan, *The Immigrant Church: New York's Irish and German Catholics, 1815–1865* (Baltimore, 1975) is a good updating of Gerald Shaughnessy, *Has the Immigrant Kept the Faith?* (New York, 1925).

9. See Yves Roby, "Charles Chiniquy," *Dictionary of Canadian Biography, vol. XII: 1891–1900* (Toronto, 1990), 189–93; and Richard Lougheed, *La conversion controversée de Charles Chiniquy, prêtre catholique devenu protestant* (Quebec, 1999).

10. See John F. Quinn, *Father Mathew's Crusade: Temperance in Nineteenth-Century Ireland and Irish America* (Amherst, Mass., 2002).

11. D. G. Paz, "Apostate Priests and Victorian Religious Turmoil: Gavazzi, Achilli, Connelly," *Proceedings of the South Carolina Historical Association* (1985): 57–69; Michael A. Gordon, *The Orange Riots: Irish Political Violence in New York City, 1870 and 1871* (Ithaca, N.Y., 1993).

12. Peter R. D'Agostino, *Rome in America: Transnational Catholic Ideology from the Risorgimento to Fascism* (Chapel Hill, N.C., 2004).

13. On those communications, see Anthony B. Lalli and Thomas H. O'Connor,

"Roman Views on the American Civil War," *Catholic Historical Review,* 40 (April 1971): 21–41.

14. For example, "La Chiesa tuttrice della libertà in America" [The Church as Guardian of Liberty in America], *La Civiltà cattolica,* ser. 6, 1 (March 18, 1865): 662–80.

15. R. Scott Appleby, *"Church and Age Unite": The Modernist Impulse in American Catholicism* (Notre Dame, Ind., 1992).

16. See especially John T. McGreevy, *Catholicism and American Freedom* (New York, 2004), and McGreevy, *Parish Boundaries: The Catholic Encounter with Race in the Twentieth-Century Urban North* (Chicago, 1996).

17. John Corrigan, *The Hidden Balance: Religion and the Social Theories of Charles Chauncy and Jonathan Mayhew* (New York, 1987).

18. Kerry S. Walters, ed., *The American Deists: Voices of Reason and Dissent in the Early Republic* (Lawrence, Kans., 1992).

19. Colin Podmore, *The Moravian Church in England* (Oxford, 1998); Rachel Wheeler, "Women and Christian Practice in a Mahican Village," *Religion and American Culture,* 13 (Winter 2003), 27–68; Jon F. Sensbach, *Rebecca's Revival: Creating Black Christianity in the Atlantic World* (Cambridge, Mass., 2005); and Peter Vogt, "'Everywhere at Home': The Eighteenth-Century Moravian Movement as a Transatlantic Religious Community," *Journal of Moravian History,* 1 (Fall 2006): 7–30.

20. Harry S. Stout, *The Divine Dramatist: George Whitefield and the Rise of Modern Evangelicalism* (Grand Rapids, Mich., 1991).

21. *Minutes of the Methodist Conferences Annually Held in America, From 1773 to 1813, Inclusive* (New York, 1813), 598–99.

22. John H. Wigger, *Taking Heaven by Storm: Methodism and the Rise of Popular Christianity in America* (New York, 1998), 81, 97.

23. *Statistics of the United States . . . in 1860,* 499.

24. Simon Schama, *Rough Crossings: Britain, the Slaves and the American Revolution* (London, 2005).

25. Sylvia R. Frey and Betty Wood, *Come Shouting to Zion: African American Protestantism in the American South and British Caribbean to 1830* (Chapel Hill, N.C., 1998).

26. W. Reginald Ward and Richard P. Heitzenrater, eds., *The Works of John Wesley,* vol. 22: *Journal and Diaries V (1765–1775)* (Nashville, 1993), 307 (for Feb. 12, 1772).

27. The primarily British sources of American antislavery are well catalogued in David Brion Davis, *The Problem of Slavery in the Age of Revolution, 1770–1823,* new ed. (New York, 1999).

28. The key work is Richard J. Carwardine, *Transatlantic Revivalism: Popular Evangelicalism in Britain and America, 1790–1865,* new ed. (Carlisle, Eng., 2005 [orig. 1978]); but further information on the figures sketched here is found in Timothy Larsen, ed., *Biographical Dictionary of Evangelicals* (Downers Grove, Ill., 2003).

29. Stephen Marini, "From Classical to Modern: Hymnody and the Development

of American Evangelicalism, 1737–1970," in *Singing the Lord's Song in a Strange Land: Hymnody in the History of North American Protestantism,* ed. Edith L. Blumhofer and Mark A. Noll (Tuscaloosa, Ala., 2004), 10, 18.

30. Charles I. Foster, *Errand of Mercy: The Evangelical United Front, 1790–1837* (Chapel Hill, N.C., 1960), 275–79.

31. *Report of the Proceedings of the Conference, Held at Freemasons' Hall, London, From August 19th to September 2nd Inclusive, 1846. Published by Order of the Conference* (London, 1847).

32. Edward H. McKinley, *Marching to Glory: A History of the Salvation Army in the United States, 1880–1992,* 2nd ed. (Grand Rapids, Mich., 1995).

33. Washington Gladden, *Social Salvation* (Boston, 1902), 237; and Gladden, *The Christian Pastor and the Working Church* (New York, 1906), 450.

34. Charles R. Henderson, "A Half Century After Thomas Chalmers," *American Journal of Theology,* 4 (Jan. 1900): 52.

35. James T. Kloppenberg, *Uncertain Victory: Social Democracy and Progressivism in European and American Thought, 1870–1920* (New York, 1986), 207–8.

36. Patricia R. Hill, *The World Their Household: The American Women's Foreign Mission Movement and Cultural Transformation* (Ann Arbor, Mich., 1985); and William R. Hutchison, *Errand to the World: American Protestant Thought and Foreign Missions* (Chicago, 1987).

37. Joan Jacobs Brumberg, *Mission for Life: The Story of the Family of Adoniram Judson* (New York, 1980).

38. *Ecumenical Missionary Conference, 1900* (New York, 1900).

39. Charles W. Forman, "The Americas," *International Bulletin of Missionary Research,* 6 (April 1982): 54.

40. James T. Campbell, *Songs of Zion: The African Methodist Episcopal Church in the United States and South Africa* (Chapel Hill, N.C., 1998).

TEACHING NINETEENTH-CENTURY AMERICAN RELIGION IN A GLOBAL CONTEXT

J. D. BOWERS

The issue of American exceptionalism—the extent to which the nation's various institutions, practices, and beliefs were unique—has long been examined in the study of American religion. One need only look at the contrasting viewpoints offered in two recent works to see the issue's prominence. Mark Noll's *America's God* (2002) makes the case for theological and institutional developments shaped by unique American circumstances, while E. Brooks Holifield's *Theology in America* (2003) presents the same period, from the founding to the Civil War, as one shaped by a lengthy and sustained heritage from abroad.

Though Noll clearly sees the dominant trend of the century as American religion following a new, isolated path, he does not completely dismiss a global context for the nation's religious developments and acknowledges that there were some substantial exchanges that continued to define the course of the nation's religious development. As he adroitly notes in the accompanying essay, "Nineteenth-Century Religion in World Context," there is no dearth of subjects when it comes to discussing and teaching about the global dimensions of American religion in the nineteenth century. Religious groups that were uniquely American—Mormons, African Americans, Unitarians, communal societies, just to name a few—still operated within a framework that was shaped by migrations, intellectual exchange, and transnational events, making it relatively easy, topical, and important to include considerations of the global dimensions of American religion in the introductory U.S. history course. The sheer diversity and breadth of America's nineteenth-century global context and developments was inspired by the tenets of a worldwide faith network of exchanges in morals and practices that transcended national boundaries. Despite what we may have been taught about the nation's political stance throughout the century, Noll's essay clearly reminds us that the United States came of age not in isolation but as one cast member among many on the world stage.

To achieve an understanding of the way in which the rest of the world shaped the direction of America's religious developments, I place great emphasis on the international dimensions of the religious crusade against slavery, the lingering connections and conversations across the oceans between members of various denominations, and the migration of religious believers as they sought out America as a place for the culmination of their communal and utopian visions.

RELIGION AND SLAVERY

The majority of students tend to have a very narrow understanding of slavery. Slavery was, they think, uniquely American, practiced only on the American plantation within a "cotton culture," and brought entirely to an end with the conclusion of the American Civil War. Few students are ever introduced to the religious dimensions of the slave institution—both those that defended and rejected its presence—or the complex religious experiences of the slaves themselves. It is one thing to talk about slavery as being wrong, but another to establish that its practice and eventual demise had religious connotations and understandings. For students, this is often the hardest leap to make. Fortunately, the literature connecting slavery and religion is plentiful, as is the literature that establishes the quest for civil and individual liberties—the duties of man and citizen often exemplified by terms such as "liberty," "equality," and "justice"—as a quest for the application of God's laws on earth.

"What does the Bible say about slavery?" is an excellent first question to ask students. One need only turn to the book itself (and a good concordance) to find multiple mentions of slavery and then seek to discern how Christians throughout the nineteenth century would have interpreted those statements. Genesis, Exodus, Leviticus, and Deuteronomy all make explicit or implicit mention of the practice of slavery, which was used as the foundation for the southern apologists. The writings of the Reverend Frederick Ross of Alabama put forth a common argument in the defense of slavery on the basis of its sanctioning by God revealed through scripture. Though it is not surprising to students that southern ministers would hold views that were aligned with their upbringing and regional culture, they often find it remarkable to learn that Ross gave numerous public speeches throughout the North to standing-room-only audiences.[1] More important, this document serves as the foundation for a discussion on the way religion was used throughout the nineteenth century in service of one's social and political beliefs.

Never one to allow the defenders of slavery to have the last word, I also ask my students to examine the plentiful writings of those who turned the proslavery arguments on their head, evoking the same biblical accounts and extending the Christian principles and objectives in pursuit of abolition. Authors such as the Reverend George Cheever, Alexander McLeod, Theodore Dwight Weld, James Freeman Clarke, and Robert Dale Owen all produced a sizable body of literature on the subject.[2] Cheever's writings, to take just one example, rejected the southern view as one that was based upon preconceived notions of what they wanted the Bible to say, rather than actually reading for context and relevance, thus allowing the book to reveal its meaning. Slavery, he argued, was not sanctioned by God, so far as it was then being practiced by man.

I have my students read the following two comparative excerpts:

Ross, *Slavery Ordained by God* (1857)
The relation of the master and slave is not sin; and that, notwithstanding its admitted evils, it is a connection between the highest and lowest races of man, revealing influences which may be, and will be, the most benevolent for the ultimate good of the master and slave. . . .

God took occasion to give to the world the rule of the superior over the inferior. *He cursed him. He cursed him* [Ham] *because he left him unblessed.* . . . Ham was cursed to render service, forever. . . .

God sanctioned slavery then, and sanctions it now.

[Southerners] hold from God, individually and collectively, the highest and the noblest responsibility ever given by Him to individual private men on all the face of the earth. For God has intrusted to them to train millions of the most degraded in form and intellect, but at the same time, the most gentle, the most amiable, the most affectionate, the most imitative, the most susceptible of social and religious love, of all the races of mankind—to train them, and to give them civilization, and the light and the life of the gospel of Jesus Christ.[3]

Cheever, *God Against Slavery* (1857)

But those men who prefer slavery along with freedom, slavery for others and freedom for themselves, and whose plan is to combine both, and give them the same sanction and the same rights everywhere, would be glad to find some support of slavery, some shield for it in God's word; and, if any one could demonstrate from God's word that slavery is right, he might do that from the Pulpit *ad infinitum* and they would not regard it at all as political preaching, but as simply the genuine meekness of wisdom preaching peace by Jesus Christ, and the very perfection of gospel conservatism.

There are many who, without the least wincing, will hear you preach about the slavery of sin, but not one word will they endure about the sin of slavery. . . .

I am more than ever convinced of the right and duty of every preacher of God's word to preach on this Subject, as contained in His word, and to show the people how He regards it; and the providence that directs and overrules all things is manifesting more clearly than ever the wickedness of the attempt to shield slavery from the reprobation of God's word, by denouncing every mention of it as political preaching. That outcry is more likely to cover up a jealousy against religion in politics, than any real hatred of politics in religion. To the law and to the testimony: should not the people seek unto their God? And if their leaders speak not according to His word, it is because there is no light in them. . . .

Involuntary servitude was forbidden by the divine law [Exodus 21:16, Deuteronomy 24:7], and the service appointed by the constitution of the Jewish state was a free service. . . .

There had been, from time to time, great and gross transgressions of this benevolent constitution; and God had incessantly denounced his vengeance, by the prophets, against such oppressions. . . .

This dreadful revolution and usurpation [sin] they [the people of Judah] now [in the King Zedekiah era] resolved upon—king, princes, priests, and the whole oligarchy of masters [in defiance of God and warnings by Jeremiah]. . . .

Now, the transaction of this marked and mighty sin, and God's tremendous, almost instantaneous, wrathful judgment against it, were, for the sudden illumination of wickedness and justice in our fallen world, like a sun shot into chaos. . . .

> It [Judah's permanent national destruction] came like a whirlwind; it was all
> over with them; there was no more reprieve, no more forbearance [by God];
> the choice of slavery instead of freedom, and oppression instead of justice and
> humanity, as the policy of the nation, filled up the measure of their iniqui-
> ties, and exhausted the last drop in the allotted patience and long-suffering
> of God.[4]

Thus students are given two contrasting views from which they can explore the differences between the two sides and understand and assess the
full spectrum of religious-based rejections and defenses of slavery.

Furthermore, as Noll points out, the century was often one of importance
in terms of the institutionalization of African American churches, building
upon the international examples and often leading blacks to migrate abroad
in order to freely practice their religion. But there is another side to the story
as well, one that is increasingly revealed through the collaboration of historians, archeologists, and anthropologists, and that is the continuation and
influence of African customs and practices within the United States.

Though a great deal of focus is often placed on the conversion of the nation's blacks to Christianity, we are increasingly becoming aware of the extent
to which African religious practices were sustained, even among those who
had been Christianized. To address this, I guide my students to the writings
of Frederick Douglass. Douglass's life is a global case study in itself, for his
tale of slavery and freedom must entail the recognition that he was assisted in
his quest for personal freedom by numerous English supporters in 1845–1847
when, in a gesture of their disdain for American slavery, audiences and bene-
factors throughout England contributed the necessary funds to legally buy
Douglass out of bondage, assuring him the status he had personally, illegally,
established when he ran away.

A careful reading of Douglass reveals a great deal about how the wider
world was still at work in America's slave society. In his most widely read
autobiography, *Narrative of the Life of Frederick Douglass,* he recounts a story
about meeting Sandy Jenkins, a slave, who gives him a talisman to carry, literally and metaphorically, into battle with his master Covey, to assure him of
victory and freedom from the abuse that he had long suffered under this most
hated of all masters.[5] By comparing this first and initial retelling of the account with the same in his later writing, *My Bondage and My Freedom,* where
the story gets told in more detail, students are presented with the religious
dimensions of his encounter with Sandy—the contrast between Christian and
African beliefs, the role of conjurers, and the persistence of African religious

customs within the American slave community. Herein, we learn that Sandy was "famous" among the slave community, as "an old advisor . . . a religious man" who believed in a system for which Douglass had "no name." Sandy was, noted Douglass, "a genuine African." And he proposed that Douglass take up a root that held mystical power, in order to protect himself from the abusive Covey. Douglass, a Christian, was uncertain. Sandy assigned a meaning and power to the root that Christians believed constituted an ascriptural act of "divination" and was therefore "sinful." But Sandy's standing within the community, and the fact that Covey and Douglass's mutual Christian beliefs failed to cause the former to act according to its principles, led Douglass to take up the root nevertheless. Douglass wins the physical and mental battle that later ensues between the two men, but he still struggles when it comes time to explain how he was victorious. His Christian beliefs lead him to assign more rational reasons, yet he is never able to explain away the power of the root or Sandy's importance to the African American community of free and enslaved blacks on the Eastern Shore of Maryland.[6] Therein students see the wider world of religion and religious practice at work in ways that are rarely so visible given our lack of sources on African slave religion.

SUSTAINED DENOMINATIONAL CONNECTIONS

To get my students thinking about the broader and lasting connections between the religious people of the United States and their European brethren, I have them read several passages on Unitarianism. Once called "an indigenous religion" by scholars who sought to establish its American credentials, Unitarianism actually had much broader international roots and connections.[7] The early competition between English, Socinian Unitarian theology as defined and practiced by Joseph Priestley, himself an immigrant to the United States in 1794, and the more American, Arian Unitarian theology is an excellent case study to explore. I begin with questions such as, "When does a religion begin?" and "Why would a religion seek to assert uniquely American origins?" To address these issues I turn to Thomas Belsham's *Memoirs of the Late Rev. Theophilus Lindsey . . . [with] a general view of the progress of the Unitarian Doctrine in England and America*. In the later pages of this work Belsham rejects the New England Unitarian theology as insufficient "polytheism" and calls those who believe otherwise "blind to the plain consequences of their own opinions." "I cannot," he concludes, "very consistently class Arians with Unitarians."[8] This passage allows me to query my students on what role an English account of an American religious group would play. As they dissect the larger passage, in which Belsham rejects the denials of an English legacy, by also reading a history of the development of Unitarianism in America, it becomes clear that not only were New England Unitarians fighting against the "orthodox" of New England for the ownership of churches and defending their particular beliefs against substantial Trinitarian opposition, but they were also being forced to account for their beliefs by others, primarily Englishmen and English immigrants to America, who also called themselves Unitarians and who were not in theological agreement. The lesson concludes with a reading of William Ellery Channing's famous Baltimore Sermon, in which he clearly wrestles with the consequences of the English involvement in American liberalism.[9]

An examination of Catholicism also provides my students with a fruitful and productive way of understanding the global dimensions of the nation's religious past. As Noll points out, Catholics went through an "Americanist" crisis late in the nineteenth century, one that provoked papal rebuke and a reassertion of Catholic doctrine. Allowing students to read passages from the Encyclical of Pope Leo XIII, *Testem Benevolentiae Nostrae,* promulgated late in the century, gives them an understanding of the struggles. Leo's declaration that, "there are among you some who conceive and would have the Church in America to be different from what it is in the rest of the world," is in itself enough to get my students to wrestle with the first part of the term *Roman Catholicism*.[10] I also distribute copies of two writings, one from 1856 and another from 1894, that put the controversy into context. William Brownlow's *Americanism Contrasted with Foreignism, Romanism, and Bogus Democracy* and Lucian Johnston's article in *The Catholic World*, "Americanism vs. Ultramontanism," allow me to ask further questions about their understanding of the role of religion in American individual and public life.[11] Brownlow blasts the "system of Popery" as deceitful and corrupt and shows that its designs were to undermine the nation's adherence to democracy and freedom. Johnson, of course, counters with his argument that the Church was liberal, accommodating, and cosmopolitan, providing American Catholics with a divine and essential faith that promoted the American quest.[12] Fortunately for us teachers, this controversy has longstanding roots and modern connotations. I begin by asking: "What does it mean to adhere to a religion that is not American?" "Does it undermine the nation if one has loyalties to an organization from abroad?" The questions are provocative and timely, allowing us to discuss the contrasts between civic nationalism and religious liberty.

But this late-in-the-century crisis is much more important when it is taught in conjunction with the earlier Catholic controversy over trusteeism. "What role should the laity have in the power of a church?" is the question that sets up the matter. The lay trustee question arose in the early years of the century and embroiled the clergy and laity in a dispute over who controlled church property, income, and ultimately authority. The precipitating series of events had to do with the nation's separation of church and state, leading to a corporate status for religious institutions whereby they were granted distinct corporate privileges that required them to adhere to corporate structures and regulations. This led to questions about who owned the church property as well as who had the right to retain and/or dismiss the clergy. Other American denominations, such as the Congregationalists, put this power entirely in the hands of the local groups. The Catholic Church, however, could not suffer such a breach of its apostolic authority; to wit, I give my students excerpts from a sequence of exchanges between Pius VII, his brief *Non Sine Magno,* and the Archbishop of Baltimore, Ambrose Marechal. Together these two writings spell out, in detail, how the progression of American institutions and practices led to results that often undermined the bishop and the Church and the response to it by those in charge. As Pius wrote, the American Protestant practice of unchecked lay authority almost always resulted in "abuses and dissensions" and was, for Catholics, frighteningly, "a practice *new and unheard* of in the church."[13] Again, students are engaged by questions of the relationship between church and state, power and authority, and the role of the people in deciding their own religious directions. Somehow it does not always square for them to understand that nearly a quarter of our nation's people, despite some differences of opinion, still profess adherence to a powerful and global institution that is centered abroad and one in which all vestiges of power flow to Rome.

PROPAGATING THE GOSPEL

Many religious believers came to the United States seeking the full and unfettered expression promised by the founding principles, while many of those already here continued to reach out to others to spread the word and fulfill their theological mission to proselytize. In both instances, the United States was clearly the middle ground in a larger context.

The University of California, Davis, has posted Roland Marchand's remarkable (for their diversity, depth, and dedication) collections of primary sources online for all to use. His case studies include (but are by no means limited to religious topics) antinomianism, communalism, and John Brown. I have repeatedly used his collection on the communal New Harmony Society to get my students to ask and answer questions about the role of the nation as a religious refuge from persecution, religious ideals for society's advancement, and the intermingling of religious, political, and economic forces.[14] Through his collected sources on New Harmony, I lead my students to explore the questions on the role of religion in addressing the problems of expansion, exceptionalism, and expression. "Why did people feel that faith-based communities would solve their social and political feelings of disassociation?" is the first question to start with. That is often followed by questions such as "To what extent was religion the driving force or was it tangential?" and "Were these societies places of social or religious experimentalism?" leading, of course, to conclusions about how and why some failed and some succeeded. The questions I ask about New Harmony could be equally applied to many of the other groups—Shakers, Amana, Oneida—as well.

I also like to have my students explore the community of Bishop Hill, Illinois. Relatively unknown on the national scene, its story is one of sustained global connections and consequences. The leader, Eric Janson, wrote his own catechism and rejected the connections between the Catholic Church and state in Sweden, the precise reason he opted for immigration to the United States. Thus my students can examine the contrast between societies where the state reigned supreme and the potential that the United States held for those who suffered under such an arrangement. Eventually Janson's efforts transcended the simple pursuit of religious freedom and moved into the realm of experimentalism, leading to declarations that he was "standing in Christ's stead" and that his efforts would "far exceed that of the work accomplished by Jesus and his apostles." Such talk, not to mention his worldly actions, soon got him into trouble, and he was assassinated. But his story compares well with that of the Mormons, whose leader was controversial but whose origins were entirely American. Janson's efforts, though short-lived, led to the immigration of more than one thousand Swedes to the Illinois prairie, beginning the great Swedish movement that defined much of the upper Midwest.[15]

Spreading the faith also occurred in the Pacific as American denominations developed sophisticated procedures for recruiting and sending missionaries to Hawaii and the rest of Oceania. The role that religion played throughout the process of national expansion and, ultimately, imperialism, can be clearly seen by turning students toward readings that reveal the intentions and actions of the missionaries. "To what extent were the missionaries serving two gods—the God of their faith and the god of civic nationalism?" is the first question to put forth. Over the years, I have amassed a collection of relevant and poignant sources that I direct my students to read: Samuel Bartlett's *Historical Sketch of the Hawaiian Mission and the Missions of Micronesia and the Marquesas Islands,* the writings of the Polynesian missionary Ta'unga, and the records of the Hawaiian annexation hearings before the U.S. Senate in 1898.

Excerpts from Bartlett are easily used to establish how Americans thought of themselves and how they saw their religion as the saving grace of many foreign peoples.

Bartlett, *Sketch of the Hawaiian Mission* **(1869)**

The nation practiced human sacrifice . . . they were a race of perpetual thieves . . . wholesale gamblers . . . drunkards. Thoroughly savage, they seemed almost destitute of fixed habits.

The sick were abandoned to die of want and neglect. Maniacs were stoned to death. Captives were tortured and slain. The whole system of government and religion was to the last degree oppressive. The lands, their products, and occupants, were [ruled by] a crushing system of restrictions, called *tabus* (6).

Even after the reputed success of the missionaries, however, Bartlett finds that much still remains to overshadow the bright and marvelous aspect of missionary work.

But, of course, they have their drawbacks. The Sandwich Islands are not Paradise, nor even America. The stage of civilization is, as it must be, far below that of our own country. The old habits still shade into the new. Peculiar temptations to intemperance and licentiousness come down by inheritance. Foreign interventions and oppositions have still been grave hindrances. Church members but fifty years removed from a state of brutalism can not and do not show the stability, intelligence, and culture of those who inherit the Christian influences of a thousand years (13).[16]

Together these documents allow students to confront the realities of religious expansion and Protestant exceptionalism. It has long been said, half in jest and half in truth, that the missionaries went to the islands of the Pacific to do good and that they did well. Thus I ask my students to consider: "How was it that the religious mission of these ministers turned into a quest to Americanize a foreign people?" and "What role did the people of the Pacific play in the process?" and conclude with the question, "How did ministers of the cloth become ministers of state and eventually the leading force in the annexation of Hawaii and U.S. imperialism?" There is no question that, by the end of the century, the nation's quest for territorial and economic growth were steeped in religious significance, both in terms of those who promoted the nation's quest as one ordained by God and those who opposed it on the grounds that God never advocated the destruction of others.

CONCLUDING THOUGHTS

As Noll relates, American religion was immersed in a transnational context and meaning; his historiographical essay relates far more instances than can be examined or considered in this abbreviated space. But I have attempted to introduce the reader to a few writings and ways to teach students about some of those topics covered by Noll as well as others that are unique to my own teaching focus. It is my hope that these two complementary essays lend themselves easily to adoption and adaptation in the classroom for others who are seeking to add the crucial global dimension to their instruction in the nation's religious history of the nineteen century.[17]

Notes

1. Rev. Frederick A. Ross, *Slavery Ordained by God* (1859), excerpted in Robert Edgar Conrad, ed., *In the Hands of Strangers: Readings on Foreign and Domestic Slave Trading and the Crisis of the Union* (University Park, Pa., 2001), 373–80. See also the specific biblical passages and the additional apologist writings of Thornton Stringfellow and Alexander McCaine in Mason I. Lowance, ed., *A House Divided: The Antebellum Slavery Debates in America, 1776–1865* (Princeton, N.J., 2003), 51–87.

2. See George Cheever, *God Against Slavery* (1857) online at <http://medicolegal .tripod.com/cheevergvs.htm>. For the writings of McLeod, Weld, Clarke, and Owen, see Lowance, ed., *A House Divided*, 88–115. Weld's writings may also be accessed at <http://medicolegal.tripod.com/weldbas.htm>.

3. F. A. Ross, *Slavery Ordained by God* (Philadelphia, 1857), 67–68.

4. George Cheever, *God Against Slavery* (New York, 1857), iv–v.

5. Frederick Douglass, *Narrative of the Life of Frederick Douglass, An American Slave, Written by Himself,* ed. Benjamin Quarles. (Cambridge, Mass., 1988), 97–105.

6. Douglass, *My Bondage and My Freedom,* ed. Phil S. Foner (New York, 1969), 233–49.

7. For the indigenous interpretations of Unitarianism's origins see the introduction to Conrad Wright, *The Beginnings of Unitarianism in America* (Boston, 1955) and the preface to Conrad E. Wright, *American Unitarianism, 1805–1865* (Boston, 1989); for the English roots and legacy in America, see J. D. Bowers, *Joseph Priestley and English Unitarianism in America* (University Park, Pa., 2007).

8. Thomas Belsham, *Memoirs of the Late Rev. Theophilus Lindsey . . . [with] a general view of the progress of the Unitarian Doctrine in England and America* (London, 1812), 209–12.

9. William Ellery Channing, "Unitarian Christianity," 1819 (also known as the "Baltimore Sermon") and many other writings of Channing at <http://www.americanunitarian.org/channing.htm>.

10. *Testem Benevolentiae Nostrae*, Papal Encyclicals Online, <http://www.papalencyclicals.net/Leo13/l13teste.htm>.

11. Both writings can be found at the *Making of America*/University of Michigan Digital Library Text Collections Web site: <http://quod.lib.umich.edu/m/moagrp/>.

12. William Gannaway Brownlow, *Americanism Contrasted with Foreignism, Romanism, and Bogus Democracy* (Nashville, 1856), 5–8; Lucian Johnston, "Americanism vs. Ultramontanism," *The Catholic World*, 731–43.

13. These writings can be found in Peter Guilday, *The Life and Times of John England* (2 vols., New York, 1927), vol. 1, 356–57, and J. T. Ellis, ed., *Documents of American Catholic History* (Milwaukee, 1956), 219–21.

14. Roland Marchand's collections of primary sources for university, high school, and middle school students is without compare. The case studies may be accessed at <http://marchand.ucdavis.edu/>.

15. For teaching about Bishop Hill, see Michael A. Mikkelsen, *The Bishop Hill Colony: A Religious Communistic Settlement in Henry County, Illinois*, Johns Hopkins University Studies in Historical and Political Sciences, 10th ser., 1 (Baltimore, 1892) and George M. Stephenson, *Religious Aspects of Swedish Immigration: A Study of Immigrant Churches (Minneapolis, 1932)*.

16. Samuel Bartlett, *Historical Sketch of the Hawaiian Mission and the Missions of Micronesia and the Marquesas Islands* (Boston, 1869); Ta'unga, *The Works of Ta'unga: Records of a Polynesian Traveller in the South Seas, 1833–1896*, ed. R. G. and Marjorie Crocombe (Honolulu, 1968), 1–42, 86–101, 126–37; U.S. Senate, 55th Congress, 2nd Sess.: Dec. 6, 1897 to July 8, 1898, *Congressional Record*, "Annexation of the Hawaiian Islands," July 6, 1898, 6693–6712.

17. Anyone wishing easy access to the teaching materials mentioned in this essay is free to e-mail the author at jbowersi@niu.edu. He will gladly provide those who do so with a page that links all of the readings in an electronic format.

CHAPTER 5

The Shawnee Indian leader Tenskwatawa
(the Prophet) "shared visions that promised to
revitalize American Indian cultures demoralized by
colonial oppression." (Library of Congress, Prints
and Photographs Division, LC-USZC4-3419.)

RETURNING THE WEST TO THE WORLD

STEPHEN ARON

So long has "the West" stood for America that it is hard to imagine it as part of the Americas. Likewise, so long has its history been associated with the westward expansion of the United States that it is difficult to envision the West as a place shaped by movements from other directions. Yet to understand how the West became a West (and not a "North," a "South," or an "East") and how it became American requires that we recover a history in which it was not always "ours" and is still not exclusively ours. By returning the West to the world, we recapture a history that was more international than national and far less exceptional than has often been assumed.

The notion that the westward expansion of the United States made this nation what it is and its people who they are has broad and deep roots, but it was Frederick Jackson Turner who gave this idea its most powerful and enduring scholarly spin. In his 1893 essay on "The Significance of the Frontier in American History," Turner boldly asserted that the "the advance of American settlement westward explain[ed] American development," nurturing the growth of democracy and nourishing the spirit of individualism and enterprise. Movements west held the key to "effective Americanization"—a process that Turner limited to the transformation of "European" into "American." In short, Turner's "frontier thesis" insisted that what was uniquely American about the United States was owed to its westward expansion.[1]

More than a century of criticism has knocked Frederick Jackson Turner's thesis from the scholarly pedestal it once occupied. Few historians now accept that westward expansion alone explained the patterns of the American past. Not many argue for an American exceptionalism based exclusively on a frontier or western heritage.[2]

But if the West and the process of westward expansion no longer play such large roles in manifesting one nation's destiny, these acquire fresh significance when restored to the intersection at which the destinies of many nations, peoples, and empires converged. To that end, historians must first reckon with the multiple colonial enterprises that sought to expand their domains across North America. From this multicolonial perspective, the history of expansionism in North America is more easily linked to imperial currents that flowed from Europe to the Americas and across much of the globe from the sixteenth through the nineteenth centuries. Those connections, in turn, open up possibilities for comparing the colonialisms that evolved in North America and elsewhere during this era. Finally, in the twentieth century and into the twenty-first, the West has retained its international position, both as a crossroads of peoples and as a terrain for global dreams.

Returning the West to the world begins by acknowledging its contested origins in what Americans call the "colonial era." Of course, when Americans think about that period, they do not typically think about the West. Year after year, this lesson gets driven home to me when I ask students in my course on the history of the American West what images and individuals they most closely identify with colonial America. Always they have responded with Pilgrims (at the first Thanksgiving), Pocahontas (as drawn by Disney animators), and patriots (led by George Washington). No surprises here: depictions of Pilgrims, Pocahontas, and patriots remain staples of American popular culture, and they figure prominently in a colonial history that commences with the founding of Virginia and Massachusetts and culminates with the independence of the United States. Still, I remain surprised that no student has added "missions" to this list, an omission that is especially puzzling because the vast majority of my students are from California. That means back in fourth grade almost all of them built an elaborate diorama of a mission. When prompted, students remember in great detail the experience of constructing missions from sugar cubes, popsicle sticks, egg cartons, and whatever else could be scrounged from parents' kitchens. Yet despite this most memorable of grade school projects, missions do not enter their vision of colonial history. In their view, the history of colonial America happened exclusively on the Atlantic Coast and involved only the thirteen mainland British American colonies that became the original United States. From this vantage point, the interior of the continent, lying west of the seaboard colonies, was only a West awaiting annexation by the United States.

Not that long ago, that is how most scholars conceived the field too. But recent work has forwarded a broader vision, spanning continent, hemisphere, and even oceans. Increasingly more typical are colonial surveys that bring all of North America into sight, that juxtapose Portuguese, Swedish, Russian, Dutch, French, and Spanish brands of colonialism alongside the imperial endeavors of the British, and that tie colonies in the Americas to trading systems that drew the products and people of Europe, Africa, and Asia together. Moreover, from this wider view, stretching from Canada to the Caribbean and Mexico to Alaska, what was merely a West from the perspective of the Atlantic coastal colonies becomes a South, a North, and an East.[3]

In fact, the interior of North America was not west at all for many of the people who lived there or moved there. It was instead the focus of prolonged rivalries between European empires, principally Spanish, French, and British, that emerged in the seventeenth century and intensified in the eighteenth. Into the nineteenth century, much of the continent remained up for grabs, with the designs of European empire builders then competing with those of westward-minded Americans. We must always keep in mind that the ultimate making of the American West required the breaking of rivals' claims on the land.[4]

From the start, expansionist schemes followed varying paths into and inside North America. For the Spanish, prior colonial experiences in Mexico guided expectations about building empires based on the extraction of mineral resources and the exploitation of native labor. In moving north, however, Spanish colonizers found lands without gold or silver and with Indian inhabitants not easily mastered. Like the Spanish, French empire makers laid claim to a vast domain in the interior of North America. But like the Spanish North, French colonists sparsely populated an arc of settlement reaching from the St. Lawrence Valley, across the Great Lakes, and down the Mississippi River. These settlers were especially dependent on the good will of Indians, for only with the partnership of native men and women could traders acquire the furs and skins that were the principal export of New France. In contrast with the North American claims of the Spanish or French, the British mainland colonies quickly established much larger European populations and more equal sex ratios. Compared with their Spanish and French brethren, English men consorted with Indian women far less frequently. Rising colonial numbers also fed increasing demand for land, creating tensions with Indian claimants, though on the eve of the American Revolution, British settlements had barely penetrated the Appalachian Mountains.[5]

All of these expansionist projects were entangled with one another and with the countercolonial aspirations of diverse Indian peoples. In Madrid, Paris, and London, and in colonial capitals, imperial authorities elaborated grand strategies and displayed maps with impressive boundaries, but the actual situation in the North American interior defied their projections. Again and again, the programs designed by distant metropolitan officials could not be enforced on Indian peoples who maintained the power to draw their own borders and protect their own rights. Through the eighteenth century across most of North America, Europeans could not dictate, but instead had to negotiate, their relations with Indians.[6]

For indigenous peoples, the territories over which European empires vied were not "North," "South," or "West" but homelands, though a number of Indians were themselves relatively recent arrivals to the region. Into the nineteenth century, Indians pursued a variety of paths to resist dispossession and dependency at the hands of one or another colonial invader. These included migrations, accommodations, confederations, and revitalizations. All proved successful for a time, especially so long as one or another European power lent support to their cause. But once imperial rivals withdrew from what the American republic claimed as its west, Indian options narrowed.[7]

As the world, in the sense of imperial competition, retreated, the pace of westward expansion accelerated. In the century and a half after the founding of Jamestown, colonial settlements spread inland less than two hundred miles. The treaty that ended the American Revolution assigned the United States a western boundary at the Mississippi River, but for several decades, the republic's control over this first American West was tenuous. Only after the War of 1812 did Britain relinquish its interest in the lands south of the Great Lakes and did American settlers complete their occupation of the country between the Appalachians and the Mississippi (and complete as well the removal of Indians from that region). By then, the United States had also acquired an immense new West beyond the Mississippi River. By mid-century, American pioneers reached the Pacific, and in the century's second half, they filled in what was now indisputably the United States' West. In 1890, the extent of settlement was such that the Census Bureau declared the American frontier closed, an announcement that Frederick Jackson Turner determined marked the end of "the really American part of our history."[8]

As the preceding paragraphs have emphasized, what Turner deemed "really American" was international before it became national. Not until the West ceased to be a zone of inter-imperial rivalry did it become manifestly American. Nor did this "effective Americanization" make the history of westward expansion particularly exceptional. To the contrary, the frontier processes that unfolded across North America readily—and sometimes uncomfortably—equate with numerous episodes of colonization and resistance around the globe.[9]

The most frequent comparisons are with other European "settler societies." Here, the United States' northern neighbor, Canada, stands both geographically and historically as the nearest point of reference. Canada, too, had a history of westward expansion, though Canadian historians have often stressed the differences between their frontier and that of the United States. In contrast with the United States, Canada's more forbidding West required greater government effort to attract settlers, and even then western Canada boasted a much smaller population than the western United States. Fewer in number, late-nineteenth-century homesteaders on the Canadian prairie put less pressure on native landholdings, and displacements of Indians did not provoke the same level of conflict and bloodshed as in the United States. Still, Canada and the United States shared much with one another and with other settler societies like Australia and New Zealand that had common roots in "Anglo" traditions of law, economics, and governance. These societies all evolved as well into "neo-Europes," that is, nations outside of Europe where persons of European ancestry came to dominate demographically. Such settler societies did best in temperate zones around the globe, where the climate eased the transplantation of European people, as well as of their familiar crops and livestock.[10]

The dominance of newcomers came, of course, at the tragic expense of natives. By the end of the nineteenth century, the number of Indians in the United States had fallen to around 250,000. Although historians disagree on how high the pre-Columbian population might have been, the general consensus is that Indian numbers plummeted by 90–95 percent in the four centuries after 1492. By no means was this demographic catastrophe unique to North American Indians. Across the hemisphere, a similar collapse occurred, as waves of epidemic diseases decimated natives who lacked immunity to the germs brought by newcomers. A key difference, though, was that much of Spanish and Portuguese America, especially those colonies situated in tropical regions that were less hospitable to European transplantations, did not become neo-Europes. Instead, generations of intercourse between Europeans, Indians, and imported African slaves created societies where mixed-race ancestry was the rule.[11]

Diseases took their toll beyond the Americas, most destructively among Australian Aborigines, but these depopulations were largely an unwitting product of European colonizations. The calls for extermination and the policies of expulsion were deliberate and often state-sponsored assaults on indigenous peoples. In the nineteenth century, the United States government maintained that military campaigns against Indians were retaliatory actions and that removal from homelands and confinement to reservations were humane policies devised to save and civilize natives. Today, though, "ethnic cleansing" would seem a more appropriate designation for the violence and forced relocations that accompanied American westward expansion. Applying that term facilitates comparisons with a host of historical and contemporary episodes, albeit ones that Americans may not want to see as parallel to their own. Consider, for example, the lessons that later expansionists took away from America's "success." As Charles Bright and Michael Geyer have pointed out, the American program of spatial expansion and economic development served as a "model" for Germans and Japanese, who "imagined themselves doing in the twentieth century what they thought Americans had done in the nineteenth: conquering a territorial hinterland" and purging it of "savage inhabitants" to transform it into "a source of food and resources, a controllable inland market, and a homeland for a growing population organized for maximum production."[12]

Illuminating parallels may also be drawn between the ways in which native peoples resisted colonial domination. Migration was one option that natives employed to get away from invaders. Others sought accommodations that might allow a measure of autonomy or secure a place within colonial society. Still others fought back, with confederations occasionally developing among previously divided indigenous groups. Often these confederacies were inspired by charismatic prophets, whose dreams emphasized the power of ritual to purify and protect followers and restore precolonial conditions. In North America, the most notable Indian prophets included Popé, Neolin, Tenskwatawa, and Wovoka, who, though emerging at different times and in different corners of the continent, shared visions that promised to revitalize Indian cultures demoralized by colonial oppression. None of these countercolonial strategies was exceptional to American Indians. From Africa to Asia, direct European imperialism—or even indirect pressure on traditional societies brought about by increased contact with European commerce and ideas—prompted responses similar to those of American Indians. Not surprisingly, then, these histories of anticolonial struggle witnessed the emergence of powerful prophetically inspired movements such as Wahhabism in the Arabian Peninsula or the Taiping and Boxer Rebellions in China that, despite their disparate context and content, bore considerable resemblance to the uprisings spurred by Popé, Neolin, Tenskwatawa, and Wovoka.[13]

The records of resistance make for fruitful comparison between the American West and the world, but these revitalization movements were not connected to one another. Taiping Rebels knew nothing of Tenskwatawa. Wovoka was wholly unaware of Wahhabism. Their prophecies drew on local traditions, and their ambitions were not in any respect global.

At the same time, the West and its people were in most respects becoming ever more worldly. The transoceanic connections that European empires created did not disappear when the United States consolidated its political control over the region. During the second half of the nineteenth century, the resources of the American West were pulled more deeply into the world economy. The West remained, too, a land of many peoples. Indeed, recent scholarship has accented the region's racial and ethnic diversity and made that the centerpiece of western American exceptionalism. In the West, Asians coming east, Hispanics coming north, and Indians both long established and newly removed mingled with westering white and black Americans and European immigrants. Absent this multiracial complexion that gave the region its distinctive character, the West, in historian Richard White's judgment, "might as well be New Jersey with mountains."[14]

Beginning in the late nineteenth and continuing through the twentieth century, a variety of measures were taken to make the population of the West less worldly. In the 1850s, the California legislature passed a foreign miners' tax that was intended to keep immigrants out of the state's gold fields. Two decades later, white Californians blamed Chinese workers for economic hard times. Bowing to popular pressures from white westerners, the government of the United States implemented the Chinese Exclusion Act in 1882. This was followed by a series of laws contrived to keep other Asians out, all enacted well before the United States moved to restrict immigration from Europe. In the second half of the twentieth century, immigration restrictionists shifted their focus to the West's southern border, seeking to stop people from Latin America from entering the United States. But the border patrol has never stopped the flow of immigrants coming to "El Norte," and, in the wake of immigration reform in 1965, the West became again an east open to Asians. Over the last four decades, increased immigration has made not only the West more worldly, but also the rest of the nation. In fact, at the start of the twenty-first century, New Jersey, now boasting growing Latin American and Asian American populations, has come to look more like the West—though still without the mountains.[15]

Nowhere was the changing ethnic composition of the American West more dramatic than in Los Angeles, which had been the "whitest" of major U.S. cities until it became the destination for millions of migrants after the 1965 Immigration Act. By the end of the twentieth century, two out of five Los Angelenos were foreign-born, and more than 40 percent of residents were of Hispanic descent. Likewise, the proportion of Asians jumped fivefold in the years after 1965. So great and so diverse was the flood of immigrants into Los Angeles that at century's end the city's public schools enrolled children who spoke nearly one hundred different languages.[16]

It is fitting that the world has now come to Los Angeles, because it was Los Angeles, more than any other place, that gave the West, or more accurately "the western," to the world. True, even before the birth of Hollywood, Buffalo Bill's spectacular touring shows gave Europeans a taste of the "Wild West." But it was cinema that magnified the spectacle and multiplied the audience for westerns. For decades, westerns reigned as Hollywood's dominant product, thrilling not only generations of American moviegoers, but also providing tens of millions of people around the globe with a West to fire imaginations.

And when Hollywood stopped making westerns, directors elsewhere began making their own. Take the so-called "spaghetti westerns," of which there were hundreds produced in Italy in the 1960s. The most famous of these were made by the Italian director Sergio Leone. These were filmed in Spain, based on Japanese samurai movies, and starred a cast of American, Italian, and Yugoslav actors. What a striking example of how the western belongs to the world.[17]

So, it should be clear, does the West. Its history has long belonged to the world. For centuries before it became just "the West," it lured European expansionists, and its products were linked to trading routes across the Atlantic and Pacific. The westward expansion of the United States in the nineteenth century created clearer boundaries, but these borders remained permeable to the flows of people and goods to and from distant shores. In the twentieth century, the western gave the West a mythic profile that struck a powerful chord worldwide. And in our day, the American West is more than ever a place of global convergence.

Bibliographical Essay

More than seventy years ago, Herbert E. Bolton, in "The Epic of Greater America," *American Historical Review*, 38 (April 1933): 448–74, called for returning the American West to the world by putting its history in a broader hemispheric context. Although Bolton's suggestion did not stimulate much hemispheric work by historians of the American West, Latin Americanists were more responsive. Some good examples of this scholarship are collected in David J. Weber and Jane M. Rausch, eds., *Where Cultures Meet: Frontiers in Latin American History* (Wilmington, Del., 1994). Beyond the Americas, historians of the American West have engaged in a number of "comparative frontier" projects. Among the most notable of these is *The Frontier in History: North America and Southern Africa Compared*, edited by Howard Lamar and Leonard Thompson and cited in endnote 9, which pairs essays on North American and South African frontiers and which inspired James O. Gump, *The Dust Rose Like Smoke: The Subjugation of the Zulu and Sioux* (Lincoln, Nebr., 1994). Equally first-rate for the comparisons and connections it draws between gold rushes in Australia and North America is David Goodman, *Gold Seeking: Victoria and California in the 1850s* (Stanford, Calif., 1994). Also worthy of attention for their wider-ranging geography and chronology are George Wolfskill and Stanley Palmer, eds., *Essays on Frontiers in World History* (College Station, Tex., 1983), and Bradley J. Parker and Lars Rodseth, eds., *Untaming the Frontier in Anthropology, Archaeology, and History* (Tucson, 2005).

Over the last twenty years, however, many "new western historians" have turned on Frederick Jackson Turner, eschewing his frontier framework in favor of a regional perspective on the history of the American West. Foremost among these critics is Patricia Nelson Limerick, whose *The Legacy of Conquest: The Unbroken Past of the American West* (New York, 1987) makes for an especially engaging read. Yet, Limerick has recently signaled her own interest in returning the West to the world. Instead of limiting the comparisons and connections to shared frontier histories, Limerick's "Going West and Ending Up Global," *Western Historical Quarterly*, 32 (Spring 2001): 5–23, focuses on common legacies of colonialism and environmental transformation.

Indeed, historians of the environment have recognized that ecosystems do not usually conform with regional or national boundaries. Taking cues from Richard White, "The Nationalization of Nature," *Journal of American History*, 86 (Dec. 1999): 976–86, environmental historians have experimented with a variety of scales, including transnational ones. Jared Diamond, in *Guns, Germs, and Steel: The Fates of Human Societies* (New York, 1997), provides the largest of all scales to explore and explain how environmental advantages underwrote European conquest of the Americas, as well as much of human history.

As this article emphasizes, one need not leave North America to take account of the international dimensions of western American history. The idea that colonial America, which extends beyond British America to encompass the entire continent, was international before it became national informs Karen Ordahl Kupperman, "International at the Creation: Early Modern American History," in Thomas Bender, ed., *Rethinking American History in a Global Age* (Berkeley, Calif., 2002), 103–22. That insight also shapes Alan Taylor's *American Colonies: The Settling of North America,* cited in endnote 3, and Robert V. Hine and John Mack Faragher, *The American West: A New Interpretive History* (New Haven, Conn., 2000), which, more so than any other recent western history textbook, considers all of North America's colonial frontiers. The convergence of Spanish, French, British, and American colonial regimes in the middle Mississippi Valley is the subject of Stephen Aron, *American Confluence: The Missouri Frontier from Borderland to Border State* (Bloomington, Ind., 2006).

The broad syntheses presented by Taylor and Hine and Faragher can be profitably supplemented with survey texts that focus on a single frontier, yet accent the international dimensions of the West before it was fully an American West. David J. Weber, *The Spanish Frontier in North America* (New Haven, Conn., 1992) and John L. Kessell, *Spain in the Southwest: A Narrative History of Colonial New Mexico, Arizona, Texas, and California* (Norman, Okla., 2002) are two excellent ones that update the tradition of borderlands studies initiated by Bolton. David J. Weber, *The Mexican Frontier, 1821–1846: The American Southwest Under Mexico* (Albuquerque, 1982), examines the Mexican north before its acquisition by the United States. Valuable as well for its binational approach is Andrés Reséndez, *Changing National Identities at the Frontier: Texas and New Mexico, 1800–1850* (Cambridge, Eng., 2004). For New France, W. J. Eccles, *The Canadian Frontier, 1534–1760,* rev. ed. (Albuquerque, 1983), is a fine overview. Exploring the expansion of the French into the Great Lakes region and the accommodations they reached with Indian peoples, Richard White, *The Middle Ground: Indians, Empires, and Republics in the Great Lakes Region, 1650–1815* (Cambridge, Eng., 1991), is a seminal interpretation that has profoundly influenced a generation of scholarship about intercultural relations in North America and around the globe. A sterling example of that influence is Alan Taylor, *The Divided Ground: Indians, Settlers, and the Northern Borderland of the American Revolution* (New York, 2006), a poignant account of the shifting relations between Britain, the United States, and Iroquois Indians in the 1780s and 1790s. Moving further forward in time and farther west in space, Jeffrey Ostler, *The Plains Sioux and U.S. Colonialism from Lewis and Clark to Wounded Knee* (Cambridge, Eng., 2004), links nineteenth-century American westward expansion and Indian resistance to similar currents around the globe.

That the West remained international even after it was incorporated into the United States is a major theme of much recent work, particularly on the Southwest. For a sampling, see David G. Gutiérrez, "Migration, Emergent Ethnicity, and the 'Third Space': The Shifting Politics of Nationalism in Greater Mexico," *Journal of American History,* 86 (Sept. 1999): 481–517, and Samuel Truett and Elliott Young, eds., *Continental Crossroads: Remapping U.S.-Mexico Borderlands History* (Durham, N.C., 2004).

Finally, the place of the West in the world's imagination has sparked many interesting contemplations, diverse examples of which include S. Ilan Troen, "Frontier Myths and Their Applications in America and Israel: A Transnational Perspective," *Journal of American History,* 86 (Dec. 1999): 1209–30; Robert W. Rydell and Rob Kroes, *Buffalo Bill in Bologna: The Americanization of the World, 1869–1922* (Chicago, 2005), and Kevin Mulroy, ed., *Western Amerykanski: Polish Poster Art and the Western* (Los Angeles, 1999).

Notes

1. Frederick Jackson Turner, "The Significance of the Frontier in American History," in his *The Frontier in American History* (New York, 1920), quotations on 1 and 4. This essay has been reprinted in scores of books and can be found online at <http://xroads.virginia.edu/~HYPER/TURNER/>. For discussions of the intellectual roots of the "frontier thesis," see Richard White, "Frederick Jackson Turner and Buffalo Bill," in *The Frontier in American Culture: An Exhibition at the Newbury Library, August 16, 1994–January 7, 1995,* ed. James B. Grossman (Chicago, 1994), 7–65; John Mack Faragher, "'A Nation Thrown Back Upon Itself': Frederick Jackson Turner and the Frontier," in *Rereading Frederick Jackson Turner: "The Significance of the Frontier in American History" and Other Essays,* ed. Faragher (New York, 1994), 1–10.

2. Hundreds of books and articles have been written critiquing one or another aspect, or all, of Turner's frontier thesis. For an excellent analysis of these debates, see Kerwin Lee Klein, *Frontiers of Historical Imagination: Narrating the European Conquest of Native America, 1890–1990* (Berkeley, Calif., 1997).

3. The best new survey that takes a continental approach to colonial history is Alan Taylor, *American Colonies: The Settling of North America,* reprint (New York, 2002, 2001).

4. I elaborate on the relationship between the "making" of an American West and the "breaking" of the claims of imperial rivals in Stephen Aron, "The Making of the First American West and the Unmaking of Other Realms," in *A Companion to the American West,* ed. William Deverell (Malden, Mass., 2004), 5–24.

5. D. W. Meinig, *The Shaping of America: A Geographical Perspective of 500 Years; Volume 1: Atlantic America, 1492–1800* (New Haven, Conn., 1986), provides an excellent survey of the geography of European colonial expansion in North America.

6. Colin G. Calloway, *One Vast Winter Count: The Native American West before Lewis and Clark* (Lincoln, Nebr., 2003), offers an exceptional synthesis of American Indian history prior to the nineteenth century in what became the American West.

7. For a more extended explanation of the relationship between imperial rivalries and Indian countercolonial strategies, see Jeremy Adelman and Stephen Aron, "From Borderlands to Borders: Empires, Nation-States, and the Peoples in Between in North American History," *American Historical Review,* 104 (June 1999): 814–41. See also the responses to this article in "Forum Essay: Responses; Borders and Borderlands," *American Historical Review,* 104 (Oct. 1999): 1221–39.

8. Turner, "Significance of the Frontier," quotation on 4.

9. Those comparisons become easier once "frontier" is more specifically defined. As critics have pointed out, vague and shifting definitions deprive historians of the analytical precision needed for useful comparison. Worse still would be to adopt Turner's rendering of the frontier as "the meeting point between savagery and civilization." Shorn, however, of such ethnocentric baggage, the frontier is more simply a meeting point. For greater clarity, I follow Howard Lamar and Leonard Thompson, who define frontier as the meeting point between peoples of differing ways and from distinct polities, where no single authority has established hegemony and fixed control over clearly demarcated borders. See Howard Lamar and Leonard Thompson, "Comparative Frontier History," in *The Frontier in History: North America and Southern Africa Compared*, eds. Lamar and Thompson (New Haven, Conn., 1981), 7–8.

10. Walter Nugent, "Comparing Wests and Frontiers," in *The Oxford History of the American West*, eds. Clyde A. Milner II, Carol A. O'Connor, and Martha A. Sandweiss (New York, 1994), 803–33. For interpretations that emphasize the differences between Canadian and U.S. expansionism, see J. M. S. Careless, *Frontier and Metropolis: Regions, Cities, and Identities in Canada before 1914* (Toronto, 1989); Gerald Friesen, *The Canadian Prairies: A History* (Toronto, 1984).

11. On the consequences of the "Columbian exchange" and the creation of "neo-Europes," see Alfred Crosby, *Ecological Imperialism: The Biological Expansion of Europe, 900–1900* (Cambridge, Eng., 1986).

12. Charles Bright and Michael Geyer, "Where in the World Is America? The History of the United States in the Global Age," in Thomas Bender, ed., *Rethinking American History in a Global Age* (Berkeley, Calif., 2002), quotation on 81. A Commission of Experts established by the Security Council of the United Nations to investigate interethnic violence in the Balkans in the early 1990s defined "ethnic cleansing" as "a purposeful policy designed by one ethnic or religious group to remove by violent and terror-inspiring means the civilian population of another ethnic or religious group from certain geographic areas. To a large extent, it is carried out in the name of misguided nationalism, historic grievances, and a powerful driving sense of revenge. This purpose appears to be the occupation of territory to the exclusion of the purged group or groups." See Commission of Experts, Final Report (S/1994/674), available online at <http://www.ess.uwe.ac.uk/ comexpert/III-IV_D.htm>. For studies that explore "ethnic cleansings" in North America, see John Mack Faragher, *A Great and Noble Scheme: The Tragic Story of the Expulsion of the French Acadians from Their American Homeland* (New York, 2005); Gary Clayton Anderson, *The Conquest of Texas: Ethnic Cleansing in the Promised Land, 1820–1875* (Norman, Okla., 2005).

13. Gregory Evans Dowd, *A Spirited Resistance: The North American Indian Struggle for Unity, 1745–1815*, paperback ed. (Baltimore, 1993); Robert L. Tignor et al., *Worlds Together, Worlds Apart: A History of the Modern World from the Mongol Empire to the Present* (New York, 2002), 239–69.

14. Richard White, "Race Relations in the American West," *American Quarterly*, 38 (1986), 394, 416, quotation on 397. For an excellent survey of the peopling of the American West, see Walter Nugent, *Into the West: The Story of Its People* (New York, 1999).

15. Roger Daniels, *Guarding the Golden Door: American Immigration Policy and Immigrants Since 1882* (New York, 2004).

16. For a provocative set of articles on Los Angeles as a global city, see "Los Angeles and the Future of Urban Cultures," *American Quarterly,* 56 (Sept. 2004).

17. For Buffalo Bill, see Louis Warren, *Buffalo Bill's America: William Cody and the Wild West Show* (New York, 2005). For Sergio Leone, see Christopher Frayling, *Once Upon a Time in Italy: The Westerns of Sergio Leone* (New York, 2005).

STRATEGIES FOR TEACHING THE AMERICAN WEST IN A GLOBAL CONTEXT

OMAR VALERIO-JIMENEZ

Growing up in Texas along the U.S.–Mexico border, I learned informally about the influence of Mexico on Texas and American western history by absorbing lessons on vaqueros, rodeos, and *corridos*. Unfortunately, the history I was supposed to learn in public schools was more provincial and tended to emphasize Texas and United States exceptionalism while ignoring the role of Mexican Americans in history. As a college professor, I have sought to incorporate the history of underrepresented peoples and the history of the American West in several of my courses. In the first part of the U.S. survey, I devote five to six class sessions to western history topics by linking developments in the American West to broader issues in U.S. and world history. Stephen Aron's essay gave me several useful ideas about incorporating a world perspective into teaching about the American West. In the future, I plan to assign his essay, design discussions that focus on the global influences of the region, and show a documentary that makes links to world history.

Portraying the American West as an indigenous homeland and as a contested space of Indian and European colonial powers helps explain American territorial expansion. Introducing indigenous territorial rights early in the semester helps students understand the fallacy that white Americans expanded westward into "virgin wilderness." Fortunately, several recent United States survey textbooks begin by focusing on Indian societies *before* European settlers began arriving in the Americas.[1] While covering sixteenth-century developments, I discuss the Pueblo Indians' territorial rights to the area that would become New Mexico. I show students photographs of the multistoried structures at Mesa Verde to explain how the Pueblo Indians were among the first people in the American West who built "planned communities."[2] Aron's essay can be used to demonstrate the contested origins of the United States and to place indigenous revolts in comparative perspective. He explains that indigenous nations responded to European incursions by migrating, accommodating, or rebelling. On the week that we discuss King Philip's War, I plan to ask students to compare that event to the Pueblo revolt of 1680. Students will read a summary of these rebellions and articles about the Pueblo revolt before dividing into groups to discuss their causes.[3] Several textbooks also introduce Spanish colonialism of Mexico's Far North in early chapters, which will allow me to discuss various European colonization efforts. Aron's essay will also be useful for a class discussion on the significance of Indian nations' migrations into and within the territory. This discussion will complicate territorial rights by exploring the reactions of indigenous nations of the Southwest to the migrations of Indians from the Southeast and Midwest, following their expulsions by European colonists. Another useful exercise is to ask students to discuss Aron's point about the fluidity of colonial demarcations owing to Indians' power to contest colonial authority throughout the eighteenth century.

Students have found it useful to compare Spanish and French "frontiers of inclusion" to the British "frontiers of exclusion" because it explains the relationship that each colonial power had with various Indian nations. The "frontier of inclusion" policy sought to incorporate Indians as laborers, subjects, traders, and mates. By contrast, the "frontier of exclusion" policy generally excluded Indians from British and American societies in favor of removing indigenous people from their native lands.[4] Understanding the Spanish plan to use missions, presidios, and pueblos to colonize Mexico's Far North also explains the presence of these structures throughout the American West (and parts of the Southeast), and of Spanish-language place names. Comparing European colonial projects places the competition for North America, and the Americas in general, in a world perspective. Finally, a comparison of the Spanish and British policies toward Indians also helps dispel the "Black Legend" myth of Spanish colonialism, which combined anti-Catholic and anti-Spanish views with propaganda about Spanish cruelty toward indigenous people.[5] The need for colonial officials to negotiate with indigenous nations can also be illustrated by comparing the French and Spanish frontiers of inclusion. The Canadian and Mexican national governments struggled to attract colonists to their borderlands partly because indigenous nations posed a serious challenge to their authority. Aron's characterization of American military campaigns against Indians and their removal onto reservations as comparable to the "ethnic cleansing" followed by the Germans and Japanese is sure to generate discussion. Such a comparison would also convince students about the relevance of studying the American West in a global context.

Examining American westward expansion in a global context also challenges popular notions of the American West. By comparing American westward expansion to colonial conquests elsewhere in the world, students can discover similarities that discount American uniqueness. European colonization of Africa, Asia, and Latin America has aggravated ethnic conflicts, transmitted disease, and increased inequality, as did American westward expansion. Similarly, European conquests have depended on large government outlays.[6] I ask students to evaluate the implied viewpoint of the term "westward expansion," the image of how the American West was settled by white Americans, and the wars fought to obtain control of the area. I lead the class discussion on these questions before students read about westward expansion in order to motivate them to question their assumptions. We begin by discussing "manifest destiny" after reading John O'Sullivan's definition of the term.[7] Students generate a list of advantages and disadvantages related to American belief in manifest destiny. Though it served to unite white Americans, this view was detrimental for the people of color encountered by westward-moving Americans. Discussing how Americans justified violence through their belief that God was on their side can lead students to question contemporary armed struggles where people waging war hold similar beliefs. I ask students to reevaluate their image of the American West. Influenced by movie and television portrayals, students usually characterize white settlers as rugged people, independent ranchers, and gun-toting cowboys. These views allow me to challenge the traditional myths of the American West by explaining Richard White's argument that this region was one of the most dependent on federal government intervention.[8] From military conquest and railroad development to land distribution and restrictive immigration laws, the federal government was heavily involved in helping white Americans gain control of the American West. Other useful discussion questions include:

- Was it the "West" for the Pueblo, Ute, or Gabrielino Indians?
- How might Mexicans refer to the region known as the "American West"?
- Why was the Texas Revolution fought? How is the Texas Revolution related to the U.S.-Mexican War? On which side did Texas-Mexicans fight?
- Who started the U.S.-Mexican War? Why was it fought?
- What were the consequences of U.S. victory?

A global comparison can also highlight how race and racism have been employed to justify conquest. Like westward-moving Americans, European colonists in Africa, Asia, and Latin America employed violence to dispossess indigenous people, whom they characterized as "barbarians." In addition to its active role in conducting numerous wars against Indians, the U.S. government also helped dispossess Mexicans. A discussion of the U.S.-Mexican War not only illustrates the U.S. government's large role in gaining control of the American West, but also highlights the racial and ethnic views of white Americans. In the colonial survey, I devote two class sessions to discussing the war and its impact by linking the war to larger issues, including immigration, sectional conflict over slavery, and nativism.[9] Students gain a deeper understanding of the views prevalent at mid-century by reading several documents and discussing them in groups. The congressional debates surrounding the U.S.-Mexican War are quite useful in exploring Americans' racial views of Mexicans and Indians. After students read parts of speeches by Senators John Calhoun and John Dix, I ask them to explain why Calhoun was opposed to incorporating "all of Mexico" while Dix favored it.[10] By reading the congressmen's speeches, students gain a thorough understanding of the ways manifest destiny influenced (and was influenced by) white Americans' racial perceptions. Students are often surprised at the racial views expressed by these congressmen, and they often become interested in learning more about the racial assumptions of white Americans in the mid-nineteenth century.[11]

To highlight the global links to the American West, I have shown parts of a documentary on the San Patricios, a group of soldiers who defected from the U.S. Army because of the abuse they suffered from fellow soldiers who held nativist and anti-Catholic views.[12] Composed of Irish and German immigrants, the San Patricios fought alongside the Mexican military until several were captured in Mexico City and executed for treason. Students in my courses are fascinated with the San Patricios, so we have had great discussions about nativism and the role of immigrant soldiers in the U.S. military. I have linked this topic to world history by discussing the factors (for example, the Irish potato famine) that spurred immigration from Europe. Examining nativism against Irish and German immigrants helps students understand the role of anti-Catholicism in the nineteenth century, and also lays a foundation for a discussion of how European Americans eventually enjoyed the privileges of whiteness while Mexican Americans were largely excluded.[13] In discussing the war, I point out that it contributed to the sectional struggle over the expansion of slavery into western territories. I have also linked the debates on westward expansion to the political differences between Whigs and Democrats, Jefferson's vision of an agrarian republic, the Wilmot Proviso, and James Polk's expansionist presidential platform.

Finally, I have used the U.S.-Mexican War to discuss political opposition and civil disobedience. Students are often surprised to learn that the war generated significant opposition from the U.S. public, and that the Whigs (including Abraham Lincoln) criticized the conflict as "Mr. Polk's War." Students have had fruitful discussions after reading sections of Henry David Thoreau's essay "Civil Disobedience."[14] This influential essay, explaining Thoreau's opposition to an "unjust" war, would later shape the views of Mahatma Gandhi and Martin Luther King Jr.[15] A global approach can also change the way that I teach the history of California's Gold Rush. The discovery of gold created a population boom as more than seventy thousand newcomers arrived in California from other parts of the United States and regions of the world. I plan to emphasize the global links of this large-scale immigration/migration by discussing the arrival of miners from China, France, Chile, and Mexico. Susan Johnson's *Roaring Camp* discusses the global forces that led men to leave their country of origin and the trade links that facilitated this migration.[16] I have previously assigned portions of *Roaring Camp* and asked students to discuss the interethnic tensions among the newcomers, Mexicans, and Miwok Indians. The mining camps' diversity would not last because nativist sentiments eventually led to the passage of the Foreign Miner's Tax (1852), targeting Chinese, Mexican, Chilean, and French miners. Widespread nativism also led to the creation of the Workingman's Party and the passage of the Chinese Exclusion Act (1882). The Gold Rush also contributed to the image of California and of the American West throughout the world. I plan to ask students to contrast the experience of "foreign" miners with the image of the American West presented in typical western films.

I will not have enough time to implement each of my proposed plans.

Therefore, I will attempt to include some of my plans within lessons on immigration, the development of the railroad, and industrial labor. Placing the American West in a global context is worthwhile because it will enhance students' understanding of U.S. and world history.

Notes

1. Some textbooks that cover precontact indigenous societies are: John Mack Faragher, Mari Jo Buhle, Daniel Czitrom, and Susan H. Armitage, *Out of Many: A History of the American People,* 3rd ed. (Upper Saddle River, N.J., 2000), 14, 18–19; Jacqueline Jones, Peter H. Wood, Thomas Borstelmann, Elaine Tyler May, and Vicki L. Ruiz, *Created Equal: A Social and Political History of the United States,* 2nd ed. (New York, 2006), 5–41; Philip J. Deloria, Patricia Nelson Limerick, Jack N. Rakove, and David Burner, *This Land: A History of the United States* (Maplecrest, N.Y., 2003), 2–59.

2. The Pueblos' permanent housing structures led Spanish explorers to call the area Nuevo Mexico because the region most resembled settled indigenous communities of central Mexico.

3. A summary of the Pueblo Revolt of 1680 and King Philip's War is found in chapter 3 of *Out of Many.* A very useful anthology with articles and discussion questions is David J. Weber's *What Caused the Pueblo Revolt?* (Boston, 1999).

4. The frontiers of inclusion and exclusion are discussed in Robert V. Hine and John Mack Faragher, *The American West: A New Interpretive History* (New Haven, Conn., 2000), 37–38, 57; Faragher et al., *Out of Many,* 52.

5. For instructors who wish to obtain more background on the Spanish colonization, I suggest several articles on the Spanish borderlands that appeared in the issue of the *OAH Magazine of History* from summer 2000, titled "The Spanish Frontier in North America"—see *OAH Magazine of History* (Summer 2000) 14:4. This issue includes a historiography article by David J. Weber; several articles by borderlands historians on missions, communities, and mestizo societies, and excellent lesson plans by secondary-school teachers. For a succinct discussion of the "Black Legend" myth, see Iris H. W. Engstrand's "How Cruel Were the Spaniards?" in this summer 2000 issue. A more thorough examination of the "Black Legend" is found in chapter 12, "The Spanish Legacy and the Historical Imagination," in David J. Weber, *The Spanish Frontier in North America* (New Haven, Conn., 1992).

6. A useful comparison of frontiers in the United States and Latin America can be found in David J. Weber and Jane M. Rausch, eds., *Where Cultures Meet: Frontiers in Latin American History* (Wilmington, Del., 1994).

7. An excerpt from John O'Sullivan's Democratic Review and some useful discussion questions can be found at: <http://www.historytools.org/sources/manifest _destiny.pdf>.

8. Richard White, *"It's Your Misfortune and None of My Own": A History of the American West* (Norman, Okla., 1991), 57–59.

9. For a useful overview and lesson plans on the U.S.-Mexican War, visit the PBS Web site created to accompany a two-part documentary on the war at: <http://www.pbs.org/kera/usmexicanwar/educators/>. The lack of knowledge about the U.S.-Mexican War among students reminds me that this is the United States' "forgotten war." Numerous monographs and textbooks inaccurately refer to the conflict as the "Mexican War," and therefore reveal the authors' U.S.-centric approach to the study of Mexico's Far North (or the United States West). U.S.-based scholars might be surprised to learn that Mexican scholars refer to the war as "The War of North American Invasion." A discussion on the public's general lack of knowledge of the U.S.-Mexican War and the Treaty of Guadalupe Hidalgo can be found in Richard Griswold del Castillo, "The U.S.-Mexican War: Contemporary Implications and Mexican American Civil and International Rights," in Iris H. W. Engstrand, Richard Griswold del Castillo, and Elena Poniatowska, eds., *Culture y Cultura: Consequences of the U.S.-Mexican War, 1846–1848* (Los Angeles, 1998), 76–96.

10. Clyde A. Milner III, Anne M. Butler, and David Rich Lewis, eds., *Major Problems in the History of the American West* (Boston, 1997), 160–63.

11. A useful article to explain the links between manifest destiny and racial views is Thomas Hietala's "The Myths of Manifest Destiny," in Milner et al., *Major Problems in the History of the American West,* 169–81.

12. Mark Day, *The San Patricios* (Vista, Calif., 1996). Information about this documentary is available at: <http://www.dayproductions.com/theSanPatricios.html>. As an alternative, I have also shown segments of the movie *One Man's Hero* (video and DVD from MGM, 2000), but factual inaccuracies, poor acting, and an unnecessary love story mar this Hollywood version.

13. David R. Roediger, *The Wages of Whiteness: Race and the Making of the American Working Class* (New York, 1991); Matthew Frye Jacobson, *Whiteness of a Different Color: European Immigrants and the Alchemy of Race* (Cambridge, Mass., 1998); Neil Foley, *The White Scourge: Mexicans, Blacks, and Poor Whites in Texas Cotton Culture* (Berkeley, Calif., 1997).

14. The original essay and several academic articles analyzing Thoreau's writings can be found at: <http://thoreau.eserver.org/civil.html>.

15. Stanley Wolpert, *Gandhi's Passion: The Life and Legacy of Mahatma Gandhi* (New York, 2001), 68, 72; Faragher et al., *Out of Many,* 404–5.

16. Susan Lee Johnson, *Roaring Camp: The Social World of the California Gold Rush* (New York, 2000), 57–95.

CHAPTER 6

Few Americans lived in large cities, like Philadel-
phia, in 1800. "Second Street North from Market
St. with Christ Church, Philadelphia," from *The
City of Philadelphia . . . as It Appeared in the
Year 1800 . . .*, by William Birch and Sons. (Library
of Congress, Prints and Photographs Division,
LC-USZC4-554.)

DRIVEN TO THE CITY
URBANIZATION AND INDUSTRIALIZATION IN THE NINETEENTH CENTURY

STUART M. BLUMIN

It is not generally noticed that Frederick Jackson Turner invokes "the complexity of city life" as early as the second paragraph of his vastly influential essay, "The Significance of the Frontier in American History." Nor is it widely noted that references to the city and to America's "manufacturing civilization" are sprinkled throughout his attempt to prove that the original and ongoing encounter with the wilderness was the shaping force in American national development. Turner's rather dark, fin de siècle announcement that "the frontier is gone, and with its going has closed the first period of American history" invites anxious attention to an inevitable urban-industrial future in the twentieth century and beyond. But the city as both commercial center and workshop is present—one might even say emphasized—throughout Turner's "first period," as the crucial site of history's advance from the primitive to the modern. Turner's key point is not that cities were insignificant in pre-twentieth-century America, but that they grew out of a frontier experience that left a permanent, *native* imprint upon them.[1]

Turner first presented his essay in 1893. Before the century had closed (and before the "Turner thesis" had taken hold among historians), a quite different statement about the nature and meaning of American urbanization appeared under the title *The Growth of Cities in the Nineteenth Century: A Study in Statistics*.[2] Adna Ferrin Weber was perhaps not even aware of Turner's essay when he compiled and analyzed available statistics of urban concentration; in any case, the assumptions and conclusions of *The Growth of Cities* are strikingly opposed to those of "The Significance of the Frontier in American History." Weber begins his statistical compilation with American data, but he quickly moves on to Europe, and from there, so far as the data were available to him, to the rest of the world. More important, Weber insists that urbanization, even in its American manifestation, is a global phenomenon. Cities arise and grow for many of the same reasons, and often in a similar fashion, all across the world, and are linked in various ways within a growing network of regional, national, and international exchange. Weber, indeed, finds an interesting way of conveying the global character of urbanization, even within an essentially Western frame. His book begins by comparing two young British offshoots at opposite ends of both the century and the planet: the United States in 1790 and Australia in 1891. Both had populations of just under four million. But while the Americans of 1790 who lived in cities of 10,000 people or more accounted for only 3 percent of the country's total population, Australians living in comparably sized places in 1891 amounted to 33 percent. The difference was one of *time,* not *place*—the America we see here lay at the threshold of the nineteenth-century urban revolution; Australia at its full development.[3]

As the phrase "urban revolution" suggests, an important element of Weber's book is the well-substantiated claim that cities and urban systems were growing very rapidly during the nineteenth century, and that the significance of this growth was of the first order, particularly in the Western world. In western Europe, for example—which was already partly urbanized at the start of the century—the population continued to be driven to cities, enlarging towns and cities of all sizes, increasing the urban proportions of nearly every country, and creating urban majorities within Britain and parts of Germany. In England and Wales, the proportions of the population living in cities larger than 10,000 increased from 21 percent in 1801 to 62 percent in 1891; those living in cities of 100,000 or more increased from fewer than 10 percent to nearly a third. (Table 6.1.) In more rural France, where only a tenth of the population lived in cities of 10,000 or more in 1801, and fewer than 3 percent lived in Paris and other cities exceeding 100,000, the proportions had risen to 26 percent and 12 percent by 1891. (Table 6.2.) Outside Europe, only a tiny fraction of the world's populations had lived in cities at the start of the nineteenth century, but in many nations the urban proportion grew into impressive minorities—to select three South American examples: 30 percent in Uruguay, 28 percent in Argentina, and 17 percent in Chile. In new countries such as the United States, this meant the creation of many new urban centers, a number of which—think here of Chicago and San Francisco—grew rapidly into great cities. By 1890, when some 28 percent of the American population lived in cities of 10,000 or more (another 10 percent were counted in smaller cities and towns of 2,500 to 10,000), more than 15 percent had come to reside in cities larger than 100,000.[4] At the start of the nineteenth century, no American city had even approached that population threshold. (Table 6.3.) By the century's end, a newly consolidated New York City could boast a population of nearly 3.5 million.[5] New York was (and is) exceptional, but we should see it as occupying the tip of a now tall and wide pyramid of more than 1,700 urban places, from great cities to small country towns, that spread across the American landscape.

As the European statistics suggest, significant and sustained urbanization did not begin with the nineteenth century, nor did it end at the century's close. Rather, the period of Weber's analysis represents the "take off" of a global

TABLE 6.1.
CHANGING CONCENTRATION OF POPULATION IN NINETEENTH-CENTURY ENGLAND AND WALES.

Living in cities greater than 10,000		Living in cities greater than 100,000	
1801	21%	1801	10%
1891	62%	1891	33%

TABLE 6.2.
CHANGING CONCENTRATION OF POPULATION IN NINETEENTH-CENTURY FRANCE.

Living in cities greater than 10,000		Living in cities greater than 100,000	
1801	10%	1801	3%
1891	26%	1891	12%

TABLE 6.3.
CHANGING CONCENTRATION OF POPULATION IN NINETEENTH-CENTURY UNITED STATES.

Living in cities greater than 10,000		Living in cities greater than 100,000	
1790	3%	1790	0%
1890	28%	1890	15%

phenomenon of enormous significance, intensifying in Europe, where it is most easily observed in its early stages, and spreading through other parts of the world to the point where, in most global regions, significant patterns of rural-urban migration and urban development lay the foundations for the quantitatively more dramatic transformations of the twentieth century. The more impressive global urbanization statistics of the twentieth century should not distract our attention from this nineteenth-century "take off," and from the most obvious question that emerges from Weber's statistics: Why did it happen? What drove so many people, in so many parts of the world and in so sustained a fashion, from farms and villages to new lives in cities and towns? Weber's own initial approach to this question is a rather coy avoidance of the most obvious answer, through a well-chosen projection: "The business man's answer would probably be short and trenchant, 'Steam.'"[6]

Cities have grown, Weber reminds us, through all of recorded human history, and in response to a variety of forces, including changes in agriculture and developments in commerce that should be obvious even to the unreflective and forward facing "business man," focused so resolutely on belching industrial smokestacks. But Weber cannot and does not resist circling back to industrialization driven by liquid water as well as by steam as the principal source of the more rapid urbanization of the nineteenth century. More than a century later, we can look back on these phenomena and come to the same conclusion. Perhaps, too, with greater historical distance, we can offer the bolder thought that the conjuncture of urbanization and industrialization forms the infrastructure of the modern world—that these large, intersecting forces, played out through the lives of millions of ordinary people, lay at the very core of what we believe separates our own lives from those lived through the ages of human history.

The relationship between urbanization and industrialization is at once simple and complex. At its simplest level, it is the concentration of people in geographic space that results from the partial transfer of a workforce from agriculture, which spreads cultivators across the land, to manufacturing, which brings them into close proximity within crowded factories and in workers' neighborhoods immediately beyond the factory gates. That closer proximity, even from the recruitment of workers to a single factory on each of the mill sites and existing townscapes across a given nation, can account for a portion of the urbanization in an era of expanding industrial output. Manufacturing of all kinds and at virtually any degree of intensity is more labor intensive than the long-distance commerce that underlay the development of cities in any region's preindustrial era. More simply put, the factory, the mill, or the congeries of outworking shops, is a more powerful population magnet than even the busiest of import-export businesses, particularly in the era when the latter sent as many of its workers out across the globe as it drew to its dock and warehouse. But the individual factory or "putting out" network constitutes only the beginning of the story. Location economics tells us that industrial firms will themselves tend to group together, as they seek the same transactional efficiencies by locating at or near sources of capital, labor, managerial skill, information, products of ancillary firms, transportation breakpoints, municipal services, and, as Weber's "business man" would quickly add, power, including great piles of inexpensive coal. These efficiencies can be realized in a variety of ways, but the most common solution, especially during the nineteenth century, was to locate either in an existing city or on an adequate mill site not too far from the city's various resources. Hence, most nineteenth-century industrialization occurred within the city, greatly magnifying the size and complexity of existing seaport and river towns, and calling into existence a number of new factory and mill towns within the geographic orbit of older cities. In each case the addition to the city of not one but many industrial firms magnified as well the secondary and tertiary effects of agglomeration—the demand by industrial businesses for banking and advertising, insurance and shipping, and by the new industrial workers for housing, food, clothing, entertainment, organized religious experience, and other urban and neighborhood services. These brought to the city not only new large businesses but also carpenters and bricklayers, butchers and bakers, tailors and second-hand clothing dealers, actors and prostitutes, honest preachers and religious charlatans, in numbers never before seen. The great cities would remain the most complex and would continue to grow beyond limits that even Weber predicted they would soon reach. But even the simpler, single-industry mill towns would become larger and more varied—not mere mill sites but real additions to an urban network expanding in response to the new industrial economy's need for workers, and to the needs of those workers for goods and services they could not, or could no longer, provide for themselves.

The effects of industrialization on urbanization are still more complicated, and extend even to the land, and to countries that did not significantly experience industrial growth within their own borders (recall those South American urban statistics). Agricultural workers were not merely drawn to the city; many were also pushed there by changes in farming that are traceable in no small measure to industrialization as a global phenomenon, and to more integrated international markets in food, fiber, and other products that developed in concert with expanding industrial production and distribution. The invention and production of new agricultural machinery in some of those labor-hungry urban factories "industrialized" farming by mechanizing and consolidating farms that now needed fewer hands per acre. More important, new techniques and institutions of both production and transportation reduced worldwide agricultural prices, driving large numbers of marginal farmers from the land and into cities in search of a new livelihood. In many places, from Italy to China, it drove them to other countries, too, including the United States, and increased the ethnic complexity of the cities in which they came to reside. And there is a smaller-scale effect that is less widely entered into this equation of industrialization and rural-urban migration. Within the rural landscapes of various countries, the appearance of factory-made goods in local markets removed a number of economic functions from the home and from gristmills and other rural workshops, drawing farmers and other rural producers into nearby towns to receive, store, insure, advertise, and sell the cloth, the prepackaged flour, and the other "store bought" goods that now arrived from city factories and mills far beyond the local horizon. Even without a factory in sight, in other words, new forms and quantities of industrial production could create urban life. The broad base of the urban pyramid was as much the product of industrialization as was its narrow top.

All of this takes us back to the idea that the specifically American history of the nineteenth-century urban revolution, and of the industrial revolution we have now joined to it, is international in two senses. First, what was happening in the United States was happening elsewhere as well, most obviously in England, the birthplace of the Industrial Revolution and the country with the most impressive urban statistics, but in varying degrees in other parts of the West and in other regions of the world. And second, American industries and cities were *linked* to the economies of many other nations in a global system of extraction, production, finance, and exchange. In its earliest stages, American industrial development, even when it occurred within established seaports, actually reduced recurring exchanges beyond the sea by making the young nation less dependent on imports of a variety of manufactured goods. But the sheer scale and complexity of the maturing urban-industrial economy meant that remaining linkages, along with many new ones, would soon grow well beyond the value of those reduced or lost in the name of national self-sufficiency. America was, of course, never self-sufficient, and it became less so with the passage of time. And if it was, as Turner insisted, in some senses an inward-looking nation, shaped in part by the frontier experiences and dreams of parts of its population, it was also a city-dwelling, industrial-capitalist nation, linked to the wider world. Did the frontier define "the first period of American history"? I would propose that the growth of cities and an urban-based industrial economy, bearing only the weakest imprint of a sometimes long-forgotten wilderness experience, was the more powerful force.

The textbook version of the American industrial revolution begins with the English immigrant Samuel Slater's ingenious (and from the British point of view, criminal) reconstitution of cotton-spinning machinery of the sort he had worked with in the mills of Lancashire, for the firm of Almy and Brown in Providence, Rhode Island, in 1790. The numerous small spinning mills that Slater helped build in southern New England during the next few years constituted the first significant cluster of industrial production in the United States, but they were soon dwarfed by the results of a more extensive (and similarly illegal) copying of English technology by Boston merchant Francis Cabot Lowell. Lowell, in association with a number of other wealthy Boston merchants, built the first fully integrated American cotton mill, ten times the size of any of Slater's spinning mills, in Waltham, Massachusetts, in 1814, and the success of this enterprise led in turn to a cluster of still larger mills on the banks of the Merrimack River, less than thirty miles from Boston. The reliance of these mills on water power precluded their construction in Boston itself, but the farms and woods that initially surrounded them should not obscure the urban capitalization and control of these institutions. And in any case, the farms and woods did not last long. The mills on the Merrimack were soon surrounded by America's first industrial satellite city, appropriately named Lowell.[7]

Mechanized cotton mills provide the most dramatic and easily understood exemplars of early American industrialization, but the story of the emergence and development of the American economy's manufacturing sector is actually a good deal more varied than the traditional "textile paradigm" allows, and, in the aggregate, even more closely connected with the growth of cities. In nearly all other product areas, industrialization proceeded not from the sudden injection of impressive new production technologies but from the highly varied attempts of city-based merchants and enterprising artisans to gather and ship inexpensive, American-made goods to rapidly expanding inland markets. Turnpikes, canals, river steamboats, and railroads dramatically reduced the costs of reaching these markets, and businessmen sought to reduce expenses further by lowering production costs in any way they could. Although this often involved subdividing production tasks, as did the sequence of water-powered machines in the large textile mills, in most instances it only gradually resulted in the incorporation of heavy machinery, and it most often did not require the building of water-powered mills outside the city. Indeed, by the time most industries reached the stage of large-scale mechanization, advances in productivity based on the deskilling of tasks and the piecemeal introduction of large or small machines in small "manufactories" and outworking shops were long established. In many industries, it was not until after the Civil War that the large-scale factory began to supplant these smaller and less mechanized workplaces, and by then the spread of coal-fired steam engines made it less likely that production would migrate from the city to mill sites in the countryside.

The traditional association of industrialization with the large, mechanized factory has somewhat obscured the importance of earlier and less easily understood changes in modes of production, and of the pre–Civil War years in which most of them occurred. Even apart from textiles, it was in the three or four decades preceding the war that the most significant transitions from craft-based to industrial processes occurred; indeed, as Thomas Cochran long ago established, the Civil War itself, once thought to be the indispensable catalyst to American industrial development, is more properly understood as a disruption of changes well underway.[8]

Economic statistics of the antebellum era are far from reliable, but they suggest that during the two decades before the war the manufacturing sector of the economy grew far more rapidly than agriculture, mining, or construction, rising from perhaps one-sixth of total commodity output in 1840 to approximately one-third in 1860, even in the face of impressive expansion in each of the other sectors. Not coincidentally, these were also the decades of the most impressive relative urban growth in U.S. history. City and town populations nearly doubled during the 1840s, and then increased by about 75 percent (from a larger base) in the 1850s.[9] Cities and industrial workshops of all sizes and types were "taking off," and an element central to both developments was a vast expansion of foreign immigration, mainly from Ireland and Germany. Mostly poor refugees from famine, economic dislocation, and political conflict, these immigrants provided cheap labor for city-based factories, manufactories, and outwork shops, at a propitious moment for industrial entrepreneurs seeking to lower production costs.

Foreign immigration of this sort was, despite its striking differences from more local migrations from farm to city, part of the ongoing migration of rural people to industrializing cities. This process would continue through the rest of the century and beyond, shaped by new crises of various sorts, but driven most fundamentally by the changing demands for labor in a global economy that wanted fewer farmers and more industrial and other urban workers. In the United States, cities and the industrial sector of the economy would continue to grow and to reinforce each other's growth. By the end of the nineteenth century, manufacturing would account for more than half of the value of goods grown, mined, built, and produced, and the numbers of people living in cities and towns would account for some 40 percent of the total population. This pattern of reinforcing urban-industrial growth would continue into the next century, and then change in response to new technologies and the new overall structures of a postindustrial economy. But as America entered the twentieth century, the continuing coalescence of urbanization and industrialization would constitute the most fundamental force shaping the nation's everyday life. This force had developed relentlessly over a long period, and its result was a revolution in the way most Americans lived, and in the way the nation as a whole related to the larger world.

Bibliographical Essay

As this essay suggests, Adna Ferrin Weber, *The Growth of Cities in the Nineteenth Century: A Study in Statistics,* reprint (Ithaca, N.Y., 1967, 1899) remains the basic source for understanding the global patterns of nineteenth-century urbanization. American urbanization is described more fully in a number of more recent textbooks, among which are Howard P. Chudacoff and Judith E. Smith, *The Evolution of American Urban Society,* 5th ed. (Upper Saddle River, N.J., 2000); and David R. Goldfield and Blaine A. Brownell, *Urban America: A History,* 2nd ed. (Boston, 1990). Blake McKelvey, *American Urbanization: A Comparative History* (Glenview, Ill., 1973) contains a more complete array of urban growth statistics than either of these texts, but is topically less comprehensive. Two books by the geographer Allan R. Pred provide fascinating materials for understanding how a system of American cities emerged even before the Civil War, and how this system worked to channel and enhance the movement of goods, people, and information. These books are: *Urban Growth and the Circulation of Information: The United States System of Cities, 1790–1840* (Cambridge, Mass., 1973), and *Urban Growth and City-Systems in the United States, 1840–1860* (Cambridge, Mass., 1980). William Cronon expands upon Pred's insights, and carries them further along in time, in *Nature's Metropolis: Chicago and the Great West* (New York, 1991). A very different kind of study of the nineteenth-century American city is Gunther Barth, *City People: The Rise of Modern City Culture in Nineteenth- Century America* (New York, 1980). Barth's book, which focuses on characteristic urban institutions, can be read as a complement to Pred's and Cronon's studies of urban-rural systems.

Industrialization and its connections with the American city can be approached most broadly through several essays in Stanley L. Engerman and Robert E. Gallman, eds., *The Cambridge Economic History of the United States*, vol. 2, *The Long Nineteenth Century* (Cambridge, Eng., 2000) and, perhaps more easily, in Walter Licht, *Industrializing America: The Nineteenth Century* (Baltimore, 1995). Licht's survey can be complemented by his more focused study of labor markets and migration: *Getting Work: Philadelphia, 1840–1950* (Cambridge, Mass., 1992). There are a large number of studies, like the latter, that examine industrialization and industrial workers within specific urban settings. Some of the more rewarding of these are: Thomas Dublin, *Women at Work: The Transformation of Work and Community in Lowell, Massachusetts, 1826–1860* (New York, 1979); Philip Scranton, *Propriety Capitalism: The Textile Manufacture at Philadelphia, 1800–1885* (Cambridge, Eng., 1984); Sean Wilentz, *Chants Democratic: New York City & the Rise of the American Working Class, 1788–1850* (New York, 1984); Richard B. Stott, *Workers in the Metropolis: Class, Ethnicity, and Youth in Antebellum New York City* (Ithaca, N.Y., 1990); Roy Rosenzweig, *Eight Hours for What We Will: Workers and Leisure in an Industrial City, 1870–1920* (Cambridge, Eng., 1983).

Most of these historical studies discuss some aspect of the quantitative dimensions of urbanization and industrialization, but none is as comprehensive, or as useful for quantitative research projects, as the small number of available statistical compendia. An older work of this type, the U.S. Bureau of the Census's *The Statistical History of the United States from Colonial Times to the Present* (Stamford, Conn., 1965), is available only in book form, but other collections can now be read on the Internet. A quite new edition of an older compendium, Susan B. Carter et al., eds., *Historical Statistics of the United States: Earliest Times to the Present,* millennial ed. (Cambridge, Eng., 2006), is available in five published volumes, and at <http://www.cambridge.org/us/americanhistory/hsus/>. This is a pay-per-view site. U.S. government sites can be examined without cost. The most relevant site is <http://www.census.gov/prod/www/abs/decennial/index.htm>. This site contains photoreproductions of the original published volumes reporting and analyzing each decennial U.S. census, and contains links to other useful sites within the public domain.

Notes

1. Turner's essay has been republished in many places after its initial appearance in the 1893 *Proceedings of the Historical Society of Wisconsin*. It is the first chapter of the author's essay collection, *The Frontier in American History* (New York, 1920, 1899), 1–35.

2. Adna Ferrin Weber, *The Growth of Cities in the Nineteenth Century: A Study in Statistics,* reprint (Ithaca, N.Y., 1967).

3. Ibid., 1.

4. Ibid., 144–45.

5. Blake McKelvey, *American Urbanization: A Comparative History* (Glenview, Ill., 1973), 24, 73.

6. Weber, *Growth of Cities*, 158.

7. Thomas Dublin, *Women at Work: The Transformation of Work and Community in Lowell, Massachusetts, 1826–1860* (New York, 1979), 14–22.

8. Thomas C. Cochran, "Did the Civil War Retard Industrialization?" in Ralph Andreano, ed., *The Economic Impact of the American Civil War* (Cambridge, Mass., 1962), 148–60.

9. McKelvey, *American Urbanization*, 37.

AMERICAN INDUSTRIALIZATION, 1870–1920

TEACHING FROM LOCAL, NATIONAL, AND INTERNATIONAL PERSPECTIVES

BETTY A. DESSANTS

My approach to teaching industrialization in the United States during the late nineteenth and early twentieth centuries has always been through a mix of local and national history, with not much more than a nod to the international perspective on the issue. Virtually all of my students have studied world history in two required freshman surveys and, as a result, I can assume at least a familiarity with industrialization in a global context. Yet I have not taken advantage of the kind of comparative history that Stuart Blumin's essay suggests could be done on this rich topic.

As I began to write this brief description of my teaching approach to the topic, I thought about how I might add this third viewpoint to what I already teach on the national and local character of industrialization. Because I begin my semester-long U.S. survey course after the Civil War, my focus on the period 1870–1920 is narrower than Blumin's analysis of the entire nineteenth century.[1] Yet my approach raises many of the same issues connecting industrial change, urbanization, and the movement of people within and across national and international boundaries. Drawing on primary documents, I also suggest using a comparative analysis of working conditions in England and the United States, and entrepreneurial attitudes of Japanese and American businessmen toward their work, to demonstrate similarities and differences in the development of national economies.

I encourage students to think about the various aspects of the process of industrialization that reach beyond the factory. How and why was the United States able to industrialize so quickly and so expansively between approximately 1870 and 1920? We answer this question through an analysis of seven components of industrialization and their interaction:

1. Availability and exploitation of natural resources
2. Superior transportation and communication
3. Technology
4. Human resources (increased population, immigration)
5. Capital investment and business practices
6. Consumerism and sales techniques
7. Minimal government regulation of the economy

This framework allows students to make sense of the complexity of economic change and recognize the interaction between environment, people, and institutions during this historical period. I use a variety of illustrations for each of the components—for example, the creation of the trust, the use of "cutthroat competition" as business practices, the development of advertising, and the new types of stores that fed middle-class consumerism. This framework might also be used to illustrate the linkages, across both national and global contexts, between immigration, migration, economic change, finance, and urbanization as discussed in Blumin's essay.

The second and third classes in my triad consider the impact of industrialization on the lives of working people. In broad terms, we examine conditions for urban factory workers, for tenement and sweatshop labor, and more specifically, for women and children. How did working people respond to industrialization? To answer this, we analyze and compare the appeals of the Knights of Labor, the American Federation of Labor, and the International Workers of the World. We also discuss the problem of building a European-style class consciousness among workers who often measured their economic mobility by consumerism. Finally, we look at the challenges of urban life, the problems of city government, the emergence of mass culture, and the growing disparity of wealth as evidenced by the living conditions of urban upper-, middle-, and working-class people.

Armed with this broad background, students then look more closely at the local yet also international stories of industrialization through a discussion of Thomas Bell's novel, *Out of This Furnace,* which was published in 1941.[2] Drawing on the experiences of his own family, who settled in Braddock, Pennsylvania, Bell traces the lives of three generations of Slovak immigrants who lived in Braddock and worked in the steel mills near Pittsburgh between 1880 and the 1930s. Because I teach in Pennsylvania and many of my students are from the state, I often have students who recognize members of their own families in Bell's characters. The novel resonates with them because their great-grandfathers worked in the steel industry or their great-grandparents emigrated from Eastern Europe. I generally assign the book at the beginning of the semester, so the students are reading it during our three classes on industrialization. I often require a paper on the novel's first two parts (I reserve parts three and four until our discussion of labor and the Great Depression), which prepares them for the class discussion.

The beauty of *Out of This Furnace* is that while touching on every aspect of my seven components of industrialization, it also keeps students interested and engaged in the topic (indeed, I have had students call the novel "a page-turner" on their course evaluations). From the perspective of Blumin's essay, *Out of This Furnace* also demonstrates his point that "marginal farmers" in areas that did not industrialize sought work where they could find it, even if that meant transforming themselves into factory labor in other countries. Pushed by their poverty in rural Hungary and drawn by family connections in the United States, Bell's immigrants became part of the global exchange of labor, industrial development, transportation, and urbanization.

Work in the steel mills and life in a new urban environment created as many problems, however, as opportunities. Much of our class discussion of the book centers around the disparity between the expectations of immigrant workers and the hard realities they faced on a daily basis in their homes, social communities, and places of work. We also discuss the process of assimilation and Americanization, and the differences in each generation's expectations of "the American dream." Specifically, I pose the following questions:

1. What types of difficulties did Bell's workers face in the steel industry?
2. How did Bell's immigrants adjust to American society? What helped or hindered their assimilation into American life?
3. What was the relationship of Bell's characters to "Americanization?"

4. What were the means of social and economic escape for immigrant workers?
5. What were their visions of the future? How and why did these visions differ for successive generations?
6. How did immigrant workers respond to employers, unions, and collective activity among workers?
7. How did the public and the government respond to unions? How did Bell's characters view the government?
8. Do you think Bell's workers consciously saw themselves as a working class? Would they have joined the IWW? What were their views of the American Federation of Labor?
9. What roles did women play in industrialization in the late nineteenth century? How would you characterize their position in working-class immigrant society?
10. Bell's book is a novel rather than a work of history. How might we deal with fiction as historical representation?

We usually have a lively discussion and rarely get to all of the questions in one class period. If I have time (or sometimes in the next class), I show them a twenty-minute video, *Out of This Furnace: A Walking Tour of Thomas Bell's Novel,* narrated by David Demarest.[3] Students can see what Braddock looks like today and how the decline of the steel industry affected the town.

Although my local and national approaches touch on several issues that have international dimensions, such as immigration and unionization, I have not addressed the question of the processes and impact of industrialization in a comparative global context. One way to do this might be through a comparison of working conditions in England and the United States during their respective periods of marked increase in industrial work. Excerpts from the various government investigations of working conditions, particularly for children, in textile mills and mines in both the United States and Great Britain provide good comparisons.[4] Although their testimonies were separated by almost fifty years, the workers in both places faced similar problems of long hours, low wages, and irregular employment. The documents also reveal the necessity of an entire family working just to make ends meet, although the British testimonies present more detailed descriptions of child labor in mines and mills. Workers' testimonies suggest the debilitating effects of working conditions on traditional family structure, gender roles, education, and economic status. They also show how technological development within textile mills impacted the availability of steady work and working conditions in both countries.

Students should soon realize that working conditions in industrializing nations had comparable qualities that raised similar concerns among workers themselves and social reformers in the larger society. The British government responded in the 1830s and 1840s with a series of laws limiting child labor in textile mills and mines, and eventually restricting the working hours of women and children in all textile factories. In the United States, progressive reformers at the state and federal levels took the same route between 1890 and 1920. Many American students have little understanding of how the United States lagged behind England and western Europe in terms of both industrial development and reform during the nineteenth and early twentieth centuries.

This comparative approach could also be used to compare and contrast attitudes of American and Japanese businessmen toward their workers, business concerns, and responsibility to the larger society during the late nineteenth century. Two documents that reveal these similarities and differences are Andrew Carnegie's "Gospel of Wealth" (1889) and Iwasaki Yataro's 1876 letter to his employees in the Mitsubishi conglomerate.[5] Carnegie concludes that disparities of wealth and rigidity in class structure are an inevitable result of the progress of "civilization" and the "law of competition." Individuals may suffer but society as a whole only benefits from the "wonderful material development, which brings improved conditions in its train." Private businessmen bear the responsibility of administering their good fortune for the betterment of society as a whole. Carnegie's emphasis is on the efforts and achievements of individual workers and businessmen; the nation and national government are of little consequence in his understanding of industrial development.[6]

Like Carnegie, Yataro implores his employees to work hard and accept what must be done to build their company into a strong competitor. But Yataro diverges from his American counterpart as he emphasizes the national imperative of industrialization and the community of purpose of workers and owners. Yataro explains to his employees that in order to build his shipping company into a force that can compete with foreign rivals who want to monopolize Japan's coastal trade, "there is no other alternative but to eliminate unnecessary positions and unnecessary expenditures." In real terms, this means jobs will be cut and hard work will be required of those employees who remain. In the end, not only will the Mitsubishi company strengthen, but success will be "a glorious event for our Japanese Empire." Yataro appeals to his workers' national pride as they labor to help the Japanese Empire "let its light shine to all four corners of the earth."[7] Students might note that although Carnegie and Yataro have similar ideas about the necessity of hard work and individual sacrifice in economic development, the ends of those efforts produced very different conceptions of the role of business and industry in national society for the United States and Japan.

I always teach from an international and comparative perspective in my world history course without giving much thought to its necessity. The nature of world history demands it. Furthermore, a comparative approach often forces students to analyze historical material in a more sophisticated way. Perhaps a more internationalized U.S. survey course will help not only to break down the parochialism that can easily infuse the survey, but will also teach our students to think more critically about their past and present.

Notes

1. My survey course (U.S. since 1865) meets for three fifty-minute classes weekly and has thirty-five to forty students. During almost every class, students engage in some discussion, usually based on required documents, historiographical excerpts, and supplementary reading (for example, historical monographs, novels, or memoirs). After assigning a textbook narrative and supplementary primary sources, I present an analysis at the national level of the process and impact of industrialization. I usually devote three classes of lecture and discussion to this part of the study.

2. Thomas Bell, *Out of This Furnace,* with an afterword by David P. Demarest Jr. (Pittsburgh, 1976). A useful article on Slovak immigrants, their work in the steel mills, and unionization is M. Mark Stolarik, "Slovak Americans in the Great Steel Strike," *Pennsylvania History,* 64 (Summer 1997), 407–18. Thanks to Robert Shaffer, my Shippensburg University colleague, for alerting me to this article.

3. *Out of This Furnace, A Walking Tour of Thomas Bell's Novel,* produced by Steffi Domike (Pittsburgh, 1990).

4. "Testimony Before Parliamentary Committees of Working Conditions in England," in Alfred J. Andrea and James H. Overfield, eds., *The Human Record, Sources of Global History,* Vol. 2: *Since 1500,* 5th ed. (Boston, 2005), 267–72; "Immigrant Thomas O'Donnell Laments the Worker's Plight, 1883," in Elizabeth Cobbs Hoffman and Jon Gjerde, eds., *Major Problems in American History,* Vol. 2: *Since 1865,* 2nd ed. (Boston, 2007), 64–66.

5. "Steel Magnate Andrew Carnegie Preaches a Gospel of Wealth, 1889," in Hoffman and Gjerde, eds., *Major Problems in American History,* 66–68; Iwasaki Yataro, "Letter to Mitsubishi Employees," in Andrea and Overfield, eds., *Human Record,* 353–56.

6. "Steel Magnate Andrew Carnegie Preaches a Gospel of Wealth, 1889," 66–68.

7. Yataro, "Letter to Mitsubishi Employees," 353–56.

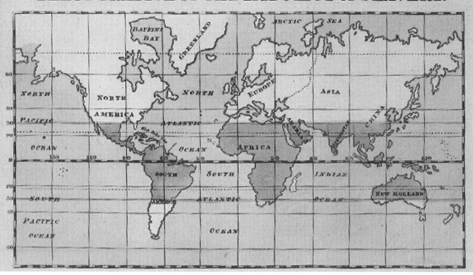

CHART OF THE WORLD,
ON MERCATOR'S PROJECTION.
ILLUSTRATIVE OF THE IMPOLICY OF SLAVERY.

CHAPTER

Reflecting a concern about global slavery, this early-nineteenth-century map illustrates sugar-producing areas around the world where slave labor was used. (Library of Congress, Prints and Photographs Division, LC-USZC4-3650.)

THE AMERICAN CIVIL WAR, EMANCIPATION, AND RECONSTRUCTION ON THE WORLD STAGE

EDWARD L. AYERS

Americans demanded the world's attention during their Civil War and Reconstruction. Newspapers around the globe reported the latest news from the United States as one vast battle followed another, as the largest system of slavery in the world crashed into pieces, as American democracy expanded to include people who had been enslaved only a few years before.[1]

Both the North and the South appealed to the global audience. Abraham Lincoln argued that his nation's Civil War "embraces more than the fate of these United States. It presents to the whole family of man, the question, whether a constitutional republic, or a democracy . . . can, or cannot, maintain its territorial integrity." The struggle, Lincoln said, was for "a vast future," a struggle to give all men "a fair chance in the race of life."[2] Confederates claimed that they were also fighting for a cause of worldwide significance: self-determination. Playing down the centrality of slavery to their new nation, white southerners built their case for independence on the right of free citizens to determine their political future.[3]

People in other nations could see that the massive struggle in the United States embodied conflicts that had been appearing in different forms throughout the world. Defining nationhood, deciding the future of slavery, reinventing warfare for an industrial age, reconstructing a former slave society—all these played out in the American Civil War.

By no means a major power, the United States was nevertheless woven into the life of the world. The young nation touched, directly and indirectly, India and Egypt, Hawaii and Japan, Russia and Canada, Mexico and Cuba, the Caribbean and Brazil, Britain and France. The country was still very much an experiment in 1860, a representative government stretched over an enormous space, held together by law rather than by memory, religion, or monarch. The American Civil War, played out on the brightly lit stage of a new country, would be a drama of world history. How that experiment fared in its great crisis—regardless of what happened—would eventually matter to people everywhere.

More obviously than most nations, the United States was the product of global history. Created from European ideas, involvement in Atlantic trade, African slavery, conquest of land from American Indians and European powers, and massive migration from Europe, the United States took shape as the world watched. Long before the Civil War, the United States embodied the possibilities and contradictions of modern Western history.

Slavery was the first, most powerful, and most widespread kind of globalization in the first three centuries after Columbus. While colonies came and went, while economies boomed and crashed, slavery relentlessly grew—and nowhere more than in the United States. By the middle of the nineteenth century, the slave South had assumed a central role on the world stage. Cotton emerged as the great global commodity, driving factories in the most advanced economies of the world. The slaves of the South were worth more than all the railroads and factories of the North and South combined; slavery was good business and shrewd investment.

While most other slave societies in the hemisphere gradually moved toward freedom, the American South moved toward the permanence of slavery. Southerners and their northern allies, eager to expand, led the United States in a war to seize large parts of Mexico and looked hungrily upon the Caribbean and Central America. Of all the slave powers—including the giants Brazil and Cuba, which continued to import slaves legally long after the United States— only the South and its Confederacy fought a war to maintain bondage.[4]

Ideas of justice circulated in global intercourse just as commodities did, and those ideas made the American South increasingly anomalous as a modern society built on slavery. Demands for universal freedom came into conflict with ancient traditions of subordination. European nations, frightened by revolt in Haiti and elsewhere and confident of their empires' abilities to prosper without slavery, dismantled slavery in their colonies in the Western Hemisphere, while Russia dismantled serfdom.

Black and white abolitionists in the American North, though a tiny despised minority, worked with British allies to fight the acceptance of slavery in the United States. A vision of the South as backward, cruel, and power-hungry gained credence in many places in the North and took political force in the Republican Party. The global economy of commodities and ideology, demanding cotton while attacking slavery, put enormous and contradictory strains on the young American nation.[5]

Meanwhile, a new urge to define national identity flowed through the Western world in the first half of the nineteenth century. That determination took quite different forms. While some people still spoke of the universal dreams of the French and American Revolutions, of inalienable attributes of humankind, others spoke of historical grievance, ethnic unity, and economic self-interest. Many longed for new nations built around bonds of heritage, imagined and real.[6]

White southerners, while building their case for secession with the language of constitutions and rights, presented themselves as a people profoundly different from white northerners. They sought sanction for secession in the recent histories of Italy, Poland, Mexico, and Greece, where rebels rose up against central powers to declare their suppressed nationhood, where native elites led a "natural, necessary protest and revolt" against a "crushing, killing union with another nationality and form of society."[7]

As the South threatened to secede, the Republicans, a regional party themselves, emphasized the importance of union for its own sake, the necessity of maintaining the integrity of a nation created by legal compact. It fell to the United States, the Republicans said, to show that large democracies could survive internal struggles and play a role in world affairs alongside monarchies and aristocracies.[8]

Once it became clear that war would come, the North and the South seized upon the latest war-making strategies and technologies. From the outset, both sides innovated at a rapid pace and imported ideas from abroad. Railroads and telegraphs extended supply lines, sped troop reinforcements, and permitted the mobilization of vast armies. Observers from Europe and other nations watched carefully to see how the Americans would use these new possibilities. The results were mixed. Ironclad ships, hurriedly constructed, made a difference in some southern ports and rivers, but were not sufficiently seaworthy to play the role some had envisioned. Submarines and balloons proved disappointments, unable to deliver significant advantages. Military leaders, rather than being subordinated by anonymous machinery, as some expected, actually became more important than before, their decisions amplified by the size of their armies and the speed of communication and transport.[9]

The scale and drama of the Civil War that ravaged America for four years, across an area larger than the European continent, fascinated and appalled a jaded world. A proportion of the population equal to five million people today died, and the South suffered casualties at a rate equal to those who would be decimated in Europe's mechanized wars of the twentieth century.

The size, innovation, and destructiveness of the American Civil War have led some, looking back, to describe it as the first total war, the first truly modern war. Despite new technologies and strategies, however, much of the Civil War remained old-fashioned. The armies in the American Civil War still moved vast distances on foot or with animals. The food soldiers ate and the medical care they received showed little advance over previous generations of armies. The military history of the Civil War grew incrementally from world history and offered incremental changes to what would follow. Although, late in the war, continuous campaigning and extensive earthen entrenchments foreshadowed World War I, Europeans did not grasp the deadly lesson of the American Civil War: combining the tactics of Napoleon with rapid-fire weapons and trenches would culminate in horrors unanticipated at Shiloh and Antietam.[10]

Diplomacy proved challenging for all sides in the American crisis. The fragile balance of power on the Continent and in the empires located there limited the range of movement of even the most powerful nations. The Confederacy's diplomatic strategy depended on gaining recognition from Great Britain and France, using cotton as a sort of blackmail, but European manufacturers had stockpiled large supplies of cotton in anticipation of the American war. British cartoonists, sympathetic to the Confederacy, ridiculed Abraham Lincoln at every opportunity, portraying him as an inept bumpkin—until his assassination, when Lincoln suddenly became sainted. Overall, the North benefited from the inaction of the British and the French, who could have changed the outcome and consequences of the war by their involvement.[11]

Inside the United States, the change unleashed by the war was as profound as it was unexpected. Even those who hated slavery had not believed in 1861 that generations of captivity could be ended overnight and former slaves and former slaveholders left to live together. The role of slavery in sustaining the

Confederacy through humbling victories over the Union created the conditions in which Abraham Lincoln felt driven and empowered to issue the Emancipation Proclamation. The Union, briefly and precariously balanced between despair and hope, between defeat and victory, was willing in 1862 to accept that bold decision as a strategy of war and to enlist volunteers from among black Americans.[12]

The nearly two hundred thousand African Americans who came into the war as soldiers and sailors for the Union transformed the struggle. The addition of those men, greater in number than all the forces at Gettysburg, allowed the Union to build its advantage in manpower without pushing reluctant northern whites into the draft. The enlistment of African Americans in the struggle for their own freedom ennobled the Union cause and promised to set a new global standard for the empowerment of formerly enslaved people. The world paid admiring attention to the brave and disciplined black troops in blue uniforms.[13]

The destruction of American slavery, a system of bondage of nearly four million people in one of the world's most powerful economies and most dynamic nation-states, was a consequence of world importance. Nowhere else besides Haiti did slavery end so suddenly, so completely, and with so little compensation for former slaveholders.[14] Had the United States failed to end slavery in the 1860s the world would have felt the difference. An independent Confederate States of America would certainly have put its enslaved population to effective use in coal mines, steel mills, and railroad building, because industrial slavery had been employed before secession and became more common during wartime. Though such a Confederacy might have found itself stigmatized, its survival would have meant the evolution of slavery into a new world of industrialization. The triumph of a major autonomous state built around slavery would have set a devastating example for the rest of the world, an encouragement to forces of reaction. It would have marked the repudiation of much that was liberating in Western thought and practice over the preceding two hundred years.[15]

Driven by the exigencies of war, northern ideals of color-blind freedom and justice, so often latent and suppressed, suddenly if briefly bloomed in the mid-1860s. The Radical Republicans sought to create a black male American freedom based on the same basis as white male American freedom: property, citizenship, dignity, and equality before the law. They launched a bold Reconstruction to make those ideals a reality, their effort far surpassing those of emancipation anywhere else in the world. The white South resisted with vicious vehemence, however, and the Republicans, always ambivalent about black autonomy and eager to maintain their partisan power, lost heart after a decade of bitter, violent, and costly struggle in Reconstruction. Northern Democrats, opposing Reconstruction from the outset, hastened and celebrated its passing.[16]

If former slaves had been permitted to sustain the enduring political power they tried to build, if they had gone before juries and judges with a chance of fair treatment, if they had been granted homesteads to serve as a first step toward economic freedom, then Reconstruction could be hailed as a turning point in world history equal to any revolution. Those things did not happen, however. The white South claimed the mantle of victim, of a people forced to endure an unjust and unnatural subordination. They won international sympathy for generations to follow in films such as *Birth of a Nation* (1915) and *Gone With the Wind* (1939), which viewed events through the eyes of sympathetic white southerners. Reconstruction came to be seen around the world not as the culmination of freedom but as a mistake, a story of the dangers of unrealistic expectations and failed social engineering. Though former slaves in the American South quietly made more progress in landholding and general prosperity than former slaves elsewhere, the public failures of Reconstruction obscured the progress black southerners wrenched from the postwar decades.[17]

When the South lost its global monopoly of cotton production during the Civil War, governments, agents, and merchants around the world responded quickly to take the South's place and to build an efficient global machinery to supply an ever-growing demand in the world market. As a result, generations of black and white sharecroppers would compete with Indian, Brazilian, and Egyptian counterparts in a glutted market in which hard work often brought impoverishment. The South adapted its economy after the war as well. By the 1880s, the South's rates of urban growth, manufacturing, and population movement kept pace with the North—a remarkable shift for only twenty years after losing slavery and the Civil War—but black southerners were excluded from much of the new prosperity.[18]

The destruction of slavery, a major moral accomplishment of the United States Army, of Abraham Lincoln, and of the enslaved people themselves, would be overshadowed by the injustice and poverty that followed in the rapidly changing South, a mockery of American claims of moral leadership in the world. Black southerners would struggle, largely on their own, for the next one hundred years. Their status, bound in an ever-tightening segregation, would stand as a rebuke to the United States in world opinion. The postwar South and its new system of segregation, in fact, became an explicit model for South Africa. That country created apartheid as it, like the American South, developed a more urban and industrial economy based on racial subordination.

Americans read about foreign affairs on the same pages that carried news of Reconstruction in the South. Even as the southern states struggled to write new constitutions, Secretary of State William Henry Seward purchased Alaska in 1867 as a step toward the possible purchase of British Columbia. President Grant considered annexation of Santo Domingo, partly as a base for black southern emigration; he won the support of black abolitionist Frederick Douglass, who wanted to help the Santo Domingans, but was opposed by Radical Republican Senator Charles Sumner.

Americans paid close attention to Hawaii in these same years. Mark Twain visited the islands in 1866, and Samuel Armstrong—the white founder of Hampton Institute, where Booker T. Washington was educated—argued that Hawaiians and former slaves in the South needed similar discipline to become industrious. At the same time, Seward signed a treaty with China to help supply laborers to the American West, a treaty that laid the foundation for a large migration in the next few decades. In 1871, American forces intervened militarily in Korea, killing 250 Korean soldiers. The leaders of the Americans admitted they knew little about their opponents, but brought to the conflict the same racial assumptions that they brought to their dealings with all non-Europeans everywhere. Koreans—like Hawaiians, Chinese, American Indians, and African Americans—needed to be disciplined, taught, and controlled.

No master plan guided Americans in their dealings with other peoples. In all of these places, the interests of American businessmen, the distortions of racial ideology, and hopes for partisan political advantage at home jostled with one another. As a result, the consequences of these involvements were often unclear and sometimes took generations to play out. Nevertheless, they remind us that Americans paid close attention to what was happening elsewhere, whether in the Franco-Prussian War (1870–1871), where the evolution of warfare continued to become more mechanized and lethal, or the Paris Commune (1871), where some thought they saw the result of unbridled democracy in chaos and violence—and wondered if Reconstruction did not represent a similar path.

Many people around the world were surprised that the United States did not use its enormous armies after the Civil War to seize Mexico from the French, Canada from the English, or Cuba from the Spanish. Conflict among the great powers on the European continent certainly opened an opportunity, and the United States had expanded relentlessly and opportunistically throughout its history. Few Americans, though, had the stomach for new adventures in the wake of the Civil War. The fighting against the American Indians on the plains proved warfare enough for most white Americans in the 1870s and 1880s.[19]

The United States focused its postwar energies instead on commerce. Consolidated under northern control, the nation's economy proved more formidable than ever. The United States, its economic might growing with each passing year, its railroad network and financial systems consolidated, its cities and towns booming, its population surging westward, its mines turning out massive amounts of coal and precious minerals, its farms remarkably productive, and its corporations adopting new means of expansion and administration, became a force throughout the world. American engineers oversaw projects in Asia, Africa, and Latin America. American investors bought stock in railroads, factories, and mines around the globe. American companies came to dominate the economies of nations in Latin America.[20]

Americans became famous as rich, energetic, and somewhat reckless players amid the complexity of the world. As the Civil War generation aged, younger men looked with longing on possible territorial acquisitions in their own hemisphere and farther afield. They talked openly of proving themselves, as their fathers and grandfathers had, on the battlefield. Some welcomed the fight against the Spanish and the Filipinos in 1898 as a test of American manhood and nationalism. The generation that came of age in 1900 built monuments to the heroes of the Civil War but seldom paused to listen to their stories of war's horrors and costs.

The American Civil War has carried a different meaning for every generation of Americans. In the 1920s and 1930s leading historians in a largely isolationist United States considered the Civil War a terrible mistake, the product of a "blundering generation." After the triumph of World War II and in the afterglow of the cold war, leading historians interpreted the Civil War as a chapter in the relentless destruction of slavery and the spread of democracy by the forces of modernization over the forces of reaction. Recently, living through more confusing times, a number of historians have begun to question straightforward stories of the war, emphasizing its contradictory meanings, unfulfilled promises, and unintended outcomes.[21]

The story of the American Civil War changes as world history lurches in unanticipated directions and as people ask different questions of the past. Things that once seemed settled now seem less so. The massive ranks, fortified trenches, heavy machinery, and broadened targets of the American Civil

War once seemed to mark a step toward the culmination of "total" war. But the wars of the twenty-first century, often fought without formal battles, are proving relentless and boundless, "total" in ways the disciplined armies of the Union and Confederacy never imagined.[22] Nations continue to come apart over ancient grievances and modern geopolitics, the example of the United States notwithstanding. Coerced labor did not end in the nineteenth century, but instead has mutated and adapted to changes in the global economy. "A fair chance in the race of life" has yet to arrive for much of the world.

The great American trial of war, emancipation, and reconstruction mattered to the world. It embodied struggles that would confront people on every continent and it accelerated the emergence of a new global power. The American crisis, it was true, might have altered the course of world history more dramatically, in ways both worse and better, than what actually transpired. The war could have brought forth a powerful and independent Confederacy based on slavery or it could have established with its Reconstruction a new global standard of justice for people who had been enslaved. As it was, the events of the 1860s and 1870s in the United States proved both powerful and contradictory in their meaning for world history.

Bibliographical Essay

Surprisingly, no one book covers all themes of this essay. To understand this era of American history in global context, we need to piece together accounts from a variety of books and articles. For recent overviews of different components of these years, see Jay Sexton, "Towards a Synthesis of Foreign Relations in the Civil War Era, 1848–1877," *American Nineteenth-Century History*, 5 (Fall 2004): 50–73, and Amy Kaplan, *The Anarchy of Empire in the Making of U. S. Culture* (Cambridge, Mass., 2002).

Robert E. May, in the introduction to the book he edited, *The Union, the Confederacy, and the Atlantic Rim* (West Lafayette, Ind., 1995), provides a useful summary of the larger context of the war. Though it is older, the perspective of D. P. Crook, *The North, the South, and the Powers, 1861–1865* (New York, 1974) brings a welcome worldliness to the discussion. On the crucial debate in Britain, see Howard Jones, *Union in Peril: The Crisis Over British Intervention in the Civil War* (Chapel Hill, N.C., 1992) and R. J. M. Blackett, *Divided Hearts: Britain and the American Civil War* (Baton Rouge, La., 2001).

James M. McPherson offers characteristically insightful, and hopeful, analysis in several places. Perhaps the single best focused portrayal of the interplay between events in the United States and in the Atlantic world is in his *Crossroads of Freedom: Antietam* (Oxford, 2002). McPherson's essay, "'The Whole Family of Man': Lincoln and the Last Best Hope Abroad," in May, ed., *The Union, the Confederacy, and the*

Atlantic Rim, makes the fullest case for the larger significance of the war in encouraging liberal movements and belief around the world.

Peter Kolchin's *A Sphinx on the American Land: The Nineteenth-Century South in Comparative Perspective* (Baton Rouge, La., 2003) offers an elegant and up-to-date survey that puts the conflict in the larger context of emancipation movements. A useful overview appears in Steven Hahn, "Class and State in Postemancipation Societies: Southern Planters in Comparative Perspective," *American Historical Review,* 95 (Feb. 1990): 75–98.

Another pioneering work is Drew Gilpin Faust, *The Creation of Confederate Nationalism: Ideology and Identity in the Civil War South* (Baton Rouge, La., 1988). Faust changed historians' perspective on nationalism in the South, which had been considered largely fraudulent before her account. Building on Faust are two recent books that offer fresh interpretations: Anne S. Rubin, *A Shattered Nation: The Rise and Fall of the Confederacy, 1861–1868* (Chapel Hill, N.C., 2005) and Susan-Mary Grant, *North Over South: Northern Nationalism and American Identity in the Antebellum Era* (Lawrence, Kans., 2000).

On the much-debated issue of the relative modernity and totality of the Civil War, see Stig Förster and Jörg Nagler, eds., *On the Road to Total War: The American Civil War and the German Wars of Unification, 1861–1871* (Washington, D.C., 1997); the essays by Stanley L. Engerman and J. Matthew Gallman, Earl J. Hess, Michael Fellman, and Richard Current are especially helpful. Brian Holden Reid, in *The American Civil War and the Wars of the Industrial Revolution* (London, 1999), offers a concise but insightful portrayal of the war in larger military context.

For a powerful representation of the role of slavery in this history, David Brion Davis's works are all helpful. His most recent account synthesizes a vast literature in an accessible way: *Inhuman Bondage: The Rise and Fall of Slavery in the New World* (New York, 2006).

Excellent examples of what might be thought of as the new global history appear in Sven Beckert, "Emancipation and Empire: Reconstructing the Worldwide Web of Cotton Production in the Age of the American Civil War," *American Historical Review,* 109 (Dec. 2004): 1405–38; and Gordon H. Chang, "Whose 'Barbarism'? Whose 'Treachery'? Race and Civilization in the Unknown United States–Korea War of 1871," *Journal of American History,* 89 (March 2003): 1331–65.

Notes

1. For other portrayals of the Civil War in international context, see David M. Potter, "Civil War," in C. Vann Woodward, ed., *The Comparative Approach to American History* (New York, 1968), 135–45; Carl N. Degler, *One Among Many: The Civil War in Comparative Perspective,* 29th Annual Robert Fortenbaugh Memorial Lecture (Gettysburg, Pa., 1990); Robert E. May, ed., *The Union, the Confederacy, and the Atlantic Rim* (West Lafayette, Ind., 1995); Peter Kolchin, *A Sphinx on the American Land: The*

Nineteenth-Century South in Comparative Perspective (Baton Rouge, La., 2003). My view of the workings of world history has been influenced by C. A. Bayly, *The Birth of the Modern World, 1780–1914: Global Connections and Comparisons* (Malden, Mass., 2004). Bayly emphasizes that "in the nineteenth century, nation-states and contending territorial empires took on sharper lineaments and became more antagonistic to each other at the very same time as the similarities, connections, and linkages between them proliferated" (p. 2). By showing the "complex interaction between political organization, political ideas, and economic activity," Bayly avoids the teleological models of modernization, nationalism, and liberalism that have dominated our understanding of the American Civil War.

2. Lincoln quoted in James M. McPherson, *Abraham Lincoln and the Second American Revolution,* reprint (New York, 1992, 1991), 28.

3. The seminal work is Drew Gilpin Faust, *The Creation of Confederate Nationalism: Ideology and Identity in the Civil War South* (Baton Rouge, La., 1988). For an excellent synthesis of the large literature on this topic, see Anne S. Rubin, *A Shattered Nation: The Rise and Fall of the Confederacy, 1861–1868* (Chapel Hill, N.C., 2005).

4. For a useful overview, see Robert W. Fogel, *Without Consent or Contract: The Rise and Fall of American Slavery* (New York, 1989).

5. David Brion Davis, *Slavery and Human Progress* (New York, 1984); Davis, *The Problem of Slavery in the Age of Revolution, 1770–1823* (Ithaca, N.Y., 1975), and Davis, *Inhuman Bondage: The Rise and Fall of Slavery in the New World* (New York, 2006).

6. For helpful overviews of the global situation, see Steven Hahn, "Class and State in Postemancipation Societies: Southern Planters in Comparative Perspective," *American Historical Review,* 95 (Feb. 1990): 75–98, and Hahn, *A Nation Under Our Feet: Black Political Struggles in the Rural South From Slavery to the Great Migration* (Cambridge, Mass., 2003).

7. Quoted in Faust, *Creation of Confederate Nationalism,* 13.

8. There is a large literature on this subject, not surprisingly. A useful recent treatment is Susan-Mary Grant, *North Over South: Northern Nationalism and American Identity in the Antebellum Era* (Lawrence, Kans., 2000). Peter Kolchin also offers penetrating comments on nationalism in *A Sphinx on the American Land,* 89–92.

9. Brian Holden Reid, *The American Civil War and the Wars of the Industrial Revolution* (London, 1999), 211–13; John E. Clark Jr., *Railroads in the Civil War: The Impact of Management on Victory and Defeat* (Baton Rouge, La., 2001); Robert G. Angevine, *The Railroad and the State: War, Politics, and Technology in Nineteenth-Century America* (Stanford, Calif., 2004).

10. For a range of interesting essays on this subject, see Stig Förster and Jörg Nagler, eds., *On the Road to Total War: The American Civil War and the German Wars of Unification, 1861–1871* (Washington, D.C., 1997).

11. See D. P. Crook, *The North, the South, and the Powers, 1861–1865* (New York, 1974); R. J. M. Blackett, *Divided Hearts: Britain and the American Civil War* (Baton

Rouge, La., 2001); James M. McPherson, *Crossroads of Freedom: Antietam* (Oxford, 2002); May, ed., *The Union, the Confederacy, and the Atlantic Rim;* and Charles M. Hubbard, *The Burden of Confederate Diplomacy* (Knoxville, Tenn., 1998).

12. See Allen C. Guelzo, *Lincoln's Emancipation Proclamation: The End of Slavery in America* (New York, 2004).

13. See Joseph T. Glatthaar, *Forged in Battle: The Civil War Alliance of Black Soldiers and White Officers* (New York, 1990). ·

14. See Leon Litwack, *Been in the Storm So Long: The Aftermath of Slavery,* 1st Vintage ed. (New York, 1980, 1979) and the major documentary collection edited by Ira Berlin, Leslie S. Rowland, and their colleagues, sampled in *Free At Last: A Documentary History of Slavery, Freedom, and the Civil War* (New York, 1992).

15. See Davis, *Slavery and Human Progress,* for a sweeping perspective on this issue.

16. The classic history is Eric Foner, *Reconstruction: America's Unfinished Revolution, 1863–1877* (New York, 1988). I have offered some thoughts on Reconstruction's legacy in "Exporting Reconstruction" in *What Caused the Civil War? Reflections on the South and Southern History* (New York, 2005).

17. On the legacy of Reconstruction, see David W. Blight, *Race and Reunion: The Civil War in American Memory* (Cambridge, Mass., 2001).

18. For a fascinating essay on the South's loss of the cotton monopoly, see Sven Beckert, "Emancipation and Empire: Reconstructing the Worldwide Web of Cotton Production in the Age of the American Civil War," *American Historical Review,* 109 (Dec. 2004): 1405–38. On South Africa: John W. Cell, *The Highest Stage of White Supremacy: The Origins of Segregation in South Africa and the American South* (Cambridge, Eng., 1982) and George M. Fredrickson, *White Supremacy: A Comparative Study in American and South African History* (New York, 1981).

19. See the discussion in the essays by Robert E. May and James M. McPherson in May, ed., *The Union, the Confederacy, and the Atlantic Rim.*

20. For the larger context, see Eric J. Hobsbawm, *The Age of Empire, 1875–1914* (New York, 1987) and Bayly, *Birth of the Modern World.*

21. I have described this literature and offered some thoughts on it in the essay "Worrying About the Civil War" in my *What Caused the Civil War?*

22. Reid, *American Civil War,* 213.

TEACHING THE CIVIL WAR FROM A GLOBAL PERSPECTIVE

TED DICKSON

My interest in studying the Civil War began to develop when I was one of James McPherson's students at Princeton University. Yet the Civil War is one area of the survey course that has always frustrated me because I can never spend as much time on it as I would like. With the help of Philip Paludan and others, however, I have developed a set of lesson plans that are fairly comprehensive, and after reading Ed Ayers's essay, I have made further adjustments to broaden both student understanding and the scope of coverage within my time limits.

Our unit on the Civil War begins with a review of its causes through a four-day role-playing simulation on the events of 1844–1861. We then examine the course of the war through the following one-day lessons:

1. **Why did the North win the Civil War** (part 1)? This lesson includes maps and a chart of advantages enjoyed by each side.

2. **The experience of war.** Why did the soldiers fight? This lesson includes primary sources such as Civil War songs, Mathew Brady's photographs, and Winslow Homer's drawings and paintings.

3. **Why did the North win the Civil War** (part 2)? Students present seven turning points—the border states, Manassas, the *Trent* affair and ironclads, Antietam, emancipation, the July days of Gettysburg and Vicksburg, the election of 1864—and argue which was most significant to the outcome of the war.

4. **Lincoln as war president.** Students discuss emancipation, suppression of dissent, Republican programs during the war, and the Gettysburg Address.

5. **Morality and war.** Students discuss the morality of actions taken during wartime, including the total-war strategies of William T. Sherman and Philip Sheridan and the treatment of prisoners by Henry Wirz and Nathan Bedford Forrest.

Throughout these lessons I intersperse clips from the PBS–Ken Burns *Civil War* series. In some survey classes, I show the film *Glory* in its entirety as a transition from the Civil War to Reconstruction. The students also complete a group project that requires them to write letters to and from the home front in which they discuss a variety of events and themes from the war (such as the role of women).

Given the small amount of time I have available to teach the Civil War, I struggle with how to incorporate something new. If, as Ayers concludes, "the events of the 1860s and 1870s proved both powerful and contradictory in their meaning for world history," how do I ensure that my students have a sense of these multiple meanings, especially those that define national identity and the broader context of the destruction of slavery?

First, I now place more emphasis on the global perspective that was included in my lessons. I enrich the turning points lesson by ensuring that the students presenting the *Trent* affair discuss "cotton diplomacy" and that the students presenting emancipation consider its diplomatic effects. In addition, each turning point has a card with one or two illustrations. These cards are used for the part of the lesson in which students are asked to rank the turning points in order of importance. An illustration on the emancipation card is of African American soldiers and the other is the cartoon of Lincoln playing his last card in the British magazine *Punch*. I now make sure that each group of students explains the illustration as part of their presentation. I also modified the lesson "Why did the North win the Civil War (part 2)?"

to include a brief evaluation of the long-range impact of the Civil War on military strategy and technology.

Second, I significantly changed two of the lessons. The lesson on the experience of war previously focused on Civil War song lyrics as a way to examine why the soldiers fought. I begin by defining initial, sustaining, and combat motivation. Initial motivation is why a soldier enlists. Sustaining motivation is why a soldier stays in the army (and perhaps reenlists). Combat motivation is why soldiers are willing to actually fight. We then examine lyrics from, and listen to, "Battle Cry of Freedom" (Union and Confederate versions), "The Bonnie Blue Flag," "We Are Coming Father Abraham," "The Battle Hymn of the Republic," and "Lorena." From these songs, students are able to identify a variety of initial and sustaining motivations. We also discuss other motivations such as money (including bounties) and the draft.[1]

To globalize this lesson, I added two songs: "The Song of the Splintered Shillelagh" and "Give Us a Flag." This leads to discussions of why Irish immigrants and African Americans, while apparent social rivals, both claimed that they were fighting for freedom. This comparison has even more resonance when we discuss the New York City draft riots of July 1863, which began as a protest by Irish Americans against the draft and quickly became about race. At least 119 people were killed; the majority were African American. This event could be discussed as part of the introduction of initial motivation or elsewhere in the unit. We also compare and contrast the ideas of freedom in these additional songs with those found in the other songs.[2]

DOCUMENT A: GIVE US A FLAG

(written by a member of Company A of Robert Gould Shaw's African American 54th Massachusetts Volunteer Infantry in 1863)

> Fremont told us, when this war was first begun,
> How to save this Union, and the way it should be done,
> But Kentucky swore so hard, and old Abe he had his fears,
> So that's what's the matter with the Colored Volunteers.

> [Chorus] Give us a flag all free without a slave,
> We will fight to defend it as our fathers did so brave,
> Onward boys, onward, it's the year of the jubilee,
> God bless America, the land of liberty.

Little Mack went to Richmond with three hundred thousand brave—
Said keep back the negroes and the Union he would save;
But Mack he was defeated, and the Union now in tears,
Is calling for the help of the Colored Volunteers.

[Chorus]

Old Jeff he says he'll hang us if we dare meet him armed—
It's a very big thing, but we are not at all alarmed:
He has first got to catch us before the way is clear,
And that's what's the matter with the Colored Volunteers.[3]

DOCUMENT B: SONG OF THE SPLINTERED SHILLELAGH

'Twas the night before battle and, gathered in groups,
The soldiers lay close at their quarters,
A-thinking, no doubt, of their loved ones at home
Of mothers, wives, sweethearts and daughters.

With a pipe in his mouth sat a handsome young blade,
And a song he was singing so gaily,
His name was Pat Murphy of Meagher's Brigade
And he sang of the land of Shillelagh.

Said Pat to his comrades, it looks quare to see
Brothers fighting in such a strange manner;
But I'll fight 'til I die, if I never get killed
For America's bright starry banner.

[Chorus]

Far away in the west rode a dashing young blade
And the song he was singing so gaily,
'Twas honest Pat Murphy of the Irish Brigade
And the song of the splintered shillelagh.

Well, morning soon broke and poor Paddy awoke
He found rebels to give satisfaction
And the drummer was beating the Devil's sad tune
They were calling the troops into action.

[Chorus]

Then the Irish Brigade into battle was seen,
Their blood for the cause shedding freely
With their bayonet charges they rushed on the foe
With a shout for the land of shillelagh.

[Chorus]

The day after battle, the dead lay in heaps
And Paddy lay bleeding and gory,
With a hole in his breast where some enemy's ball
Had ended his passion for glory.

No more in the camps will his letters be read
Nor his voice be heard singing so gaily
For he died far away from the friends that he loved
And far from the land of shillelagh.[4]

Possible Discussion Questions:

1. Why did African Americans want to fight? What factors influenced the Union's decision to use black troops?
2. Why did Irish Americans want to fight? What factors influenced the Union's recruitment (and drafting) of Irish soldiers? Why would an Irish immigrant who had fled persecution want to fight in the Union Army? How does that relate to the situation in Ireland?
3. Compare and contrast the motives of African American and Irish American soldiers.

The next step in the lesson is to have the students read Document C to get more depth of understanding in their answers to question 2.

DOCUMENT C: PETER WELSH TO MARY WELSH, FEB. 3, 1863

(Peter Welsh was an Irish-born carpenter and a private in the 28th Massachusetts of the Irish Brigade. Mary was his wife. Peter wrote this letter to his wife and father-in-law back in Ireland, who criticized his decision to fight for the black Republican administration. Peter was killed in action in 1864.)

This is my country as much as the man who was born on the soil. I have as much interest in the maintenance of . . . the integrity of the nation as any other man. . . . This is the first test of a modern free government in the act of sustaining itself against internal enemys . . . if it fails all tyrants will succeed the old cry will be sent forth from the aristocrats of europe that such is the common lot of all republics. . . . Irishmen and their descendents have . . . a stake in [this] nation . . . America is Irlands refuge Irlands last hope destroy this republic and her hopes are blasted.[5]

Teachers should use Ed Ayers's article to help frame their answers to these questions and to consider what freedom meant to different Americans. The recent exhibit "New York Divided" at the New-York Historical Society has added to my understanding of the second question. The text of the exhibit states that after Bull Run "New York officials, financed by local merchants, offered enlistees bonuses up to $777 (equal to two years' wages for laborers). Irishmen mobbed the U.S. consulate at Dublin, willing to don the blue uniform to obtain ship passage and a chance at citizenship." The discussion of these questions adds depth and nuance to our discussion of motivation as well as setting up the next lesson on Lincoln as war president and the idea of the "last best hope."[6]

To further emphasize the global significance of the Union victory in the Civil War, I will add two documents to the lesson on Lincoln as war president. The first is the quote with which Ayers begins his essay and the second is from Lincoln's message to Congress in December 1862.

DOCUMENT D

Abraham Lincoln argued that his nation's Civil War "embraces more than the fate of these United States. It presents to the whole family of man, the question, whether a constitutional republic, or a democracy . . . can, or cannot, maintain its territorial integrity." The struggle, Lincoln said, was for "a vast future," a struggle to give all men "a fair chance in the race of life."[7]

DOCUMENT E: ABRAHAM LINCOLN, ANNUAL MESSAGE TO CONGRESS, DECEMBER 1, 1862, CONCLUDING REMARKS

Is it doubted, then, that the plan I propose, if adopted, would shorten the war, and thus lessen its expenditure of money and of blood? Is it doubted that it would restore the national authority and national prosperity, and perpetuate both indefinitely? Is it doubted that we here—Congress and Executive—can secure its adoption? Will not the good people respond to a united, and earnest appeal from us? Can we, can they, by any other means, so certainly, or so speedily, assure these vital objects? We can succeed only by concert. It is not "can any of us imagine better?" but, "can we all do better?" The dogmas of the quiet past, are inadequate to the stormy present. The occasion is piled high with difficulty, and we must rise—with the occasion. As our case is new, so we must think anew, and act anew. We must disenthrall ourselves, and then we shall save our country.

Fellow-citizens, we cannot escape history. We of this Congress and this administration, will be remembered in spite of ourselves. No personal significance, or insignificance, can spare one or another of us. The fiery trial through which we pass, will light us down, in honor or dishonor, to the latest generation. We say we are for the Union. The world will not forget that we say this. We know how to save the Union. The world knows we do know how to save it. We—even we here—hold the power, and bear the responsibility. In giving freedom to the slave, we assure freedom to the free—honorable alike in what we give, and what we preserve. We shall nobly save, or meanly lose, the last best hope of earth. Other means may succeed; this could not fail. The way is plain, peaceful, generous, just—a way which, if followed, the world will forever applaud, and God must forever bless.[8]

The discussion of these documents centers on questions such as:

1. Why does Lincoln think the outcome of the Civil War is significant to the rest of the world?
2. What did Peter Welsh think? Do you think he had read Lincoln's December 1862 address?
3. How might the outcome of the war and emancipation affect other countries such as Brazil, Russia, Great Britain, and Prussia?
4. How might the world have been different if the South had won the Civil War?

Because we have discussed slavery and globalization and the abolitionist response extensively, these questions resonate with my students in interesting ways.

Finally, the Reconstruction section of Ed Ayers's essay lends itself to a few interesting teaching opportunities. In the conclusion of our discussion of Reconstruction, my students are asked to evaluate the entire Civil War period based on this question: "Some historians have argued that the Civil War lasted from 1850, when the Fugitive Slave law was passed as part of the Compromise of 1850, until 1877, when the Compromise of 1877 resulted in the last Union troops leaving the South—if you accept the premise that the Civil War was a twenty-seven-year conflict, then who won?" As Ayers points out in his essay, this question has even more resonance when considered in a world context or as a counterfactual. For example: Was Reconstruction a turning point in

U.S. history? In world history? Could it have been? How did the resulting system of Jim Crow influence the world's view of the United States?[9]

In addition, when I teach imperialism I make an explicit connection between Wounded Knee, *Plessy v. Ferguson,* Chinese exclusion, and the question of citizenship that arose in the *Insular Cases.* Now I ask students to compare Thomas Nast's 1879 cartoon "Every Dog has his day" with Dalrymple's 1898 cartoon "School Begins."[10]

These ideas have been a good start to globalizing my presentation of the Civil War. They follow logically from the previous lesson on the Declaration of Independence, and help my students begin to understand the "powerful and contradictory" meanings of the war. I will continue to work on broadening my scope, such as including other comparative examples in the Morality and War lesson. I will also encourage my colleagues teaching world history to compare Lincoln, Bismarck, and the leaders of the Meiji Restoration as well as including the United States in their discussions on both emancipation and apartheid.

Notes

1. This conceptual framework is based on work by John Lynn as interpreted by James McPherson, *For Cause and Comrades: Why Men Fought in the Civil War* (New York, 1997), 12–13.

2. Both of these songs are available on iTunes, as are most of the songs I use in this lesson. I prefer Bobby Horton's recordings of Civil War songs and Richie Havens's version of "Give Us a Flag." Jed Marum's version of "Pat Murphy" is also available at iTunes and has interesting lyrics. My students are already familiar with nativism and bigotry against immigrant Irish Catholics from our discussions of the San Patricio Brigade (Irish soldiers who deserted from the American army and fought as a unit in the Mexican Army during the war with Mexico), the opposition to annexing all of Mexico, and the Know Nothings. The group Black 47 has recorded an interesting song on the San Patricio Brigade that is also available on iTunes.

3. Steven H. Cornelius, *Music of the Civil War Era* (Westport, Conn., 2004), 97–98.

4. These are the lyrics as found at <http://www.traditionalmusic.co.uk/folk-song-lyrics/Song_of_the_Splintered_Shillelagh.htm>. In *Music of the Civil War Era,* Steven Cornelius also analyzes an Irish song, "Kelly's Irish Brigade," which is written from the Confederate point of view and has a different take on liberty. Additional background information on the motivations of Irish American soldiers can be found in Barnet Schecter, *The Devil's Own Work: The Civil War Draft Riots and the Fight to Reconstruct America* (New York, 2005).

5. James McPherson, *For Cause and Comrades: Why Men Fought in the Civil War* (New York, 1997), 113–14, and the accompanying footnote that appears on page 217.

6. *New York Divided: Slavery and the Civil War,* Exhibit at New-York Historical Society, New York City, November 17, 2006–September 3, 2007. For further research on this topic, see Thomas Bender, *A Nation Among Nations: America's Place in World History* (New York, 2006), especially the chapter titled, "Freedom in an Age of Nation Making." For a more comparative approach, see Carl Guarneri, *America in the World: United States History in a Global Context* (Boston, 2007).

7. As quoted by Ed Ayers in preceding essay from James M. McPherson, *Abraham Lincoln and the Second American Revolution,* reprint (New York, 1992, 1991), 28.

8. This document can be found at Abraham Lincoln Online: <http://showcase .netins.net/web/creative/lincoln/speeches/congress.htm>.

9. At the 2007 OAH Annual Meeting, Glenda Gilmore delivered a paper titled "The Nazis and Dixie" in which she discussed how Nazi leaders compared their treatment of Jews with the treatment of African Americans in the South.

10. The Thomas Nast cartoon can be found at: <http://museum.msu.edu/ Exhibitions/Virtual/ImmigrationandCaricature/7572–289.html> and the Dalrymple cartoon "School Begins" can be found at: <http://www.vcdh.virginia.edu/solguide/ VUS09/vus09a03.html>.

CHAPTER 8

This woodcut image of a male slave in chains appears on the 1837 broadside publication of John Greenleaf Whittier's antislavery poem, "Our Countrymen in Chains." The design was originally adopted as a seal of the Society for the Abolition of Slavery in England in 1787. (Library of Congress, Rare Book and Special Collections Division, LC-USZ62-44265.)

WORLDS OF REFORM

DANIEL T. RODGERS

The nineteenth and twentieth centuries were the great age of the nation-state. This was the era in which the structures of the modern states were refined and their powers to conscript, tax, regulate, and coerce were elaborated. The new states forged new popular nationalisms, planted new identities in their citizens' consciousness, and absorbed political ambitions. They developed policy regimes said to be rooted in deep, distinctive structures of national character and values.

But for all their power to absorb and focus politics, the nation-states were never as politically self-contained as their leaders represented them to be. The point is not only that the construction of the nation was itself a transnational project, made as much in processes of adaptive borrowing as by invention. Parliaments, constitutions, systems of representation, and the symbolic repertoire of nationalism itself (flags, anthems, oaths, pageantry, and the rest) were passed across the new nations. But also and just as important, the projects to modernize the existing regimes of policies and politics and to make them more just—the agendas of "reform," as historians know them—were transnational in their reach as well. Even at the height of nation-state hegemony, the networks of reform cut across the nations' borders and drew in worlds beyond them.

Take the great outburst of social reform ambitions in the early-nineteenth-century United States, when movements for the abolition of slavery, the establishment of women's rights, labor unionism, and universal suffrage challenged the established laws and mores of the new republic. One common historical interpretation roots these in the continuing dynamics of the American Revolutionary idea; other historical explanations tie them to the strains of a nascent market society or to the effects of religious revivalism. But there was not a one of the great early-nineteenth-century reform movements in the United States that was not intricately related to parallel and, for the most part, still more powerful movements elsewhere. The epicenter of the international antislavery movement in the 1830s was not William Lloyd Garrison's Boston or Lewis and Arthur Tappan's New York but William Wilberforce's and Joseph Sturge's England. Northern antislavery activists turned to England in search of connections, prestige, funds, and arguments. The term "immediatism" was the invention of a British Quaker abolitionist, Elizabeth Heyrick. The case against partial emancipation was worked out in England in critique of the experiment with postslavery "apprenticeship" in the West Indies. Antislavery agitation in the United States was the work of multiple actors: African Americans free and enslaved, remoralized white Protestant northerners, and the tremors set off by the Haitian revolutionaries. But it was the English antislavery forces, which succeeded in turning the power of the British state first against the international slave trade and then against slavery itself in the British sugar islands, that set the pace.

The workingmen's movements of the mid-nineteenth century, stocked with English, Scots, Irish, and German immigrants, were full of international borrowings, starting with the very idea of a labor union and the tactic of the strike itself. The movements' land reform enthusiasms of the 1840s (out of which the Homestead Act was eventually to emerge) were worked out in conjunction with English land reformers. The question of universal male suffrage could not be debated, after 1792, without reference to France, where a republican government elected on the basis of manhood democracy had had its first, tumultuous, modern trial. The more audacious claim that democracy should be open to women on the same grounds as men had been much less often broached on the international scene when American feminists enunciated it powerfully at Seneca Falls in 1848. But from the 1860s on, when pressure to expand male suffrage in England revived British feminism, the two movements proceeded in close association, exchanging ideas and tactics. American feminists took the lead in the 1880s and 1890s through the organization of the first international councils of women and the global assertiveness of the Women's Christian Temperance Union. With the eruption of a new repertoire of militant tactics in London in 1906, British feminists set the pace, as younger American suffragists such as Alice Paul and Harriet Stanton Blatch scrambled to bring the new British techniques and assertive action home.

The agendas of reform shifted in the generation after 1890, but their transnational character only intensified. These were the apogee years of industrial capitalism: years that witnessed the emergence of a new social landscape of transnationally mobile capital, labor, and technology, concentrated in Europe and North America but with outposts all across the globe. The exploitative aspects of these new forms of industrial life and labor, the contrast between their extraordinary productive capacities and their primitive distributional inequalities, pressed on the consciences of reformers everywhere. The new forms of poverty in the swelling, class-divided metropolises, filled with migrants from local, regional, and transnational countrysides, added to the intensity of the new reform ambitions. So did the new forms of class antagonism: the rapidly escalating scale of labor conflict, the appearance of the first international strike waves, and the rapid advance of international socialism. By the eve of the First World War, older political configurations were straining everywhere to accommodate what was now called, in a dozen different linguistic variations, the "social question." The insurgent political movements took different names—new liberals in Britain, solidarists in France, evolutionary socialists in Germany and Belgium, radicals in Argentina, laborites in Australia, progressives in the United States—but their common affinities and their hunger for means to ameliorate and control the new economic forces were unmistakable.

In this context, the networks of transnational social reform took on a new density, institutional formality, and importance. Personal friendships continued to play a pivotal role in the transnational field of reform, as they had in the benevolence networks of the nineteenth century. Religious connections remained powerful as well, sustained by the development of social doctrine in the Catholic Church after *Rerum Novarum* in 1891 and the emergence of a transnational social gospel Protestantism. Books and pamphlets, translated and reprinted across the nations, continued to be critical carriers of reform energies: Henry George's *Progress and Poverty* (read by radicals and land reformers everywhere), the Fabian Society tracts, Henry Demarest Lloyd's paean to New Zealand, *A Country Without Strikes,* Frederic Howe's *Socialized Germany,* or, still later, Marquis Childs's *Sweden: The Middle Way,* and the Beveridge Report.

Now, however, these channels were supplemented by more formally institutionalized networks. International congresses on the social problems of poverty, industrial accidents, women's labor and welfare, labor legislation, child welfare, and low-cost housing, date from the late 1880s and 1890s, drawing delegates to Paris or Brussels from as far away as Brazil, Mexico, the United States, and Japan. The best organized of these evolved into permanent, transnational associations, which circulated standards, information, and legislative models to their scattered members. Government bureaus, private foundations, university faculties, business associations, and labor alliances responded to the hunger for social facts and foreign examples with conferences, compilations of international social legislation, and missions to investigate the practical results of social reform devices abroad.

These networks rarely possessed the ability to sustain an organized international action. The simultaneous eruption of workers' demonstrations from Santiago to Paris over the execution of the Massachusetts anarchists Nicola Sacco and Bartolomeo Vanzetti in 1927 was an exception. Diplomatic attempts to coordinate national labor standards in order to level the field of relative advantage rarely came to much—though the international agreement to curb phosphorus poisoning in the match industry in 1912 was an early progressive victory. The power of the transnational social reform networks lay not in their capacity to coordinate action but in the information they carried. They laid out models and practices, agendas, and repertoires of action. They ratcheted up ambitions as reformers were encouraged to measure their labors and successes against a world of social practice.

The cumulative effect of the new transnational networks was momentous, and not only within the leading industrial nations of Europe, where they were most densely articulated. Japanese modernizers drew heavily on German social policy example. Latin American social liberals looked to French social science. Model city plans and planners left their marks on buildings and streetscapes around the globe. Not the least striking, however, was the cumulative impact of these transnational social reform networks on the United States.

Perhaps the most telling way to measure that effect is to try to imagine progressive politics in the United States in the early twentieth century exclusive of the elements that had their beginnings elsewhere in these worlds of reform.

It would be a nation without settlement houses (adapted from London examples), without charity organization societies (an English import), without factory and workplace regulation (an English innovation, widely imitated in the late nineteenth and early twentieth centuries), without systems of pooled risk and social insurance (elaborated most fully in Germany after 1881), without systems of labor dispute mediation (built on Australasian and Canadian examples), without professionalized city managers (adopted from German models), without initiative and recall elections (pioneered in Switzerland). The expert-staffed regulatory commissions, on which American progressives pinned such high hopes, were an adaptation of English and German models. The agendas of "social maternalism"—protections for women and child laborers, public health policies to promote infant health and maternity care, publicly subsidized nurseries, and family allowances to supplement the income of mothers in poverty—were, as women's historians have shown, an international production, the work of a transnational network of progressive women. The labor movement, as John Laslett, Donna Gabaccia, and other historians of the labor diaspora have shown, was—for all the differences between the peak national labor associations—an international phenomenon, a far-flung network through which tactics, experiences, and local leadership moved. At the level of political ideas, both Theodore Roosevelt's rhetoric of national efficiency and Woodrow Wilson's vocabulary of the "state" were, as James Kloppenberg and others have noted, shaped in a transatlantic intellectual conversation.

Not all the items of "reform" that circulated among the nations were, by modern standards, benign. Ideas of empire were powerful circulating commodities, as Paul Kramer and Jonathan Go have shown. Systems of labor discipline, racial and eugenic classification, hygienic engineering, criminology, and efficient racial "management" moved through them as well, from the U.S. South to the U.S.-occupied Philippines to South Africa, the European empires, and beyond. The sudden centralization of state authority after 1914, as the war governments seized on each others' examples to assume vast new powers of economic rationalization and manpower conscription, propaganda systems, and antisubversive machinery, was a project of transnational social learning as well.

In many instances, the work of these systems of circulation was relatively straightforward. The international diffusion of minimum-wage devices, designed to set a floor below which employment could be legally held to be exploitation, pure and simple, was one example. The story of modern minimum-wage legislation begins in the acute labor struggles in New Zealand in the 1890s, when judges began to stipulate legal wage minima in their labor disputes arbitration decisions. Labor activists brought a legislative variant of the idea to Australia. From there, through Fabian socialist connections, it came to England, where it was taken up by feminists aroused by the plight of low-wage women workers. British feminists pressed the importance of the idea on Florence Kelley at the international conference of consumers' leagues in Geneva in 1908. With the resources of Kelley's National Consumers' League behind it, and a brief full of internationally drawn materials commissioned by the National Consumers' League to defend it in court, it worked its way into the social legislation of more than a dozen U.S. states. The New Dealers nationalized it in the Fair Labor Standards Act of 1938.

In its international transit, neither the objects nor the mechanisms of minimum-wage legislation remained fixed. The New Zealand minimum-wage edicts were issued piecemeal, dispute by dispute, and their subjects were unionized men. The British variant, the Trade Boards Act of 1909, created special commissions for specifically named "sweated" industries to investigate the threshold of subsistence in each. Progressive Era minimum-wage legislation in the United States (though Kelley herself would have preferred otherwise) was almost exclusively applied to women. Elsewhere in the Americas, the rationales and circumstances of adoption were different still. Minimum-wage legislation came to the Canadian provinces in the wake of the wrenching labor upheavals of 1918–1919; in Argentina, minimum-wage legislation was a central pillar of Peronism; in still other parts of Latin America, minimum-wage legislation arrived through the U.S.-led Alliance for Progress. Each legislative reenactment, framed within new political and constitutional contexts, resulted in a different bundle of compromises. But the arc of transnational appropriations cannot be missed.

At other times, the transit of a reform idea or device across national lines resulted in such dramatic shifts in ends and purposes that terms like policy "diffusion" or "transfer" barely do justice to the process. Zoning for city building heights and densities was the invention of German municipal planners in the decade before 1914, when city authorities everywhere were struggling to wrest the shape of cities from the exclusive domain of land speculators and developers. They used it in Berlin and Frankfurt to try to zone cities into coherent districts for inner-city commerce, manufacturing, low-cost workers' housing, and bourgeois villa districts. Zoning came to the United States via urban reformers who had studied it closely in Germany. But it flourished in the 1920s by dropping every shred of solicitousness for low-cost housing and reshaping itself as the legal foundation for exclusive, one-class, suburban building development.

In still other instances, the efforts to bring a piece of socially progressive legislation across the borders of nation-states simply failed altogether. State-administered insurance against the costs of sickness remains, in the U.S. case, the single most striking example. Sickness insurance for wage earners was the first effectively devised form of public social insurance against the hazards of work life. As the German model of 1883 instituted it, sickness insurance was compulsory but not centralized; financed by a combination of wage taxes and employers' levies, it was administered through thousands of local associations, each contracting with its own doctors. These cautious but effective policy compromises attracted the attention of progressive reformers everywhere. Its incorporation into British social practice in 1911 (over fierce political opposition and the threat of a doctors' strike) was one of the new Liberals' most striking achievements.

U.S. experts on social insurance, studying these events closely, assumed it was only a matter of time before public sickness insurance would be realized in the United States and, indeed, all over the industrialized world. But by the time their campaign began in earnest in 1916, the field of interests they faced was different than progressives had confronted elsewhere. With commercial insurance companies much more deeply entrenched in the United States and the doctors better organized to protect their professional and entrepreneurial interests, resistance was much stiffer, even before the war enabled sickness insurance's opponents, raising the cry of a policy "made in Germany," to brand it as a ploy of German militarists, designed to sap the military and economic strength of the United States. When public health insurance schemes began to circulate internationally again in the 1920s, the U.S. effort was exhausted. The Progressive Era campaign for public health insurance shattered in the United States on issues of context and timing, not on those (timeless) differences in national values that exceptionalist explanations of American social policy have emphasized and exaggerated. But these were obstacle enough to block its passage.

Transit and transformation, incorporation and failure, imitation and adaptive reinvention: all these processes marked the global world of reform. Whether it was the feminization of the settlement house movement in Progressive Era America, or Theodore Roosevelt and Gifford Pinchot's transformation of the public forest idea from a point of city pride to a mark of high national prestige, or the move by which opponents of European-style schemes of publicly financed working-class housing whittled them down to public housing for the poor (and mortgage guarantees for the middle class), the processes overlapped.

It would be a mistake to replace older models of the origins of progressive and New Deal reform with one that focused solely on the global stage. Even the most cosmopolitan American progressives worked simultaneously on stages that were local, statewide, national, and transnational. Frederic Howe was a Cleveland (later New York City) urban reformer, a Wilsonian Democrat, and a tireless publicist of German social efficiency and municipal energy. Florence Kelley's reform career combined graduate studies in politics and economics in Zurich, an eight-year Hull House residence in Chicago, directorship of the Illinois factory inspection service, a stint as American correspondent for a major German journal of social legislation, presidency of the National Consumers' League, and a widely flung correspondence with reformers abroad.

It was in moments of local or national strain and crisis that the initiatives carried by the transnational reform networks gained their practical opportunity. The New Deal, forged in the most acute internal strain of the century, brought a raft of such measures, incubated in these transnational connections, into being. But transnational approaches to the history of reform remind historians that social strains are in themselves never sufficient explanation: that institutional and political change also hinges on shifts in ideas and agendas, in the circulating stock of imaginable policy devices, in the examples of experience-tested measures adapted or reimagined from elsewhere.

Filled by new actors and fitted to new agendas, transnational social reform networks continued to shape politics after the Progressive Era. Even at the height of cold war insularity, from the Truman through the Kennedy-Johnson years, a web of transnational connections linked the postwar European welfare states and the U.S. Democratic Party left. Other networks played a key role in the mobilization of the postwar civil rights movement, joining local struggles in the United States with anti-imperial movements in Gandhi's India and postcolonial Africa. Transnational social networks linked the student movements of the 1960s, as they do the environmental, human rights, anti-WTO, and antisweatshop movements of our own day. Since the late 1970s, a counternetwork of reformers, eager to dismantle the state-building work of the early-twentieth-century progressives and set markets "free," has relied heavily on transnational connections to sustain its ideas, sense of momentum, and supply of working policy devices. The conservative think tanks of Thatcher's Britain were critical generators of parts of the new American conservatives' reform agenda; the neoliberal showpieces for social security reform were Chile and Singapore. In turn, these networks carry the message of market efficiency worldwide. Now, as before, the worlds of reform sprawl across the nation-states.

Bibliographical Essay

For overviews of the transatlantic world of reform in the Progressive Era, the books with which to begin are Daniel T. Rodgers, *Atlantic Crossings: Social Politics in a Progressive Age* (Cambridge, Mass., 1998), from which much of this essay is adapted, and James T. Kloppenberg, *Uncertain Victory: Social Democracy and Progressivism in European and American Thought, 1870–1920* (New York, 1986), which stresses convergence in political ideas. Thomas Bender offers a fine short synthesis in chapter 5 of his *A Nation among Nations: America's Place in World History* (New York, 2006). Axel R. Schäfer, *American Progressives and German Social Reform* (Stuttgart, 2000) deals closely with linkages between German and American progressives. Mark Stears, *Progressives, Pluralists and the Problem of the State: Ideologies of Reform in the United States and Britain, 1909–1926* (Oxford, 2002) examines the dialogue between British socialist and American progressive intellectuals. Peter J. Coleman describes an aspect of the intense progressive interest in Australasia in *Progressivism and the World of Reform: New Zealand and the Origins of the American Welfare State* (Lawrence, Kans., 1987). Robin D. G. Kelley, "'But a Local Phase of a World Problem': Black History's Global Vision, 1883–1950," *Journal of American History*, 86 (Dec. 1999): 1045–77, surveys the transnational worlds in which African American progressive intellectuals and reformers moved.

The early-nineteenth-century antislavery international is described in Betty Fladeland, *Men and Brothers: Anglo-American Antislavery Cooperation* (Urbana, Ill., 1972) and David Brion Davis, *The Problem of Slavery in the Age of Revolution, 1770–1823* (Ithaca, N.Y., 1975). Bonnie S. Anderson does the same for the early women's rights movement in *Joyous Greetings: The First International Women's Movement, 1830–1860* (New York, 2000). Jamie L. Bronstein, *Land Reform and Working-Class Experience in Britain and the United States, 1800–1862* (Stanford, Calif., 1999) draws the connections between the two movements, though it stops short of Henry George's career.

The late-nineteenth- and early-twentieth-century labor diaspora is given an overview in Marcel van der Linden, "Transnationalizing American Labor History," *Journal of American History*, 86 (Dec. 1999): 1078–92, and excellent case studies in Donna R. Gabaccia, *Italy's Many Diasporas* (Seattle, 2000) and John H. M. Laslett, *Colliers Across the Sea: A Comparative Study of Class Formation in Scotland and the American Midwest, 1830–1924* (Urbana, Ill., 2000). Tony Freyer, *Regulating Big Business: Antitrust in Great Britain and America, 1880 to 1990* (Cambridge, Eng., 1992) gives a subtle reading of the interrelated British and American debates over the trusts.

Of all the phases of reform, the transnational networks that women suffragists and social maternalists made have been the most intensely studied. Margaret McFadden, *Golden Cables of Sympathy: The Transatlantic Sources of Nineteenth-century*

Feminism (Lexington, Ky., 1999) and Leila J. Rupp, *Worlds of Women: The Making of an International Women's Movement* (Princeton, N.J., 1997) stress the construction of personal friendships. Ian Tyrell, *Woman's World / Woman's Empire: The Women's Christian Temperance Union in International Perspective, 1880–1930* (Chapel Hill, N.C., 1991) and Seth Koven and Sonyaa Michel, eds., *Mothers of a New World: Maternalist Politics and the Origins of Welfare States* (New York, 1993) focus on institutions and programs. The letters between American and German women reformers collected in Kathryn Kish Sklar, Anja Schüler, and Susan Strasser, eds., *Social Justice Feminists in the United States and Germany: A Dialogue with Documents, 1885–1933* (Ithaca, N.Y., 1998) provide a fascinating, close-up glimpse into the networks of transnational feminism.

On connections between the empires: Paul Kramer, "Empires, Exceptions, and Anglo-Saxons: Race and Rule between the British and U.S. Empires, 1880–1910," *Journal of American History,* 88 (March 2002): 1315–53; and Jonathan Go and Anne L. Foster, eds., *The American Colonial State in the Philippines: Global Perspectives* (Durham, N.C., 2003). Anthony Sutcliffe surveys international aspects of the city planning movement in *Towards the Planned City: Germany, Britain, the United States, and France, 1780–1914* (Oxford, 1981).

Contemporary transnational social movements are now the subject of an extensive social science literature. For starting points: Joel Best, ed., *How Claims Spread: Cross National Diffusion of Social Problems* (New York, 2001), Donatella della Porta, Hanspeter Kriesi, and Dieter Rucht, eds., *Social Movements in a Globalizing World* (New York, 1999), and Richard Rose, *Lesson-Drawing in Public Policy: A Guide to Learning across Time and Space* (Chatham, N.J., 1993).

The largest obstacle to taking the transnational dimensions of politics seriously is the assumption that American politics are "exceptional"—driven by categorically different values than politics elsewhere. The most articulate spokesman of this point is Seymour Martin Lipset, *American Exceptionalism: A Double-Edged Sword* (New York, 1996). On the other side, see Graham K. Wilson, *Only In America? The Politics of the United States in Comparative Perspective* (Chatham, N.J., 1998), and my own "American Exceptionalism Revisited," *Raritan Review,* 24 (Fall 2004): 21–37.

TEACHING AMERICAN REFORM IN A WORLD CONTEXT

KATHLEEN DALTON

My strategies for teaching "Social Reform and the State" began with an "Aha!" moment. One fall I found myself facing a classroom filled with international students. "Aha," I realized, the course cannot be strictly an insider, national conversation anymore. It has to be comparative or global, or the students will tune out. But how would U.S. history translate?

For starters, my vocabulary was a problem. When I gave a slide lecture on Puritan theology and the debate about the religious leaders of the Massachusetts Bay Colony, I understood that I had to explain the difference between Protestant and Catholic theology and practice. I was teaching, however, in the mid-1980s, before Soviet liberalization, and a few of my students had been educated under communism. I was unprepared when a Russian student approached me after class to ask, "What is this word you used: 'God'?"

Nor could I take for granted a shared definition of what history should be or a shared preknowledge. The students from the People's Republic of China claimed history was no more than a set of facts—to them interpretation had no place in history. In addition, I could not count on students from other countries, except maybe France, to know of Benjamin Franklin. Americans are not the only people who neglect the basic history education of their young people.

We finally gained some traction on our differences by comparing national experiences, the founding of the nation-state, immigration and racial difference, the major wars and depressions. We could talk about common ground: When did industrialization occur in your country and what problems arose from it?

Then we tried to speak to each other outside the habits of nationalism, starting with the teacher promising to talk about U.S. history as "their history," to abandon the national "we" in class. A few of the European students resisted learning U.S. history altogether ("a history so short, so imperialistic!") because they did not intend to become U.S. citizens. Their attitude required me to set the U.S. story against the backdrop of world history.[1] We survived and prospered, but it left me with great respect for teachers who regularly try to broaden the scope of their U.S. survey courses. Not all of the usual survey topics translate well.

Reform is one of the most challenging topics to teach comparatively or in global terms because it can include so many different kinds of change. Before my international student class could grapple with the history of reform in the United States, we had to figure out what reform meant elsewhere. Students identified the Chinese government's abolition of foot binding as a reform and recalled the antiapartheid movement in South Africa as a reform. But would all types of change qualify as reform? Through discussion we came to a loose working definition of reform as a movement or a set of ideas being spread to change the way a society operates. In my international students class, we compared the role of the U.S. civil rights movement in challenging Jim Crow segregation, winning civil rights, and shifting racial attitudes with the antiapartheid movement and Gandhi's struggle to gain independence for India, an anticolonial movement that had to fight bigotry to win.[2] Reform became a more tangible idea when students could see the before and after pictures that showed how life changed because of reform activism.[3]

Sometimes international comparisons help highlight places around the world that remain unreformed. Students, international and American, often come to my classes without any clear understanding of the role the women's movement played in reforming the legal and educational rights of women, in the United States and elsewhere. A quick comparison of women's legal rights, educational opportunities, and job chances in 1950 and 1990 can highlight the effects of reform in the United States and other countries.[4] Even further understanding can come from taking a hard look at the widespread assumption of American cultural superiority on questions of gender. Are the rules of gender really more just or humane in the United States? How other countries see the United States surprises students. Foreign observers sometimes view the country as backward on gender, that is, disrespectful of women and oversexualized. In the 1960s, several industrialized countries witnessed a sexual revolution; the jury is still out on whom to praise or blame for the new gender atmosphere. In the United States, where voters can be whipped up into a moral panic over divorce rates, gay marriage, and the alleged decline in sexual morality, teachers need to interject more fact than fear into the classroom. Placing sexual reforms in comparative perspective may help us remove them from the fog of misunderstanding created by the U.S. culture wars. Reform has so many fascinating new meanings when you can move your vantage point beyond these familiar shores.[5]

Reform's many faces belong to different eras and economic and social conditions, and perhaps the deepest change came in the late nineteenth century and early twentieth century when industrialized nations reached a crisis of conscience.[6] To teach about progressive reform or the creation of a welfare state in a comparative or international perspective is at times challenging and requires teachable resources. Where can we turn for help? To date, despite a few admirable gestures toward token inclusion of a comparative or global perspective, U.S. history texts remain annoyingly nation-centered.[7]

Therefore, the Rodgers essay proves especially valuable because it shows us that the United States struggled with the same problems as other industrialized countries. The reform of so-called laissez-faire capitalism via the creation of the welfare state meant that the state assumed responsibility for protecting its citizens from poisonous medicines, hunger, unemployment, poverty, certain types of labor exploitation, and sickness. But many welfare state models exist. The American choice to travel down the "low services" path brought higher infant mortality rates and higher death rates because of lack of universal medical care. How can we see U.S. choices in perspective without comparing them with the ways that other industrialized countries organized their welfare states?

Understanding reform history requires us to remember the worlds of Charles Dickens and Jacob Riis. Pausing to ask our students to suggest major domestic problems the United States and other developing countries faced helps us discuss possible solutions that have been found. For example, how did the widespread use of child labor in factories become illegal? How did so many governments decide to end a profitable labor system like slavery? How were city and state governments convinced that it was their job to stop landlords from building firetrap buildings? How and when did the majority of industrialized nations decide to protect consumers by providing government inspection of medicines and foods?

The Rodgers essay invites us to question our texts. He raises a valid point about the incompleteness of traditional explanations for the rise of antebellum reform in all its variety. Though dislocations brought about by industrialization and urbanization coincided with the Second Great Awakening in stirring up reformers, nation-bound economic and religious explanations for the mushrooming of reform societies are insufficient explanations. We know that new reform ideas were not original to the American abolitionists who met with their British counterparts and learned from them. After all, Elizabeth Cady Stanton was an observer (her husband a delegate) at the World's Anti-Slavery Convention in London when she and Lucretia Mott began to talk about the need for a U.S. women's rights convention. Students with access to the *American National Biography* or a good online encyclopedia could take the major antebellum reformers and in a one-night assignment ask whether they had been in contact with reformers from other countries.

A common way for teachers to internationalize the history of reform is to use examples of reformers and reforms that belong to more than one national story. From the late eighteenth century, Olaudah Equiano (Gustavus Vassa) speaks to us as a transnational phenomenon, documented by a convenient online eyewitness account. As a West African captive, a slave and then freedman in the Americas, a sailor who witnessed wars for empire, and then as a British abolitionist and influential author, Equiano defies our habit of categorizing people and topics by national boundaries. Equiano serves as an international example of a slave and a reformer.[8] In class I have used Equiano's *Narrative* to ask groups of students to find what systems of ideas he defends in opposition to the commodification of slaves for profit in the world of Atlantic commerce. The majority of them discover in his text that he invokes Christian ethics to challenge the justice of slavery, and some also see him using the ethics of his Ibo culture or Enlightenment standards of reason and justice to critique the code of the slave traders and planters. What moral ideas does he use to call into question an economic system that the plantocracy in Parliament and Congress wanted to perpetuate? How many generations of reformers did it take to bring about the banning of the slave trade and the abolition of slavery?

Teachers will use common sense to pick which transnational reform stories work best in their classrooms. The most accessible transatlantic reform links for survey courses are the ties between British and American suffrage movements. After working with Emmeline Pankhurst, founder of the Women's Social and Political Union in Britain, Alice Paul brought direct action, militance, and careful lobbying to the stalled U.S. suffrage movement.[9] Students can delve into a selective comparison of suffrage movements around the world.[10] Why did woman suffrage wait so much longer in some countries? Was woman suffrage always tied to universal manhood suffrage, and where did opposition to women's rights come from? Why did the Nazis associate women's public activities with social decay? What took the Swiss so long to grant woman suffrage? Have gender gaps emerged elsewhere comparable to the gap in U.S. voting behavior in the Reagan era?

Women's history, now so often accepted as part of the U.S. survey, is central to understanding the history of reform from an international perspective. Women reformers from Jane Addams to Florence Kelley found some of their best ideas—the settlement house movement and the minimum wage—in the example of Toynbee Hall and the German labor movement. Women peace activists and environmental reformers crossed national boundaries and thought internationally.

Besides the time we spend in the U.S. survey on antebellum reform, the biggest expanse of time we spend on reform history is on progressivism. If my students were to read Daniel Rodgers's essay, I would divide them into working groups and ask three groups to go over the article. One group could simply list the reforms he mentions and what they tried to achieve. Another group could pull out his critique of the way reform is usually explained, and the last group could find his central arguments in favor of a global perspective. Once they came to terms with the main outlines of his argument, I would ask the groups to agree or disagree with what he said.

Another alternative for delving into the global history of progressive reform is to make it as tangible, concrete, and biographical as possible. For example, Theodore Roosevelt comes in handy as an example of a politician whose privileged life afforded him plenty of international education of the grand tour variety. But his story became more interesting when he was buttonholed by Florence Kelley and educated on international ideas about how minimum-wage laws could raise workers out of poverty. Theodore Roosevelt grew as a reformer when Jacob Riis took him through tenements to see why reform laws were needed. After his presidency Roosevelt went abroad once more and talked with David Lloyd George and continental reform thinkers and activists with whom he could compare reform agendas. When I teach progressivism and the 1912 election, I use the story from my biography of Roosevelt to describe how he and Jane Addams tried to invoke international comparisons to embarrass Americans into voting for a welfare state.[11]

Research as a strategy for making progressive reform may work best in a library where research treasure hunts, in pairs or teams, can be arranged. Students can use the *American National Biography* or the *Dictionary of American Biography* and *Notable American Women* in a reference room or selected Internet sites.[12]

Student partners could be given the names of reformers and asked to find out:

1. What did the reformer find wrong with American society?
2. What reforms did this reformer advocate from 1890 to 1920?
3. Where did this reformer learn about possible solutions to such problems? Was the reformer connected via travel, associations, reading, or friendship with reformers from other countries?
4. A bonus question: can you find any examples of the reformer writing about how America compares to other countries in terms of reform?

This assignment could be adapted to an oral report or a paper, depending upon the size of the class and the teacher's goals.

Because the historiography of the Progressive Era still suffers from some previous political historians' conflation of progressive reform with party politics, especially Progressive Party ideas, the usual suspects covered in texts and reference sources are still not selected as broadly as they could be. Founders of the N.A.A.C.P. qualify as reformers, and so do a lot of people who worked on state reforms and moral reforms.

REFORMERS (most of them easy to find in reference sources):

Gifford Pinchot
Florence Kelley
Ida B. Wells-Barnett
John Dewey
Margaret Dreier Robins
Carrie Chapman Catt
Robert M. LaFollette
Samuel "Golden Rule" Jones
Newton D. Baker
Jane Addams

Jacob Riis
Louis Brandeis
Woodrow Wilson
Theodore Roosevelt
W. E. B. Du Bois
Alice Paul

As a way to bring individual stories together, the class could talk about what a welfare state is and why that generation of reformers believed it was necessary. Can students answer this challenging question: What happens to poor people and unemployed people without a welfare state?

The final challenge for teachers is teaching the history of New Deal reform in international or comparative context. A good foundation for understanding the exceptional U.S. reforms of the 1930s is included in the Fall 2001 issue of the *OAH Magazine of History,* which offered an introduction to online resources.[13] Alonzo L. Hamby's *For the Survival of Democracy: Franklin Roosevelt and the World Crisis of the 1930s* tells the story of economic recovery in Germany, Great Britain, and the United States and can shed light on how relief in Britain and unemployment benefits and public housing reforms in Germany stifled protest while riots and demonstrations ran loose in the United States.[14] The "reform from the top down" model implicit in Hamby's study is informative but not the only way to understand New Deal reform.[15] Similarly, the latest phase of reform history, welfare state retrenchment, can be studied comparatively with good effect.[16]

Certainly the contributors to this volume would agree that teaching U.S. history in a comparative or international perspective is worthwhile, but no one should pretend that scholars or teachers have the one best way to do so figured out. As U.S. survey teachers, our intellectual and pedagogical creativity can often be derailed by the tyranny of testing, whether state dictated or college entrance driven. In too many places, teachers who want to innovate face huge classes and inadequate libraries, and state history curriculum frameworks that inhibit intellectual creativity. Keeping open to new trends in teaching, nevertheless, keeps us from stagnation and burnout. As civic education for the twenty-first century, U.S. history should not be taught ethnocentrically or in the spirit of the ancient Chinese emperors, with the assumption that we live in the Middle Kingdom and are, therefore, the center of all that is good and true. Reform comparisons, as Rodgers's essay shows us, can open up conversations about what the United States has in common with other industrialized countries.

Recommended Resources

In addition to resources listed in the footnotes, a good starting point would be Ronald G. Walters, *American Reformers, 1815–1860* (New York, 1997); Steven Mintz, *Moralists and Modernizers: America's Pre–Civil War Reformers* (Baltimore, 1995); an older book still worth reading, Eric F. Goldman, *Rendezvous with Destiny: A History of Modern American Reform* (New York, 1966), on reforms related to welfare, Robert C. Lieberman, *Shaping Race Policy: The United States in Comparative Perspective* (Princeton, N.J., 2005).

Students can be assigned to search the excellent Digital History Web site for primary documents: <http://www.digitalhistory.uh.edu/social_history/social_history.cfm>.

See also the World History Association link: <http://www.thewha.org/links.php>.

Another way to teach American reform in a world context would be to start with the world and then insert American details: Kevin Reilly, *The West and the World: A History of Civilization: From 1450 to the Present* (New York, 2003).

The Bridging World History Web site of the Annenberg Foundation offers segments on immigration reform, who freed the slaves, and progressivism and has useful teaching material connected with the PBS series *People's Century*: <http://www.learner.org/channel/courses/worldhistory/>. The Bill Moyers New York Public Affairs Television Group is working on a multiprogram series on the Progressive Era that promises to be a useful tool for teaching about reform.

Notes

1. See Elaine Scarry, "The Difficulty of Imagining Other People," in Martha C. Nussbaum, *For Love of Country*, Joshua Cohen, ed. (Boston, 2002), 98–110.

2. See an effective comparative history Web site: <http://edsitement.neh.gov/view_lesson_plan.asp?id=326>; <http://www.obs-us.com:80/obs/english/books/Mandela/Mandela.html>; the Gilder Lehrman Web site has excellent material on comparative slavery and British and American suffrage movements.

3. Reform is a huge topic in world history, e.g., Wahabist reforms, Gregorian reforms, etc. See chapter 2, Patrick Collinson, *The Reformation: A History* (New York, 2006).

4. Alice Kessler-Harris, *In Pursuit of Equity: Women, Men, and the Quest for Economic Citizenship in Twentieth-Century America* (New York, 2001); Ian Christopher Fletcher, Laura E. Nym Mayhall, and Philippa Levine, eds., *Women's Suffrage in the British Empire: Citizenship, Nation, and Race* (London and New York, 2000). For a world timeline of suffrage, see <http://www.ipu.org/wmn-e/suffrage.htm>.

5. Does the United States suffer from greater female dependence on men and more hostility toward gender equality? Janeen Baxter and Emily W. Kane, "Dependence

and Independence: A Cross-National Analysis of Gender Inequality and Gender Attitudes," *Gender and Society*, 9 (April 1995): 193–215. Rebecca J. Cook, ed., *Human Rights of Women: National and International Perspectives* (Philadelphia, 1994); Yvonne Yazbeck Haddad and John L. Esposito, eds., *Islam, Gender, and Social Change* (New York, 1998); Susan Moller Okin, ed., with respondents, ed. Joshua Cohen, Matthew Howard, and Martha C. Nussbaum, *Is Multiculturalism Bad for Women?* (Princeton, N.J., 1999). Stephanie Coontz, "A Pop Quiz on Marriage," *New York Times*, Feb. 19, 2006. On comparative reform, see Gösta Esping-Andersen, *The Three Worlds of Welfare Capitalism* (Princeton, N.J., 1990); Peter Flora and Arnold J. Heidenheimer, eds., *The Development of Welfare States in Europe and America* (New Brunswick, N.J., 1982).

6. Eugenics and "civilizing" Native Americans are examples of the dark side of reform, Steven Mintz, e-mail to the author, June 10, 2007; for the effects of Clinton-era welfare reform and its comparability to other nations, see Jill Duerr Berrick, "Marriage, Motherhood and Welfare Reform," *Social Policy and Society*, 4 (April 2005): 133–45.

7. A short textbook usable in the U.S. history survey is Carl Guarneri, *America in the World: United States History in Global Context* (New York, 2007); highly recommended, too, is Guarneri, *America Compared: American History in International Perspective*, vol. 1 to 1877, vol. 2 since 1865 (New York, 2004); Allen Davis wrote the best textbook version of a globalized, up-to-date section on "The Progressive Movement in a Global Context" in Gary B. Nash and Julie Roy Jeffrey et al., *The American People: Creating a Nation and a Society*, 7th ed. (New York, 2006), but so far no textbook does more than sidebar comparative and international history.

8. Equiano can speak as an eyewitness via his online version: <http://www .gutenberg.org/etext/15399>, or use the documentary *The Son of Africa* by California Newsreel.

9. Kathryn Sklar and Thomas Dublin, eds., "Women and Social Movements in the United States, 1600–2000" (online resource). See the subscription site: <http:// alexanderstreet6.com/wasm>; Agents of Social Change: <http:///www.smith.edu/ libraries/libs/ssc/exhibit>.

10. For British and American suffrage history: <http://www.historynow .org/03_2006/ask2f.html>; Martin Pugh, *Women and the Women's Movement in Britain, 1914–1959* (New York, 1992); Jane Rendall, *The Origins of Modern Feminism: Women in Britain, France, and the United States, 1780–1860* (New York, 1984); For European suffrage documents: <http://www.dhr.history.vt.edu/eu/mod02_vote/ index.html>.

11. Kathleen Dalton, *Theodore Roosevelt: A Strenuous Life* (New York, 2002).

12. See Richard A. Marius and Melvin E. Page, *A Short Guide to Writing About History*, 6th ed. (New York, 2006), for a term-paper guide that offers a sample research paper and practical advice on how to construct sentences and paragraphs, as well as framing a thesis that can be defended with evidence and argument.

13. Paul Chamberlin, "Using the Web to Explore the Great Depression," *OAH Magazine of History* (Fall 2001): 66–67.

14. Alonzo L. Hamby, *For the Survival of Democracy: Franklin Roosevelt and the World Crisis of the 1930s* (New York, 2004).

15. Jeff Manza, "Political Sociological Models of the U.S. New Deal," *Annual Review of Sociology,* 26 (2000): 297–322; Gary Gerstle, "The Protean Character of American Liberalism," *American Historical Review,* 99 (Oct. 1994): 1043–73.

16. On retrenchment, see Robert Henry Cox, "The Social Construction of an Imperative: Why Welfare Reform Happened in Denmark and the Netherlands but Not in Germany," *World Politics,* 53 (April 2001): 463–98; Paul Pierson, "The New Politics of the Welfare State," *World Politics,* 48 (Jan. 1996): 143–79.

CHAPTER

A Mexican citizen immigrating to the United States in 1912. (Library of Congress, Prints and Photographs Division, LC-USZ62-97491.)

CROSSING NATIONAL BORDERS
LOCATING THE UNITED STATES
IN MIGRATION HISTORY

SUZANNE M. SINKE

In 1909 Jantje Enserink van der Vliet entered the United States, headed for a rural Dutch American community. Depending on how you define it, she was or was not a part of U.S. immigration. Her story, and that of her spouse Cornelis van der Vliet, began in the Netherlands, where Jantje, the oldest and only daughter of a widower, was keeping house for her farmer father and eight younger brothers. Cornelis came to stay with the Enserinks for a few months to learn about farming techniques unfamiliar to him before he embarked on a journey for South Africa, where he hoped to become a farmer himself. In 1903 he made his way south to live with the Dutch-descended Afrikaners, and for the next three years he moved from one rural district to another, with little success at farming. He attributed part of his failure to a lack of a spouse. Cornelis decided to try elsewhere and went via England to Canada, where he got a job doing railroad construction. His interest in farming, however, was unabated, and this time he wanted to make sure he had a suitable spouse. He had not been on his railroad job long before he wrote back to Jantje Enserink, asking her to marry him.

In 1907 Cornelis returned to the Netherlands to marry Jantje and bring her back to Canada. There were many Dutch migrants going to North America in this period, and those interested in farming were slightly more likely to go to Canada than the United States owing to land availability. When Jantje arrived at their new home outside Fort William she found she was the only woman in a work camp, and that the house she expected to share with Cornelis would also house six relatives/friends, for whom she would do the cooking and cleaning. Not long thereafter Jantje's health began to go downhill, so Cornelis suggested she go to the United States, specifically to Minnesota, where his sister lived on a farm with her husband and child. Whatever Jantje's "illness," she had a miscarriage not long after arriving in Minnesota, and while there she learned that Cornelis had died of appendicitis while working on the railroad. Seeing no reason to go back to Canada, Jantje remained in the United States, continuing to live with Cornelis's sister and doing housework for wages as well. A little more than a year later Jantje Enserink van der Vliet headed back to the Netherlands, where she got a job as a housekeeper.[1] As the Van der Vliets' story shows, the study of people who cross national borders encourages historians to think beyond national histories and the terms that are caught up in them.

Individual lives linked to broader factors encouraged or discouraged migration across borders. Two factors that were prominent in this case were economics and familial ties. Economic circuits brought farmers in the Netherlands into competition with those elsewhere, dimming future prospects for someone like Cornelis Van der Vliet, the son of a farmer. Land prices, cost of living, wages: these were pieces of information that made their way across borders to potential migrants in the nineteenth and twentieth centuries. Cornelis sought to take advantage of the economic activity associated with rebuilding after the Anglo-Boer War. Ethnic ties meant Van der Vliet could expect to be able to function in Afrikaans-speaking segments of South Africa. But he came as a carpetbagger of sorts, at a time when at least some Afrikaners were disgruntled with the lack of support the Netherlands had provided during the war and distrustful of those who came afterward. This situation, and his single status, made farming more difficult. When his attempts in South Africa failed, he turned to North America and to railroad work in order to amass an economic base. Railroads were part of the infrastructure linking various parts of the world; at the same time, they offered opportunities for men (and less often women) to earn a living—if they survived. Cornelis recruited several relatives and friends to join him in Canadian railroad work when he went back to the Netherlands to marry.

Meanwhile, Jantje Enserink became part of an international marriage market when Cornelis wrote from Canada asking her to wed. Perhaps there had been signs of romance before; perhaps she was tired of caring for her younger brothers. There were many women, especially in rural areas of the Netherlands, who wanted to marry but had few opportunities owing to the lack of young men with reasonable economic prospects. Marriage to an international migrant, or migrating alone with hopes of marriage, became an alternative. Familial motivations—joining spouses, parents, and other relatives, as well as trying to escape marriage and/or family duties—were major forces for migration. In other words, individual stories such as that of Cornelis and Jantje Enserink van der Vliet illustrate how economic systems and family ties crossed borders. Other migrants, notably refugees, add other categories of linkage, but the basic principle of migrants as challenges to national histories remains.

To label Jantje Enserink van der Vliet an immigrant to the United States would be technically accurate, but misleading. "Immigration" typically has implied a person moving across a national border to live in a new country, a one-way movement. Because there were many who returned to their homelands, particularly after transportation innovations made this easier and less expensive in the mid-nineteenth century, scholars have increasingly used migration as the term to cover those moving, sometimes back and forth many times and from one location to others, as Cornelis and Jantje Enserink van der Vliet did. A further caveat in terms of defining migration is that many migrants did not cross national boundaries, but faced major cultural differences nonetheless. When Jantje went to live with her in-laws in Minnesota she joined a Dutch-speaking farming community complete with church. Would that have been a more difficult transition than one of her likely alternatives had she remained in the Netherlands—going to work in a major urban center there? Stories like this suggest the need for a continuum of adjustment.

For that reason, recent scholars often pay less attention to national boundaries than to cultural connections and disconnections. Immigration historian Dirk Hoerder used the title *Cultures in Contact* (2002) for his recent prize-winning history of migration, which spanned a millennium and the globe. Hoerder defined migration broadly, to include any move beyond the parental home, though his focus for the study went beyond the individual level to discuss ten circuits, "webs" of connection of commerce and knowledge, which spurred people to move extensively—across the Atlantic or Pacific, for example. These webs meant people, money, goods, and ideas moving in different directions—blending, clashing, changing.

AN OVERVIEW OF U.S. IMMIGRATION

The United States was connected into these webs of migration, although its importance within each system varied across time. Prior to independence it connected into the Atlantic system through two major streams of migration: people taken as slaves primarily from western Africa, and migrants from Europe, particularly the British Isles and German-speaking states (including many indentured servants). North America was a minor destination in the slave trade, dwarfed by the plantation economies of the Caribbean and parts of South America. In 1808, furthermore, the importation of slaves from Africa officially ended for the United States, one small part of an ongoing battle to outlaw the slave trade internationally. The other stream of migration to the United States, from Europe to the new nation, continued. By the 1840s the United States was also connecting into the Pacific migration system, with some men (and very few women) coming from southeastern China until racially motivated exclusion acts curtailed this movement.

The largest migration to the United States (and to North America more generally) throughout the nineteenth century and into the twentieth came from Europe. German speakers and Irish, along with smaller groups from other parts of northern and western Europe, predominated early in the nineteenth century. They were part of a group of "moving Europeans," responding to various economic, religious, and political opportunities and changes.[2] The majority who moved nevertheless remained in Europe. Others sought opportunities elsewhere, like Cornelis van der Vliet; and yet others followed these individuals (albeit sometimes reluctantly, like Jantje Enserink). In the circuits of connection from Europe, the United States attracted the largest number of transatlantic migrants, but not necessarily the largest for all groups or per capita: Argentina had a much higher proportion of migrants (58 percent foreign born and their children in 1914); Canada was comparable to the United States in terms of growth rates and started offering land on the prairies around the time that farms became harder to get in the United States.[3] The national border along the 49th Parallel made less difference to the Van der Vliet families moving to North America than did the issue of where they could find work and land.

By the late nineteenth century, migrants to the United States increasingly sought urban and industrial employment opportunities, or connections to those that had them. In the United States this shift in predominance to industrial labor coincided with a shift in the proportion of migrants from southern and eastern Europe, whom policy makers called "new immigrants" even though many from western Europe in this period also fit this pattern. The shift to steam transportation and the expansion of railroad lines contributed to making migration easier and cheaper, and hence led to a major expansion in the numbers of migrants, many of whom returned to their homelands, and sometimes came back again. Factory and domestic service work might not support a family in the United States, but at least in some cases it could provide sustenance for an individual plus a chance to send remittances back to others in areas where dollars translated into a higher standard of living.

As a consequence of the Spanish-American War, the United States became more enmeshed in the Pacific migration system, particularly through the acquisition of Hawai'i, and control of the Philippines. Escalating racial tensions led to a ban on the migration of workers from Japan in 1908, and then to the Asian-barred zone in 1917, directing a number of potential Asian migrants to other nations like Peru and Brazil. In general, after the turn of the twentieth century, the U.S. elite increasingly raised questions about immigration, expanding this to include issues about the suitability of southern and eastern European migrants living in the United States. These concerns culminated in the restrictive national quota acts of the 1920s. Thus Asian exclusion set the precedent for the overall curtailment of immigration.

Meanwhile, during the 1910s the Mexican Revolution spurred migration north, particularly into the southwestern United States, the land that had once been part of Mexico. Mexican migration continued at mid-century through the bracero program. Farm and factory laborers on these guest-worker visas established links into the U.S. economy that outlived the programs. Migration circuits continued, particularly though not exclusively for low-wage jobs in construction, factories, housekeeping, and child care. The combination of both documented and undocumented migration from Mexico constituted the largest national migration circuit for the United States late in the twentieth century and a major political issue—illegal immigration.

Shifts in U.S. immigration policy through the mid-twentieth century eliminated some of the most glaring anti-Asian bias, but in the major global migrations tied to decolonization movements—often involving people going from Asia and Africa to former colonial powers—the United States remained peripheral. It was not until the Hart-Celler Act of 1965 that patterns in the United States shifted more significantly. Under that legislation, family reunification and skills preferences constituted the highest priorities, though national quotas—now all equal—continued for all countries. Overall this led to an upsurge in immigration, particularly from Asia and Latin America, and to a division between highly skilled and unskilled migrants. The United States again became a major magnet for migration, though certainly not the only one.

RECENT APPROACHES TO MIGRATION

Since the early 1990s *transnationalism* has become the leading phrase to refer to migrant lives among anthropologists and sociologists who have pioneered studying post-1965 migration to and from the United States. The term *trans-nationalism* goes back much longer, as does this kind of scholarship among immigration historians, but studies that go beyond national boundaries have gotten a boost because of it. Typically transnationalism refers to ongoing connections across borders: economic, political, religious, social. For example, Rhacel Salazar Parreñas's *Servants of Globalization* (2001), a study of Filipinas migrating to do domestic work in Los Angeles and Rome in the late twentieth century, showed how parenting roles crossed borders—transnational motherhood—both for paid caregivers who served families in richer nations and for the children they left behind. What we now label *emotional work* across borders existed in the letters of the Van der Vliets as well: "Oh, dear ones, I know that you care about me so much, and how gladly I would speak to you. I can imagine what you must have thought: 'Jantje will not be able to bear that without God's support.'"[4] For the nineteenth century, transnational fatherhood was a common phenomenon, and men who sent money and advice—and sometimes returned—illustrated how people managed to maintain relationships across borders.

Scholars from other nations who focus on migration to North America often chronicle the impact of returnees and remittances on a region of extensive out-migration. The interest in migration as a field of study has surged in Europe, with the formation of a number of museums and institutes devoted to the topic. Research indicates that a significant number of migrants going to the United States might mean higher land prices in Galicia, or fewer marriage opportunities in a small Sicilian town, or a growing middle class in Mount Lebanon. The "American," a term for returned migrants that existed in many languages, became a common character in many parts of Europe in the nineteenth century.[5] This person was typically less deferential to authorities than before and used conspicuous consumption to illustrate the wealth he (and less often she) had gained. The term at times even applied to people who had not migrated, but who acted the way "Americans" did. Letters, often read and circulated in public venues, contributed strongly to this kind of image-making. They could create a "culture of migration" that scholars of more recent times have charted among Mexican migrants.

Letters that migrants sent back and forth reflected their positions in more than one cultural world. The authors, many with minimal literacy in the nineteenth century, compared wages and prices and described marital prospects, living and working conditions, gender roles, and sometimes political and religious opportunities. Historians today can draw upon many published collections of these letters, some with elaborate annotation about places and people. Many of Cornelis van der Vliet's contemporaries, for instance, can be found in *Dutch American Voices: Letters from the United States 1850–1930*.[6] These works, which trace individuals from place to place, typically focus on binational comparisons. Some, however, include multinational locations, such as one of Poles going to either Brazil or the United States in the early 1890s.[7]

Comparisons of one national or ethnic group in several locations has become more common under the label *diaspora*, a term that initially referred to groups after forced expulsion (Jews, Africans caught in slavery), but that has grown to sometimes include people from one national background residing elsewhere, including later generations. In the latter form it is frequently just another version of the nation-state paradigm.[8] Sometimes the diasporic connection is seen in language, as with the characters translated as "overseas Chinese." Adam McKeown's study of Chinese migrants in Peru, Chicago, and Hawai'i in the early 1900s makes one of the strongest cases for expanding national histories to incorporate a population overseas, and for the ways in which migrants themselves create and sustain transnational contacts.[9] To follow this model, we would need much more rigorous study of U.S. citizens who have moved elsewhere, as well as ongoing attention to how people who have taken on "American" identity have brought this back to their places of origin.

One of the best exemplars of a study of people from one nation who historically go to many locations is the "Italians everywhere" project that has united scholars from several countries to compare and contrast migrations to several continents, as well as the impact of migration on the sending regions.[10] While the "Italians everywhere" project is largely qualitative, examining labor, gender, and sexuality, there are numerous demographic projects that take advantage of ships' lists, census data, and the like, to trace large groups of individuals who left no other records. The creation of the Trans-Atlantic Slave Trade Database (1999), available on CD-ROM, has been particularly helpful in providing basic demographic information for comparison throughout the

Atlantic world in the European colonial era. For scholars of colonial America, it means we currently have more accessible data on transportation of slaves into parts of North America than we do of nonslaves.[11] The Dutch are one of many groups for whom demographic data about emigration in the nineteenth century exists. As Robert Swierenga showed after having studied these emigration records, *the* place to go for a male Dutch farmhand like Cornelis van der Vliet at the turn of the twentieth century was North America, either the United States or Canada—South Africa was clearly third. The Dutch East Indies, in contrast, attracted more well-educated young men from urban backgrounds, who had sufficient class status to get positions in the colonial bureaucracy.[12]

The examples above suggest some specific ways to link U.S. history into a broader world through the study of migration. Letter collections and individual accounts typically provide at least binational comparisons, as do many monographs that connect sending and receiving areas. Larger diaspora projects (both quantitative and qualitative) compare persons moving from one nation or region to several others, thus changing the definition of nation to include people outside national boundaries. Such studies typically incorporate the impact of migration (to the United States or elsewhere) on areas from whence migrants originated. The most ambitious projects see linkages beyond national terms more broadly—like the webs of "cultures in contact" that Hoerder describes. In them the story of Jantje Enserink van der Vliet crosses national borders to illustrate larger migration patterns.

Bibliography

Irish Immigrants in the Land of Canaan: Letters and Memoirs from Colonial and Revolutionary America, 1675–1815. Edited by Kerby A. Miller, Arnold Schrier, Bruce D. Boling, and David N. Doyle. New York, 2003. This annotated collection of writings by early migrants to North America is organized primarily by occupation as well as topics specific to migration and contains a solid index. The original texts may be a bit challenging for students.

News from the Land of Freedom: German Immigrants Write Home. Edited by Walter D. Kamphoefner, Wolfgang Helbich, and Ulrike Sommer. Translated by Susan Carter Vogel. Ithaca, N.Y., 1991. A heavily annotated collection of letters, mainly from the nineteenth century, this book illustrates information about the United States and lives of migrants there as conveyed to relatives and friends elsewhere.

Between the Lines: Letters Between Undocumented Mexican and Central American Immigrants and their Families and Friends. Translated, edited, and with an introduction by Larry Siems. Tucson, 1992. This collection of transcribed letters in the original (mainly Spanish) along with their English translations provides a late-twentieth century counterpart to the other letter collections, but without the annotations.

Separate Lives, Broken Dreams, <http://www.naatanet.org/separatelivesbroken dreams/>. Related to the 1993 documentary of the same name, this site provides a short history of Chinese exclusion in the United States. It includes interactive primary sources such as immigration and court records (with commentary) and cartoons for illustration, and an annotated bibliography of Web sites related to Chinese American life. The site provides an important corrective to an image of welcome often related to immigration.

Dirk Hoerder, *Cultures in Contact: World Migrations in the Second Millennium.* Durham, N.C., 2002. Hoerder's hefty work (almost eight hundred pages of small print) outlines migration systems across time. It is the best current work in English on historical migration patterns. Teachers may be drawn particularly to the excellent maps and to the sections that place migration to and from the United States in a much broader context.

Robin Cohen, *Global Diasporas: An Introduction.* Seattle, 1997. This text is relatively short and accessible and aimed at a college audience. The attention is global, although several of the diasporas Cohen covers include migrants to the United States.

Digital Histories: Ethnic America, <http://www.digitalhistory.uh.edu/historyonline/ethnic_am.cfm>. This online textbook provides a timeline of U.S. immigration policy and a number of firsthand immigrant accounts, with an emphasis on African American, Asian American, Native American, and Mexican American voices.

Exploring Amistad at Mystic Seaport, <http://amistad.mysticseaport.org/timeline/atlantic.slave.trade.html>. The Web site includes a basic timeline of the Atlantic slave trade and international efforts at abolition. Source documents and lesson plans introduce students to capture in Africa, sale in the Caribbean, trial in the United States, and then the move back to Sierra Leone. Compare to the following entry regarding the *Kate Hooper.*

Robert J. Plowman, "Voyage of the *Kate Hooper.*" Available from the National Archives and Records Administration at: <http://www.archives.gov/publications/prologue/print_friendly.html?page=summer_2001_coolie_ship_kate_hooper_1_content.html&title=NARA+|+Prologue+|+Prologue%3A+Selected+Articles>. This article concerns a U.S. ship carrying Chinese indentured servants to Cuba. It illustrates the "coolie trade" and how the United States reacted to it. Together with the Amistad site, this article makes for a good discussion of unfree labor and the legal rights of migrants.

The Ulster American Folk Park, <http://www.folkpark.com/>. The Web site for this open-air museum in Northern Ireland focuses on migration from this area to North America in the eighteenth and nineteenth centuries and includes a virtual walking tour of the buildings and living history activities related to them. The children's corner includes an Atlantic crossings game about migration in the age of sail. The site is a good example of emigration-related museums outside the United States.

The Philippine History Site, <http://opmanong.ssc.hawaii.edu/filipino/index.html>. This site provides an overview of the Philippine Revolution and Philippine-American War as well as Filipino migration to the United States throughout the twentieth century. This case illustrates changing immigration categories and the split nature of migration between highly educated and manual workers through the twentieth century.

Global Korean Network of Los Angeles, <http://www.gknla.net/main/projects/history/history_project.htm>. Although the goal of this nonacademic site is to link all people of Korean descent worldwide, much emphasis is on the United States. It includes a history page devoted to Korean migration to many parts of the world. These are linked to a number of articles about these migrations. The section on Changho Ahn, better known by his pen name "Dosan" and leader of the Korean Independence Movement Overseas, exemplifies the role of migrant populations in homeland politics.

Beth-Hatefutsoth: The Nahum Goldmann Museum of the Jewish Diaspora, <http://www.bh.org.il/>. This site, in English and Hebrew, includes high-quality online exhibitions on Jews in a variety of locations around the world. It demonstrates the connections to family histories and to community links (rather than national ones) that are common in diasporic identity.

National Geographic Xpeditions: Migration Station, <http://www.nationalgeographic.com/xpeditions/hall/index.html?node=36>. This site provides a basic geographic discussion of migration with interactive maps for some nineteenth- and twentieth-century migrations. It provides a lesson plan on U.S. migration in the late twentieth century as well as one on how people make the decision to stay or to go based on European examples, including ones where migration is illegal and where potential migrants face political persecution.

Notes

1. Frank Verbrugge, ed., *Brieven uit het Verleden/Letters from the Past,* manuscript, Calvin College, 42, 78, 98. The story of Enserink and Van der Vliet also appears in Suzanne M. Sinke, *Dutch Immigrant Women in the United States, 1880–1920* (Urbana, Ill., 2002).

2. Leslie Page Moch, *Moving Europeans: Migration in Western Europe since 1850,* 2nd ed. (Bloomington, Ind., 2003).

3. For a quick introduction to transatlantic comparisons, see Walter T. K. Nugent, *Crossings: The Great Transatlantic Migrations, 1870–1914* (Bloomington, Ind., 1992).

4. Jantje Enserink van der Vliet to (three) Female Friends, July 2, 1910, in Verbrugge, *Brieven,* 162.

5. Mark Wyman, *Round-Trip to America: The Immigrants Return to Europe, 1880–1930* (Ithaca, N.Y., 1993).

6. Herbert J. Brinks, ed., *Dutch American Voices: Letters from the United States, 1850–1930* (Ithaca, N.Y., 1995).

7. Witold Kula, Nina Assorodobraj-Kula, and Marcin Kula, *Writing Home: Immigrants in Brazil and the United States, 1890–1891,* ed. and trans. Josephine Wtulich (Boulder, Colo., 1987).

8. On the use of *diaspora,* see Kevin Kenny, "Diaspora and Comparison: The Global Irish as a Case Study," *Journal of American History,* 90 (June 2003): 134–62. For definitions, see Robin Cohen, *Global Diasporas: An Introduction* (Seattle, 1997).

9. Adam McKeown, *Chinese Migrant Networks and Cultural Change: Peru, Chicago, Hawaii, 1900–1936* (Chicago, 2001).

10. Donna Gabaccia wrote about one part of this project in an article entitled "*Gli italiani nel mondo*: Italy's Workers around the World," *OAH Magazine of History,* 14 (Fall 1999): 12–16.

11. On this topic, see David Eltis, ed., *Coerced and Free Migration: Global Perspectives* (Stanford, Calif., 2002).

12. Immigration Records: Dutch in America, 1800s, Family Tree Maker's Family Archives, CD #269, Broderbund, Neth., 2000.

STRATEGIES FOR TEACHING THE HISTORY OF MIGRATION TO THE UNITED STATES IN A GLOBAL CONTEXT

LOUISA BOND MOFFITT
AND TED DICKSON

Traditional approaches to teaching immigration usually come in standard, well-recognized packages that deal with early colonization, the slave trade, the "old" and "new" immigration of the nineteenth and early twentieth centuries, and, if time does not run out at the end of the school year, a quick nod to the Immigration Act of 1965 and its impact. Suzanne Sinke urges an approach that presents the teaching of migration as a series of cycles that are intertwined with each era of history, moving in many directions at once. She urges teachers to avoid presenting migrants during any era or to any place as people who simply came to stay, completely leaving whatever they had behind them. A more complex lens is appropriate.

In United States history, no discussion of migration would be complete without an evaluation of the ways in which Americans accept and resist the new realities of an increasingly diverse population. Migration and settlement need to be seen as national phenomena, rather than ones relegated to ethnic pockets here and there. Certainly discussions of migration need to factor in global religious, political, and economic forces that led large numbers of people to relocate. Issues of assimilation, nativism, and immigration policy are far more complex when immigration is viewed as transnational migration.

Sinke suggests that developing the ability to see the interconnected nature of migrations is essential to a realistic understanding of the world today. National borders have become more porous as people cross and recross boundaries looking for work, escaping oppression, reuniting with family, and even looking for marriage partners. How did and how will society accommodate those cultural aspects of immigrant life that remain strong and important, though they might be at odds with local mores? What has been and what will be the impact of the Internet, the cell phone, instant international news, and the jet plane on the ties people feel between themselves and their family members in other parts of the world as migration continues into the new century?

In teaching migration as more of a global phenomenon, we want our students to begin thinking of migration as circuits rather than one-way streets. The concept of global migration should be introduced early in the year, so the different circuits can be examined and traced as the course progresses. The challenge will be to get students to recognize the circuits, and to place themselves within the ones that relate to their families. One key to teaching migration is to get students to make personal connections with real people.

Our introduction to migration begins with a discussion of the following questions to prompt students to address migration in a global perspective and to begin what Sinke calls "a continuum of adjustment."

1. What are the different ways to define migration?
2. Is migration a one-way movement?
3. Are there migrants who do not cross national borders but face cultural differences?
4. How do we compare the experiences of one ethnic group in several locations?
5. Are there ongoing connections among immigrant groups across borders?
6. How does technology affect migration?
7. Why might migration be a better term than immigration?

To begin the actual lesson, we go to the Ellis Island Web site: <http://www.ellisisland.org> and go to *Ellis Island—The Immigrant Experience—The Peopling of America*. There we download and print the immigration chart showing waves and number of immigrants to North America from pre-1790 through 2000. We then enlarge the line graph to make a display for one of the bulletin boards in our classroom. The display will remain throughout the year, and students will complete it as we progress through the course.

After explaining the purpose of the bulletin board display to the class, we introduce some of the essential vocabulary used in the discussion of migration: push and pull factors (including economic circuits and ethnic and familial ties), chain migration, "birds of passage," transnational parenthood, assimilation, nativism, ethnic enclaves, and naturalization. The initial activity for the students will be to spend a day in the computer lab working with a different section of the Ellis Island Web site: <http://www.ellisisland.org>. We divide the class into six small teams and direct each to the *Genealogies* icon and then the *American Family Immigration History* icon, where they find the stories of six people who traced their family histories back to countries of origin. Each team examines one of the stories and completes Chart A for that individual. The assigned individuals include Margaret Feeny, Char McCargo Bah, Byron Yee, Alex Woodle, Mary Seville, and Jennifer Petrino. On returning to class, each group presents its findings to the others and places its person's ancestor in the appropriate place on the bulletin board timeline. The other students take notes on each group's presentation.

Next, we introduce a number of different major migration circuits that will be a part of the United States survey during the year. A working list might include the following ten circuits:

1. The settlers who came across the Atlantic before the American Revolution, the "moving Europeans."
2. Those caught up in the transatlantic slave trade.
3. Those moving from Latin America into North America before 1850.
4. Those coming to the West Atlantic Rim, the Caribbean, and the Louisiana area from 1500 to 1800.
5. The migration and displacement of American Indians from 1600 to 1900.
6. The wave of immigrants from Great Britain and northern Europe from 1800 to 1860.
7. The beginnings of Asian immigration to the Pacific Coast from 1800 to 1882.
8. Immigrants arriving from the 1880s through 1924 from southern and eastern Europe and Asia.
9. Immigrants who came from Mexico in the early 1900s through the 1960s.

10. Immigrants who arrived after 1965 from Asia, Latin America, Central America, and other places around the globe.

Students are asked to identify these circuits on the bulletin board timeline as well. Each of the six groups that worked with the Ellis Island site then decides to which circuit its particular case study belonged. As we reach each of these periods of migration in the survey, we incorporate further discussion of the issues that we first raised about migration. We also examine the popular and public policy responses to each immigration circuit.

This lesson could be incorporated at a number of places in the survey. If used near the beginning of the course, perhaps as part of the discussion of the first circuit, this activity can introduce themes that will be used throughout the survey. Alternatively, the lesson could be used during the study of circuit eight. In this case, we would begin by telling the story of Cornelis and Jantje Enserink van der Vliet to raise questions about migration before explaining the vocabulary of migration. This approach enables us to use the previous circuits to explain the concepts and sets up discussion of the other circuits later in the survey.

Finally, we want to reemphasize that students learn about migration more effectively when the subject becomes personal. Teachers may consider asking each student to build a family genealogy as the year progresses, with the goal of finding his/her family's place in the timeline and determining which circuits apply to their relatives. To conduct this research, students should be encouraged to use some of the same techniques used by the six case studies they looked at earlier, beginning with interviews of relatives. To get them started, provide students with a copy of the *Four Generation Family Tree* chart from the Ellis Island Foundation and ask them to work with their families to complete as many of the listed generations as possible. As the students place their own stories into the proper places along the timeline, they will also see the families of classmates. It is hoped they will discern the patterns of connection, of fluidity, and of cross-cultural exchanges that show migration to be a living part of history rather than a series of static moments in a textbook. Alternatively (again, perhaps on circuit eight), students could be asked to write a story about an immigrant. In completing this assignment, students should use the vocabulary of migration (supplementing those listed above with: steerage, Ellis and Angel Islands, detention, and so forth), and include the following topics: decision to leave, experiences on the journey, choosing a new home, and adjusting to a new land or moving again. Another approach could be to divide up the circuits and have student teams study each circuit rather than an individual immigrant (see table 9.2). An alternate summary activity would be to have students write an editorial on immigration (perhaps in the context of a public policy debate) in which the editor must use details and experiences from other students' stories or from multiple circuits.

These ideas allow us to present the complexities of migration history in ways that teach students to conceive it in a global context and to make personal connections.

TABLE 9.1. ELLIS ISLAND DATA RETRIEVAL CHART

Name of family history researcher	
Specific ancestor investigated	
Ancestor's country of origin	
What motivated this person to search for this relative?	
What documents, agencies, and sources were helpful in the search?	
Where specifically did the ancestor originate?	
Where did this ancestor live after coming to the United States? Did he or she ever make a trip back to the country of origin, and if so, why?	
What specific connections were found between the searcher and the country and family of origin?	
Of what larger immigration circuit was this ancestor a part?	

TABLE 9.2. IMMIGRATION CIRCUIT

Country or countries of origin	
Reasons for immigration	
Primary years of migration	
Approximate numbers arriving during primary immigration	
Skills brought, jobs sought	
Religions	
Race	
Other significant ethnic characteristics	
Location of primary settlement	
Subsequent movement within the U.S. or to other countries	
How they were received in America	
Political situation they encountered when they arrived	
—Foreign policy	
—Domestic policy	
Leaders, significant figures	
Impact on the economy in the United States	
Impact on the economy in the country they left	
Other decades of major immigration	
Percentage of the U.S. population today	

The following online sources may help students with their genealogical research.

American Civil Liberties Union: <http://www.aclu.org>
America Friends Service Committee: <http://www.afsc.org>
American Immigration Control Foundation: <http://www.cfw.com>
Americas Watch: <http://www.hrw.org>
Angel Island: <http://www.angelisland.org>
Center for Human Rights and Constitutional Law:
    <http://www.centerforhumanrights.org>
Center for Immigration Studies: <http://www.cis.org>
Ellis Island: <http://www.ellisisland.org>
Family History: <http://www.familysearching.org>
Federation for American Immigration Reform: <http://www.fairus.org>
Genealogy: <http://www.ngsgenealogy.org>
Immigration: <http://www.immigrantships.net>
Immigration Debate: <http://www.ImmigrationDebate.com>
Immigration Forum: <http://www.immigrationforum.org>
Immigration Pathfinder (National Cathedral School): <http://207.238.30/library/
    pathfinders/Immigration.htm>
Internet Modern History Sourcebook: U.S. Immigration:
<http://www.fordham.edu/halsall/mod/modsbook28.html>
Latino Issues Forum: <http://www.lif.org>
League of United Latin American Citizens: <http://www.lulac.org>
Migration and Refugee Service: <http://www.nccbuscc.org/mrs>
Migration News of North America: <http://www.migration.ucdavis.edu>
National Archives: <http://www.archives.gov>
National Council of La Raza: <http://www.nclr.org>
National Immigration Forum: <http://www.immigrationforum.org>
National Immigration Law Center: <http://www.nilc.org>
National Network for Immigration and Refugee Rights: <http://www.nnirr.org>
National Population: <http://www.npg.org>
Social Contract: <http://www.thesocialcontract.com>
U.S. Border Control: <http://www.usbc.org>
U.S. Numbers: <http://www.NumbersUSA.com>
Yale–New Haven Teachers' Institute: Immigration and American Life:
<http://www.yale.edu/ynhti/curriculum/nits/1999/3>

CHAPTER 10 ☰

A. Phillip Randolph. In 1941, Randolph, Bayard Rustin, and A. J. Muste proposed a march on Washington to protest racial discrimination in the armed forces. The march was cancelled after President Roosevelt issued Executive Order 8802, creating the Fair Employment Practices Committee. (Library of Congress, Prints and Photographs Division, *New York World-Telegram and the Sun* Newspaper Photograph Collection, 1963, LC-USZ62-119495.)

THE CIVIL RIGHTS MOVEMENT IN WORLD PERSPECTIVE

KEVIN GAINES

The Mighty Sparrow, a calypso performer from Trinidad, sang in 1963, at a perilous juncture during the civil rights movement, "I was born in the USA but because of my color I'm suffering today." "The white man preaching democracy but in truth and in fact it's hypocrisy," Sparrow continued, warning that he was "getting vexed." His proposed solution was the song's up-tempo refrain: "So—we want Martin Luther King for president!" Sparrow put his irreverent humor to deadly serious purpose, his song indicting both temporizing U.S. officials during the Birmingham crisis and a nation far from ready to elect a black president. Recorded for Caribbean audiences, including immigrants to the United States, Sparrow's topical song reminds us, along with a number of recent studies, that the activities of King and the civil rights movement were keenly observed by audiences all over the world.

Until quite recently, U.S. historians were accustomed to thinking of the civil rights movement within a domestic U.S.-based framework. But in its time, the movement had global dimensions that were abundantly clear to many contemporaries, including Sparrow, King, and others, as this essay will show. Recent scholarship has engaged the way in which the consciousness of civil rights leaders and black activists was in fact a *worldview,* a framework linking local and global events and perspectives. At the same time, that scholarship has yet to make a discernible impact in college and secondary school U.S. history textbooks. If the civil rights movement is covered in undergraduate surveys or high school classes (and sadly, we should not assume that even the most basic history of the movement is routinely taught), its story often remains a nation-based account of the response of presidential administrations to southern racial upheavals, with King as the movement's main protagonist.

That our understanding of the movement should emphasize a domestic U.S. narrative is not surprising. The violence that confronted civil rights demonstrators in Birmingham, Selma, Mississippi, and other battlegrounds jolted the conscience of many throughout the nation. The sacrifices of those who died, and the traumas borne by their survivors, should never be forgotten. That said, viewing the civil rights movement within an international frame need not displace the memory of those who fought to end racial segregation on U.S. soil. Historians who examined the conditions that led many unsung local people in the South to risk their lives and livelihoods in opposing Jim Crow have learned that global events often informed the outlook and aspirations of activists.[1] Black World War II veterans, energized by the global struggle against fascism, were at the vanguard of postwar demands for voting rights in the South. They and others were also inspired by national independence struggles in Africa and Asia. One of those veterans, Medgar Evers, the director of the NAACP branch in Jackson, Mississippi, admired the Kenyan nationalist leader Jomo Kenyatta.[2] The Freedom Singers, a vocal ensemble made up of Student Nonviolent Coordinating Committee (SNCC) activists working to organize black Mississippians to demand voting rights despite the constant threat of vigilante terror, paid tribute to the armed resistance employed by Kenyan nationalists.[3] Such examples remind us that the local and the global are not antithetical. Rather, they complement each other.

By viewing the black freedom movement within a global frame, scholars and teachers may gain an enhanced appreciation of the motivations of those who challenged the racial status quo. Such a recontextualization also enables us to comprehend the limits, as well as the achievements, of civil rights strategies and reforms. In his discussion of the movement's mixed legacy, Thomas Holt has noted that South African and Brazilian freedom movements during the 1960s consciously aligned themselves with organized labor, while the U.S. civil rights movement severed its partnership with labor, a strategy that crucially limited the forms of freedom and citizenship that were imaginable in the U.S. context.[4] In addition to prompting a reconsideration of the movement's tactics, an engagement with the global context of decolonization, the emergence of new African and Asian nations from European colonial rule during the 1950s and 1960s reveals a wider spectrum of political consciousness and debate among black activists. Within that wider world of black movement activism, even as student sit-ins and nonviolent direct action campaigns spread throughout the South during the early 1960s, northern urban black activists were fighting discrimination in employment and housing, and had been doing so since World War II.[5] Here again, the local and the global were inseparable. Activists based in New York, Chicago, and other cites followed the decolonization of Africa just as avidly as they demanded equality on the local and national level. Their outlook was reflected in the views of such prominent figures as James Baldwin, Lorraine Hansberry, and Malcolm X, all of whom faulted the federal government for its failure to enforce and implement civil rights law.

Viewing the black freedom movement within the context of decolonization and African national liberation movements goes beyond acknowledging the origins of the movement's tactic of nonviolent direct action in the Gandhian philosophy of Satyagraha employed by Indian nationalists' struggle against British colonialism. Such a global reframing highlights the tension between U.S. conceptions of civil rights reforms, understood in terms of color blindness, or formal civil and political equality, and an evolving postwar international discourse of human rights, whose definitions of rights potentially embraced broader social needs such as income, housing, and health care. Arguably, this broader conception of social rights contained within human rights discourse partially informed Malcolm X's attempt, after he was forced out of the Nation of Islam, to substitute an internationalist rhetoric of human rights for that of civil rights.

To reconsider the U.S. black freedom movement within an international arena of political change is to discover that the status of African Americans in U.S. society has long been, and remains relevant for, U.S. foreign affairs.[6] It could not be otherwise, given America's superpower status since World War II. From the global war against fascism to the Cold War, to the present U.S. occupation of Iraq, the situation of African Americans has often symbolized, for Americans and overseas audiences, depending on one's perspective, either a color-blind American dream of racial progress or a nightmare of exclusion mocking the nation's democratic ideals. More recently, a global perspective of a different sort found expression after the U.S. government's abandonment of African Americans stranded in New Orleans by Hurricane Katrina. That debacle led many Americans and overseas observers to compare the federal government's feckless performance to that of a third-world country. The chronic conditions of poverty, ill health, and official neglect exposed by the storm suggest the limits of triumphalist accounts of the civil rights movement in the U.S., and likewise, claims of victory in the Cold War. Arguably, the destruction of much of New Orleans can be attributed in part to the diversion of manpower and resources—for maintaining the levee system before the storm and emergency management after—to the wars in Iraq and Afghanistan, wars that have their roots in the Cold War policy of arming proxies to fight such enemies as the Soviet Union.[7] The conjuncture of the Cold War and America's aspirations for global hegemony, the U.S. civil rights movement, and the decolonization of Africa was a momentous one. For Thomas Borstelmann, it led to a paradoxical divergence between domestic and foreign policy; though the Johnson administration could credit itself for passing landmark civil rights and voting rights legislation, its indulgent policy toward repressive white minority governments in southern Africa paved the way for substantial U.S. financial investments in those latter-day colonial societies.[8] The debacle of the Vietnam War justifiably looms large in our assessment of LBJ's foreign policy, but the civil rights era also saw the subversion of African nationalist aspirations by the United States and other Western powers. Following such civil rights activists as Robert Moses, who linked the cause of black freedom in the United States with opposition to the Vietnam War, our account of the era must accommodate not only the sacrifices of the many who braved jail, beatings, and death in civil rights struggles at home, but also the catastrophic toll on African and Asian victims of carpet bombing, "low intensity" proxy wars, and covert operations of U.S. foreign policy. A global approach to the civil rights movement fundamentally challenges us to ponder what is at stake in the teaching and writing of this history. Studying the black freedom movement within a global perspective can better prepare students to understand contemporary global affairs, helping them draw connections between postwar U.S. history and the histories of Africa, Asia, and the Middle East.

The joint enterprise of teachers and students to "connect the dots" between ostensibly disparate histories—of labor and civil rights, and domestic and foreign policy—becomes more palpable when we adopt, as the wartime examples above suggest, the perspective of what Jacquelyn Hall has called "the long civil rights movement," marking the genesis of the movement well before the landmark events of the 1954 *Brown v. Board of Education* decision and the Montgomery bus boycott a year later, and emphasizing the movement's evolution from reformist goals to an agenda of radical social change under King's leadership.[9] As Patricia Sullivan has shown, during the 1930s, federal New Deal reform and relief programs shifted the balance of power away from southern "states' rights" ideology, creating an opening in that region for labor organizing, civil rights activism, and demands for voting rights.[10] During World War II, civil rights and labor organizations joined hands as struggles for equality in the South and nationwide attacked segregation in housing, the workplace, and at the polls.[11] African Americans supported the Fair Employment Practices Commission (FEPC), a federal agency mandated to safeguard African American rights in the workplace. The FEPC was established in 1941 by President Franklin D. Roosevelt's Executive Order 8802, as a concession to the pressure brought by A. Philip Randolph's march on Washington movement. In addition, blacks in civilian life and the armed forces championed the Double V campaign publicized by African American newspapers and civil rights organizations, which insisted that victory at home against Jim Crow segregation was essential for victory in the global war against fascism.

As evidenced by the Double V campaign, the movement itself responded to, and was shaped by, world events. During the war, African American civil rights leaders and organizations rhetorically anchored their cause to the global momentum of decolonization, as newly independent nation-states emerged from European colonial rule in Asia and Africa. But the postwar world, and the fortunes of emergent Asian and African nations, as well as those of the civil rights movement, came increasingly under the sway of the Cold War struggle between the United States and the Soviet Union. The Cold War did not simply influence the rhetoric of the movement. By stifling domestic criticism and dissent, the Cold War also limited the range of possibilities for social reform, restricting the goals of the movement to formal civic and political equality. Although the march on Washington movement demanded jobs along with freedom, its goals maintained an exclusive focus on obtaining federal legislation to ban racial discrimination in civic and political life.

The Cold War held a double-edged significance for the civil rights movement. In declaring segregation in public schools unconstitutional, the Supreme Court's unanimous decision in *Brown* enshrined the Cold War understanding that racial equality at home was a vital component of U.S. foreign policy and national security. But segregationists could and did marshal Cold War anticommunism to discredit the movement and its leadership. In their reliance on the federal government as an ally to secure civil rights legislative reforms, King and other leaders of the mainstream civil rights organizations maintained a discreet silence on U.S. foreign policy and the deepening U.S. war in Vietnam. By 1967, having achieved the hard-won legislative victories of the Civil Rights and Voting Rights Acts, King set about restoring the link between civil rights and economic justice. King could no longer refrain from criticizing the Vietnam War, which squandered resources needed to combat poverty and the effects of discrimination in the workplace and housing in the urban North and nationwide. The Vietnam War and opposition to it on a global scale had contributed to King's transformation from reformer to revolutionary.

The very fact that the world was watching the civil rights movement during the 1950s and 1960s ensured the responsiveness of otherwise reluctant U.S. policymakers to the demands of the black freedom movement. Throughout the modern civil rights movement, spanning the administrations of Truman, Eisenhower, and Kennedy, U.S. State Department officials endorsed civil rights, seeking to convince foreign audiences of the nation's commitment to eradicating systemic barriers to the full participation of African Americans in public life. Yet news media accounts of all-too-frequent incidents of racism broadcast to foreign audiences throughout the 1950s and early 1960s were a chronic headache for U.S. foreign-policy makers. Whether from acts of discrimination against African diplomats traveling Route 40, the corridor between New York and Washington, or from the full-scale unrest ignited by the violence authorities unleashed upon nonviolent civil rights demonstrators throughout the Jim Crow South, as was the case in Birmingham, such racial upheavals, U.S. officials feared, undermined their assertions that the United States was the leader of the "Free World." The persistence of racism was America's Achilles' heel in its competition with the Soviet Union for the allegiance of new nations having recently emerged from European colonial empires.

Sparrow's identification with King's and other African Americans' struggle for equality was also part of a tradition of black internationalism dating back to the interwar years, as peoples of African descent forged solidarities across geographical and historical divides. The example of New Negro radicalism in the United States during the 1920s, especially the mass movement led by the Jamaican-born Marcus Garvey, had inspired the anticolonial movements in Africa and the Caribbean that had shaped Sparrow's worldview. That internationalist consciousness was energized throughout the black world by Italy's invasion of the sovereign African nation of Ethiopia in 1935.[12] As World War II accelerated the collapse of European empires in Asia and Africa, African

American civil rights and civic organizations lent support to African anti-colonial movements, espousing what Penny Von Eschen has called a vibrant "politics of the African diaspora" that linked demands for equality in the United States with African national liberation movements.[13] Throughout the 1950s and 1960s, such prominent African Americans as the singer and actor Paul Robeson, the scholar W. E. B. Du Bois, the boxing champion Joe Louis, and later, of course, Martin Luther King Jr., were household names among people of African descent worldwide. Likewise, many black Americans avidly followed in the black press the political exploits of Kwame Nkrumah, leader of the nationalist movement in the British Gold Coast colony, and also Jawaharlal Nehru, the first prime minister of India, and Jomo Kenyatta of Kenya.

As the Cold War transformed the Soviet Union from wartime ally to post-war nemesis, a wartime black popular-front alliance of African American civil rights organizations, the labor movement, and African nationalist parties came under official suspicion. African Americans' advocacy of African anticolonial movements and their democratic aspirations clashed with U.S. foreign-policy makers bent on extending their influence over Africa's labor and raw materials. The allied victory over global fascism was not accompanied by the demise of Jim Crow segregation in the U.S. South, as most African American civic leaders, journalists, and soldiers had hoped. The political backlash of the Cold War pushed a number of figures to relocate, like the novelist and ex-communist Richard Wright, who moved to France in 1946, where he could speak, write, and work with West Indian and African nationalists beyond the reach of House Un-American Activities Committee (HUAC) investigations.

The Cold War and its loyalty investigations had served as a warning to actual or potential critics. But if U.S. officials sought to keep internal dissent from overseas audiences, news coverage of violent outbursts by white southerners could not so easily be embargoed. U.S. officials sought a propaganda counteroffensive that would help audiences abroad view outbreaks of racial unrest as aberrations within a narrative of steady progress in race relations. *Brown,* the product of a protracted legal struggle waged by civil rights attorneys against Jim Crow "separate but equal" doctrine, was crucial for this narrative. But while it allowed U.S. foreign-policy makers to proclaim to critics abroad that desegregation was the law of the land, *Brown* did not prescribe a plan for implementation.

Without an official federal strategy for integration, mass activism would be needed to desegregate public life in the Jim Crow South. The mobilization of African Americans in the Montgomery movement had desegregated that city's public transportation system and catapulted its leader, Martin Luther King Jr., to national prominence. But King and other civil rights leaders seemed to falter in the face of white southern resistance and an Eisenhower administration unwilling to enforce *Brown*. When Ghana (formerly the British-controlled Gold Coast colony) achieved its independence in March 1957, its prime minister, Kwame Nkrumah, invited King and other civil rights leaders and African American dignitaries as a show of support for the struggle for equality in the United States. In doing so, Nkrumah also acknowledged African American leaders' support for nationalism in the Gold Coast and throughout Africa. Many attended, including A. Philip Randolph, Adam Clayton Powell, and Ralph Bunche. In Ghana, ironically enough, King achieved the high-level contact with the Eisenhower administration that he and other civil rights leaders had vainly sought back home when he encountered Vice President Richard Nixon, head of the U.S. delegation. With his wife Coretta, King lunched with Nkrumah, and upon their return, King linked Ghana's independence to their own struggles: "Ghana tells us that the forces of the universe are on the side of justice. . . . An old order of colonialism, of segregation, discrimination is passing away now. And a new order of justice, freedom and good will is being born."[14] King informed his audience that Nkrumah encouraged African Americans to move to Ghana and contribute to building the new nation. Over the 1950s and 1960s, some three hundred African Americans did so, establishing an expatriate community whose destiny was closely tied to the political fortunes of Ghana under Nkrumah's leadership.

King's understanding of the civil rights cause as a global issue, if not his optimism, was reinforced by the turmoil in Little Rock, Arkansas, in 1957, as menacing white mobs gathered outside that city's Central High School to prevent the enrollment of nine African American youths, thus desegregating the school. President Eisenhower hesitated to intervene, prompting an angry condemnation by jazz musician Louis Armstrong of the president and the state's segregationist governor, Orval Faubus, for inflaming the situation. Amid damaging worldwide press coverage of the crisis, Eisenhower finally sent in federal troops to restore order and to allow the students to attend school. The international implications of the civil rights issue were on King's mind when he announced plans for the Pilgrimage for Prayer in Washington, where a crowd of twenty thousand assembled at the Lincoln Memorial in May 1957 to demand federal enforcement of *Brown*. "[T]he hour is getting late," King warned, "[f]or if America doesn't wake up, she will one day arise and discover that the uncommitted peoples of the world will have given their allegiance to a false communistic ideology." King insisted that civil rights was not some "ephemeral, evanescent domestic" matter to be exploited by segregationists for immediate political gain, but an "eternal moral issue" that would determine the outcome of the Cold War. Vice President Nixon used similar logic, warning that continued discrimination against African Americans undermined U.S. influence in Africa, which he regarded a crucial terrain of the superpower struggle against international communism.

Not everyone subscribed to such stark visions of Cold War conflict, nor did others feel compelled, as King and his advisors did, to promote the image of Christian piety to deflect charges of communist influence on the movement. Several prominent African American intellectuals and artists viewed the U.S. black struggle for equality within the changing global order of decoloniza-tion, including sociologist E. Franklin Frazier, expatriate novelists Richard Wright and James Baldwin, playwright Lorraine Hansberry, and others. How might African Americans redefine themselves and their relation to modern political change in America and Africa? Would they become unhyphenated Americans, or in gaining formal equality would they enact their U.S. citizen-ship in solidarity with African peoples and promote a broader definition of socioeconomic justice at home and abroad, one that might contribute to the democratization of American society?[15]

Frazier, Hansberry, Baldwin, and, increasingly, the Nation of Islam minister and national spokesman Malcolm X were voicing in their respective ways the frustration of African Americans in the urban North, where, since World War II, local civil rights activists had opposed discrimination in housing, labor unions, and the workplace, making little headway against white-controlled municipal governments, police departments, school systems, neighborhood associations, and labor unions. The plight of northern urban African Ameri-cans mired in slum conditions while wealth, opportunity, and the American dream lay beyond their reach, led many to look to Africa as the foundation for their identity, rather than an American nation still largely defined by the indignities and brutality of Jim Crow. As an alternative to what some regarded as the Scylla of integration and the Charybdis of separatism, black radical writers, artists, and activists, including Hansberry, Maya Angelou, Julian Mayfield, Amiri Baraka (then Leroi Jones), and others advocated a new Afro-American nationalism, defined by an independent critique of Cold War liberalism, a sense that integration would not address the plight of northern urban blacks, and an anti-imperialist critique of U.S. foreign policy conso-nant with that of the Afro-Asian bloc in the United Nations. That emergent Afro-American nationalism had its most dramatic expression in the demonstration in February 1961 in the gallery of the United Nations Security Council by African Americans, including Angelou and Baraka, following the announcement of the death of Patrice Lumumba, the democratically elected prime minister of the Congo, whose independence from Belgium was marred by civil disorder fomented by Belgium. The demonstrators were outraged that Lumumba's ouster, disappearance, and murder occurred with the apparent complicity of the U.N. peacekeeping mission. The assassination of Lumumba, who had traveled to Washington and to the U.N. in a vain appeal for diplomatic support, would remain a decisive event for those northern urban black militants and radicals whose political consciousness had been shaped by the decolonization of Africa.

Malcolm X would become the most prominent spokesman for those northern blacks sympathetic to Afro-American nationalism. The demonstration at the U.N., the most prominent of many protests condemning Lumumba's death throughout the United States and worldwide, would become a defining moment for Malcolm and his generation. In the near term, U.S. officials regarded the demonstration as proof that those involved and others were susceptible to the influence of international communism. The secular Afro-American radicals involved in the demonstration could not have been further in temperament from the organization that most effectively tapped the disaffection of urban blacks, the Nation of Islam (NOI). Under the leadership of Elijah Muhammed, born Elijah Poole in rural Georgia, the NOI diverged from orthodox Islam, capitalizing on America's racial divide. The NOI's view that whites were devils made sense to those mired in the endemic poverty and exclusion of Jim Crow segregation in the urban North. Muhammed urged NOI members to eschew political activism, but Malcolm, his leading spokesman, intensified his criticism of the Kennedy administration during the Birmingham crisis of 1963. Malcolm's harsh rhetoric—he dismissed the March on Washington for Jobs and Freedom as a public relations event stage-managed by the Kennedys—had garnered headlines and FBI surveillance.

Malcolm's notoriety and his apparent disregard for the NOI's apolitical stance had opened a breach between him and Muhammed, along with those rival ministers who considered themselves Muhammed's rightful heirs. Instructed by Muhammed to refrain from public comment on the death of President Kennedy, Malcolm told a New York audience that Kennedy had fallen victim to the violence his administration had unleashed throughout the world. Calling the assassination a matter of "chickens coming home to roost," Malcolm's provocative claim led to his ouster from the NOI. Malcolm spent much of the eleven months remaining to him traveling throughout

Africa and the Middle East. His travels and discussions with members of diplomatic corps and African heads of state informed his rejection of the idea of innate white racism. Malcolm addressed audiences throughout Europe, Africa, and the United States, his analyses focusing on institutionalized racism at home and abroad, and positing a universal moral standard of justice and human rights. Though unable to live down his media reputation as an extremist, Malcolm's critical posture would help shape African American leadership and civil rights organizations' attempts to influence U.S. foreign policy in Africa. At the Oxford Debate Union in December 1964, Malcolm condemned the recent military offensive by Belgium, backed with U.S. air support, against Congolese nationalists. That mission, described in the press as the humanitarian rescue of European hostages seized by Congolese rebels against the Belgian-controlled central government, resulted in the slaughter of some three thousand Congolese civilians. The Belgium-U.S. intervention in the Congo was widely condemned by African officials at the United Nations. African American civil rights leaders, including King, A. Philip Randolph, Roy Wilkins, James Farmer, Whitney Young, and Dorothy Height, pressed the Johnson administration to withdraw its support for the Congolese central government. For its part, the administration refused to meet with these prominent civil rights leaders who comprised the American Negro Leadership Conference on Africa. A White House memorandum of January 1965 referred to LBJ's desire to "discourage emergence of any special Negro pressure group (a la the Zionists) which might limit [the administration's] freedom of maneuver."[16] For Johnson, the achievement of civil rights reforms in the United States seemed to require the acquiescence of black leadership on African and foreign affairs.

At Oxford, Malcolm condemned the "cold-blooded murder" of Congolese civilians and linked that use of organized violence to the unredressed violence wielded by white extremists in Mississippi, where charges against the accused killers of three civil rights workers (James Chaney, Andrew Goodman, and Michael Schwerner) the previous summer had recently been dropped. Aided by fellow activists in Harlem, Malcolm founded the Organization of Afro-American Unity, a secular organization whose agenda for liberation sought to address local conditions within an internationalist framework. Malcolm also sought a rapprochement with civil rights organizations, sharing platforms with SNCC activists in Harlem and Selma, Alabama. In East Africa, Malcolm held court with SNCC activists, including John Lewis. Upon his return, Malcolm, the son of Garveyite parents, told a Harlem audience that although a physical "return" to Africa was impractical, Afro-Americans should migrate "spiritually, culturally, and philosophically" to Africa. By this he meant that for African Americans, a sense of black and "African" cultural identification was essential for the achievement of equal citizenship. Malcolm's death in 1965 at the hands of assassins incited by NOI death threats brought a swift end to that fledgling organization.

Though unable to build an organization that remotely matched the influence of the NOI, black movement activists increasingly followed Malcolm's example in envisioning an international terrain of black struggle and liberation. As if emulating Malcolm's pilgrimage, SNCC activists, including Robert Moses and Fannie Lou Hamer, toured Africa, nursing their disillusionment at the defeat, as they perceived it, of their attempt to unseat the all-white Mississippi delegation at the 1964 Democratic Convention. While the sight of black officials exercising power and leadership in black majority societies was inspiring, they, like Malcolm, were dismayed by the reach of U.S. propaganda, whose rosy portrayals of progress clashed with their experience of violent resistance to their demands for voting rights in Mississippi and elsewhere throughout the South.[17]

As SNCC became bogged down in disputes over organizational structure and ideology, Moses gravitated toward the burgeoning anti–Vietnam War movement.[18] Here, it is crucial to note that antiwar statements by Moses, and later, King, were matters of sharp disagreement and conflict within the civil rights movement. A world of political differences may have separated youthful SNCC militants from the gray eminences of the civil rights establishment, but members of both camps could voice strong objection to criticism from the likes of Moses and King against U.S. foreign policy. In their view, antiwar statements at such a crucial juncture were diversions from the steadfast pursuit of freedom at home. The realities of a movement under siege and the urgent cause of voting rights justified, to some black activists, reticence on matters of U.S. foreign policy.

Given the unwillingness of the Johnson administration to countenance an independent African American critique of U.S. foreign policy, it seems fitting to recall an assessment of global affairs by Richard Wright in his novel *The Outsider* (1953) that uncannily speaks to our present condition. Casting a pox on both houses of American capitalism and Soviet communism as totalitarian systems of exploitation, Wright, in the guise of his protagonist, claimed that those systems contained the seeds of the destruction of Western progress and modernity. The few hundred years of "freedom, empire-building, voting, liberty, democracy" would yield to a "more terrifyingly human" future. "There will be . . . no trial by jury, no writs of habeas corpus, no freedom of speech, of religion—all this is being buried, and not by Communists or Fascists alone, but by their opponents as well. All hands are shoveling clay onto the body of freedom before it even dies, while it lies breathing its last."[19] Those secular Cold War belief systems would be undermined by greed, corruption, and cynicism, and would be rejected by much of the world's population, replaced by the rise of new forms of religious fundamentalism.

In this and other writings, Wright seems to have sensed that civil rights—integration and formal equality envisioned solely within the U.S. terrain—would not be enough. Wright helps us understand how devastating was the eclipse of the movement's abandoned vision of socioeconomic justice that King had tried to restore. Yet this was more than a matter of the lack of an alliance between labor unions and the black freedom movement. The liberating impact of the civil rights movement was limited, as well, by the Cold War's containment, by the U.S. and Western powers, of the democratic aspirations of the formerly colonized world, and the eclipse of an expansive international democratic vision of freedom emanating from the civil rights movement from such powerful exponents as King and Malcolm. The death of those figures, and the ideological defeat of their global vision of liberation, with its religious underpinnings, resulted in the moral and political vacuum left by the end of the Cold War, a vacuum ominously filled by religious fundamentalisms at home and abroad. And so it is at the end of 2006 that as the Roberts Court is poised to interpret the *Brown* decision in a manner that undermines the pursuit of integration, the global and the local merge once again in the return of the bodies of U.S. servicemen and women killed in Iraq and Afghanistan to their hometowns.

Bibliographical Essay

Teaching the international dimensions of the civil rights movement through music offers a powerful means of exposing students to the immediacy and contingency of consciousness as it is lived. The album containing the Mighty Sparrow's "Martin Luther King for President" contains other topical songs, including a tribute to President Kennedy after his assassination, and commentary on Khrushchev and the Cold War. These songs are found on a compilation album, "The Mighty Sparrow Sings True Life Stories of Passion, People, Politics," Scepter International SI-9001. The song "Oginga Odinga" can be found on the album *The Freedom Singers Sing of Freedom Now!* Mercury Records, MG 20924. In part owing to her association with SNCC activists, during the 1960s Nina Simone's music reflected the militancy of many younger blacks, while also foregrounding issues of Afro-American nationalism and gender equality. Her music is widely available on compact disc reissues, and the relevant selections are discussed in Ruth Feldstein, "'I Don't Trust You Anymore': Nina Simone, Culture, and Black Activism in the 1960s," *Journal of American History*, 91 (March 2005): 1349–79.

Teachers of the civil rights movement in world perspective would do well to begin with the work of Brenda Gayle Plummer. Her book, *Rising Wind: Black Americans and U.S. Foreign Affairs, 1935–1960* (Chapel Hill, N.C., 1996) extensively details African Americans' involvement with international affairs from the Italian invasion of Ethiopia to the emergence of newly independent African nations at the dawn of the civil rights movement. Penny Von Eschen's *Race Against Empire: Black Americans and Anticolonialism, 1937–1957* (Ithaca, N.Y., 1997) foregrounds the broad-based support among African Americans for anticolonial movements in Africa during World War II, with an emphasis on the black press as a forum for wide-ranging commentary on global affairs. Von Eschen argues that in response to Cold War strictures, civil rights leaders downplayed linkages with African nationalist movements. Instead, they increasingly argued that desegregation was essential for winning the Cold War.

Nikhil Pal Singh, *Black Is A Country: Race and the Unfinished Struggle for Democracy* (Cambridge, Mass., 2004) builds upon the work of Plummer and Von Eschen with his intellectual history of African American intellectuals' sustained engagement with issues of race and democracy in a global arena since the 1930s. Singh's introduction asks students to rethink the legacy and popular memory of Martin Luther King and the civil rights movement. Singh places the often forgotten radicalism and "world perspective" of Martin Luther King during the later phase of his career within the context of earlier efforts by W. E. B. Du Bois (and others) to bring a global perspective to bear on their critiques of American democracy, as Du Bois did in the coda to his 1935 study *Black Reconstruction,* positing the post-Reconstruction repression of African American citizenship rights and colonial systems of exploitation founded on white supremacy as a unitary historical phenomenon. The active role Du Bois sought in advancing a vision of equality in the United States and world order defined by self-determination for colonized peoples at the conference devoted to crafting the United Nations charter is detailed by David L. Lewis, *W. E. B. Du Bois—the Fight for Equality and the American Century, 1919–1963* (New York, 2000) in chapter 14 of the second volume.

Studies of local movements have probed the significance of international events on the perspective of movement activists. Besides John Dittmer's *Local People: The Struggle for Civil Rights in Missouri* (Urbana, Ill., 1994), there is Timothy B. Tyson's *Radio Free Dixie: Robert F. Williams and the Roots of Black Power* (Chapel Hill, N.C., 1999), a pathbreaking study of the North Carolina NAACP official who gained notoriety for advocating armed self-defense among blacks. Tyson is attentive to Williams's adept use of Cold War internationalism during the late 1950s in what became known as the "kissing case" (in which two African American boys were jailed on charges of rape for "playing house" with white female playmates) to pressure federal intervention by attracting international condemnation on that travesty and to publicize other such crises facing African Americans. In *To Stand and Fight: The Struggle for Civil Rights in Postwar New York City* (Cambridge, Mass., 2001), Martha Biondi reminds us of the centrality of struggles against racial discrimination in labor and the workplace, and also notes that internationalism was part and parcel of the political vision of the black popular front. Her account notes the paradox of the intensification of racial segregation in the urban North at the very moment that legal racial barriers were being dismantled in the South. Eric Burner, *And Gently He Shall Lead Them: Robert Parris Moses and Civil Rights in Mississippi* (New York, 1994) provides an account of Moses's evolving internationalism and his incorporation of an antiwar position in his work for SNCC. *Lost Prophet: The Life and Times of Bayard Rustin* (New York, 2000), John D'Emilio's biography of the pacifist who served as an advisor to King during and after the Montgomery movement, notes the importance of his encounter with national independence movements in India and Africa. Rustin's involvement in nuclear disarmament protests in Africa was integral to his—and the movement's—vision of nonviolent direct action.

Also building on earlier work on African Americans and U.S. foreign relations, Mary Dudziak's study, *Cold War Civil Rights: Race and the Image of American Democracy* (Princeton, N.J., 2000) established the importance of viewing the *Brown* decision as a legal event embedded in national and international diplomacy and geopolitics, and the civil rights movement as profoundly exposed to the political winds of the Cold War. *Brown* was a landmark, but its reliance on extrajudicial arguments, such as the need to maintain the image of the United States as the leader of the "Free World" overseas, illustrates that constitutional law cannot be separated from sociopolitical conditions. The subtitle of Dudziak's book is instructive, for she extensively portrays U.S. policymakers as more concerned with defending the image of American democracy than enforcing federal desegregation laws.

Viewing the civil rights movement in world perspective necessitates a reperiodization of sorts. Just as our understanding of *Brown* as the genesis of the modern civil rights movement is called into question by the framework of "the long civil rights movement," and complicated further by the impact of the Cold War, so must we consider the extent to which African American consciousness and U.S. domestic- and foreign-policy makers were responding not only to the black freedom movement in the United States but also to the decolonization of Africa, including such events as what became known as the Congo Crisis. For Malcolm X, Lorraine Hansberry, Amiri Baraka, and a generation of Afro-American nationalists, the death of Lumumba was as formative as any of the hallmark civil rights campaigns and crises that occurred in the South. James Meriwether's *Proudly We Can Be Africans: Black Americans and Africa, 1935–1961* (Chapel Hill, N.C., 2002) captures the mood of those who looked to the new Africa of modern nation-states as an important basis for American civic identity. The impact of the Congo Crisis is detailed in Plummer, Meriwether, and in my recent study, *American Africans in Ghana: Black Expatriates and the Civil Rights Era* (Chapel Hill, N.C., 2006). Newsreel footage of the demonstration of African Americans in the gallery of the United Nations Security Council can be seen in the documentary *Ralph Bunche: An American Odyssey* (William Greaves Productions). One of the participants in that demonstration, Maya Angelou, provided an account of the demonstration in her evocative, if not always historically accurate memoir, *The Heart of a Woman* (New York, 1981), which describes the transformative potential of the new Africa on African American identity. In *The Cold War and the Color Line,* (Cambridge, Mass., 2001), Thomas Borstelmann provides an account of the Congo Crisis from the standpoint of U.S. officialdom. Borstelmann argues that Eisenhower officials' racial attitudes toward the besieged Congolese prime minister Patrice Lumumba were decisive in their refusal to extend political or military support. While silent on the administration's racial perceptions of Lumumba, Stephen E. Ambrose notes Eisenhower's approval of a CIA plot to assassinate Lumumba in *Eisenhower* (New York, 1983).

My study *American Africans in Ghana* resituates such familiar figures as King and Malcolm X within the framework of decolonization in Africa. As one of several African American honored guests, King visited the nation of Ghana in 1957 for that former British colony's independence ceremonies. A valuable contemporary account of King's visit to Ghana is in Lawrence D. Reddick, *Crusader Without Violence: A Biography of Martin Luther King Jr.* (New York, 1959). See also the relevant documents on King's visit to Ghana collected by Clayborne Carson, senior editor, *The Papers of Martin Luther King Jr. volume 4, Symbol of the Movement January 1957–December 1958* (Berkeley, Calif., 2000), particularly King's sermon on the birth of Ghana. While in Ghana, King met with Prime Minister Kwame Nkrumah and other Ghanaian nationalist leaders, as did Malcolm X during his own visit in 1964. By 1964, the optimism of the moment of independence was a distant memory, shattered by violent repression of nationalists in the Congo and in South Africa. Ghana was under siege from internal and external opposition, and Nkrumah had eroded civil liberties with a repressive domestic security apparatus after two assassination attempts. And in the U.S. setting, African American liberals and radicals who sought to influence U.S. foreign policy toward Africa clashed with the U.S. liberal establishment over the very terms and content of African American political consciousness and citizenship. For teaching purposes, I recommend chapter 6 of my book, *American Africans in Ghana,* on Malcolm X's visit to Ghana, which details his ouster from the Nation of Islam, his engagement with African affairs, and the impact the latter had on his ideas for mobilizing U.S. blacks.

Notes

1. Stuart Burns, ed., *Daybreak of Freedom: The Montgomery Bus Boycott* (Chapel Hill, N.C., 1997) frames that event in the context of the national independence struggle in the Gold Coast, West Africa.

2. John Dittmer, *Local People: The Struggle for Civil Rights in Mississippi* (Urbana, Ill., 1995).

3. "Oginga Odinga," a selection from the Freedom Singers album, *Freedom Now,* describes the SNCC activists' meeting with the Kenyan nationalist leader and politician, who had been brought to the United States by the State Department.

4. Thomas Holt, *The Problem of Race in the 21st Century* (Cambridge, Mass., 2000), xx.

5. Martha Biondi, *To Stand and Fight: The Struggle for Civil Rights in Postwar New York City* (Cambridge, Mass., 2003); Matthew J. Countryman, *Up South: Civil Rights and Black Power in Philadelphia* (Philadelphia, 2006); and Jeanne Theoharis, Komozi Woodard, and Matthew Countryman, eds., *Freedom North: Black Freedom Struggles Outside the South, 1940–1980* (New York, 2003); Jeanne Theoharris and Komozi Woodard, eds., *Groundwork: Local Black Freedom Movements in America* (New York, 2005).

6. Gerald Horne, *Black and Red: W. E. B. Du Bois and the Afro-American Response to the Cold War, 1944–1963* (Albany, N.Y., 1986); Brenda Gayle Plummer, *Rising Wind; Black Americans and U.S. Foreign Affairs, 1935–1960* (Chapel Hill, N.C., 1996); Penny M. Von Eschen, *Race Against Empire: Black Americans and Anticolonialism, 1937–1957* (Ithaca, N.Y., 1997); Azza Salama Layton, *International Politics and Civil Rights Policies in the United States, 1941–1960* (Cambridge, Eng., 2000); Mary L. Dudziak, *Cold War Civil Rights: Race and the Image of American Democracy* (Princeton, N.J., 2000); Carol Anderson, *Eyes Off the Prize: The United Nations and the African American Struggle for Human Rights* (Cambridge, Eng., 2003).

7. Mahmood Mamdani, *Good Muslim, Bad Muslim: America, the Cold War, and the Roots of Terror* (New York, 2004).

8. Thomas Borstelmann, *The Cold War and the Color Line: American Race Relations in the Global Arena* (Cambridge, Mass., 2001).

9. Jacquelyn Dowd Hall, "The Long Civil Rights Movement and the Political Uses of the Past," *Journal of American History,* 91 (March 2005): 1233–63.

10. Patricia Sullivan, *Days of Hope: Race and Democracy in the New Deal Era* (Chapel Hill, N.C., 1996).

11. Robert Korstad and Nelson Lichtenstein, "Opportunities Found and Lost: Labor, Radicals and the Civil Rights Movement," *Journal of American History,* 75 (Dec. 1988): 786–811; Robert Rodgers Korstad, *Civil Rights Unionism: Tobacco Workers and the Struggle for Democracy in the Mid-Twentieth Century South* (Chapel Hill, N.C., 2003); see also Biondi, *To Stand and Fight;* and Countryman, *Up South.*

12. Winston James, *Holding Aloft the Banner of Ethiopia: Caribbean Radicalism in Early Twentieth-Century America* (New York, 1999); James H. Meriwether, *Proudly We Can Be Africans: Black Americans and Africa, 1935– 1961* (Chapel Hill, N.C., 2002).

13. Von Eschen, *Race Against Empire,* 1997.

14. Kevin K. Gaines, *American Africans in Ghana: Black Expatriates and the Civil Rights Era* (Chapel Hill, N.C., 2006), 83–84.

15. Gaines, "E. Franklin Frazier's Revenge: Anticolonialism, Nonalignment, and Black Intellectuals' Critiques of Western Culture," *American Literary History,* 17 (2005): 506–29.

16. Gaines, *American Africans in Ghana,* 218.

17. Clayborne Carson, *In Struggle: SNCC and the Black Awakening of the 1960s* (Cambridge, Mass., 1982).

18. Eric R. Burner, *And Gently He Shall Lead Them: Robert Parris Moses and Civil Rights in Mississippi* (New York, 1994).

19. Richard Wright, *The Outsider* (New York, 1965), 366.

THE CIVIL RIGHTS MOVEMENT AND THE COLD WAR CULTURE IN PERSPECTIVE

PINGCHAO ZHU

Three years ago I taught a two-semester university course on globalization. This experience convinced me that, from its beginning, U.S. history has been interconnected with world history. Kevin Gaines's essay, which places the civil rights movement in the context of decolonization and the Cold War, demonstrates this point. By using his essay in the classroom, teachers can provide students with a broader perspective that will help them better understand the many ways international and local events are related and oftentimes interconnected.

Challenges in teaching the civil rights movement from a global (or international relations) perspective obviously come from different directions. Teaching according to conventional wisdom, in Gaines's words, would confine the civil rights movement "within a domestic U.S.-based framework." In this format, a string of events from early slavery, the Civil War, the Emancipation Proclamation, Reconstruction, the civil rights movement, and the 1964 Civil Rights Act seem to say it all about African Americans' long struggle for freedom and equality. Previously, I would teach the civil rights movement more or less along this outline. As an "obvious story," it appears to have little relevance to the Cold War's international developments. Pedagogically, Gaines sees an advantage teachers and students can gain by putting the black freedom movement within a global framework. "Such a recontextualization," according to Gaines, "also enables us to comprehend the limits, as well as the achievements, of civil rights strategies and reforms." As national independence movements in Africa, communist expansion in Asia, and racial oppression in the United States continued to make headlines, especially during the 1960s, reforming the American "moral character" would become an urgent issue on the U.S. Cold War agenda. Paradoxically, Gaines also suggests that the Cold War itself limited the strategies the civil rights activists could pursue.[1]

Gaines's discussion covers primarily the 1960s, which is a critical time period and can easily include many issues in the U.S. history survey course. I present the "The Cold War and the Civil Rights Movement" in three major phases, with each phase using one class period. The first phase focuses on the examination of a mix of primary documents and scholarly writing to give students a sense of national impact and international implication of the civil rights movement.[2] Gaines's essay serves as a departure point to unfold an ever-expanding civil rights movement against the background of a turbulent world that was deeply clouded by Cold War tension. I help students identify several important themes (or questions) in Gaines's essay:

1. Do you see a transformation in the civil rights movement from "reformist goals to an agenda of radical social change under Martin Luther King's leadership?"
2. What does Gaines mean when he suggests that "the Cold War held a doubled-edged significance for the civil rights movement?"
3. Why does Gaines characterize news media coverage of the civil rights movement as "a chronic headache for U.S. foreign-policy makers?"
4. How would you describe the relationship between Lyndon Johnson's administration and black leaders in terms of U.S. civil rights reforms?
5. What were the limits of the civil rights movement at the international level? Did the ideological aspirations of the civil rights movement at home and the U.S. Cold War policy abroad (for example, containment of and crusade against communism) contradict each other?

These questions force students to think critically about the important issues raised by Gaines. Class discussion is an effective format to involve students and encourage an exchange of views in the classroom.

The first phase of my teaching strategy involves the efforts of civil rights activists to place their aims in a global context. In *Cold War Civil Rights: Race and the Image of American Democracy,* Mary Dudziak addresses issues and developments during the 1960s—at a time when the civil rights movement and the Vietnam War collided. Dudziak suggests that "by 1966 Vietnam had replaced American race relations as an important matter of international concern."[3] In the classroom, I emphasize several landmark achievements, including the Civil Rights Act of 1964, Martin Luther King's Nobel Peace Prize in December 1964, and the Voting Rights Act of 1965, which were overshadowed by chronic protests against U.S. involvement in Vietnam. This intensifying racial division raised international concerns about the "moral" contradiction within American government and society.

Additionally, King's speech, "Beyond Vietnam: A Time to Break Silence," on April 4, 1967, at Riverside Church in New York City indicated that since the mid-1960s, he was becoming increasingly critical of American Cold War policy in general and strategies in Vietnam in particular.[4] It is important to point out to students that King connected the civil rights movement at home to the war in Vietnam and America's image in the world.

King's call for finding "new ways to speak for peace in Vietnam and justice throughout the developing world" was followed by the Detroit riot in July 1967. At this point, I direct students to revisit Gaines's essay where the author argues that it was the Vietnam War and the accompanying global opposition that "contributed to King's transformation from reformer to revolutionary." In sum, the Dudziak and King readings show students how the civil rights movement and the Cold War corresponded to each other at a global level.

The Civil Rights Act of 1964 also illustrates the Cold War dimensions of the civil rights movement. While reading the text of the act, I ask students to answer the following question: In what ways were civil rights laws important to American foreign policy? Both Martin Luther King and Malcolm X sought international help, including the United Nations, to pressure the U.S. government to improve race relations and end racial discrimination. I divide students into four small groups to identify different provisions in the act and to analyze how the changes carried implications for U.S. foreign policy. I expect different responses: some students applaud the legislative accomplishment, while others comment that African Americans would later insist that only radical ideas would result in radical change. Malcolm X, for example, commented in his 1965 speech on "Prospects for Freedom": "In '64, what was it? The civil-rights bill. Right after they passed the civil-rights bill, they murdered a Negro in Georgia and did nothing about it; murdered two whites and a Negro in Mississippi and did nothing about is. So that the civil-rights bill has produced nothing where we're concerned. It was only a valve, a vent, that was designed to enable us to let off our frustrations. But the bill itself was not designed to solve our problems . . . it was designed to lessen the explosion."[5] Malcolm X's statement best represents the radicalization of the American civil rights movement, which also reflected the emerging Afro- American nationalism and the divisions among African American leaders in the movement.

The second phase of my teaching strategy involves dividing students into groups, with each group examining a civil rights movement in another country. Though the civil rights movement in the United States is the most well-known, it was only one of many civil rights movements around the globe. Therefore, in order to contextualize the U.S. civil rights movement, it is important to have students examine international events during and prior to the 1960s.

While Gaines's essay deals with a much broader framework of not only governmental responses but also the ideological climate that shaped the civil rights leaders' tactics, the student investigations should help them obtain detailed information about specific events in the context of the Cold War and in connection to civil rights issues at home. I divide students into four groups and have each conduct an investigation of one of the following issues:

1. Ghana independence
2. Congo independence
3. Martin Luther King's position toward U.S. involvement in Vietnam
4. Communist responses to and the reports on the civil rights movement in the United States

Each group reports its findings and conclusions to the class in terms of their issue's respective goals, historical significance, impact on the region, global effect, and applicable connection to other similar movements. Following the group reports, the students should discuss how they would answer the following two questions.

1. The first discussion question explores the significance of more than twenty African nations declaring independence from European colonial rule (mainly British or French) during the 1960s. Are there parallels between the U.S. civil rights movement and the African national independence movements?

This question relates Gaines's suggestion that studying the African American struggle for equality "within the changing global order of decolonization" can help students better understand how political consciousness of many civil rights activists, especially "those northern urban black militants and radicals," was "shaped by the decolonization of Africa." One of the major features of the Cold War was that the United States and the Soviet Union "fought" numerous regional wars through their armed proxies in Africa, Latin America, and Asia. For the United States, a national independence movement, if won with the forming of a democratic regime, could contribute to the deterrence of growing Soviet control in these regions. I believe that the case study of Congo independence from Belgium in June 1960 and the Congo Crisis shortly after best explains the point that American support of national independence was largely determined by our Cold War interests in the region. I direct students to explore two aspects of African independence:

a) Patrice Lumumba's Independence Day speech.[6]

b) The role the CIA played in handling the Congo Crisis and the coup to oust and murder Patrice Lumumba—the first nationally elected prime minister of Congo.

Lumumba's radical voice and his call for "fundamental liberties" forced the United States to reconsider supporting a "moderate camp" in the new Congo. According to the CIA studies, the U.S. needed to find a compromise between two extremes: the Belgium-supported mining companies (Moise Tshombe) and the allegedly pro-Soviet Patrice Lumumba. In David Gibbs's view, "The CIA found a midpoint between these two extremes. It helped Joseph Mobutu—then a nationalist member of the Congolese forces—become a third alternative."[7] In a 1964 speech, Malcolm X called Tshombe "a cold-blooded murderer" of Lumumba and blamed the United States for Congo's chaotic situation.

Along with Gaines's discussion of King's link to Ghana's struggle against colonialism, segregation, and discrimination, I want students to also understand his argument about the tradition of black internationalism, which "had inspired anticolonial movement in Africa and the Caribbean," and would energize social and political consciousness in the civil rights movement in the United States.

2. The second discussion question involves how the U.S. involvement in Vietnam divided American society. What were the "moral contradictions" of the U.S. policy in Southeast Asia, as indicated by Martin Luther King? How did the communists use the African American civil rights movement for propaganda purposes?

China is a useful place to start answering these questions. The 1960s was also a crucial decade in China. Since the late 1950s, China began to experience ideological difficulties with the Soviet Union over Khrushchev's criticism of China's economic policy and his denunciation of Stalin. Although China could not afford to completely break away from the Soviet Union, it found a potential ally in the international black community. According to the communist theory, the working classes around the world share common interests and a similar class consciousness in the struggle against economic and military injustice. The Chinese communists interpreted the civil rights movement as a fight by African Americans against U.S. imperialist oppression. The Chinese viewed the movement sympathetically and used it as a convenient overture for courting support from the international black community. Incidentally, Gaines argues that the civil rights movement was silent on the labor perspective. To explore the connection between labor and civil rights, students should be encouraged to answer the following question: How did civil rights leaders address labor issues in their discourse of promoting socioeconomic justice in America?

In early August 1963, two weeks before the March on Washington, Mao Zedong, the Chinese communist leader, issued a declaration through the *People's Daily,* an official newspaper of the Chinese Communist Party and the government. Mao called upon people of the world to support African Americans in their struggle against racial discrimination in the United States. He also argued that American democracy was hypocritical and served only the interests of the ruling class. Most important, Mao connected the U.S. civil rights movement to various national independence, anticolonialist, and anti-imperialist movements. This type of criticism from Asia and Africa became a major foreign policy concern for the United States.

At this time, I ask the class to read a quotation from Gaines's essay and think about how the Cold War politics stood out in the civil rights movement in different ways:

> King insisted that civil rights was not some "ephemeral, evanescent domestic" matter to be exploited by segregationists for immediate political gain, but an "eternal moral issue" that would determine the outcome of the Cold War. Vice President Nixon used similar logic, warning that continued discrimination against African Americans undermined U.S. influence in Africa, which he regarded a crucial terrain of the superpower struggle against international communism.

Both John Kennedy and Lyndon Johnson tried to postpone addressing civil rights issues when facing an escalating U.S. commitment in Vietnam. Kennedy, for example, said that he "wanted to improve racial relations, without getting us too far out front."[8] Gaines also points out that Johnson realized "the achievement of civil rights reforms in the U.S. seemed to require the acquiescence of black leadership on African and foreign affairs."

When Martin Luther King spoke publicly against the war, the civil rights movement, like antiwar protests, was blamed for having weakened America's ability to contain communism and win the Cold War. Gaines refers to this tension in his discussion of the "sharp disagreement and conflict within the civil rights movement." He argues that "the realities of a movement under siege and the urgent cause of voting rights justified, to some black activists, reticence on matters of U.S. foreign policy." Still, King's words were powerful and explicit:

> The bombs in Vietnam explode at home: They destroy the hopes and possibili-
> ties for a decent America. . . . It is estimated that we spend $322,000 for each
> enemy we kill in Vietnam, while we spend in the so-called War on Poverty
> in America only about $53 for every person classified as poor.[9]

On another occasion, King expounded, "so we have repeatedly faced with the cruel irony of watching Negro and white boys on TV screens as they kill and die together for a nation that has not been unable to seat them together in the same school."[10] As the war in Vietnam dragged on with no solution, more Americans began to question U.S. intentions in Southeast Asia. This situation became a propaganda opportunity for America's Cold War enemies. They capitalized on the civil rights leaders' criticism of U.S. involvement in Vietnam in an effort to fan international and domestic opposition to U.S. foreign policy. At this point, I give students the opportunity to research communist propaganda statements such as Hanoi's assertion that "the African-Americans' struggle" was a "second front to weaken U.S. imperialism," China's view of "class struggle in the U.S.," and Moscow's broadcast of an imminent "civil war" in the United States.[11]

With enough background discussion, the students can discuss King's position on the U.S. involvement in the Vietnam War and communist manipulation of America's racial problems specifically in the context of the civil rights movement. This project provides students with something they do not often hear or read about but might find interesting and eye-opening.

The third phase of the teaching strategy examines how world events and the civil rights movement complemented each other in the 1960s. For this examination, I have the class read the following excerpt from Mao Zedong's speech on the assassination of Martin Luther King on April 4, 1968:

> Some days ago, Martin Luther King, the African American clergyman, was
> suddenly assassinated by the U.S. imperialists. Martin Luther King was an
> exponent of non-violence. Nevertheless, the U.S. imperialists did not on that

account show any tolerance towards him, but used counter-revolutionary violence and killed him in cold blood. . . . It has touched off a new storm in their struggle against violent repression sweeping well over a hundred cities in the United States, a storm such as has never taken place before in the history of the country.

The storm of African American struggle taking place within the United States is a striking manifestation of the comprehensive political and economic crisis now gripping U.S. imperialism. It is dealing a telling blow to U.S. imperialism, which is beset with difficulties at home and abroad.

The African American struggle is not only a struggle waged by the exploited and oppressed black people for freedom and emancipation, it is also a new call to all the exploited and oppressed people of the United States to fight against the barbarous rule of the monopoly capitalist class. It is a tremendous support and inspiration to the struggle of the people throughout the world against U.S. imperialism and to the struggle of the Vietnamese people against U.S. imperialism. On behalf of the Chinese people, I hereby express resolute support for the just struggle of the black people in the United States.[12]

Mao's speech—which remained an anti-U.S. imperialist statement within the communist camp throughout the Cold War—represented the communist strategy of using the racial issue to create anti-U.S. propaganda. I give students the opportunity to study and analyze several political terminologies used in Mao's statement in order to understand communist Cold War ideology and strategy.

Facing a growing communist challenge, and needing to rehabilitate its image as the world's first democracy, the U.S. government was forced to re-evaluate its Cold War strategy. Thus the momentum of the civil rights movement pushed reform to a higher level. At the end of this teaching strategy, I have the students discuss the following question: What features did Cold War consciousness, class consciousness, and African American consciousness share?

In conclusion, I examine why civil rights legislation was so important to American foreign policy, and in so doing help students understand the Cold War was an international event and the black freedom movement had a global context. The paths of the two histories interconnect in a number of ways and illustrate the bigger picture of world politics and global developments. Gaines emphasizes that studying the civil rights movement from a global perspective "can better prepare students to understand contemporary global affairs, helping them draw connections between postwar U.S. history and the histories of Africa, Asia, and the Middle East." His essay is an effective reading assignment in both U.S history survey and upper-division U.S. diplomacy courses. Additionally, the civil rights movement in the context of decolonization and the Cold War can be an interesting topic in a course on globalization. Students in the U.S. survey class can find more interesting subjects and issues to explore beyond the American boundary. In other words, globalizing U.S. history is not only inevitable, but also a breath of fresh air.

Notes

1. Mary L. Dudziak indicates that "in spite of the repression of the Cold War era, civil rights reform was *in part* a product of the Cold War." See *Cold War Civil Rights, Race and the Image of American Democracy* (Princeton, N.J., 2000), 12.

2. In addition to Kevin Gaines's essay, a few primary sources, articles, and books also focus on this topic. King's speech on April 4, 1967, at Riverside Church in New York City can be found in the Web site at <www.ssc.msu.edu/~sw/mlk/brkslnc.htm>. King's "Nobel Prize Acceptance Speech" on December 10, 1964, is available in James M. Washington, ed, *A Testament of Hope: The Essential Writings and Speeches of Martin Luther King Jr.* (New York, 1986), 224–26. Secondary sources include Mary Dudziak, *Cold War Civil Rights: Race and the Image of American Democracy* (Princeton, N.J., 2000); Thomas Borstelmann, *The Cold War and the Color Line: American Race Relationship in the Global Arena* (Cambridge, Mass., 2003); David Gibbs, "Misrepresenting the Congo Crisis," *African Affairs,* 95 (July 1996): 453–59.

3. Dudziak, *Cold War Civil Rights,* 242.

4. See Web site at <www.ssc.msu.edu/~sw/mlk/brkslnc.htm>.

5. George Breitman, ed., *Malcolm X Speaks, Selected Speeches and Statements* (New York, 1965), 151.

6. See Web site at <http://www.africawithin.com/lumumba/independence_speech.htm>.

7. Gibbs, "Misrepresenting the Congo Crisis," 456–57.

8. Bruce J. Dierrenfield, *The Civil Rights Movement* (New York, 2004), 83.

9. Martin Luther King's speech from PBS series, *LBJ: The American Experience* (1991). In Dierrenfield's book, however, the numbers are $500,000 and $35, respectively (page 128).

10. King, "Beyond Vietnam," April 4, 1967, <www.ssc.msu.edu/~sw/mlk/brkslnc.htm>, 3.

11. Dierrenfield, *The Civil Rights Movement,* 243.

12. Mao Zedong, "Statement in Support of the African American Struggle against Violent Repression" (Beijing, 1968), 1–3.

CHAPTER 11

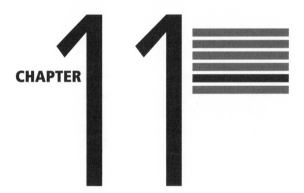

"The First Vote," by A. R. Waud, originally appeared in *Harper's Weekly*, November 16, 1867. (Image courtesy of the Library of Congress, Prints and Photographs Division, LC-USZ62-19234 [5-21].)

RACE AND CITIZENSHIP

At first sight, the concepts of race and citizenship are at odds with each other. Citizenship is premised on equality and uniformity, while race is inseparably bound up with inequality and difference. Yet the two emerged in close historical proximity and have been constant companions ever since, so we need to look beyond the semblance of inconsistency to seek the basis on which such a contradictory pairing should cohere.

We are all familiar with the notion that the modern concept of citizenship came to fruition in the eighteenth century and was particularly associated with the American War of Independence and the French Revolution. The idea that race has a cognate history is more surprising. This is because the concept of race has always figured as a natural endowment, which has placed it beyond the realm of human intervention. To begin to understand the workings of race, therefore, we should lift it out of the realm of nature and examine it as a human ideological invention that has served distinct purposes in particular historical contexts. To chart its ideological workings, it is useful to distinguish between race as an idea or concept—which is largely an outcome of classificatory natural science—and that idea as it has been put into social practice, which is an inherently political process. I term this latter process *racialization*. *Race* involves both the idea of race and the practical racialization of particular social groups—which, as we shall see, has varied widely according to context. When we recognize that race is not a universal condition but a historically particular set of constructs that vary from country to country, and even in application to different populations within the same country, we denaturalize race. To this end, the chapter will first sketch the emergence of the idea of race before moving on to consider some of the different ways in which racialization has operated in two countries: Australia and the United States. We will also consider the different ways in which black people and Native Americans have been racialized within the United States. Having illustrated the sociohistorical variability of race in this way, the chapter will come back to the relationship between race and citizenship.

THE IDEA OF RACE

To say that we can date the emergence of the idea of race from the late eighteenth century is not to suggest that Europeans failed to recognize and act on observable phenotypical differences before that time. Precursors are legion. One only has to cite Othello. Nor is it to pretend that an overland journey from Botswana to Finland would fail to suggest a significant degree of anatomical-geographical correlation. The point is, rather, that the mere fact that people have differentiated between human collectivities does not mean that they have subscribed to the ideology that today we call *race*. (It would be hard to establish a connection between Othello and the bell curve, for instance.) The idea of race is but one historically distinctive mode of collective differentiation. Though most if not all of its ingredients can be found in earlier classifications, race combines these elements into a particular ideological mix that we do not encounter before the eighteenth century.

The feature that sets the idea of race apart from other ideological constructs, and that embeds it in the late eighteenth century, is its merger of two central but otherwise distinct strands of Enlightenment discourse. Race reconciled the great taxonomies of natural science with the political rhetoric of the rights of man. There is obvious tension between the hierarchical structuring of Enlightenment classifications and the formal equality that constitutes citizenship in liberal-democratic theory. As a taxonomy par excellence, however, race provided a set of categorical boundaries that enabled hierarchical distinctions to be made within the otherwise universal category of mankind. In particular, as a separate race, blacks were not part of the universal "man" who was the bearer of Jeffersonian rights.

The science of race originated as comparative craniology, which received its first systematic expression in 1795 with the publication of the third edition of Johann Friedrich Blumenbach's *De Generis Humanae Varietate,* in which Blumenbach categorized humanity, in the taxonomic manner of Linnaeus and Buffon, as a single species that was divided into five varieties (Caucasian, Mongolian, Ethiopian or Negroid, American, and Malay), distinguished according to the criteria of hair type, skin color, body structure, and, especially, the shape of the skull as viewed from above (the *norma verticalis*). From here, it was a short step to the invidious hierarchies of nineteenth-century scientific racism.

As Edmund Morgan and other U.S. historians have shown, the concept of race also enabled slaveholding founding fathers such as Washington and Jefferson to proclaim universal liberties without apparent embarrassment. The prestige of natural science afforded the most authoritative of warrants to a contradictory ideology that tolerated the enslavement of Africans as a condition of American freedom. In the nineteenth century, a hotchpotch of scientific theories was recruited to the cause of bolstering racial discrimination. The doctrine of polygenesis, for instance, held that black people and Indians were separate species to white people, descended from "different Adams." As such, they were entitled to different standards of treatment. As the nineteenth century wore on, an assortment of scientific variations on the doctrine of progress hardened into a consensus generally known as Social Darwinism, whereby nonwhite races were seen to be held back at various stages in the evolutionary history that Europeans had already passed through. Accordingly, nonwhite people were congenitally inferior to whites, whose mission it was to govern and uplift them. The bell curve has a long history.

RACIALIZATION

Social Darwinism was equally influential in nineteenth-century Australia. Rather than providing a justification for enslaving Aboriginal people, however, the same doctrine explained their disappearance. Aborigines were held to be denizens of the Old Stone Age. In the form of whites, they were encountering their immeasurably distant future, a people who had been selectively improved by millennia of progress. Accordingly, it was inscribed in the natural order of things that Aborigines would simply fade away—their decimation was not their white invaders' fault. Though premised on the same body of doctrine, therefore, the racialization of black Australians assigned them a destiny that was very different from the one that was prescribed for black people in the United States. Yet it was very similar to the destiny that U.S. racial ideology assigned to Indians, who were, of course, classified as red rather than black. When it comes to the practical racialization of subordinated social groups, therefore, we need to look beyond natural-scientific categories (color, genes, bodily characteristics, and so forth) to the social contexts in which the idea of race was activated. In this case, it is clear that the distinction that counts is that between native peoples and those who have been enslaved.

In Australia and in the United States, white authorities have generally accepted—even targeted—native people's physical substance (typically represented as blood) for assimilation into their own stock. In both countries, native people have resisted assimilation, asserting criteria other than blood quanta as bases for group membership and identity. When it has come to black people's physical substance, on the other hand, it has only been in the past few decades that U.S. authorities have dispensed with the most rigorous procedures for insulating the white bloodline. Moreover, with some exceptions, black groups in the United States have themselves affirmed the "one-drop rule," maintaining an inclusive membership policy that, apart from anything else, has kept up group numbers. Thus it is clear that, if the idea of race has some coherence, this is not reflected in the practical racialization of subordinate social groups, which varies from case to case.

Because race is an inherently classificatory practice, a good way to probe its workings is to see what happens when the classifications break down. The classic situation in which this occurs is when people from different racial groups combine to produce offspring, a phenomenon that is often termed miscegenation, meaning "mixed generation." Miscegenation threatens the very basis of a racial order, confusing the boundaries between rulers and ruled, colonizer and colonized, masters and slaves. Accordingly, the dominant race characteristically polices miscegenation in ways that reveal much about the racial order in question. For instance, Australia was established as a British settler colony. Settler colonialism is not a temporary procedure. Invasion is a structure, not an event. The colonizers come to stay. Rather than prioritizing native labor, their overriding goal is to replace the natives on their land. Thus we can characterize the governing logic of settler colonialism as a logic of elimination.

In Australia, the logic of elimination has had three principal historical manifestations. At the outset, when Europeans first reached a given Aboriginal group's territory, the outcome was invariably violent, with Aborigines being killed or removed in large numbers. Apart from outright homicide, starvation and introduced disease were major factors in the frontier attrition of Aboriginal populations. Once the dust had settled on the frontier and white settlement had been established, policy generally shifted to one of geographical confinement, with Aboriginal people—at least, those not required to service the white economy—being gathered together on missions or reserves. The rhetoric accompanying this policy differed considerably from the bloodthirsty talk of marauding savages that had accompanied the violence of the frontier. Rather, missionaries were held out as "smoothing the pillow of a dying race." Nonetheless, the practical consequences of the policy were no less consistent with the logic of elimination, because confining Aboriginal people to fixed locations had the effect of vacating their traditional territory and rendering it available for white settlement. The third manifestation of the logic of elimination in Australia was the policy of Aboriginal assimilation, which prevailed for most of the twentieth century. Under this policy, the "Aboriginal problem" was to be eliminated through Aborigines being incorporated into white society. The policy operated both genetically and culturally. In its crude, genetic form, it provided for Aboriginal people with white ancestry to be removed from Aboriginal society and incorporated into white society—as the policy was often summarized, they would be "bred white." In Australia, therefore, miscegenation became a conduit to whiteness, with pale skin serving as a pretext for Aboriginal children to be taken from their families and adopted out to whites. Clearly, therefore, the racialization of Aboriginal people, whereby white ancestry makes one white, has to be understood in the broader context of the logic of elimination that is the foundational characteristic of Australian settler colonialism. Genetics are not involved. If Aboriginal genes really had been believed to be inferior, as Social Darwinist propaganda held them to be, then official policy would not have sought to incorporate them into the white gene pool.

The Australian case could not contrast more sharply with miscegenation discourse as it has been applied to black people in the United States. Here, rather than white blood conducing to whiteness, the reverse has been the case: any amount of African inheritance, no matter how remote and regardless of phenotypical appearance, has entailed an individual being classified black. This policy, generally known as the one-drop rule, reached its zenith in the twentieth century with the hysterical policing of white blood that characterized the Jim Crow era. Just as the assimilation policy in Australia reflects the logic of settler colonialism, so is the one-drop rule a direct legacy of slavery. With short-lived exceptions, notably in Maryland, the offspring of a slave was born a slave. The logic of this situation was brutally simple—chattel slaves were valuable commodities, which meant that whites could augment plantation owners' property by impregnating their female slaves. In the wake of slavery, this policy became thoroughly racialized, with black blood coming to overwhelm all others, no matter what the relative proportions involved.

The contrast becomes even clearer when we move, within the United States, to miscegenation discourse as it has been applied to Native Americans. Here the resemblance to Australia is thoroughgoing. Despite the practice of treaty making, which did not occur in Australia, Indians have experienced frontier violence, removal (usually as a consequence of treaties), confinement to reservations, and, crucially, assimilation, in a manner that is only too familiar to an Australian historian. The only major difference between the two histories is the absence of an allotment program in Australia, reflecting the fact that Aboriginal people's ownership of their land was not acknowledged, which meant that there was no native property to allot. So far as assimilation is concerned, however, the two histories are strikingly similar, right down to the centrality of blood quantum requirements. "Mixed-blood" Indians were especially targeted to lose their land under the allotment policy that was generalized to all Indians at the end of the nineteenth century. To this day, blood quanta continue to aggravate the miseries of tribal enrolment. Rather than one drop of black blood making an individual black, white ancestry jeopardizes Native Americans' Indian-ness. Regardless of the national difference, where U.S. Indian policy has been concerned, the conformity with the Australian pattern is striking. Clearly, the common ground lies in the fact that Native Americans, like Aboriginal people in Australia, are settler-colonized natives. Their involuntary contribution to the settler nation has been their land rather than their labor. This basic historical difference informs the antithetical ways in which blacks and Indians have been racialized in the United States.

RACE AND CITIZENSHIP

The policy of assimilating Indians culminated in 1924, with the passing of an act that extended U.S. citizenship to all Native Americans. Strikingly, 1924 also saw a high-water mark in Jim Crow racial codification in the form of the Virginia antimiscegenation statute, which barred white people from marrying other than white people. As if to dramatize the discrepant ways in which blacks and Indians were being racialized, however, this act conceded the so-called Pocahontas exception, whereby certain categories of white/ Indian unions were specifically exempted from its otherwise draconian catalog of proscriptions. For Indians, citizenship and racialization converged. Both conduced to assimilation, the ultimate and least redressable mode of elimination. Conversely, rather than converging with their citizenship, black people's racialization could not have conflicted with it more violently. The racist terror of Jim Crow was above all directed toward undoing the formal equality that black people's citizenship entailed. The difference could not be clearer. Black people did not have to be equal to be exploited. Their inclusion did not add millions of acres to the national estate.

Thus we return to the question of equality, and the relationship between citizenship and race. I propose a modification to Edmund Morgan's analysis of the relationship between race and slavery, one that depends on the distinction between race and racialization. As Morgan showed, the idea of race provided white men with an alibi for slavery. When that idea first emerged, therefore, it was secondary to slavery, for which it furnished a justification. With slavery in place, full-blown racialization was relatively redundant. There was no doubt as to who was in control. Lynchings were rare and southern slaveholders rubbed shoulders *(inter alia)* with their household slaves. What, then, when slavery was abolished? This, I wish to argue, is the key factor in the racialization of black people.

Prior to emancipation, which occurred piecemeal in the northern states well before the Civil War produced the final emancipation of slaves in the South, the juridical condition of slavery had not been absolute. In particular, manumissions had taken place on an individual basis. By dismantling the boundary that had previously separated a free black from a slave, emancipation changed all this. In place of enslaved people, a new and more inclusive subordinate category emerged, one that, being defined by race, did not admit the awkward exceptions and contradictions that manumission had entailed for the peculiar institution of slavery. Emancipation, in short, cancelled out the exemption—you could be an ex-slave but you could not be ex-black. In bringing a form of freedom to black people, the ending of slavery also completed their racialization.

On this basis, it is not surprising that antiblack riots, segregation, and a range of discriminatory practices that foreshadowed the Jim Crow regime should have become established well before the Civil War in northern states that had introduced emancipation. Jim Crow was not to emerge in the South until the 1880s. As James Stewart, Joanne Melish, and other historians have recently documented, however, a new apparatus of discrimination that Stewart calls "racial modernity" had emerged in the North by the 1830s. Racial modernity deployed a rhetoric of essential and unchangeable racial inferiority to justify an oppressive regime that practically ensured that, though emancipated, black people in the North were by no means equal. In this light, I venture the hypothesis that the historical function of race was to restore the inequality that citizenship had theoretically abolished. Race, we may conclude, is a pathological by-product of democracy.

Bibliography

Johann Friedrich Blumenbach. *De Generis Humanae Varietate Nativa liber,* 3rd ed. (Göttingen, 1795), partly translated as "On the Natural Varieties of Mankind" in T. Bendyshe, ed., *The Anthropological Treatises of Johann Friedrich Blumenbach* ... (London, 1865).

Edmund S. Morgan, *American Slavery, American Freedom: The Ordeal of Colonial Virginia* (New York, 1975, see especially pages 1–3, 326–41, 380–87) is the classic account of the harmony between the enunciation of revolutionary ideals and the institution of slavery. Morgan had earlier outlined his perspective in an article, "Slavery and Freedom: The American Paradox," *Journal of American History,* 59 (1972): 4–29.

Joanne Pope Melish, *Disowning Slavery: Gradual Emancipation and "Race" in New England, 1780–1860* (Ithaca, N.Y., 1998) traces and contextualizes the growth and development of racial thought and practice in antebellum New England.

James Brewer Stewart's articles, "The Emergence of Racial Modernity and the Rise of the White North, 1790–1840," *Journal of the Early Republic,* 18 (1998): 181–217, and "Modernizing 'Difference': The Political Meanings of Color in the Free States, 1776–1840," *Journal of the Early Republic,* 19 (1999): 691–712 examine the crisis in racial definitions and race relations that developed in the North in the late 1820s and, as Stewart put it, "exploded in the North during the early 1830s."

Richard J. Herrnstein and Charles Murray, *The Bell Curve: Intelligence and Class Structure in American Life* (New York, 1994). Let us just say, read with care.

Further Reading

This chapter extends a perspective that I began to develop in two previous articles, both of which are much denser than this one: Patrick Wolfe, "Land, Labor, and Difference: Elementary Structures of Race," *American Historical Review,* 106 (2001): 866–905, and "Race and Racialisation: some thoughts," *Postcolonial Studies,* 5, no. 1 (2002): 51–62.

There are many general histories of race and racism. An excellent recent account, which deals with racism in the United States, South Africa, and Nazi Germany, is concise, lucid, and a model of comparative scholarship: George M. Fredrickson, *Racism: A Short History* (Princeton, N.J., 2002).

Kenan Malik, *The Meaning of Race: Race, History and Culture in Western Society* (London, 1996) is a sophisticated, clearly written, theoretically informed, and wide-ranging account of the historical career of the idea of race in Western discourse.

George L. Mosse, *Toward the Final Solution: A History of European Racism* (Madison, Wisc., 1985) is a clear, authoritative, and passionately argued account of the development of race and racism in European thought from the Enlightenment through Count Gobineau and Houston Stuart Chamberlain to Hitler.

Ivan Hannaford, *Race: The History of an Idea in the West* (Baltimore, 1996) is a lengthy but impressively comprehensive account of European discourses on strangers and foreigners from the ancient world to the modern era, presented to sustain the not-unprecedented contention that the modern concept of race was a product of the eighteenth century.

Stephen Jay Gould, *The Mismeasure of Man* (New York, 1981) is an authoritative, lively, incisive account of the presuppositions, follies, and downright distortions that sustained the nineteenth-century obsession with craniology, the bedrock of scientific racism.

Discussions of racial discourse in the United States are far too numerous to cite. Most discuss Euroamerican treatment of either black people or Native Americans. Few discuss them together. Exceptions include Ronald Takaki, *Iron Cages: Race and Culture in Nineteenth-Century America* (New York, 1979) and Gary Nash, *Red, White, and Black: The Peoples of Early North America*, 3rd ed. (Englewood Cliffs, N.J., 1992).

Winthrop D. Jordan, *White Over Black: American Attitudes Toward the Negro, 1550–1812* (Williamsburg, Va., 1968) is the classic account of European and white American discourses on Africans and the relationship between racial ideologies and slavery. Though no doubt a great work, this book suffers from an oddly ahistorical tendency to attribute white views of Africans to primordial European cultural attitudes to darkness.

Audrey Smedley, *Race in North America: Origin and Evolution of a Worldview* (Boulder, Colo., 1999), which does not deal with Canada and only tangentially discusses the racialization of Indians, is nonetheless a wide-ranging and well-written synthesis of disciplinary approaches that recounts and invalidates the scientific claims of racial discourse in the United States.

David Brion Davis, *The Problem of Slavery in the Age of Revolution* (Ithaca, N.Y., 1975) is an elegant and impeccably sourced historical elaboration of Morgan's analysis of the contradictory relationship between American ideals of liberty and the persistence of slavery.

Michael A. Morrison and James Brewer Stewart, eds., *Race and the Early Republic: Racial Consciousness and Nation-Building in the Early Republic* (New York, 2002) is an excellent collection of fresh, insightful, and innovative essays on a comprehensive range of racial issues in the first half century following the American War of Independence.

Alden T. Vaughan's article, "The Origins Debate: Slavery and Racism in Seventeenth-Century Virginia," *Virginia Magazine of History and Biography,* 97 (1989): 311–54 is a masterful summary of a complex and often acrimonious debate, which preoccupied the American historical profession from the 1950s to the 1970s, over the origins of racial thinking and its relationship to slavery in colonial North America.

David Roediger, *The Wages of Whiteness: Race and the Making of the American Working Class* (London, 1991) traces the production and maintenance of white consciousness among the white working class in the United States. In many ways a pioneering work, this book set the scene for a plethora of subsequent studies that showed that, rather than being taken for granted, whiteness had to be carefully articulated and maintained.

Matthew Fry Jacobson, *Whiteness of a Different Color: European Immigrants and the Alchemy of Race* (Cambridge, Mass., 1998) recounts the fascinating history of how the boundaries of whiteness expanded and shifted in the United States as large-scale immigration threatened to blur the boundaries between whites and others.

Jack D. Forbes, *Africans and Native Americans: The Language of Race and the Evolution of Red-Black Peoples* (Chicago, 1993) is a laborious and, in places, overwhelmingly detailed account of the development of racial categories in America, focusing on the classification of people combining Indian and African inheritances. Though a cover-to-cover read is not advisable, the book is an extraordinary repository of information.

Though not interrogating the concept of race, Leon Litwack, *North of Slavery: The Negro in the Free States, 1790–1860* (Chicago, 1961) opened historians' eyes to the mistreatment of black people in the antebellum North. As such, it provided a detailed complement to C. Vann Woodward's classic civil rights–era text, *The Strange Career of Jim Crow* (Oxford, 1957), which remains indispensable to an understanding of white discourses on black people in the United States.

F. James Davis, *Who Is Black? One Nation's Definition* (University Park, Pa., 1991) presents an exhaustive account of the one-drop rule. Davis overlooks some important counterexamples, though, so his account should be approached with caution. Paulini Murray's compendium, *States' Laws on Race and Color* (Athens, Ga., 1997, originally 1950), can be consulted with confidence.

On white attitudes, law, and policies concerning Native Americans, the extensive works of Vine Deloria Jr. are apt, authoritative, and informative. See, for instance, Vine Deloria Jr. and David E. Wilkins, *Tribes, Treaties, and Constitutional Tribulations* (Austin, Tex., 1999) or Sandra Cadwallader and Vine Deloria Jr., eds., *The Aggressions of Civilization: Federal Indian Policy since the 1880s* (Philadelphia, 1984).

Russel Lawrence Barsh and James Youngblood Henderson, *The Road: Indian Tribes and Political Liberty* (Berkeley, Calif., 1980) is a sequential account of the development of Indian law from colonial times up to the 1970s. The analysis is sharp and critical, expressed in economical if somewhat legalistic prose.

On the policy of Indian assimilation, Frederick E. Hoxie, *A Final Promise: The Campaign to Assimilate the Indians, 1880–1920* is authoritative and lucidly argued, though I for one find the proposition that the U.S. government turned away from assimilation in the early twentieth century hard to accept. The classic work on allotment and the Dawes campaign of assimilation is a report that was commissioned by the framers of the Indian Reorganization Act of 1934: D. S. Otis, *The Dawes Act and the Allotment of Indian Lands,* F. P. Prucha, ed. (Norman, Okla., 1973, originally 1934).

The voluminous writings of Francis Paul Prucha are thorough, reliable, and informative. In places, however, Father Prucha's conservatism comes close to apologizing for oppression. See especially his master work, *The Great Father: The United States Government and the American Indians,* 2 vols. (Lincoln, Nebr., 1984, abridged ed. 1986).

TEACHING CITIZENSHIP AND RACE

ORVILLE VERNON BURTON

I have found students to be very interested in issues of race, citizenship, liberty, and freedom, and how these concepts have changed over time. Knowledge of these issues is crucial, especially in a democratic society. For this reason, I appreciate Patrick Wolfe's "Race and Citizenship" article for its comparison of the United States and Australia. Too often, scholars address history at what we think of as the national or transnational level without consciously realizing that these "higher, broader" levels are in fact intellectual constructs rather than concrete realities. At the same time, it is also true that no history, properly understood, is merely local. Though a historian may usefully compare groups within a region, or regions within a country, I applaud the effort to make comparisons across the globe.

One teaching strategy is to relate historical issues of race and citizenship to present-day issues of affirmative action and minority rights. Wolfe's view that "Race . . . is a pathological by-product of democracy" is thought provoking and challenging. Many students will want to contest his findings, and that is where the learning begins. I have found that students engage in learning when they, individually and as a class, work from our nation's documentary record. In other words, they learn when they determine for themselves how race and citizenship interact. I begin by insisting that students seek some agreement on definitions. Generally, we deal with such terms as race and citizenship in the context of the changing meanings of freedom and liberty. Therefore, it is important for students to see how definitions vary and how these variations affect an argument. I want students, for example, to confront George Frederickson's distinction between societal and intellectual racism.[1] It is often surprising to students to see how difficult it is to define terms. This awareness carries over when students seek to discover what writers meant by certain terms throughout history.

Wolfe mentions the importance of racial/ethnic group statistics. I have found that the slave trade and enslavement is an excellent opportunity to introduce students to the importance of quantitative reasoning with historical data. Demographic profiles can allow students to compare the United States and Latin America in terms of the number of whites and persons from Africa. They also may want to look at the number of women and the difference that can make in creating community expectations. Comparing America's one-drop rule—that is, any American with African American ancestors was considered black—with the fact that other societies lacked such a rule helps students understand and critique racial constructs. I also ask students to examine the comparative reader edited by Eugene Genovese and Laura Foner. The essays compare different countries' physical treatment of slaves, access to freedom and emancipation, and incorporation within a society as citizens.[2]

Wolfe relates the development of race to changing ideas of science. When students see how science and colonial ambitions combined to "affirm" the "White Man's Burden," how phrenological examination of Aboriginal skulls and skeletons "proved" that they were a degenerate race, sure of imminent extinction and incapable of profiting from the benefits of European civilization, they can then ask questions about their own cultural certainties. Students who see how anxieties about population increase, industrialization, and the growth of cities found expression in the knowledge scientists produced are then likely to reflect on how their own understanding and uses of new technologies might be subject to the influences of wider economic and cultural forces. Australian scholar Paul Turnbull's Web site on Captain Cook's voyages (<http://southseas.nla.gov.au/about.html>) and essays on science and colonial ambitions allow an American audience insight into the particular problems and opportunities of teaching with computers and on employing comparative historical information.

Wolfe suggests that "the relative numbers of the populations" help determine both admission to citizenship and racialization. A question that students love to debate is why Africans were successfully enslaved in North America but Native Americans were not. They are usually surprised to learn just how widespread Native American slavery was, and how Native Americans were sold away from the colonies as slaves. Students enjoy learning about Squanto's travels from continent to continent before he greeted the Pilgrims at Plymouth Plantation. Students in the survey are also surprised to learn about the differences between slave systems among Indians and the one that developed for racialized slavery in the United States. They learn that not only did Indians hold slaves, but a number of free blacks enslaved other blacks as well. Exploring the various motives for owning slaves and what slavery meant for different groups is always a good discussion and a good test as to how much students understand about the complications of race, citizenship, and cultures.

For Native American history, I have used a teaching strategy of my colleague Fred Hoxie. Hoxie has students read the United Nations General Assembly Resolution adopted December 9, 1948, "Convention on the Prevention and Punishment of the Crime of Genocide." They then debate whether the U.S. treatment of Indians fits the definition of genocide as defined in Article 2. I also like my students to debate the meaning of "assimilation," as discussed in Wolfe's article.

I borrowed another successful teaching strategy from Heather Cox Richardson. In addition to any history textbook chapters on Andrew Jackson, Richardson has students read Jackson's veto of the Bank of the United States, his State of the Union address on the Cherokee removal, Ralph Waldo Emerson's protest of the Cherokee removal, and a selection from Black Hawk's autobiography.[3] Then Richardson asks the students: "Did Jackson truly represent the American people?" "Should the president do what those who elected him want, or does the president have an obligation to do what is right for everyone?" Richardson asks her students to think about the Inuit Circumpolar Conference's charge that the United States is violating their human rights by promoting global warming.[4] She asks them to imagine what Americans will think about the subject two hundred years from now. Anyone who teaches Indian removal realizes that it is easy for students to identify with Native Americans and condemn Jackson for the Indian removal. What Richardson wants her students to realize is that the United States makes similar decisions all the time and it is not just the president or Congress who is responsible, but all of us as a country. When students face the Inuit charge that we are destroying the Inuit culture because of our personal refusal to deal with global warming, students will recognize that we make similar decisions to Jackson's. I cannot think of a better way to teach about race and citizenship in a global context.

Wolfe proposes that the concept of race was created in the eighteenth century at the same time that ideas of citizenship and the nation-state were developing. One good teaching strategy is to ask the students which came first, racism or slavery. They usually come to see that whichever answer they choose defines and shapes a particular interpretation of race relations. Is racial prejudice the inherent and automatic reaction of European and African people meeting for the first time, or was it the system of slavery that wrought prejudice? In considering this dilemma, I found it particularly effective to have students read selections of Shakespeare's *Othello* and descriptions of Caliban, the creature in thrall to Prospero in *The Tempest*. I display an image from the fifteenth century that depicts the "Four Theaters of the Earth" with four women representing Europe, Asia, Africa, and America, and ask students to interpret how peoples from different parts of the world are imagined by Europeans.[5] I also like to use a section from Mark Twain's *The Adventures of Huckleberry Finn* where Huck decides to break the law and risk eternal damnation for his friend, the runaway slave, Jim.[6] I have students unpack the meaning of that wonderful passage and particularly how religion, as Huck was taught, reinforced an unjust law, and what logic of conscience enabled Huck to resist the law and the threat of hell.

For decades, the topic of race relations was taught through the dichotomy of blacks and whites. But as we become more aware of the many sides and forms of racism in our multiethnic society, this dichotomy no longer rings true. I have now found some success in asking students to define whiteness and white privilege.[7] I also distinguish between racism and what John Higham outlined in *Strangers in the Land* as "nativism," and how other ethnic groups struggled with the meaning of citizenship.[8] I have the students ponder why historians wrestling with these issues might have come up with the theories they did at a particular time.

For definitions of citizenship, I want students to examine the earliest documents so that they can begin to map out how ideas of belonging to a community developed in America. In 1619, African slaves were sold into the colony of Virginia. That same year Jamestown established a republican assembly, the

House of Burgess, one of the oldest law-making bodies in the world. From this beginning, the vote was central to liberty, self government, and citizenship, yet that vote and consequent representative citizenship sanctioned racial slavery.[9] Throughout my teaching on citizenship and race, I emphasize that the study of suffrage is central to understanding what constitutes citizenship and how race influences who has a meaningful vote. According to Wolfe, "Race restored the social inequality that citizenship had theoretically abolished." To verify or to refute this proposition, I encourage students to investigate early state constitutions. Students, working together in groups, discover why and how male citizens were denied voting rights unless they held property, an idea of freedom rooted in the political philosophy of the Founders. They will find that in 1800 no free state limited the right to vote on the basis of race. But every state that entered the Union after that year (except Maine) restricted suffrage to white males. This usually surprises students, and they want to find out why. The United States, said a delegate to the convention that disfranchised Pennsylvania's black population, was "a political community of white persons." In effect, race, which had not been an earlier factor in suffrage, became a boundary when property ceased as a requirement defining which American men were to enjoy political freedom. Again, my strategy is to relate it to today. Does property or wealth have any effect today on voting? On who might run for office?

As Wolfe explains, the federated form of government with state and federal definitions is crucial for defining race and citizenship and its complications and ambiguities. The Constitution is, of course, the central document for understanding citizenship. But I also make available for students at least two state constitutions, one from the North and one from the South, to see how the federated system defined citizenship and how a state could impede the citizenship of a minority group through the regulation of voting even when the federal Constitution guaranteed that citizenship.[10] An interesting way to continue this discussion in a global context would be to compare these definitions of race and citizenship with other constitutions. Students could be divided into groups to research the constitutions of South Africa (perhaps both the 1996 and 1983 constitutions), Australia, and Brazil. Students could also research issues of suffrage and racial policy.[11]

In teaching the first half of the survey course, I do not end the discussion of citizenship and race at the traditional breaking point of 1877, but rather with the legal retreat from the idealism of the Civil War when the Supreme Court affirmed legal segregation in *Plessy v. Ferguson* (1896). The Court found that segregation was legal as long as the separate facilities for blacks were not

234 · TEACHING CITIZENSHIP AND RACE

inferior to those for whites. This completed the process that Wolfe points out, "in bringing a form of freedom to black people, the ending of slavery also completed their racialization." Only one judge on the Supreme Court dissented from the majority opinion, Justice John Harlan, the son of a former North Carolina slaveholding family. And yet students are very surprised to read that he could not embrace the notion of equal citizenship without caveat.[12] We use Harlan's dissent to discuss and try to understand the exclusion of Asians from citizenship and the attempts to deter their immigration to the United States.

Wolfe challenges the conceived wisdom of history tests by examining their theoretical bases. He explains the importance of "social context," which is essential to historical analysis. The comparisons and contrasts in Wolfe's article give nuance to the construction of race and the inclusion in citizenship.

Notes

1. George Frederickson, *The Black Image in the White Mind: The Debate on Afro-American Character and Destiny, 1817–1914* (New York, 1971).

2. Eugene Genovese and Laura Foner, eds., *Slavery in the New World: A Reader in Comparative History* (Englewood Cliffs, N.J., 1969).

3. See <http://millercenter.virginia.edu/scripps/digitalarchive/speechDetail/42?PHPSESSID=594ed714206175cf07a546daa43bec70> (last accessed July 19, 2007); <http://www.presidentialrhetoric.com/historicspeeches/jackson/stateoftheunion1831.html> (last accessed July 19, 2007); <http://www.fordham.edu/halsall/mod/blackhawk.html> (last accessed July 19, 2007). David M. Robinson, ed., *The Political Emerson: Essential Writings on Politics and Social Reform* (Boston, 2004).

4. See <http://news.mongabay.com/2005/1208–icc.html> (last accessed July 22, 2007).

5. I also assign varying interpretations by well-respected historians such as Edmund Morgan's *American Slavery, American Freedom: The Ordeal of Colonial Virginia* (New York, 2003) and the arguments of Winthrop Jordan, *White Over Black: American Attitudes toward the Negro, 1550–1812* (Chapel Hill, N.C., 1968).

6. Mark Twain, *The Adventures of Huckleberry Finn* (New York, 1953).

7. I introduce some of the arguments of Thomas Holt, Frederick Cooper, and Rebecca Scott, *Beyond Slavery: Explorations of Race, Labor, and Citizenship in Postemancipation Societies* (Chapel Hill, N.C., 2000). Also, Barbara Fields, *Slavery and Freedom on the Middle Ground: Maryland during the Nineteenth Century* (New Haven, Conn., 1985) and the ideas of my colleague David Roediger on whiteness, such as *Colored White: Transcending the Racial Past* (Berkeley, Calif., 2002).

8. John Higham, *Strangers in the Land: Patterns of American Nativism, 1860–1925* (New Brunswick, N.J., 1955).

9. See <http://www.virtualjamestown.org/>.

10. Most state constitutions are available online at the official state Web site or at a state's official archive. Soon the Center for the Study of Democratic Governance at the University of Illinois, <http://www.csdg.uiuc.edu/>, will make available the constitutions of 177 countries. These constitutions will be completely searchable and a valuable resource for comparison of citizenship across countries.

11. These constitutions are available on the Internet: South Africa: <http://www .info.gov.za/documents/constitution/index.htm>; Brazil (in English): <http://www .v-brazil.com/government/laws/constitution.html>; Australia: <http://www.aph.gov .au/senate/general/constitution/> (last accessed July 24, 2007).

12. "There is a race so different from our own that we do not permit those belonging to it to become citizens of the United States. Persons belonging to it are, with few exceptions, absolutely excluded from our country. I allude to the Chinese race." <http://historymatters.gmu.edu/d/5484/> (last accessed July 22, 2007).

CHAPTER 12

Louis "Satchmo" Armstrong's European travels earned him the title of "Ambassador Satch" and inspired the U.S. State Department's jazz tours, which included Armstrong's 27-city tour of the African continent. (Library of Congress, Prints and Photographs Division, *New York World-Telegram & Sun Photograph Collection*, LC-USZ62-127236.)

GLOBALIZING POPULAR CULTURE IN THE "AMERICAN CENTURY" AND BEYOND

PENNY M. VON ESCHEN

In November 2005, the first monument to martial arts expert and film star Bruce Lee was unveiled in Mostar, Bosnia (one day before a second monument was displayed in Hong Kong). Honoring Lee as a symbol of "loyalty, skill, justice, and friendship," the organizers also intended the life-sized bronze statue as a "rebuke to the ongoing use of public spaces to glorify the country's competing nationalisms." As one of them put it, "the monument is an attempt to question symbols old and new, by mixing up high grandeur with mass culture and kung fu."[1] It was critical that Lee was neither Croatian, Serb, nor Muslim, and that his statue faced north, favoring neither east nor west in a city that had been divided and at war over such identities.

How might the commemoration of Bruce Lee in Bosnia help us think about globalization and popular culture? The historian Vijay Prashad has discussed the cultural significance of Lee for different audiences across multiple continents.[2] Lee was born in San Francisco in 1940, the child of Chinese

Opera stars. The family returned to Hong Kong in 1941, where Lee grew up under Japanese occupation and then British colonialism. Sent back to the United States for schooling, Lee emerged as a Hollywood phenomenon in the short-lived television series *The Green Hornet*. When studio executives, who could only imagine an Asian as a sidekick and not in a more powerful role, blocked his attempts to develop his own series, Lee returned to Hong Kong in 1971, where he made a series of martial arts films, including *The Chinese Connection* and *Enter the Dragon*. If Lee needed to escape the racist constraints of Hollywood to make his films, ironically, his worldwide fame depended on the circulation and distribution power of Hollywood, which released *Enter the Dragon* in 1973, one month after Lee's untimely death at the age of thirty-two.

I begin with the story of Bruce Lee because I think his career and status as a cultural icon illustrate the possibilities as well as the challenges of teaching the globalization of popular culture. Lee's career illuminates multiple global flows and helps us identify questions that are critical to inquiries into popular culture in a globalizing world. It also helps us to appreciate some of the most important developments among historians of culture and globalization. Historians have increasingly argued that globalization is a process that has profoundly shaped the development of U.S.-American culture. Bruce Lee's career was the product of globalization, beginning with the movements of people and capital across national borders during more than a century of Chinese immigration to the United States that created the audience as well as the economic infrastructure necessary for Lee's father's work with the Chinese Opera. As a result of Lee's influence in popularizing the study of martial arts in the United States, the number of American-born girls and boys in karate schools today may rival the numbers of children on baseball diamonds in the United States. It is clear that processes of globalization have transformed U.S.-American popular culture as much as the circulation of American culture—from its films and music, to Coca-Cola and baseball—has influenced peoples and nations outside the United States.

Cultural historians have insisted that popular culture never imposes a unitary meaning on audiences but is contested, recontextualized, and reinterpreted as it circulates in specific local, regional, and national contexts.[3] Much of the earlier literature on the global circulation of American popular culture had taken for granted that its impact made the rest of the world more like the United States. But despite the extraordinary power of U.S. culture industries and the U.S. state and economy throughout the twentieth century—and especially in the post-1945 period on which this essay focuses—the production, circulation, and reception of American culture abroad cannot be reduced to a notion of "Americanization." Though Hollywood gave Bruce Lee an audience far larger than the Hong Kong film industry could have provided in the 1970s, the U.S. film industry could not dictate how audiences perceived Lee. Released in the context of the war in Vietnam and continuing third world struggles for liberation in Asia, Africa, and Latin America, the films turned Lee into an instant icon of rebellion against Western and Soviet domination. For audiences from Calcutta to Los Angeles and Hong Kong to New York, Lee embodied antiracist and anti-imperialist yearnings.[4]

In "American Empire and Cultural Imperialism: A View From the Receiving End," historian Rob Kroes argues that European consumers of American culture have not only cracked and appropriated American codes, but that in the circulation of mass culture, "the very slogans chosen by sales departments" are "semantically unstable" and may well carry a message different from that intended. The message of "Freedom of Choice" can be powerfully inverted to read as "choice of freedom," turning advertising strategies into a "civics lesson" with an antiauthoritarian call. American consumer culture is therefore reinterpreted and recontextualized by various audiences as they explore rebellion against parental authority and pursue a vision of personal freedom through consumption and sexual expression.[5] Moreover, Kroes points out, apparel produced in Europe that might be read as symbols of American culture, such as a New York Giants T-shirt and even clothes sporting brand names, signifies membership in an international youth culture indifferent to claims of "authenticity" that would mark these symbols as "American."[6] Indeed, the global popularity of Japanese anime and the ubiquitous Pokémon underscore the limitations in reading popular culture from a vantage point of "Americanization."[7]

What historian Victoria de Grazia usefully sums up as "the mass-produced, classically narrated feature film mainly fashioned in the giant studio systems of southern California" is an excellent topic for exploring tensions between "Americanization" and processes of globalization. Hollywood can be productively viewed as the quintessential mass culture industry, fundamentally shaped by globalization, from its shared origins in the mass production/ mass consumption Fordist economy, to its far-flung global circulation and the waning of the studio system that by the late 1960s allowed Bruce Lee to emerge as a new kind of star through the "lesser" medium of television. In *Irresistible Empire: America's Advance Through Twentieth-Century Europe*, de Grazia argues that "no American industry was more self-consciously rivalrous about its role in shaping international cultural trends, none more engaged in reaching out, responding to, and shaping consumer tastes abroad, none more aggressive in taking on the barriers and obstacles to its installation in other societies."[8] As Hollywood "communicated in the language of a new vernacular, one that was visual, animated, and eventually spoken as well, the American cinema trespassed the hard-bound lines that in Europe still divided the high and academic from popular and mass cultures." With the American film industry posing as the purveyor of "universal" values, it in fact engendered complex and intense economic and cultural competition as French, German, and Italian filmmakers responded with the creation of self-consciously national film industries. If de Grazia's sensitive exploration of these dynamics ultimately emphasizes the economic triumph of the U.S. industries, reminding us that at the turn of the twentieth century, Hollywood's market share of European film receipts was 80 to 90 percent, the historian Richard Pells has interestingly inverted the Americanization thesis. In "Is American Culture American?" Pells argues that if Hollywood became the cultural capital of the twentieth century, it was a cosmopolitan rather than exclusively American capital. Like other cultural capitals, argues Pells, "Hollywood has functioned as an international community, built by immigrant entrepreneurs and drawing on the talents of actors, directors, writers, cinematographers, editors, composers, and costume designers from all over the world." American directors in every era sought to emulate foreign directors. To cite just one example of artistic influences, the postwar American style of reliance on physical mannerism and silence in interpreting a role— exemplified by the brooding introspection of Marlon Brando—was based on an acting technique studied by Brando called "The Method," which Pells explains was "originally developed in Stanislavsky's Moscow Art Theatre in pre-revolutionary Russia."[9]

For Pells, the universalizing pretensions of Hollywood, and especially its focus on intimate emotions rather than political events, were key to its success. Along with the economic power of U.S. capitalism, the heterogeneity of the U.S. population forced the media to experiment with images and story lines that had broad appeal. This, along with American media success at "transcending internal social divisions, national borders and language barriers" by mixing up "high" and "low" cultural styles, has enhanced its appeal in an international as well as domestic context.[10] Other scholars have importantly drawn our attention to the gender and racial hierarchies masked by such universalizing claims. Christina Klein has discussed musicals such as Rodgers and Hammerstein's *South Pacific* and *The King and I* as an integral part of an outward-looking, open, popular internationalism that sought to

mobilize citizens during the Cold War. Reflected in such government programs as people-to-people exchanges as well as in middlebrow mass media
from magazines to films and novels, this emphasis on positive global connections as distinct from the ominous preoccupation with containment was
critical in forging domestic support for the ambitious global agendas of the
American century. Such musicals promoted a global vision of economic and
racial integration where "undeveloped" peoples could be integrated into the
world order on American terms, and invariably portrayed Asians as backward
and in need of superior American tutelage.[11]

Pells has further suggested that many discussions of Americanization and
globalization conflate the two terms or simplistically identify globalization
with Americanization. This is an important point for students to engage,
and his discussion of Hollywood as fundamentally shaped by globalization
offers an accessible route into these questions. Nonetheless, this vexing issue of Americanization or globalization still needs to acknowledge recurrent
charges of cultural imperialism and assertions of anti-Americanism from
around the globe, charges that certainly cannot be reduced to confusion over
Americanization and globalization. In large part, the difficulty of analytically
and historically separating these terms arises from the tangled relationships
between the culture industries and the ascendance of the United States as
an economic, cultural, and military power over the course of the twentieth
century. Well before U.S. dominance was consolidated in the aftermath of
World War II, the distinctions between globalization and Americanization
have often indeed been fuzzy, for those on the producing as well as receiving ends. From the Wilsonian legislation that freed Hollywood industries,
along with banks and other corporations, from Progressive Era restrictions
with the explicit intent of providing U.S. industries with a competitive global
advantage, to the postwar circulation of Coca-Cola, Hollywood, and comic
books, many peoples of the globe have encountered what we commonly
think of as "private industry" in the context of U.S. economic dominance,
U.S. state sponsorship, and/or through overt military presence. Drawing on
the important insights of historian Bruce Cumings about the U.S. "Archi-
pelago Empire," characterized by military bases throughout the Pacific, we
can note that such bases were one of the major vehicles for the circulation
of U.S.-American culture. In the post-1945 world, many Asians and Pacific
Islanders encountered rock 'n' roll music, Coca-Cola, and U.S. comic books
for the first time in and around U.S. bases.

In his exploration of transnational cooperation between Mexican and U.S.
political elites that characterized postwar mass-cultural programs, Seth Fein

has further demonstrated not only extensive U.S. government censorship in the making of films, but also its work with Disney and its involvement in film production in attempts to shape U.S. relations with Mexico and Latin America. In film as well as in printed material, U.S. officials believed that cartoons were the most effective way of communicating.[12] The ubiquity of Disney and Warner Brothers characters throughout Mexico and Latin America inspired the classic critique of cultural imperialism: Ariel Dorfman's and Armand Mattelart's *How to Read Donald Duck.* The authors explore the subtle ways in which the comic advocates adherence to the U.S. economic system and capitalist values and work ethic.[13] More recently, essays such as Fein's in the collection *Close Encounters of Empire,* like scholarship noted above, have questioned the one-way imposition of U.S.-American messages, focusing the interactions and Latin American agency and meaning-making in what were undeniably powerful attempts on the part of U.S. corporations to assert economic control and cultural influence.

In examining the circulation of U.S.-American culture, we are inevitably examining power relations, and it is critical that we constantly work to disaggregate the terms "America" and "American" in order to empower students to ask questions about the complexity and contradictions in the circulation of U.S. culture. If the spread of U.S.-American film, music, comics, and many consumer products was connected to U.S. economic dominance, wars, and permanent and long-standing military bases, by no means were such cultural productions and artifacts part of a unitary corporate, military, or state project. It is important to appreciate the various and sundry ways that U.S.-American culture has circulated through the globe: from Hollywood films to military bases, from State Department jazz tours and recording industries to the Coke-Pepsi wars and boxing. We also need to pay careful attention to the *multiplicity* of cultural productions and projects originating within the United States. Emphasizing the multiplicity of these projects reminds us that U.S.-American global ambition was not orchestrated or masterminded by any one group of people but was shaped by multiple and often contradictory interests, from the State Department and the Pentagon to corporations such as Coca-Cola, IBM, and General Motors, to missionaries, NGOs, Hollywood, and artists. At times the interests of any number of global actors coincided, such as during World War II when the U.S. Army gave the Coca-Cola Corporation privileged access to war and occupation zones. At other moments, interests could clash. Nonetheless, from Coca-Cola's ambition to dominate the world soft-drink market to corporate-state insistence on controlling access to resources—from oil to uranium to the numerous minerals critical for products ranging from refrigerators to vacuum cleaners, jet engines, and the material technologies of radio and film—many U.S.-American actors approached their endeavors with the unabashed intent to dominate markets and access to resources, leading to myriad charges of cultural imperialism and many reactions, such as the Coca-Cola wars of 1950 when France and Italy made concerted efforts to block the importation of Coke.

Careful attention to questions of periodization in the study of popular culture and globalization is critical if we are to untangle these issues. As in the case of film, national competition in culture industries was hardly new during the Cold War years. Yet the period beginning in the immediate aftermath of the Second World War was characterized by a powerful and competitive marking of national cultures as the United States and the Soviet Union engaged in Cold War competition over the political allegiances and resources of peoples emerging from decades of colonialism. For Time-Life owner Henry Luce and his allies, the end of World War II ushered in the "American century," when American values, culture, and consumer products would peacefully conquer the world. As the U.S. government and U.S. corporations stepped into the vacuums of power left in the vast areas of the globe that had been occupied by Germany and Japan, European colonialism collapsed in the aftermath of the war. Between 1945 and 1960, forty new nation-states emerged. As the Soviet Union sent classical orchestras and ballet companies around the world, along with emphasizing folk productions, and the United States responded with jazz, dance, and a dazzling array of other cultural forms, the development of cultural industries and the circulation of culture was part and parcel of the Cold War battle. The United States Information Agency produced and distributed films, radio programs, and vast numbers of pamphlets and news releases aimed at showing the world the superiority of the American way of life and American democracy.[14] The U.S. government even distributed transistor radios so that audiences without previous access to this technology could tune in to Voice of America and Radio Free Europe. By 1955, Voice of America brought American music and culture to an estimated thirty million people in more than eighty countries. In the next decade, this number would triple. The State Department sponsored cultural presentations involving a multitude of artists, running the gamut from jazz musicians Louis Armstrong, Duke Ellington, and Dizzy Gillespie, to dancers and choreographers Martha Graham, Alvin Ailey, and Paul Taylor, to the Cleveland Orchestra and high school marching bands, and finally to rhythm and blues and soul groups.[15] American athletes were also featured in State Department tours, and the Olympics took on the character of fierce

Cold War national competitions. Frances Stonor Saunders has demonstrated the highly porous nature of state and private boundaries by tracing the remarkable scope of CIA funding of cultural institutions from the Museum of Modern Art to radio, newspapers, and the motion picture industry.[16]

Through such private initiatives and government-industry collaboration, Cold War cultural competition was influential in the development of cultural industries such as film and music for more than two decades. In the case of jazz and the cultural presentation programs, state sponsorship brought performing artists to places that would not have been logistically viable or commercially profitable. Yet, these efforts had multiple unintended consequences. Not only did musicians bring their own agendas, from promoting civil rights and challenging State Department priorities, but their desire to connect with musicians in other countries and learn new musical styles also promoted a globalization of popular music that destabilized the purported distinctiveness of national cultures promoted by governments in this era. By the mid-1960s, the U.S. emphasis on jazz and other modernist expressions as "high art" over what they disparagingly labeled "entertainment" dissolved with the belated recognition that just as rock music had captivated youth cultures throughout the United States and Europe, rhythm and blues and soul were now immensely popular as well. Responding to the demands of youth audiences from Africa and the Eastern bloc, the State Department sent blues musicians such as Buddy Guy and Junior Wells and the jazz-inflected rock group Blood, Sweat, and Tears abroad. By the early 1970s, U.S. officials were requesting the Jackson Five and other soul groups.

Despite the government's embrace of popular culture, by the early 1970s in increasingly concentrated and commercialized culture industries, the distribution and circulation of popular culture, like the broader economy, was breaking loose from dependence on the nation-state. Nineteen seventy-eight, the last year of State Department sponsorship of cultural presentation (until its revival in 2002 in the aftermath of the terrorist attacks on September 11, 2001), witnessed the first of the now annual Jazz Yatra festivals in Bombay, India, underlining the fact that a music born of histories of slavery, colonialism, and exclusion, and based on improvisation, could not be owned by one nation.[17]

We can usefully distinguish between the immediate post-1945 period as the high point of shared interests between U.S. corporations, cultural industries, and the federal government, and much longer processes of globalization. The epochal shift in the global political economy that was marked by a breaking away of civil society from state control and regulation became manifest around the time of the 1973 energy crisis. By the end of the 1980s, with the collapse of the Berlin Wall and the Soviet Union removing yet another barrier to the flow of capital and migrants, to many it appeared that we lived in a globalized world symbolized by the transnational corporation as well as hybrid, transnational cultural productions.[18]

If manifestations of economic crisis in the 1970s and an awareness of the mobility of transnational capital appeared sudden, it was in part because the Cold War era's national competitions had obscured longer-term processes of globalization. Rather than searching for neat causal connections in these shifts, we would do well to develop questions and frameworks that allow us to trace the evolving relationships between nation-states, culture industries, and a transnational and globalizing political economy. To understand the circulation of U.S.-American culture/power throughout the globe and its effects, it is useful to highlight the ways in which divergent interests can forge alliances. For example, a corporation that at one moment may depend on the financial and military infrastructure of the U.S. government for the circulation of its products, and therefore, like Coca-Cola in the 1940s and 1950s, appears to move in tandem with the nation-state, may later come into conflict with U.S. wage, health, or environmental laws, and attempt to locate important parts of its operations outside of regulation by the federal government. This is critical in tracing the processes through which genres, products, and corporations once viewed as quintessentially American become "global" and "transnational."

In a further reminder to complicate the term "American" and to emphasize that culture is always reinterpreted by audiences, the historian Reinhold Wagnleitner has argued that it was often oppositional elements in American culture, and particularly those of African American culture, that proved most appealing to various overseas audiences.[19] Not only did jazz and rock 'n' roll foster an anticommunist counterculture in the Eastern bloc as well as western Europe, it was a counterculture that identified as much with black oppositional culture as with the government's ideas of democracy. Uta Poiger, in *Jazz, Rock and Rebels: Cold War Politics and American Culture in a Divided Germany,* has explored German adolescents' adoption of such American icons as Marlon Brando and Elvis Presley, and argued that consumer culture became a stimulus for rebellion as well as the critical delineation between the East and the West.[20]

In Africa, the Caribbean, and Brazil, the dynamics that fused political and aesthetic inspirations were perhaps even more pronounced, through a reciprocal process by which jazz, soul, and rhythm and blues inspired emerging

African popular music styles that, in turn, inspired American musicians.[21] Michael Veal, the biographer of Nigerian musician Fela, argues that Afrobeat, which Fela considered "the progressive music of the future," had grown out of a jazz-soul-highlife fusion "reconciled through modal harmonies found in traditional Yoruba genres." Fela had been influenced politically and musically by black Americans during an extended stay in Los Angeles and was further inspired by James Brown's 1970 tour of West Africa. But if Brown clearly inspired Fela, it was also clear that the influence was mutual.[22] The reverberations of inspiration and influence among Afro-diasporic musicians were extensive from the 1950s through the 1980s and continue today. Ghanaian percussionist and composer Guy Warren was inspired by modern jazz icons such as Charlie Parker. Bob Marley and other Jamaican artists were inspired by such African American soul musicians as Curtis Mayfield and Billy Stewart, and the Afro-Brazilian singer/songwriter Gilberto Gil was deeply influenced by such Jamaican musicians as Marley and Jimmy Cliff. Many American jazz musicians were influenced by Brazilian music, particularly the compositions of Antonio Carlos Jobim. And the universal and proliferating impact of hip hop and techno music, both intensely eclectic and hybrid forms, provides more recent evidence of the reciprocity in the creation and circulation of popular music.

Bruce Lee's example makes clear that though audiences interpret popular culture in their own image, it is also produced, distributed, and consumed in unequal and hierarchical relations of power. Over the past decade, historians have paid careful attention to struggles over conditions of cultural creation and production, as well as the question of who profits from popular culture, insisting that such inquiries are central to explorations of globalization and popular culture. In *Dangerous Crossroads,* historian George Lipsitz celebrates the creativity of transnational and transethnic cultural productions while also warning about the dangers of exploitation in such encounters. In "Strategic Anti-Essentialism in Popular Music," he acknowledges that Paul Simon's cross-cultural collaboration with South African musicians in *Graceland* and David Byrne's salsa- and samba-oriented *Rei Momo* brought "much needed and deserved attention" to neglected musical forms. But these collaborations did not "effectively illuminate power relations between Western artists and their sources of illumination from the third world." For Lipsitz, "the ways in which market imperatives shape the contours of the music that gets recorded and distributed internationally" must remain in the foreground of our inquiries.[23] Lipsitz further argues that "in its most utopian moments, popular culture offers a promise of reconciliation to groups divided by differences in power, opportunity and experience." Though popular culture can also exacerbate divisions and inequalities, and people sometimes "do violence to others by stealing stories and appropriating ideas, . . . they also display a remarkable ability to find and invent the cultural symbols that they need."[24]

Indeed, much of the most compelling work on globalization and popular culture has examined the hybridization of popular cultural forms. In *Global Pop: World Music, World Markets,* Timothy D. Taylor, examines the marketing category of "World Music," contending that the rubric constructs a normative center and exotic margin. Such cross-cultural impresarios as Paul Simon, Peter Gabriel, and other Western musicians who collaborate with musicians from other parts of the globe are never described as "hybrid" and never asked to defend their "authenticity," but are labeled as "rock," the most prestigious of categories.[25] Taylor also explores the work of musicians in numerous locations around the globe, including the popular Indonesian musician Rhoma Irama, who turned away from Western pop and rock in favor of Melayu music, a genre of Western/Arabic/Indian-influenced popular music, before envisioning a new musical style based on the criteria that it had to be "popular with Indonesians of different classes and backgrounds; it had to be modern, it had to be intelligible to young people everywhere; and it mustn't bear too close a relationship to western styles." Taylor also considers the complexity of resistance in the music of Djur Djura, a Kabyle (an Algerian Berber) "who takes feminist ideas to make powerful statements against patriarchy in Algeria, using music and musical sounds from all over."[26]

I conclude with Bruce Lee because, like inquiries into popular music and film, research into his role in popular culture demonstrates the ways in which explorations of globalization and popular culture are especially productive for bringing students into classrooms as knowledge producers. A quick Google search of Bruce Lee and Bosnia identifies pages of reports originating in multiple countries, thus allowing students to take up questions about the multiple meanings of Lee and how he is interpreted in different contexts. Newspapers and film journals available in online archives allow students to compare reviews of Lee's films at the time of their release in different national, regional, and local contexts. In any classroom, students will inevitably bring more knowledge about a variety of forms of contemporary popular culture than any of us do. Now, with readily available if limited access to sources from the Web and through libraries, students not only become our collaborators in knowledge production but also, through tracing the histories of even the most contemporary forms, they become historians.

Bibliographical Essay

Michael Denning's *Culture in the Age of Three Worlds* (London, 2004) offers a useful unpacking of the terms "globalization" and "culture" as well as an overview of various theoretical approaches to the concepts. While the text is too theoretical for a survey class, Denning does offer highly useful reflections on pedagogy. On page 24 he suggests three key issues for productive debate among students on global flows (worldwide distribution and reception of some cultural industry practices, the emergence of hybrid popular forms, and questions of commodification, cooptation, and resistance). He also discusses a productive class activity in which he asks students to make a list of the most valuable cultural texts since 1945. See page 31. However absurd and unanswerable, this opens up valuable discussions about processes of globalization.

George Yúdice's *The Expediency of Culture: Uses of Culture in the Global Era* (Durham, N.C., 2003) offers another important and ambitious attempt to theorize the changing role of culture in a globalizing world. Like Denning, the arguments are for the most part too complex for an introductory survey, but parts could be effectively excerpted. See, for example, chapter 4, "The Funkification of Rio," which considers the place of youth in social movements and funk music and dance as a way of dealing with racism and social exclusion. Chapter 7, "The Globalization of Latin America: Miami," offers an excellent introduction to the complexity of cultural production and performance in a global city, discussing Miami as a center for "the fusion of dance and house musics, especially the Latinization of disco, funk, rap and jungle," and demonstrating that a global corporation like MTV seeks local relevance and not homogenization. These sections could be usefully paired with the works of Timothy Taylor and George Lipsitz cited in the text, as well as Rob Nixon's wonderful *Homelands, Harlem and Hollywood: South African Culture and the World Beyond* (New York, 1994).

For work on the earlier circulation of jazz and African American culture, see Brent Hayes Edwards, *The Practice of Diaspora: Literature, Translation, and the Rise of Black Internationalism* (Cambridge, Mass., 2003). Edwards argues that developments in Paris cannot be understood as parallel to or a version of the Harlem Renaissance; rather they provided an alternative site that in turn affected developments in Harlem. See also, William A. Shack, *Harlem in Montmartre: A Paris Jazz Story Between the Great Wars* (Berkeley, Calif., 2001). On swing music and USO tours during World War II, see Sherrie Tucker, *Swing Shift: All-Girl Bands of the 1940s* (Durham, N.C., 2000), especially pages 227–58; and David W. Stowe, *Swing Changes: Big-Band Jazz in New Deal America* (Cambridge, Mass., 1994), especially pages 149–50, 157, and 159.

In addition to Victoria de Grazia's chapter on Hollywood discussed in the body of the essay, *Irresistible Empire* probes a range of topics from advertising to the transformation of the European food industry and the emergence of the Slow Food movement in Italy. Her Web site <http://www.columbia.edu/~vd19/irresistible_empire/gallery/

html> has a wonderful visual archive to accompany the book that allows students to analyze advertising and other manifestations of the changing European landscape.

Reinhold Wagnleitner and Elaine Tyler May's edited work, *Here, There, and Everywhere: The Foreign Politics of American Culture* (Hanover, N.H., 2000) is a collaboration between international scholars working on American culture and U.S.-based scholars. Numerous accessible essays allow students to enter debates about globalization and American culture through the lens of Europeans, Asians, and Africans. Many chapters engage debates on cultural imperialism and anti-Americanism and/or debates on creative reinterpretations of American popular culture abroad. I note several below to give a sense of the range of possibilities in both genre and geography: Aurora Bosch and M. Fernanda del Rincón, "Dreams in a Dictatorship: Hollywood and Franco's Spain, 1939–1956"; Giuliana Muscio, "Invasion and Counterattack: Italian and American Film Relations in the Postwar Period"; Nosa Owens-Ibie, "Programmed for Domination: U.S. Television Broadcasting and Its Effects on Nigerian Culture"; Christoph Ribbat, "How Hip Hop Hit Heidelberg: German Rappers, Rhymes, and Rhythms"; Masako Notoji, "Cultural Transformations of John Philip Sousa and Disneyland in Japan"; Gülriz Büken, "Backlash: An Argument against the Spread of American Popular Culture in Turkey." See also Carol Silverman's "'Move Over Madonna': Gender Representation and the 'Mystery' of Bulgarian Voices," in Sibelan Forrester et al., eds., *Over the Wall/After the Fall: Post-Communist Cultures Through an East-West Gaze* (Bloomington, Ind., 2004).

In addition to the discussions of the reception of film in the May and Wagnleitner collection, see Eric Smoodin, *Regarding Frank Capra: Audience, Celebrity, and American Film Studies, 1930–1960* (Durham, N.C., 2004). On celebrity and mass culture, see also S. Paige Baty's book on images of Marilyn Monroe, *American Monroe: The Making of a Body Politic* (Berkeley, Calif., 1995).

Mike Marqusee's *Redemption Song: Muhammad Ali and the Spirit of the Sixties,* (London and New York, 1999) offers a highly accessible portrayal of the career of Muhammad Ali in a global as well as broad political context. See especially chapter 4, "Beyond the Confines of America." The excellent global context provides students with background enabling them to read online and archival newspaper coverage of Ali in sources from multiple locations, including West African and British sources. Even in the most introductory survey, a short assignment involving online research from multiple international sources can be a powerful illustration of the benefits of reading American culture "from the outside in." An examination of the circulation of Muhammad Ali as a cultural and political icon can be usefully paired with a discussion of Michael Jordan's circulation as a symbol of Nike and corporate capitalism. See, Walter LaFeber's highly accessible *Michael Jordan and the New Global Capitalism* (New York, 1999).

Notes

1. Alexander Zaitchik, "Mostar's Little Dragon: How Bruce Lee Became a Symbol of Peace in the Balkans," *Reason Online*, April 2006, <http://www.reason.com/0604/cr.az.mostars.shtml>. I thank Gary Reichard, Rob Kroes, an anonymous reader, Judith Jackson Fossett, and Kevin Gaines for useful comments and suggestions.

2. Vijay Prashad, "Bruce Lee and the Anti-imperialism of Kung Fu: A Polycultural Adventure," *Positions: East Asia Cultures Critique*, 11 (Spring 2003): 51–90. See also Prashad, *Everybody Was Kung Fu Fighting: Afro-Asian Connections and the Myth of Cultural Purity* (Boston, 2001).

3. Reinhold Wagnleitner, "The Empire of Fun, or Talkin' Soviet Union Blues: The Sound of Freedom and U.S. Cultural Hegemony in Europe," *Diplomatic History*, 23 (Summer 1999): 499–524.

4. Prashad, "Bruce Lee and the Anti-imperialism of Kung Fu."

5. Rob Kroes, "American Empire and Cultural Imperialism: A View From the Receiving End," in Thomas Bender, ed., *Rethinking American History in a Global Age* (Berkeley, Calif., 2002), 295–313.

6. Ibid.

7. Joseph Tobin, ed., *Pikachu's Global Adventure: The Rise and Fall of Pokémon* (Durham, N.C., 2004).

8. Victoria de Grazia, *Irresistible Empire: America's Advance Through Twentieth-Century Europe* (Cambridge, Mass., 2005), 288.

9. Richard Pells, "Is American Culture American?" eJournal USA, February 2006, <http://usinfo.state.gov/journals/itgic/0206/ijge/pells.htm>. See also Pells, *Not Like Us: How Europeans Have Loved, Hated, and Transformed American Culture Since World War II*, reprint (New York, 1998).

10. Ibid.

11. Christina Klein, *Cold War Orientalism: Asia in the Middlebrow Imagination, 1945–1961* (Berkeley, Calif., 2003).

12. Seth Fein, "Everyday Forms of Transnational Collaboration: U.S. Film Propaganda in Cold War Mexico," in Gilbert M. Joseph, Catherine C. LeGrand, and Ricardo D. Salvatore, eds., *Close Encounters of Empire: Writing the Cultural History of U.S.–Latin American Relations* (Durham, N.C., 1998).

13. Ariel Dorfman and Armand Mattelart, *How to Read Donald Duck: Imperialist Ideology in the Disney Comic*, 2nd ed. (New York, 1984).

14. Mary L. Dudziak, *Cold War Civil Rights: Race and the Image of American Democracy* (Princeton, N.J., 2002).

15. Penny M. Von Eschen, *Satchmo Blows Up the World: Jazz Ambassadors Play the Cold War* (Cambridge, Mass., 2004).

16. Frances Stonor Saunders, *The Cultural Cold War: The CIA and the World of Arts and Letters* (New York, 2000).

17. Von Eschen, *Satchmo Blows Up the World*, chapters 7–8.

18. Charles Bright and Michael Geyer, "Where in the World is America?" in Bender, *Rethinking American History in a Global Age,* 63–99.

19. Wagnleitner, "The Empire of Fun, or Talkin' Soviet Union Blues."

20. Uta G. Poiger, *Jazz, Rock and Rebels: Cold War Politics and American Culture in a Divided Germany* (Berkeley, Calif., 2000).

21. Von Eschen, *Satchmo Blows Up the World.*

22. Michael E. Veal, *Fela: The Life and Times of an African Musical Icon* (Philadelphia, 2000).

23. George Lipsitz, *Dangerous Crossroads: Popular Music, Modernism and the Poetics of Place* (London, 1994), 60–61.

24. Ibid., 169.

25. Timothy D. Taylor, *Global Pop: World Music, World Markets* (New York, 1997), 201.

26. Ibid., 82–83, 88.

TEACHING THE GLOBALIZATION OF AMERICAN POPULAR CULTURE IN THE TWENTIETH CENTURY

LAWRENCE CHARAP

Penny von Eschen's essay reminded me of my own first experience discovering the striking effects that U.S. popular culture can have on parts of the world that most Americans rarely think about. In the early 1990s, while on an archeological dig in southern Moravia, I witnessed a peculiar ritual engaged in by the residents of the small town near the site. Every afternoon around 5:30 they gathered around a television in a local pub. The object of their fascination? A half-hour animated TV show from America: Disney's *Duck Tales*.

Students of U.S. history in particular need to be aware of the power that "American" popular culture can have beyond our borders. One of the most significant characteristics of our own time and place in the early twenty-first-century United States is the way that popular culture envelops us, infusing our lives with meanings and providing common points of reference in interpersonal interactions. Yet the ubiquity of popular culture means that the majority of us, and especially our students, have difficulty seeing it as an independent subject of inquiry. Like Disney's *Duck Tales,* popular culture is ubiquitous and banal, omnipresent and yet somehow beneath our radar as a subject for historical study.

Cultural theorists like those discussed by Von Eschen remind us of the power of culture by showing how members of other societies have taken American popular culture and used it in myriad ways, often with unintended consequences. In many places around the world, both modernity and its resulting tensions seem to be epitomized by the values enshrined in American popular culture. Students of U.S. history who understand the United States' role in the world must become aware of how something they take for granted has had a powerful and transformative effect elsewhere in the world.

TEACHING STRATEGIES

Short of taking students to a village in southern Moravia, making them realize the potential meanings within popular culture is a difficult undertaking. Von Eschen, by focusing on the reception of Western popular culture elsewhere in the world, suggests only a few places of convergence with the U.S. history survey. Moreover, the complexity and nuance involved in theoretical discussions of cultural and intellectual history are hard to handle in a survey course with even the most advanced students.

For discussions of this sort to occur, the survey course must have a strong emphasis on cultural history from the outset. Students must be exposed to many examples of visual, textual, and musical culture and asked to analyze them for both overt and implicit meanings. An appreciation for period culture and the arts provides teachers with concrete examples of what the familiar political and social events we teach *mean* to historical actors.

A second prerequisite is a strong global approach to U.S. history in the eighteenth and nineteenth century of the sort suggested by the other essays in this volume. Von Eschen's essay suggests that we emphasize the mutual influences of American and world culture on one another at any particular time. Students must see how American ideals and actions, and the idea of America itself, had profound effects on the rest of the world in the eighteenth and nineteenth centuries. They also need to appreciate in turn how the term *culture* itself connoted an exposure to aesthetic and intellectual values of the rest of the world, particularly Europe, for most of that time. For example, the idea of America as embodying progress and technological change, a theme in early twentieth-century European art, itself influenced American artists in the 1910s and 1920s, as avant-garde American writers and authors, in places as diverse as Paris and Harlem, saw their revolt against American Gilded Age values as being in part an adoption of non-American aesthetic styles, movements, and ideas.

While undoubtedly challenging for teachers, an emphasis on global events and global culture can open up students to international and comparative dimensions on U.S. history. It also allows teachers to understand foreign relations as having a crucial cultural component, a topic of increasing interest in current historical scholarship on war and diplomacy. These can produce rich rewards in student understanding by the end of the course. The two teaching strategies that follow are intended to present the complicated, recursive interplay between American popular culture and perceptions of the United States by the rest of the world in the twentieth century.

1. THE COLD WAR AND GLOBAL AMERICANISM

Von Eschen's article discusses the ironies of American efforts to propagandize against communism in the "third world" during the Cold War. The CIA, the U.S. State Department, and other U.S. agencies viewed culture as a major front in the battle with communism worldwide. Critically, these agencies sponsored activities that were not propaganda in the ordinary sense of the term. Recognizing that American artistic and intellectual expressions were sources of fascination elsewhere around the world, American bureaucrats created literary magazines and sent jazz and rock musicians on goodwill tours to Africa, Asia, and the Middle East. American musicians often had their own purposes in making such trips, which helped to lay the groundwork for a new fusion of global musical styles.

How can we explore this dimension of the Cold War in our classroom? Students should understand that the Cold War involved more than diplomatic and military moves, but was based in deep-seated political, cultural, and intellectual justifications of the American way of life—at a time when that way of life was changing profoundly. The idea that America represented modernity and progress can easily be found in American domestic political and advertising rhetoric. It also became a key part in rhetorical anticommunism at moments when American and Soviet ways of life were directly contrasted, most memorably at the 1959 "Kitchen Debate" between Vice President Richard Nixon and Soviet premier Nikita Khrushchev. (A transcript of the debate can be found at <http://www.teachingamericanhistory .org/library/index.asp?document=176> and a brief video of the exchange is currently available at <http://www.youtube.com>.)

As part of the discussion of American social and cultural change dur-ing the 1950s, students should be asked how these exhortations to prog-ress might appear to non-Western viewers of American culture. Students should also appreciate, for example, the hilarious 1956 short film "Design for Dreaming" by General Motors, viewable in its entirety at <http://www.archive.org/details/Designfo1956>. Many examples of 1950s print advertis-ing can be found online, including Ad*Access at <http://scriptorium.lib.duke.edu/adaccess/browse.html>. A guided or "jigsaw" activity leading students through these sources, such as the excellent one at <http://eprentice.sdsu.edu/F02X1/rtirsbier/webquest/student_template/s-webquest.htm> can be adapted to ask the following questions:

- How did advertisers present modernity and progress as American values?
- How might you feel about these advertisements if you came from a country in the Soviet bloc? In the developing world? What would these ads tell you about American values and expectations?
- Would the defense of Soviet values as an alternative to American cap-italism, such as the one put forward by Khrushchev in the "Kitchen Debate," be effective against these types of advertising?

Both advertising and propaganda attempt direct persuasion of their consum-ers, unlike the goodwill tours described by Von Eschen, whose messages were more open-ended. To make this point effectively with students, it would be helpful to provide examples of direct U.S. propaganda efforts in the Cold War. The National Security Archive has an excellent online "briefing book," *U.S. Propaganda in the Middle East—The Early Cold War Version,* edited by Joyce Battle, that contains more than a hundred declassified State Department documents with detailed descriptions of U.S. propaganda in Iran, Iraq, and Saudi Arabia in the early 1950s (<http://www.gwu.edu/~nsarchiv/NSAEBB/NSAEBB78/essay.htm>). Among the most useful examples are Document 20, a nine-page memorandum from 1953 describing American films, leaflets, and cartoons distributed in Iran (in violation of Iranian law) and Document 62, a 1952 U.S. Embassy dispatch describing propaganda goals and efforts in Iraq. The NSA essay discusses how the governments of both Iraq and Iran initially cooperated with anticommunist propaganda but had begun to di-verge from U.S. approaches by 1954.

Students should be encouraged to place these propaganda efforts into context with Middle East events: the independence of the state of Israel and first Arab-Israeli war in 1948–1949; the continuation in power of the pro-Western Hashemite monarchy in Iraq during these years; and the CIA-sponsored August 1953 coup that overthrew Mohammed Mossadegh's government in Iran. Such contextualization can make students aware of the many ironies inherent in the era's anticommunist propaganda efforts. A two-page Baghdad embassy communiqué from 1954 (Document 120) describes Iraqi government anticommunist propaganda as relying heavily on anti-Semitic and anti-Israel components. Here we see at work an anticommunist effort whose likely outcome could hardly be seen as benefiting friendship toward westerners or Americans in the long run.

After prereading and assigning different groups of students to read documents from different places, reassemble and have the following guided discussion:

- What seems to be the most important "message" that propaganda recipients are meant to take from these propaganda efforts? Is the United States strong, weak, good, moral, modern, etc.? Is the focus more on promoting Western values or on attacking communism?
- What do the documents tell you about underlying U.S. goals with propaganda? Do short-term goals and long-term goals differ?
- How much familiarity do the propaganda efforts show with local concerns and cultures?
- Do you think the efforts described would be effective? Why or why not?

Finally, students should be aware that the issue of worldwide perceptions of the United States has taken on a new significance in the twenty-first century. As Von Eschen shows, if the spread of American/Western films, music, and fashion in the 1950s to 1970s was seen as a useful pro-American trend in the battle against Soviet communism, it can have a very different significance today. The idea of the United States as a force of progress and modernity ironically may have succeeded all too well in parts of the world that reject Western fashions, tastes, and values as a threat to established beliefs. As Americans have slowly realized over the last few years, rejections of Western values and American power have gone together in the ideologies of al-Qaeda and other anti-American terrorist groups in the Arab world. In the wake of the attacks of September 11, 2001, the U.S. government even set up a new Arabic-language propaganda service, Radio Sawa (<http://www.radiosawa.com/english.aspx>), to play Western pop music and promote pro-American attitudes in the Arab world. A perceptive lesson on worldwide attitudes toward America might end by discussing these and similar efforts to affect world opinion in the context of the post-2001 "global war on terror."

Bibliography

Vaughan, James. *The Failure of American and British Propaganda in the Arab Middle East, 1945–1957: Unconquerable Minds.* New York, 2005.
Westad, Odd Arne. *The Global Cold War: Third World Interventions and the Making of Our Times.* Cambridge, Eng., 2006.

2. RACE AND RESISTANCE

Von Eschen emphasizes issues of race and nationalism in her discussion of American popular culture in the late twentieth century. Western popular culture is truly globalized today, a potentially homogenizing culture industry seen by much of the world as "American" in spirit and values. While this has produced an anti-Western backlash in many places, Von Eschen notes the irony that, as with Bruce Lee films, because these cultural products are global, they may be interpreted by their consumers in ways that promote a narrative of resistance. John Fiske, for example, is a leading cultural theorist whose work discusses such oppositional "readings" of culture, drawing upon anthropological research showing that Australian Aborigines identify with John Rambo from the *Rambo* films: a renegade figure fighting paternalistic/colonial authority.

How to show the complicated and interactive relationship between American culture and other world cultures? Von Eschen discusses the phenomenon of "world music," and her insights can be applied to a lesson on popular music—a subject that of course intensely interests our students.

Although a useful activity with the same lessons could be constructed from many types of world music, I suggest a period devoted to the fascinating history of Jamaican music in relation with popular music consumed within the United States. Many students today are familiar with reggae music in a variety of forms. Reggae's antecedents, ska and rock-steady, emerged in Jamaica in the 1950s and early to mid-1960s. Many music historians trace the birth of ska to Jamaicans hearing American swing and R&B by artists such as Louis Armstrong and Fats Domino on southern U.S. radio stations and on imported albums replayed in dance halls. When American music moved to rock 'n' roll, less popular with Jamaicans, native musicians came up with a new, distinctive style that put a guitar note on the second and fourth beats. In the early 1960s ska musicians created their own new music and often reinterpreted American swing standards or movie themes in the ska style.

A teaching lesson with songs can be built around the complicated cultural translations from American R&B and Hollywood, to Jamaican ska, to

Top 40 reggae. An easy starting place is Roland Alphonso's "James Bond," his 1966 version of John Barry's familiar theme from the James Bond films. A similar contrast can be made between Herbie Hancock's 1962 oft-covered "Watermelon Man" (itself seen as having a "Latin" style) with the ska version by the Baba Brooks Band (1963), showing the transformation of American R&B in the transition to Jamaican ska. These contrasts illustrate the playful fusion of cultural styles contained within ska. (Many of the songs referred to in this lesson are available for individual download from iTunes or are on readily available compilations.)

A lesson discussing cultural transformations and their implications for familiar political history might continue by discussing the transition of ska into the slower and steadier rhythms of reggae in the late 1960s and 1970s. The connection between reggae and the Rastafarian religious movement in Jamaica gave the music a strong antiracist and anticolonial cast, which in the United States helped voice themes of black nationalism and resistance. Classic reggae anthems such as "Get Up, Stand Up" (1973) or "Exodus" (1977) by Bob Marley and the Wailers can be contrasted with Marley's earlier ska work (the songs "Simmer Down" [1962] and "Judge Not" [1962] are available on iTunes).

A particularly ambitious instructor might also discuss the popularity of reggae music after it was adopted by white artists such as the Police ("Roxanne") in the late 1970s and 1980s, recapping the familiar pattern in which music seen as "black" achieves mainstream success after being adopted by white artists.

After playing these songs and discussing the history of ska, students might be asked to closely "read" them for their style and content, and to consider their meanings for American and Jamaican music consumers. Some conversation starters include:

- What kind of mood is conveyed by reggae music, ska music, and American R&B? How does each form relate to other "Western" musical styles?
- What kinds of political themes are present in popular reggae songs as opposed to ska songs? How might this influence the reception of these songs in the United States?
- Why has reggae, not ska, become the incarnation of Jamaican music most familiar to Americans, both black and white?
- Reggae has become popular in unlikely places, from the Hopi Reservation in northern Arizona to the music of the current Sri Lankan–

London artist Maya Arulpragasam (M.I.A.).[1] What aspects of reggae might appeal to disparate audiences around the world?

These lessons should allow students a full understanding of popular culture and the myriad meanings it can possess, both for Americans and for observers of the United States in the rest of the world.

Discography

Roland Alphonso, "James Bond," on *Something Special: Ska Hot Shots,* Heartbeat Records, 2000.

Herbie Hancock, "Watermelon Man," on *Takin' Off,* Blue Note Records, 1996 [1962].

Skatalites, "Guns of Navarone," on *Guns of Navarone: The Best of the Skatalites,* Trojan, 2001.

Dimitri Timokin, "The Guns of Navarone—The Legend of Navarone," *Great Themes in Dolby Surround: War!* Silva America, 1997.

Bibliography

Fiske, John. *Understanding Popular Culture.* London, 1989.

Katz, David. *Solid Foundation: An Oral History of Reggae.* London, 2003.

Notes

1. See Bruce Weber, "Reggae Rhythms Speak to an Insular Tribe," *New York Times,* September 19, 1999; Sasha Frere-Jones, "Bingo in Swansea," *New Yorker,* November 22, 2004.

CHAPTER 13

These sewing machine operators were photographed by Martha Cooper as part of a group of images taken on September 14, 1994, to document scenes of the VBF Trim Company, a Paterson, New Jersey, garment-making shop. Paterson has been associated with working-class immigrant communities for generations. (Photographed by Martha Cooper for the Working in Paterson Folklife Project, Library of Congress, American Folklife Center, WIP-MC-C086-20.)

FROM ROSIE THE RIVETER TO THE GLOBAL ASSEMBLY LINE

AMERICAN WOMEN ON THE WORLD STAGE

LEILA J. RUPP

In 1939, shortly after the outbreak of war in Europe, American pacifist and feminist Emily Greene Balch wrote from Geneva to colleagues in the Women's International League for Peace and Freedom (WILPF) about their plight. "Ringed around by a wall of violence, we draw closer together."[1] It was a hopeful statement about organizational and gender solidarity in the face of impending doom, but it can perhaps also serve as a foreshadowing of the ways that, in the more than half century since the end of World War II, women across the continents have at times been able to make connections across national differences to confront common problems, including gendered violence. From a twenty-first-century vantage point, we can look back over the decades and see how intimately connected the changes in American women's lives have been with events unfolding on the world stage and how little of what happens to women in the United States is unconnected to larger global forces.

The magnitude of the worldwide conflict that ended in 1945 with the surrender of Germany and Japan, the liberation of the concentration camps, and the unleashing of the atomic bomb had brought American women, like women elsewhere, into areas of the labor force previously reserved for men. Like Rosie the Riveter, the symbol of American women patriotically taking up factory jobs previously reserved for men, women in all of the combatant countries went to work as men left to fight. Women even made inroads into the armed forces, although not, in the United States, as combatants. Spared the devastation of bombed-out cities and the massive losses suffered by the peoples of Europe and Asia, Americans set about reestablishing "normal life," although in a vastly reconfigured global context. Men returning home sought both their jobs and the comforts of a wife at home, if they could afford it. Although many women who had moved from poorly paid service jobs into more financially rewarding factory jobs preferred to remain, employers moved to restore the prewar sexual division of labor. In fact, even as increasing numbers of white middle-class women were entering the paid labor force in the postwar years, the goal of returning women to the home became a hallmark of American life, in contrast to the Soviet bloc countries, where women were encouraged to combine paid work and motherhood. Equally striking was that the American occupation authorities in both Germany and Japan, assuming that women could serve as the foundation of democratic governments, insisted that those countries' new constitutions grant women equal rights, while the Equal Rights Amendment at home languished in congressional committees.

In the context of the cold war that followed closely on the heels of the end of hostilities, differences between the Soviet employment of women, especially in factory labor, and American domesticity took on political and diplomatic importance. Symbolic of this cultural clash was the famous "kitchen debate" between U.S. vice president Richard Nixon and Soviet premier Nikita Khrushchev in 1959 at the opening of the American National Exhibition in Moscow. Nixon praised capitalism for providing U.S. housewives with an array of consumer goods and the choice of brands of appliances while Khrushchev, although also touting domesticity, boasted about the productivity of Soviet women workers. It was a debate that laid bare the ideological and economic differences between the two systems as they competed for dominance in the world system.

One way that rivalry played out was in competition for the hearts and minds of what came to be known as the "third world." Just as the two superpowers raced to try to make over in their own image countries newly independent of colonial rule, so too, transnational women's organizations from each bloc sought to bring developing countries into their fold. The new Women's International Democratic Federation (WIDF), launched out of the communist-led resistance movements of World War II and dominated by the Soviet Union, challenged the traditional transnational women's organizations such as the International Council of Women, the International Alliance of Women, and the WILPF and competed with them at the United Nations over who really represented the world's women. The older organizations, dedicated to women's rights and peace, had long sought to make their membership "truly global" but remained dominated in terms of membership and leadership by women from western and northern Europe and the United States. The WIDF, in contrast, although founded in Paris and supported from the Soviet Union, won adherents throughout the third world through its commitment to "win and defend national independence and democratic freedoms, eliminate apartheid, racial discrimination and fascism."[2] In the United States, organizations associated with the WIDF found themselves accused of communist affiliations in the postwar crackdown.

The decade of the 1950s has indeed gone down in U.S. history as Nixon depicted it to Khrushchev—a period of prosperity, conformity, domesticity, and suburbanization. Retreating from the disruptions of war and threatened by Soviet expansion and Chinese revolution without and communist subversion within, Americans, according to the conventional story, clung to home and family life. White men, taking advantage when they could of mortgages and college educations made possible by the G.I. Bill, became "organization men" loyal to their corporate employers and took up "do-it-yourself" projects in their suburban homes on the weekends. White women stayed home in the expanding suburbs, giving birth to more children and drinking coffee with their neighbors. Such prosperity depended on U.S. domination of the world economy in the war's aftermath. Suburban mothers chastised children reluctant to clean their plates to "think of the starving children in Europe"; with European economic recovery, the line shifted to the starving children in Africa. When Michael Harrington published *The Other America* in 1962, the fact that poverty existed at home came as something of a shock to those not experiencing deprivation themselves. A decade later, the revelation of the "feminization of poverty" both in the United States and globally called attention to the economic impact of discrimination against women, the sexual division of labor, the wage gap between women and men, and women's responsibility for rearing children.

Just as the reality of poverty underlay American prosperity in the 1950s, so too the domesticity and tranquility of the 1950s was far more apparent than real. In the burgeoning civil rights movement, African American women and men organized their communities and launched determined protests against segregation and discrimination, taking heart from national liberation movements in Africa and elsewhere. From the group of mostly mothers whose challenge to the segregated school system of Topeka, Kansas, contributed to the Supreme Court decision declaring segregation inherently unequal in *Brown v. Board of Education* (1954) to Rosa Parks, who refused to move to the back of the bus in 1955 and helped launch the Montgomery bus boycott, black women played critical roles in calling the attention of the country and the world to the second-class status of African Americans. In the West, Mexican American working-class women and men also took up civic activism on the local level, like African Americans inspired by nationalist movements in the third world. Within the beleaguered union movement, in the peace movement, in the remnants of the women's movement, in the vilified Communist Party, in the homophile movement that sought acceptance for lesbian and gay Americans, women fought for social change despite the proclaimed contentment of the era.

The recognition that a great deal was going on beneath the surface calm of the 1950s goes a long way toward helping us understand the origins of the explosive decade of the 1960s. The social protest movements of the 1960s had their roots in the tensions and contradictions of the 1950s. But they also occurred in a global context, as national liberation movements increasingly freed former colonies from the grip of imperialism. Transnational connections can be glimpsed in Martin Luther King Jr.'s embrace of Gandhian nonviolence, while Gandhi himself used tactics in the Indian struggle for independence inspired by militant British women fighting for the right to vote. Or in the anthem of the civil rights movement, "We Shall Overcome," with origins in the "sorrow songs" of slaves brought from Africa, then sung by striking tobacco workers in the 1940s, and then in Arabic by Palestinians, in Spanish by members of the United Farm workers, and, in a sense going home, in the South African antiapartheid movement.

Social upheavals occurring across the globe made the year 1968 synonymous with struggles for social justice. It was in 1968, when French students threw up barricades in the Left Bank quarter and protesting Mexican students were gunned down by the government, that a group of feminists gathered in Atlantic City to protest the objectification of women in the Miss America Pageant. In what has become a legend in the history of the resurgence of feminism—and gave rise to the mistaken notion that feminists burned their bras—feminists dumped bras, corsets, and hair rollers into a "freedom trash can" and crowned a sheep Miss America.

The turmoil of the 1960s sparked renewed activism by women all around the globe, although feminist movements almost everywhere had roots reaching back to earlier struggles by women for education, civil and political rights, employment opportunities, and other legal and social changes. Sometimes, as in the United States, women in male-dominated social justice movements began to adapt class or national or racial/ethnic critiques to their own situation as women, particularly if they found themselves pushed aside or relegated to second-class citizenship after fighting alongside men for freedom and justice. Although women's movements took on different shapes in various parts of the world—liberal feminism calling for the extension of the rights of men to women, socialist feminism advocating revolutionary change, radical feminism challenging the devaluing of women and the exploitation of women's sexuality and reproductive capacity—feminist movements growing from indigenous roots and influenced as well by a transnational exchange of ideas and strategies flourished. Feminism as a world view emphasizing the equal worth of women and men, a recognition of male privilege, an understanding of the ways that gender intersects with race, class, ethnicity, sexuality, ability, and other forms of difference, and a commitment to work for social justice found footholds everywhere. In different contexts, women organized and fought for access to education and employment, for control of their bodies, and against various forms of violence against women, including in wartime.

In the United States, African American, Latina, Asian American, and Arab American women, often angered by the white, middle-class assumptions of women's movement groups, connected their struggles to those of women in the third world, taking on the term "third world women" to describe themselves. Under the auspices of the United Nations, which included the principle of equality between women and men in its charter from its founding, women from across the globe came together in a series of conferences. A meeting in celebration of International Women's Year in Mexico City in 1975 gave rise to the UN's "Decade for Women," marked by a gathering in Copenhagen in 1980 and Nairobi in 1985, followed up by a fourth international conference in Beijing in 1995. From the beginning, conflicts erupted among women. In Mexico City, Domitila Barrios de Chungara, representing an organization of Bolivian tin miners' wives, expressed shock at discussions of such issues as prostitution, lesbianism, and male abuse of women, arguing that women in her group sought to work with men to change the system so that both women and men would have the right to live, work, and organize. In these meetings, the diverse lives of women came to light and made clear the need to broaden the definition of what counted as a "women's issue."

These international meetings brought together not only official government representatives but, more productively, auxiliary forums of nongovernmental organizations. Their debates about the impact of development policies, poverty, welfare systems, population policies, imperialism, and national liberation movements on women raised consciousness among women in the United States and other industrialized nations. Women from the global South voiced criticism of the narrowly defined interpretation of gender interests often articulated by women from the affluent North in a way that resonated with the critiques of women of color in the United States. What difference does the "glass ceiling" that keeps U.S. women from reaching the top rungs of their professions make to women who have no right to land and cannot feed their families? And perhaps more troubling, who is making the clothing worn by professional women in the industrialized countries, who is cleaning their houses and caring for their children, and under what conditions? The United Nations nongovernmental gatherings helped to articulate the multiple ways that the experiences of women of different nations were intertwined, from Asian and Latin American women producing clothing and electronic products on the global assembly line for purchase by U.S. women to the international sex trade that makes prostitution and the "entertainment industry" a major employer of women in a number of Asian countries, to the immigration of women from the Philippines, Mexico, and Latin America to work in U.S. and European homes as maids and nannies while forced to leave behind their own children.

As the twentieth century drew to a close and the cold war ended, the world had come a long way from the "kitchen debate" of 1959. By the dawn of the new millennium, the divisions between the global North and South had superceded the old political rivalries, and the question of globalization's impact on women came to the fore. What happens to women's traditional work in agriculture or trade when international lending agencies require a country to gear its economy for the world market? Where does "surplus" female labor go? Connecting such questions to the employment of women in sweatshops, as domestics, and in the sex tourism industry makes clear the impact of large-scale forces on women's lives and the ties that bind women in developing countries to those in wealthy industrialized ones like the United States. The pressing questions for women all around the world are what kinds of work they do, how much they are paid, what kinds of opportunities are open to them, who does the housework and takes care of the children, how much control they have over their sexuality and reproductive capacity, and who makes decisions for the family and nation. These are the questions with which transnational feminism grapples. All point to the interconnections of gender, class, race, ethnicity, sexuality, ability, and nation. In a world in which we are still, as Emily Greene Balch lamented, "ringed around by a wall of violence," hope lies in the connections American women can make with each other and with women around the globe.

Bibliography

Evans, Sara M. *Tidal Wave: How Women Changed America at Century's End.* New York, 2003. An examination of the U.S. women's movement that emphasizes the diversity of participants, the geographical spread of activism, and the continuity of struggle.

Ferree, Myra Marx and Beth B. Hess. *Controversy and Coalition: The New Feminist Movement Across Four Decades of Change.* 3rd ed. New York, 2000. A comprehensive sociological survey of the U.S. women's movement, tracing its development over time and its changing structure and strategies.

Freedman, Estelle B. *No Turning Back: The History of Feminism and the Future of Women.* New York, 2002. An analysis of the women's movement in global perspective, surveying the emergence of feminist movements, their varied approaches to work, family, sexuality, politics, and creativity, and the diversity of views and participants that ensures the continuation of feminist struggle.

Jayawardena, Kumari. *Feminism and Nationalism in the Third World.* London, 1986. A classic work on the history of women's political struggles in Asia and the Middle East since the late nineteenth century, arguing that feminism has indigenous roots throughout the third world.

Johnson-Odim, Cheryl and Nina Emma Mba. *For Women and the Nation: Funmilayo Ransome-Kuti of Nigeria.* Urbana, Ill., 1997. A biography of a Nigerian activist involved with women's issues in her own country and transnationally through the Women's International Democratic Federation.

May, Elaine Tyler. *Homeward Bound: American Families in the Cold War Era.* New York, 1988. An analysis of the ways that the cold war affected all aspects of American women's lives in the 1950s, from sexuality and reproduction to consumerism and family life.

Meyerowitz, Joanne, ed. *Not June Cleaver: Women and Gender in Postwar America, 1945–1960.* Philadelphia, 1994. A collection of essays on diverse women's activities in the United States in the 1950s that explodes the myth of domesticity and contentment.

Miller, Francesca. *Latin American Women and the Search for Social Justice.* Hanover,

N.H., 1991. A history of women's organizing in Latin America that includes Latin American women's involvement in international women's movements.

Naples, Nancy A. and Manisha Desai, eds. *Women's Activism and Globalization: Linking Local Struggles and Transnational Politics.* New York, 2002. A collection of essays dealing with contemporary women's activism in opposition to the consequences of globalization.

Richardson, Laurel, Verta Taylor, and Nancy Whittier, eds. *Feminist Frontiers.* 7th ed. New York, 2007. A women's studies text that includes articles detailing diverse women's experiences with appearance, socialization, work, family life, sexuality, reproduction, violence, politics, and the women's movement.

Rosen, Ruth. *The World Split Open: How the Modern Women's Movement Changed America.* New York, 2000. A comprehensive study, based on oral histories and archival research, of the women's movement and its impact on American society.

Rupp, Leila J. *Worlds of Women: The Making of an International Women's Movement.* Princeton, N.J., 1997. A history of the first wave of transnational organizing among women from the 1880s to 1945, focusing on the International Council of Women, the International Alliance of Women, and the Women's International League for Peace and Freedom.

Smith, Bonnie G., ed. *Global Feminisms Since 1945.* London, 2000. A collection of essays focusing on women's movements in different parts of the world.

Dublin, Thomas and Kathryn Kish Sklar. "Women and Social Movements in the United States, 1775–2000." <http://www.womhist.binghamton.edu.> Web site on the history of women's involvement in a variety of forms of activism throughout U.S. history.

United Nations Division for the Advancement of Women. *Women Go Global: The United Nations and the International Women's Movement, 1945–2000.* CD-ROM. United Nations, 2000. An interactive CD-ROM on the events that have been shaping the international agenda for women's equality since the founding of the UN.

Notes

1. Emily Greene Balch to International Executive Meeting, November 21, 1939, WILPF papers, reel 4.

2. WIDF Constitution, quoted in Cheryl Johnson-Odim and Nina Emma Mba, *For Women and the Nation: Funmilayo Ransome-Kuti of Nigeria* (Urbana, Ill., 1997), 137.

AMERICAN WOMEN IN A GLOBAL CONTEXT

BRENDA SANTOS

Leila Rupp's article illustrates the new place of women in the United States history curriculum. She takes us from peace activism before the entry of the United States into World War II to the contemporary issues of labor in the global economy. She presents an integrated vision of women within U.S. history rather than mere sidebars on "women's role," as well as an international context that compares, contrasts, and connects American women to the world. The challenge for teachers of the survey course is to bring these two major interventions to the classroom.

Some progress has already been made on the first of these two fronts. The New Social History took some time to reach the high school classroom, but for at least the past ten years, the curriculum has placed greater emphasis on the lives of Americans who had no political or military titles, not least women. Thus far, the most evident changes have been in the area of family history. Textbooks now ask students to consider the unique struggles of enslaved women, the effects of the Great Depression on family structure, and the role of women during war. In cases of women as political actors, though, texts still typically limit discussion to the three subunits in which women have traditionally appeared: the pre–Civil War women's rights movement (with lessons structured around Susan B. Anthony, Elizabeth Cady Stanton, and the Seneca Falls Convention), the suffrage movement (focusing on the conflict between Carrie Chapman Catt of the National American Woman Suffrage Association and Alice Paul of the National Woman's Party), and the women's liberation movement in the 1960s. Rupp's discussions of women's peace activism, women's war work, and women of the civil rights movement all suggest ways we might expand our ideas about politics to include women as political. Her discussion of the "kitchen debate" alludes to the importance of a nation's ideas about gender in defining national character.

Rupp's second intervention is to place American women within an international context. In so doing, she illustrates connections that reveal both the impact of the world on American women and their mark upon it. She discusses the ways in which American women have cooperated with other women in the world to address similar problems. She also shows, in her section on the "kitchen debate," how ideas about women have figured into national politics in unexpected ways. Drawing such connections in these areas could surely strengthen the United States history curriculum.

The possibilities that Rupp presents for globalizing women's history are too numerous to discuss in detail here. So I will focus on two of the places where a global perspective promises to enrich the curriculum: the role of women at home during World War II and the "kitchen debate." In keeping with my own broader teaching philosophy, the suggestions I present here are based on an inquiry-based teaching model that centers on the use of documents as a classroom tool.

The documents at the center of the first teaching activity are World War II propaganda posters. The major aim of this lesson is to investigate the ways in which governments asked women to participate in the war effort. I begin the lesson by asking students to define the term *propaganda* and use the following prompts.

What is the purpose of propaganda?

- What forms can it take?
- What examples of propaganda have we seen in our own lives?
- In history?
- Under what circumstances might a government produce propaganda?

I then ask students to look at the poster "Are you doing all that you can?" This poster and many others are available at the Library of Congress's American Memory site: <http://memory.loc.gov/learn/features/homefront/gallery .html>.

The poster introduces the genre of World War II propaganda posters and allows the teacher to model document analysis with the entire class. (Ideally photocopies should be distributed and the image should be projected.) Depending upon the students' level of experience with primary source documents, there are several specific approaches one might take. With the most inexperienced students, I usually start a document analysis by asking students to fold a piece of paper into three sections and to label them, "What I See" (objective observations), "What I Think" (subjective observations or hypotheses), and "Further Questions."[1] After students have individually filled out their sheets, a class discussion ensues in which students learn about the historical significance of the document and about the historian's process of document inquiry. With more experienced students, I abbreviate this part of the process by observing, hypothesizing, and questioning together as a class. During the course of this discussion it is important that students notice indications that this poster was directed toward American civilians. In order to transition to the class activity, I ask the students what they think the U.S. government had in mind for American women and how they think this was similar to or different from the demands placed on women in other nations during the war.

In putting together the materials for this lesson, it is important to provide students with a variety of posters that illustrate the ways women were asked to participate in their respective country's war effort. In small groups, students will analyze several propaganda posters directed at women during the war and compile a list of specific ways in which nations called upon women to contribute to the war effort. Posters from the United States, Canada, Great Britain, and the Soviet Union are in the public domain and easily accessible online. I have been unable to locate online posters from Germany, although several books have been published on Nazi propaganda that might include useful illustrations.[2] Examples of the propaganda posters can be found at the Web sites listed in the second endnote. As groups report their findings, I compile on the board a list of the ways these posters suggest women could contribute to the war effort. A class discussion would then be structured around the following questions:

- How do the contributions asked of women during the war compare across national boundaries?
- In what ways did the war affect the lives of women?
  —What limitations did it present?
  —What responsibilities did it present?
  —What opportunities did it present?
  —What were the limits of these opportunities?
- What do these propaganda posters aimed at women tell us about the way that the Allies saw themselves as nations and as a cause? What evidence do you see in the posters? (Extend this question to the Axis powers if German, Italian, or Japanese propaganda is made available to the students. Then ask the students to compare the Axis propaganda with the Allied propaganda.)
- How accurate are these posters in telling us about the roles women took during the war? In what ways that are not depicted did women contribute? What do the posters omit? What does this tell us about the historical context in which they were produced?

The discussion might end by emphasizing the ambiguity of the posters—their call for women to take an active role in the war effort and their adherence to traditional images of women and family. In the next unit of a typical U.S. history course, the students would learn about postwar trends—conservatism, suburbanization, consumerism, and the pressure women faced to return to a wholly domestic life. Students' discussion of women during World War II would provide them some understanding of the ambiguity of the 1950s and the turbulence of the 1960s and 1970s, as women faced and challenged the domestic ideal. This first activity also provides some basis for the second activity that I suggest, in that it prompts students to think about the ways in which nations frame their national identities and goals in "domestic relationships," here the relationships between women and the men in their lives. This framing supports national policy—women's responsibility to the state—while reinforcing their place within the family.

In the second teaching activity, the students once again grapple with the connections between women, domesticity, and the state. For the second teaching activity that I offer here, this idea of the image of women and family is central. But instead of investigating what it means to women's experiences or to their status in society per se, we are primarily interested in how it contributes to the ways nations see themselves, specifically the ways the United States and the Soviet Union saw themselves during the cold war. Here

I suggest a rethinking of the way the kitchen debate reflected and constructed the United States' and the Soviet Union's respective visions of themselves, each other, and their relationship to one another.

The central document for this lesson is the transcript of the kitchen debate. It was published on the front page of the *New York Times* on July 25, 1959, and is accessible through online databases at most public libraries. Alternately, it is available on Turner Learning's "Sputnik" site: <http://www.turnerlearning.com/cnn/coldwar/sputnik/sput_re4.html>.

I begin class by asking students to read the debate, underlining the text where they see Nixon and Khrushchev discussing the differences between their two nations. The debate is just a couple of pages long transcribed and should not take too much class time to read. With a slower learning group, the teacher could assign the reading and underlining for homework. A class discussion would follow, guided by the following questions:

- According to Nixon and Khrushchev, how do their nations differ?
- Are there places in the discussion where Nixon or Khrushchev hints at similarities between the two nations? What are these similarities?
- What are the sources of tension between the United States and the Soviet Union in 1959?
- What is the importance of the setting of the kitchen debate?
- How is the setting of this debate unique?
- How is the content of this debate (the topics discussed) unique?
- What does Nixon and Khrushchev's discussion of the homes and life-styles of their people tell us about the way they see themselves?
  —What does it tell us about the way they distinguish themselves from one another?
  —How do the women of these nations figure into this debate?
- How do Nixon's comments reinforce what we know about the culture of the 1950s in the United States?
- How accurate was Nixon's depiction of domestic life in the United States? What difference did race and class make? In what ways did activists in the civil rights–black power movement, the New Left, the countercultural movement, and the women's liberation movement in the 1950s, 1960s, and 1970s challenge the way of life Nixon depicted in the debate? Consider the ways in which these movements connected their critique of domestic life to critiques of American foreign policy.

To reinforce this discussion, I ask students to consider the values on which American opposition to communism and the Soviet Union were based: free enterprise, commerce, protection of the family, and freedom of religion. I ask students how traditional ideas about women's roles could be used to defend each of these. I would then ask them to consider the openings for change in this historical moment. How did the U.S. position in the cold war and the values it promoted in opposition to communism provide opportunities for American women to transcend traditional roles? I then ask students to perform a similar thought exercise for the Soviet Union. How did ideas about women's place in society reinforce the values on which the Soviet Union based its opposition to the United States? Where are inconsistencies evident? What do these suggest about the reality of life for women and about their opportunities?

Admittedly, these questions are difficult. But considering them impresses upon students the social and cultural dimension of cold war tension, and the importance of ideas about women in defining national character. This lesson also challenges the artificial way in which historians and teachers dichotomize the stories of history into domestic versus foreign or social versus political. Because this lesson defies those categories, it could be used in a traditional course as an introduction to the cold war or the 1950s unit. Ideally, it would serve as an introduction to a unit that integrates foreign and domestic issues in the cold war era.

The lessons I have developed here only represent the beginning of how an international approach to the U.S. history curriculum promises to enrich the teaching of American women and the national experience. Rupp's article suggests several other areas for development, including pre- and postwar international women's movements. I look forward to extrapolating upon her ideas to develop my next course, placing women at the center of a truly international U.S. history.

Notes

1. For students requiring even more guidance, teachers might find the Document Analysis Worksheets developed by the National Archives helpful. They are posted on the NARA Web site: <http://www.archives.gov/education/lessons/worksheets/>.

2. See the National Museum of American History's "Produce for Victory" site: <http://americanhistory.si.edu/victory/index.htm#Contents>; Library of Congress American Memory's "On the Homefront" site: <http://memory.loc.gov/learn/features/homefront/gallery.html>; The National Archives' "Powers of Persuasion" site: <http://www.archives.gov/exhibits/powers_of_persuasion/powers_of_persuasion_home.html>; McGill University's "Canadian War Poster Collection" site: <http://digital

.library.mcgill.ca/warposters/english/index.htm>; St. Andrew's School's "Weapons on the Wall" site: <http://www.st-andrews.ac.uk/~pv/pv/courses/posters/index.html>; the University of Maryland, Baltimore County's 1930–1940s Soviet Propaganda Posters site: <http://userpages.umbc.edu/~akotovl/propaganda.html#top>; the Hoover Institution Library and Archives: <http://www-hoover.stanford.edu/hila/posters .htm>. All of the posters featured here are from these sites and in the public domain, with the exceptions of "How have you helped the front?" from International Poster Gallery Online: <http://www.internationalposter.com/thumbdir.cfm?Start Page=1&Style=&Period=WWII%2C40%2C50%2C60%2C70%2C80%2C90&Cou ntry=RU&NavBar=PosterFinder+%3A+Country+%26+Period+%3A+WWII+to +Present>; and "We are READY for the work!" from Soviet Propaganda Posters 3: <http://posters.nce.buttobi.net/russ3.htm>. For sources of German propaganda online and in print, see Calvin College's Nazi Propaganda: 1933–1945 site: <http://www.calvin .edu/academic/cas/gpa/ww2era.htm>.

CHAPTER 14

Winston Churchill, Josef Stalin, and Harry S
Truman shaking hands at the Potsdam Conference.
(The Truman Presidential Museum and Library,
63-1457-29.)

COLD WAR AND GLOBAL HEGEMONY, 1945–1991

MELVYN P. LEFFLER

We are accustomed to viewing the cold war as a determined and heroic response of the United States to communist aggression spearheaded and orchestrated by the Soviet Union. This image was carefully constructed by presidents and their advisers in their memoirs.[1] This view also was incorporated in some of the first scholarly works on the cold war, but was then rebutted by a wide variety of revisionist historians who blamed officials in Washington as well as those in Moscow for the origins of the Soviet-American conflict.[2] Nonetheless, in the aftermath of the cold war the traditional interpretation reemerged. John Gaddis, arguably the most eminent historian of the cold war, wrote in the mid-1990s that the cold war was a struggle of good versus evil, of wise and democratic leaders in the West reacting to the crimes and inhumanity of Joseph Stalin, the brutal dictator in the Kremlin.[3]

This interpretation places the cold war in a traditional framework. It is one way to understand American foreign policy between the end of World War II and the breakup of the Union of Soviet Socialist Republics (U.S.S.R.) in 1991. But for quite some time now, historians, political scientists, and economists have been studying the cold war in a much larger global context. They do so because the new documents from the Soviet Union and its former empire as well as older documents from the United States and its allies suggest that Stalin conducted a more complex and inconsistent foreign policy than previously imagined and that U.S. officials initially did not regard Stalin, notwithstanding his crimes and brutality, as an unacceptable partner with whom to collaborate in stabilizing and remaking the postwar world.

Most scholars looking at Soviet documents now agree that Stalin had no master plan to spread revolution or conquer the world. He was determined to establish a sphere of influence in eastern Europe, where his communist minions would rule. But at the same time, Stalin wanted to get along with his wartime allies in order to control the rebirth of German and Japanese power, which he assumed was inevitable. Consequently, he frequently cautioned communist followers in France, Italy, Greece, and elsewhere to avoid provocative actions that might frighten or antagonize his wartime allies. Within his own country and his own sphere, he was cruel, evil, almost genocidal, just as Gaddis and other traditional scholars suggest.[4] Yet U.S. and British officials were initially eager to work with him. They rarely dwelled upon his domestic barbarism. President Harry S Truman wrote his wife, Bess, after his first meeting with Stalin: "I like Stalin . . . . He is straightforward. Knows what he wants and will compromise when he can't get it." W. Averell Harriman, the U.S. ambassador to Moscow, remonstrated that "if it were possible to see him [Stalin] more frequently, many of our difficulties would be overcome."[5]

Yet the difficulties were not overcome. American fears grew. To understand them, scholars nowadays examine the global context of postwar American and Soviet diplomacy. They see the contest between American freedom and Soviet totalitarianism as part of an evolving fabric of international economic and political conditions in the twentieth century. After World War II, they say, U.S. leaders assumed the role of hegemon, or leader, of the international economy and container of Soviet power. To explain why, scholars examine the operation of the world economy and the distribution of power in the international system. They look at transnational ideological conflict, the disruption of colonial empires, and the rise of revolutionary nationalism in Asia and Africa. They explain the spread of the cold war from Europe to Asia, Africa, the Middle East, and Latin America by focusing on decolonization, the rise of newly independent states, and the yearnings of peoples everywhere to modernize their countries and enjoy higher standards of living. Yet the capacity of the United States to assume the roles of hegemon, balancer, and container depended on more than its wealth and strength; the success of the United States also depended on the appeal of its ideology, the vitality of its institutions, and the attractiveness of its culture of mass consumption—what many scholars nowadays call "soft power."[6]

At the end of World War II, the United States and the Soviet Union emerged as the two strongest nations in the world and as exemplars of competing models of political economy.[7] But it was a peculiar bipolarity. The United States was incontestably the most powerful nation on the earth. It alone possessed the atomic bomb. It alone possessed a navy that could project power across the oceans and an air force that could reach across the continents. The United States was also the richest nation in the world. It possessed two-thirds of the world's gold reserves and three-fourths of its invested capital. Its gross national product was three times that of the Soviet Union and five times that of the United Kingdom. Its wealth had grown enormously during the war while the Soviet Union had been devastated by the occupation by Nazi Germany. Around twenty-seven million inhabitants of the U.S.S.R. died during World War II compared to about four hundred thousand Americans. The Germans ravished the agricultural economy of Soviet Russia and devastated its mining and transportation infrastructure.[8]

Compared to the United States in 1945, the Soviet Union was weak. Yet it loomed very large not only in the imagination of U.S. officials, but also in the minds of political leaders throughout the world. It did not loom large because of fears of Soviet military aggression. Contemporary policymakers knew that Stalin did not want war. They did not expect Soviet troops to march across Europe. Yet they feared that Stalin would capitalize on the manifold opportunities of the postwar world: the vacuums of power stemming from the defeat of Germany and Japan; the breakup of colonial empires; popular yearnings for postwar social and economic reform; and widespread disillusionment with the functioning of democratic capitalist economies.[9]

During World War II, the American economy had demonstrated enormous vitality, but many contemporaries wondered whether the world capitalist system could be made to function effectively in peacetime. Its performance during their lifetimes had bred worldwide economic depression, social malaise, political instability, and personal disillusionment. Throughout Europe and Asia, people blamed capitalism for the repetitive cycles of boom and bust and for military conflagrations that brought ruin and despair. Describing conditions at the end of the war, the historian Igor Lukes has written: "Many in Czechoslovakia had come to believe that capitalism . . . had become obsolete. Influential intellectuals saw the world emerging from the ashes of the war in black and white terms: here was Auschwitz and there was Stalingrad. The former was a byproduct of a crisis in capitalist Europe of the 1930s; the latter stood for the superiority of socialism."[10]

Transnational ideological conflict shaped the cold war. Peoples everywhere yearned for a more secure and better life; they pondered alternative ways of organizing their political and economic affairs. Everywhere, communist parties sought to present themselves as leaders of the resistance against fascism, proponents of socioeconomic reform, and advocates of national self-interest. Their political clout grew quickly as their membership soared, for example, in Greece, from 17,000 in 1935 to 70,000 in 1945; in Czechoslovakia, from 28,000 in May 1945 to 750,000 in September 1945; in Italy, from 5,000 in 1943 to 1,700,000 at the end of 1945.[11] For Stalin and his comrades in Moscow, these grassroots developments provided unsurpassed opportunities; for Truman and his advisers in Washington, they inspired fear and gloom. "There is complete economic, social and political collapse going on in Central Europe, the extent of which is unparalleled in history," wrote Assistant Secretary of War John McCloy in April 1945.[12] The Soviet Union, of course, was not responsible for these conditions. Danger nonetheless inhered in the capacity of the Kremlin to capitalize on them. "The greatest danger to the security of the United States," the CIA concluded in one of its first reports, "is the possibility of economic collapse in Western Europe and the consequent accession to power of Communist elements."[13]

Transnational ideological conflict impelled U.S. officials to take action. They knew they had to restore hope that private markets could function effectively to serve the needs of humankind. People had suffered terribly, Assistant Secretary of State Dean G. Acheson told a congressional committee in 1945. They demanded land reform, nationalization, and social welfare. They believed that governments should take action to alleviate their misery. They felt it "so deeply," said Acheson, "that they will demand that the whole business of state control and state interference shall be pushed further and further."[14]

Policymakers like Acheson and McCloy, the officials who became known as the "Wise Men" of the cold war, understood the causes for the malfunctioning of the capitalist world economy in the interwar years. They were intent on correcting the fundamental weaknesses and vulnerabilities. Long before they envisioned a cold war with the Soviet Union, they labored diligently during 1943 and 1944 to design the International Monetary Fund (IMF) and the World Bank. They urged Congress to reduce U.S. tariffs. They wanted the American people to buy more foreign goods. They knew that foreign nations without sufficient dollars to purchase raw materials and fuel would not be able to recover easily. They realized that governments short of gold and short of dollars would seek to hoard their resources, establish quotas, and regulate the free flow of capital. And they knew that these actions in the years between World War I and World War II had brought about the Great Depression and created the conditions for Nazism, fascism, and totalitarianism to flourish.[15]

"Now, as in the year 1920," President Truman declared in early March 1947, "we have reached a turning point in history. National economies have been disrupted by the war. The future is uncertain everywhere. Economic policies are in a state of flux." Governments abroad, the president explained, wanted to regulate trade, save dollars, and promote reconstruction. This was understandable; it was also perilous. Freedom flourished where power was dispersed. But regimentation, Truman warned, was on the march, everywhere. If not stopped abroad, it would force the United States to curtail freedom at home. "In this atmosphere of doubt and hesitation," Truman declared, "the decisive factor will be the type of leadership that the United States gives the world." If it did not act decisively, the world capitalist system would flounder, providing yet greater opportunities for communism to grow and for Soviet strength to accrue. If the United States did not exert leadership, freedom would be compromised abroad and a garrison state might develop at home.[16]

Open markets and free peoples were inextricably interrelated. To win the transnational ideological conflict, U.S. officials had to make the world capitalist system function effectively. By 1947, they realized the IMF and the World Bank were too new, too inexperienced, and too poorly funded to accomplish the intended results. The United States had to assume the responsibility to provide dollars so that other nations had the means to purchase food and fuel and, eventually, to reduce quotas and curtail exchange restrictions. In June 1947, Secretary of State George C. Marshall outlined a new approach, saying the United States would provide the funds necessary to promote the reconstruction of Europe. The intent of the Marshall Plan was to provide dollars to like-minded governments in western Europe so they could continue to grow their economies, employ workers, ensure political stability, undercut the appeal of communist parties, and avoid being sucked into an economic orbit dominated by the Soviet Union. U.S. officials wanted European governments to cooperate and pool their resources for the benefit of their collective well-being and for the establishment of a large, integrated market where goods and capital could move freely. In order to do this, the

United States would incur the responsibility to make the capitalist system operate effectively, at least in those parts of the globe not dominated by the Soviet Union. The United States would become the hegemon, or overseer, of the global economy: it would make loans, provide credits, reduce tariffs, and ensure currency stability.[17]

The success of the Marshall Plan depended on the resuscitation of the coal mines and industries of western Germany.[18] Most Europeans feared Germany's revival. Nonetheless, U.S. officials hoped that Stalin would not interfere with efforts to merge the three western zones of Germany, institute currency reform, and create the Federal Republic of Germany. Marshall Plan aid, in fact, initially was offered to Soviet Russia and its allies in eastern Europe. But Stalin would not tolerate the rebuilding of Germany and its prospective integration into a Western bloc. Nor would he allow eastern European governments to be drawn into an evolving economic federation based on the free flow of information, capital, and trade. Soviet security would be endangered. Stalin's sphere of influence in eastern Europe would be eroded and his capacity to control the future of German power would be impaired. In late 1947, Stalin cracked down on eastern Europe, encouraged the communist coup in Czechoslovakia, and instigated a new round of purges.[19]

Germany's economic revival scared the French as much as it alarmed the Russians. The French feared that Germany would regain power to act autonomously. The French also were afraid that initiatives to revive Germany might provoke a Soviet attack and culminate in another occupation of France. French officials remonstrated against American plans and demanded military aid and security guarantees.[20]

The French and other wary Europeans had the capacity to shape their future. They exacted strategic commitments from the United States. The North Atlantic Treaty was signed in 1949 as a result of their fears about Germany as well as their anxieties about Soviet Russia. U.S. strategic commitments and U.S. troops were part of a dual containment strategy, containing the uncertain trajectory of the Federal Republic of Germany as well as the anticipated hostility of the Soviet Union. Hegemonic responsibilities meant power balancing, strategic commitments, and military alliances.[21]

Just as western Germany needed to be integrated into a Western sphere lest it be sucked into a Soviet orbit, so did Japan. U.S. officials worried that their occupation of Japan might fail and that the Japanese might seek to enhance their own interests by looking to the Soviets or the communist Chinese as future economic partners. In 1948, U.S. policy makers turned their attention from reforming Japanese social and political institutions to promoting economic reconstruction. Japan's past economic growth, they knew, depended on links to Manchuria, China, and Korea, areas increasingly slipping into communist hands. Japan needed alternative sources of raw materials and outlets for her manufactured goods. Studying the functioning of the global capitalist economy, America's cold warriors concluded that the industrial core of northeast Asia, Japan, needed to be integrated with its underdeveloped periphery in Southeast Asia, much like western Europe needed to have access to petroleum in the Middle East.[22] It was the obligation of the hegemon of the world capitalist economy to make sure component units of the system could benefit from the operation of the whole.

But, as hegemon, the United States also had to be sensitive to the worries and responsive to the needs of other countries. In Asia, as in Europe, many peoples feared the revival of the power of former Axis nations. Truman promised them that U.S. troops would remain in Japan, even as Japan regained its autonomy, and that the United States would ensure peace in the Pacific, even if it meant a new round of security guarantees, as it did with the Philippines and with Australia and New Zealand.[23]

Yet, much as American officials hoped to integrate Japan with Southeast Asia, revolutionary nationalist movements in the region made that prospect uncertain. During World War II, popular independence movements arose in French Indochina and the Netherlands East Indies. Nationalist leaders like Ho Chi Minh in Vietnam and Sukarno in Indonesia wanted to gain control over their countries' futures.[24] Decolonization was an embedded feature of the postwar international system, propelled by the defeat of Japan and the weakening of traditional European powers. Decolonization fueled the cold war as it provided opportunities for the expansion of communist influence. Third world nationalists wanted to develop, industrialize, and modernize their countries. They often found Marxist-Leninist ideology attractive because it blamed their countries' backwardness on capitalist exploitation. At the same time, the Soviet command economy seemed to provide a model for rapid modernization. Stalin's successors, therefore, saw endless opportunities for expanding their influence in the third world; leaders in Washington perceived dangers.[25]

As hegemon of the free world economy, U.S. officials felt a responsibility to contain revolutionary nationalism and to integrate core and periphery. The Truman administration prodded the Dutch and the French to make concessions to revolutionary nationalists, but often could not shape the outcomes of colonial struggles. When the French, for example, refused to acknowledge Ho Chi Minh's Republic of Vietnam and established a puppet government under

Bao Dai in 1949, the United States chose to support the French. Otherwise, Truman and his advisers feared they would alienate their allies in France and permit a key area to gravitate into a communist orbit, where it would be amenable to Chinese or Soviet influence. Falling dominos in Southeast Asia would sever the future economic links between this region and Japan, making rehabilitation in the industrial core of northeast Asia all the more difficult.[26]

In the late 1950s and 1960s Japan's extraordinary economic recovery, sparked by the Korean War and fueled by subsequent exports to North America, defied American assumptions. Yet, by then, American officials had locked the United States into a position opposing nationalist movements led by communists, like Ho Chi Minh. U.S. officials feared that if they allowed a communist triumph in Indochina, America's credibility with other allies and clients would be shattered. Hegemons needed to retain their credibility. Otherwise, key allies, like West Germany and Japan, might doubt America's will and reorient themselves in the cold war.[27]

Hegemony and credibility required superior military capabilities. Leaders in Washington and Moscow alike believed that perceptions of their relative power position supported risk taking on behalf of allies and clients in Asia and Africa. In the most important U.S. strategy document of the cold war, NSC 68, Paul Nitze wrote that military power was an "indispensable back-drop" to containment, which he called a "policy of calculated and gradual coercion." To pursue containment in the third world and erode support for the adversary, the United States needed to have superior military force.[28] Prior to 1949, the United States had a monopoly of atomic weapons. But after the Soviets tested and developed nuclear weapons of their own, U.S. officials believed they needed to augment their arsenal of strategic weapons. Their aim was not only to deter Soviet aggression in the center of Europe, but also to support the ability of the United States to intervene in third world countries without fear of Soviet countermoves.

Nuclear weapons, therefore, produced paradoxical results. Their enormous power kept the cold war from turning into a hot war between the United States and the Soviet Union. Leaders on both sides recognized that such a war would be suicidal. But at the same time, nuclear weapons encouraged officials in both Washington and Moscow to engage in risk-taking on the "periphery," that is, in Asia, Africa, the Middle East, and the Caribbean because each side thought (and hoped) that the adversary would not dare escalate the competition into a nuclear exchange.[29] When Ronald Reagan revived the determination of the United States to regain military superiority in the 1980s, he sought to use those military capabilities, not for a preemptive attack against the Soviet Union, but as a backdrop to support U.S. interventions on behalf of anticommunist insurgents from Nicaragua and El Salvador to Afghanistan and Angola. In other words, Reagan viewed superior strategic capabilities as a key to containing communism, preserving credibility, and supporting hegemony.[30]

For U.S. officials, waging the cold war required the United States to win the transnational ideological struggle and to contain Soviet power. To achieve these goals, the United States had to be an effective hegemon. This meant that the United States had to nurture and lubricate the world economy, build and co-opt western Germany and Japan, establish military alliances and preserve allied cohesion, contain revolutionary nationalism, and bind the industrial core of Europe and Asia with the underdeveloped periphery in the third world. To be effective, cold warriors believed that superior military capabilities were an incalculable asset. They focused much less attention and allocated infinitely fewer resources to disseminating their values and promoting their culture. Yet scholars of the cold war increasingly believe that America's success as a hegemon, its capacity to evoke support for its leadership, also depended on the habits and institutions of constitutional governance, the resonance of its liberal and humane values, and the appeal of its free-market and mass-consumption economy.[31]

Bibliographical Essay

The majority of governments publish primary source documents regarding the history of their foreign policy. These documents are published many decades after the fact, but we now have many documents for the 1940s, 1950s, and 1960s. For the evolution of the role of the United States in the cold war, see U.S. Department of State, *Foreign Relations of the United States* (Washington); for Britain and the cold war, see *Foreign and Commonwealth Office, Documents on British Policy Overseas*. Since the end of the cold war, the Cold War International History Project has been publishing (and distributing free of charge) primary source documents from the Soviet Union and other formerly communist nations, including the People's Republic of China. They are indispensable for understanding the global context of the cold war. See the Cold War International History Project, *Bulletin* (Washington, D.C., 1992–2004). The Central Intelligence Agency (CIA) has published several volumes of documents. See, for example, Woodrow J. Kuhns, ed., *Assessing the Soviet Threat: The Early Cold War Years* (Springfield, Va., 1997); Scott A. Koch, ed., *Selected Estimates on the Soviet Union, 1950–1959* (Washington, D.C., 1993); Ben B. Fischer, *At Cold War's End: U.S. Intelligence on the Soviet Union and Eastern Europe, 1989–1991* (Reston, Va., 1999).

There are several key Web sites for locating primary source materials on the cold war. The most important are the Cold War International History Project, <http://wwics.si.edu/index.cfm?topic_id=1409&fuseaction=library.collection>; the National Security Archive, <http://www.gwu.edu/~nsarchiv/>; the Parallel History Project for information on NATO and the Warsaw Pact, <http://www.isn.ethz.ch/php/>; and the Declassified Documents Reference Service, <http://www.galegroup.com/psm>. The Federation of American Scientists also has a Web site with valuable documents on many issues, like the nuclear arms race. See <http://www.fas.org/>. Many U.S. government agencies also have Web sites containing documents on current and past foreign policy. For the Department of State, see <http://www.state.gov/history/>; for the Department of Defense, see <http://www.defenselink.mil/>; for the Central Intelligence Agency, <http://www.cia.gov/>. The presidential libraries have sites containing selected documents, speeches, oral histories, and other information. You can access them through <http://www.archives.gov/presidential_libraries/index.html>.

For short books locating the cold war in a global context, see Robert J. McMahon, *The Cold War: A Very Short Introduction* (New York, 2003); David S. Painter, *The Cold War: An International History* (New York, 2002); Geoffrey Roberts, *The Soviet Union in World Politics: Coexistence, Revolution and Cold War, 1945–1991* (New York, 1999); Geir Lundestad, *East, West, North, South: Major Developments in International Relations since 1945,* 4th ed. (Oxford, 1999).

Many scholars are now using primary documents from the former Soviet Union and other communist countries to study the cold war. In addition to the books and articles listed in note 3, see David Holloway, *Stalin and the Bomb: the Soviet Union and Atomic Energy, 1939–1956* (New Haven, Conn., 1994); William Taubman, *Khrushchev: The Man and His Era* (New York, 2003); Hope M. Harrison, *Driving the Soviets Up the Wall: Soviet-East German Relations, 1953–1961* (Princeton, N.J., 2003). Some of the most fascinating books deal with Chinese foreign policy and the relations between Mao Tse-tung and Stalin. See, for example, S. N. Goncharov, John Wilson Lewis, and Litai Xue, *Uncertain Partners: Stalin, Mao, and the Korean War* (Stanford, Calif., 1993); Jian Chen, *Mao's China and the Cold War* (Chapel Hill, N.C., 2001).

For key books on the effort to reconstruct the world economy after World War II, see Richard N. Gardner, *Sterling-Dollar Diplomacy in Current Perspective: The Origins and the Prospects of Our International Economic Order* (New York, 1980); Herman Van der Wee, *Prosperity and Upheaval: The World Economy, 1945–1980* (Berkeley, Calif., 1986); Alfred E. Eckes and Thomas W. Zeiler, *Globalization and the American Century* (New York, 2003).

For transnational ideological conflict and the cold war, see Joyce and Gabriel Kolko, *The Limits of Power: The World and United States Foreign Policy, 1945–1954* (New York, 1972); Walt W. Rostow, *The Stages of Economic Growth: A Non-Communist Manifesto,* 3rd. ed. (New York, 1990); François Furet, *The Passing of an Illusion: The Idea of Communism in the Twentieth Century* (Chicago, 1999); Odd Arne Westad, *The Global Cold War* (Cambridge, Eng., 2005); Michael E. Latham, *Modernization as*

Ideology: American Social Science and "Nation-Building" in the Kennedy Era (Chapel Hill, N.C., 2000); David C. Engerman, *Modernization from the Other Shore: American Intellectuals and the Romance of Russian Development* (Cambridge, Mass., 2003); John Lewis Gaddis, *We Now Know: Rethinking Cold War History* (New York, 1997).

There are some wonderful studies on decolonization, revolutionary nationalism, and the cold war. See, for example, Robert J. McMahon, *Colonialism and Cold War: The United States and the Struggle for Indonesian Independence, 1945–49* (Ithaca, N.Y., 1981); Frances Gouda and Thijs Brocades Zaalberg, *American Visions of the Netherlands East Indies/Indonesia: U.S. Foreign Policy and Indonesian Nationalism, 1920–1949* (Amsterdam, 2002); Matthew James Connelly, *A Diplomatic Revolution: Algeria's Fight for Independence and the Origins of the Post–Cold War Era* (New York, 2002); Piero Gleijeses, *Conflicting Missions: Havana, Washington, and Africa, 1959–1976* (Chapel Hill, N.C., 2002). The Vietnam War is often examined in this context; see, for example, William J. Duiker, *U.S. Containment Policy and the Conflict in Indochina* (Stanford, Calif., 1994); George C. Herring, *America's Longest War: The United States and Vietnam, 1950–1975,* 4th ed. (Boston, 2002).

For power and the cold war, see Mark Trachtenberg, *A Constructed Peace: The Making of the European Settlement, 1945–1963* (Princeton, N.J., 1999); William Curti Wohlforth, *The Elusive Balance: Power and Perceptions During the Cold War* (Ithaca, N.Y., 1993); Melvyn P. Leffler, *A Preponderance of Power: National Security, the Truman Administration, and the Cold War* (Stanford, Calif., 1992). Raymond L. Garthoff has written two lengthy and illuminating books that link power and ideology. See Garthoff, *Détente and Confrontation: American-Soviet Relations From Nixon to Reagan* (Washington, D.C., 1985) and *The Great Transition: American-Soviet Relations and the End of the Cold War* (Washington, D.C., 1994).

For discussions of the end of the cold war that focus on ideas and transnational movements, see Matthew Evangelista, *Unarmed Forces: The Transnational Movement to End the Cold War* (Ithaca, N.Y., 1999); Robert D. English, *Russia and the Idea of the West: Gorbachev, Intellectuals, and the End of the Cold War* (New York, 2000); Lawrence S. Wittner, *Toward Nuclear Abolition: A History of the World Nuclear Disarmament Movement, 1971 to the Present* (Stanford, Calif., 2003).

For discussions of hegemony and soft power, see the citations in notes 5 and 29.

Notes

1. For example, see Harry S Truman, *Memoirs, Vol. I: 1945, Year of Decisions,* reprint (New York, 1965, 1955); Truman, *Memoirs, Vol. II: Years of Trial and Hope, 1946–1952,* reprint (New York, 1965, 1956); Dwight D. Eisenhower, *Mandate for Change: The White House Years, 1953–1956* (Garden City, N.J., 1963); Dean G. Acheson, *Present at the Creation: My Years at the State Department* (New York, 1969); George F. Kennan, *Memoirs,* 2 vols., paperback ed. (New York, 1967, 1972).

2. See, for example, Joyce and Gabriel Kolko, *The Limits of Power: The World and*

United States Foreign Policy, 1945–1954 (New York, 1972); for a discussion of the different historiographical approaches, see my essay, "The Cold War Over the Cold War," in Gordon Martel, ed., *American Foreign Policy Reconsidered, 1890–1993* (London, 1994).

3. John Lewis Gaddis, *We Now Know: Rethinking Cold War History* (New York, 1997).

4. For some of the best new scholarship on Stalin, see Simon Sebag Montefiore, *Stalin: The Court of the Red Tsar,* reprint (New York, 2004, 2003); Norman M. Naimark, *The Russians in Germany: A History of the Soviet Zone of Occupation, 1945–1949* (Cambridge, Mass., 1995); Vojtech Mastny, *The Cold War and Soviet Insecurity: The Stalin Years* (New York, 1996); Eduard Maximilian Mark, "Revolution by Degrees: Stalin's National Front Strategy for Europe, 1941–1947," Cold War International History Project Working Paper No. 31 (Washington, D.C., 2001); Geoffrey Roberts, "Stalin and the Grand Alliance: Public Discourse, Private Dialogues, and the Direction of Soviet Foreign Policy, 1941–1947," *Slovo,* 13 (2001): 1–15.

5. Robert H. Ferrell, ed., *Dear Bess: The Letters from Harry to Bess Truman, 1910–1959* (New York, 1983), 522; Harriman to Truman, June 8, 1945, Department of State, *Foreign Relations of the United States: The Conference of Berlin: The Potsdam Conference, 1945,* 2 vols. (Washington, D.C., 1960), 1:61.

6. For soft power, see Joseph S. Nye, *Soft Power: The Means to Success in World Politics* (New York, 2004); Nye, *The Paradox of American Power: Why the World's Only Superpower Can't Go It Alone* (New York, 2002).

7. Odd Arne Westad, *The Global Cold War* (Cambridge, Eng., 2005).

8. Paul M. Kennedy, *The Rise and Fall of the Great Powers: Economic Change and Military Conflict From 1500 to 2000* (New York, 1987), 347–72; R. J. Overy, *Russia's War* (London, 1997); Allan M. Winkler, *Home Front U.S.A.: America During World War II,* 2nd ed. (Wheeling, Ill., 2000).

9. Melvyn P. Leffler, *A Preponderance of Power: National Security, the Truman Administration, and the Cold War* (Stanford, Calif., 1992), 1–141.

10. Igor Lukes, "The Czech Road to Communism," in Norman M. Naimark and Leonid Gibianskii, eds., *The Establishment of Communist Regimes in Eastern Europe, 1944–1949* (Boulder, Colo., 1997), 29; William I. Hitchcock, *The Struggle for Europe: The Turbulent History of a Divided Continent, 1945 to the Present* (New York, 2004), 1–125.

11. Adam Westoby, *Communism Since World War II* (New York, 1981), 14–15.

12. Memo for the President, by John McCloy, April 26, 1945, box 178, President's Secretary's File, Harry S. Truman Presidential Library.

13. Central Intelligence Agency, "Review of the World Situation As It Relates to the Security of the United States," September 26, 1947, box 203.

14. Testimony by Dean G. Acheson, March 8, 1945, U.S. Senate, Committee on Banking and Currency, *Bretton Woods Agreement Act,* 79th Cong., 1st sess. (Washington, D.C., 1945), 1:35.

290 · COLD WAR AND GLOBAL HEGEMONY, 1945–1991

15. U.S. Department of Commerce, *The United States in the World Economy* (Washington, D.C., 1943); Harley A. Notter, *Postwar Foreign Policy Preparation, 1939–1945* (Washington, D.C., 1950), 128; Georg Schild, *Bretton Woods and Dumbarton Oaks: American Economic and Political Postwar Planning in the Summer of 1944* (New York, 1995).

16. Harry S Truman, *Public Papers of the Presidents of the United States, 1947* (Washington, D.C., 1963), 167–72; see also his Truman Doctrine speech, which followed a few days later, 176–80, and his special message to the Congress on the Marshall Plan, 515–29.

17. Michael J. Hogan, *The Marshall Plan: America, Britain, and the Reconstruction of Western Europe, 1947–1952* (New York, 1987); David W. Ellwood, *Rebuilding Europe: Western Europe, America and Postwar Reconstruction* (New York, 1992); Thomas W. Zeiler, *Free Trade: Free World: The Advent of GATT* (Chapel Hill, N.C., 1999).

18. John Gimbel, *The Origins of the Marshall Plan* (Stanford, Calif., 1976); Carolyn Woods Eisenberg, *Drawing the Line: The American Decision to Divide Germany, 1944–1949* (New York, 1996).

19. Geoffrey Roberts, "Moscow and the Marshall Plan: Politics, Ideology and the Onset of the Cold War, 1947," *Europe-Asia Studies,* 46 (Dec. 1994): 1371–86; V. M. Zubok and Konstantin Pleshakov, *Inside the Kremlin's Cold War: From Stalin to Khrushchev* (Cambridge, Mass., 1996), 46–53.

20. William I. Hitchcock, *France Restored: Cold War Diplomacy and the Quest for Leadership in Europe, 1944–1954* (Chapel Hill, N.C., 1998).

21. Timothy P. Ireland, *Creating the Entangling Alliance: The Origins of the North Atlantic Treaty Organization* (Westport, Conn., 1981).

22. Michael Schaller, *The American Occupation of Japan: The Origins of the Cold War in Asia* (New York, 1985); Howard B. Schonberger, *Aftermath of War: Americans and the Remaking of Japan, 1945–1952* (Kent, Ohio, 1989); John W. Dower, *Embracing Defeat: Japan in the Wake of World War II* (New York, 1999), 271–73, 525–46.

23. Leffler, *Preponderance of Power,* 346–47, 393–94, 428–32, 464–65; Roger Dingman, "The Diplomacy of Dependency: The Philippines and Peacemaking with Japan," *Journal of Southeast Asian Studies,* 27 (Sept. 1986): 307–21; H. W. Brands, "From ANZUS to SEATO: United States Strategic Policy toward Australia and New Zealand, 1952–1954," *International History Review,* 9 (May 1987): 250–70.

24. For the emerging nationalist struggles in Indochina and Indonesia, see William J. Duiker, *Sacred War: Nationalism and Revolution in a Divided Vietnam* (New York, 1995); George McTurnan Kahin, *Nationalism and Revolution in Indonesia* (Ithaca, N.Y., 1952).

25. Odd Arne Westad, "The New International History of the Cold War: Three (Possible) Paradigms," *Diplomatic History,* 24 (Fall 2000): 551–65; David C. Engerman, Nils Gilman, Mark H. Haefele, and Michael E. Latham, eds., *Staging Growth: Modernization, Development, and the Global Cold War* (Amherst, Mass., 2003).

26. Mark Atwood Lawrence, "Transnational Coalition-Building and the Making of the Cold War in Indochina, 1947–1949," *Diplomatic History,* 26 (Summer 2002): 453–80; Andrew Jon Rotter, *The Path to Vietnam: Origins of the American Commitment to Southeast Asia* (Ithaca, N.Y., 1987).

27. For the importance of credibility, see the pathbreaking article by Robert J. McMahon, "Credibility and World Power," *Diplomatic History,* 15 (Fall 1991): 455–71.

28. NSC 68, "United States Objectives and Programs for National Security," April 14, 1950, in Thomas H. Etzold and John Lewis Gaddis, eds., *Containment: Documents on American Policy and Strategy, 1945–1950* (New York, 1978), 401–2; NSC 114/2, "Programs for National Security," October 12, 1951, Department of State, *Foreign Relations of the United States, 1951: National Security Affairs; Foreign Economic Policy* (Washington, D.C., 1979), 1:187–89.

29. For Soviet policy, see A. A. Fursenko and Timothy J. Naftali, *"One Hell of a Gamble": Khrushchev, Castro, and Kennedy, 1958–1964* (New York, 1997); Aleksandr Fursenko and Timothy Naftali, *Khrushchev's Cold War* (New York, 2005).

30. Peter Schweizer, *Reagan's War: The Epic Story of his Forty Year Struggle and Final Triumph Over Communism* (New York, 2002).

31. G. John Ikenberry, *After Victory: Institutions, Strategic Restraint, and the Rebuilding of Order After Major Wars* (Princeton, N.J., 2001), 163–214; Robert O. Keohane, *After Hegemony: Cooperation and Discord in the World Political Economy* (Princeton, N.J., 1984), especially 135–81; Michael Mandelbaum, *The Ideas that Conquered the World: Peace, Democracy and Free Markets in the Twenty-First Century* (New York, 2002); Geir Lundestad, *"Empire" by Integration: The United States and European Integration, 1945–1997* (New York, 1998); Gaddis, *We Now Know.*

TEACHING THE COLD WAR

FREDERICK W. JORDAN

Classroom teachers attempting to convey an understanding of the Cold War face a daunting array of challenges.[1] Perhaps the most obvious is that as a discrete event, the topic covers roughly a half century, running from the origins of the U.S.-Soviet conflict during the Second World War until the breakup of the Soviet Union on Christmas Day, 1991.[2] This wide scope is compounded by the fact that in most United States history textbooks, wedded as they are to a chronological framework, the Cold War is not treated as an isolated topic. Rather, the events that comprised the foremost international struggle of the century tend to be interspersed with (among others) Levittown, Jackie Robinson, the Kennedy assassination, Woodstock, Watergate, gas shortages, and supply-side economics.[3] Yet another difficulty lies in the essential nature of the conflict: What exactly should we teach about the Cold War? Was the struggle one of ideologies, geopolitical power, or national cultures? Finally, as with so many historical topics, one's own political inclinations also may inform the story. Conservatives can see in the Cold War a morality tale on a worldwide scale, a triumph of good over evil that affirms the positive values of democratic capitalism. Liberals also can draw moral lessons, but might see different villains—short-sighted policy makers who, in cahoots with the military-industrial complex, initiated an expensive arms race and overseas bloodletting, and who also showed little regard for civil liberties at home.

Melvin Leffler's article provides a superb overview of the Cold War as an international struggle for global hegemony. In the process, he neatly disposes of the idea that it was merely a bilateral contest between two superpowers. Central to Leffler's analysis is the point that third parties to the conflict often found in it opportunities to advance their own interests, and that inconsistencies in both U.S. and U.S.S.R. foreign policy often allowed them to do so. There was, in John Lewis Gaddis's phrase, only "the appearance of bipolarity—weaker states discovered numerous opportunities to confront, manipulate, or blunt the superpowers' conflict to their own ends."[4] This is perhaps less apparent in the early stage of the Cold War, which was largely conducted amid the ashes of Europe in the closing years of the Second World War and during the half decade immediately following. However, as the Cold War globalized after 1949, it converged with powerful forces of nationalism unleashed by the end of World War II—a volatile mix that produced what Leffler calls "transnational ideological conflict."[5]

The inaugural point of classroom discussion of the Cold War occurs in the study of the wartime diplomacy of the Grand Alliance during the Second World War. In my classes, I have made great use of Henry Luce's famous editorial, "The American Century," originally published in the February 17, 1941, issue of *Life* magazine. Writing with the fervor of a missionary (his parents were Christian missionaries in Asia), Luce proclaimed his supreme confidence in "great American ideals," which included "a love of freedom, a feeling for the equality of opportunity, a tradition of self-reliance and independence, and also of cooperation." But he reminded Americans of his day—who at the time were not an overly receptive audience—that to whom much was given, much was expected: "It now becomes our time to be the powerhouse from which the ideals spread throughout the world and do their mysterious work of lifting the life of mankind from the level of beasts to what the Psalmist called a little lower than the angels." Such a noble endeavor would only bear fruit, Luce continued, because of American prestige throughout the world, prestige that in turn rested on the innate goodness of the American people, buttressed by their "ultimate intelligence and strength."[6] It was a clarion call to transform the world, and one that would reverberate through American foreign policy for the next sixty years at least.

Discussion of the Luce document can launch a valuable debate on the nature of American power that often continues for the remainder of the course. The discussion centers on whether U.S. power is uniformly good (many—perhaps even the majority—of my students believe it is) and whether it is unlimited (fewer of them believe it is). The first aspect engages the age-old question of American character and in many classrooms may continue a year-long discussion for those students who have been introduced to Crevecoeur and de Tocqueville earlier in the course. Is the United States "good"? Are its core values of, say, individualism, pluralism, republicanism, and commitment to free-market capitalism, "exportable?"[7]

Debate over the second aspect—the extent of American power—will recur time and time again in studying the Cold War: Can America, with such great means (however they are measured), achieve any ends that it wishes, and in any part of the world? If not, what are the constraints on its power? Are there regions that lie beyond the effective reach of the United States? Are there cultures that are impervious to American power or influence? Are the nation's resources (whether military, economic, or psychological) limited in any way? Introducing these issues at the start is important because they will resurface in virtually every subsequent Cold War development: Kennan's theory of containment, American involvement in nation building in Vietnam, the Soviet placement of missiles in Cuba, or détente, to name but a few. (It comes as no surprise that students also tend to be alert to more contemporary applications.) Furthermore, this question can be used to analyze Soviet constraints as well. The constraints include the Berlin blockade in 1948, the erection of the Berlin Wall in 1961, the split with China in the 1950s, and the invasion of Afghanistan in 1979.

These issues regarding the nature and extent of American power are at the core of two World War II events that shaped relations between the United States and the U.S.S.R.: the Yalta Conference in February 1945 and Truman's decision to drop the atomic bomb in August 1945. At Yalta, could the United States have prevented Soviet domination of postwar eastern Europe, as critics of the conference subsequently charged? A few of my students endorse the view that the United States should have conducted a "postwar war" against the communists (a view that some of them seem to have derived from watching the movie *Patton*), while others see significant limitations to what FDR could have accomplished in constructing the postwar world. A copy of the Yalta accords is an invaluable tool here because it can be used to analyze the goals of

U.S. policy makers at the conference.[8] Similarly, Soviet hopes for the postwar world are illustrated by the transcript of the Tehran Conference (the first of the "Big Three" wartime meetings in 1943) and also by a March 1945 analysis of postwar Soviet aims offered by British minister Sir John Balfour.[9]

In studying these documents, students can see that Stalin wanted postwar security and a buffer zone that would prevent another invasion of his country through central Europe. The documents also illustrate U.S. war aims. FDR sought assurances of postwar democracy in eastern Europe but was also well aware of the context of heavy fighting on Iwo Jima and the attendant need for Russian aid to help conclude the Pacific war. (The atomic bomb was not successfully tested until July 1945, which changed the balance of power again.) Teachers can stimulate discussion regarding the decision to drop the bomb by posing the revisionist argument to students that the bomb was dropped to impress the Russians as much as it was to defeat the Japanese. I have often used the documents collected in the 1988 Advanced Placement Document-Based Question, as either tools for a classroom discussion or as an assigned paper.[10]

These issues frame the examination of the next stage of the Cold War: heightened tensions between the United States and the Soviet Union in the period from 1945 to 1949. There is a wealth of documentary evidence to employ here. Kennan's famous long telegram of February 1946 has been widely reprinted in both course readers and on the Internet.[11] I have also used Winston Churchill's 1946 "Iron Curtain" speech, Harry S Truman's address to Congress in March 1947, and the Soviet rejection of the Marshall Plan.[12] These documents can further stimulate discussion on the nature of American power in two ways. First, they allow students to see the economic dimension of power, which buttresses Leffler's point that "open markets and free peoples were inextricably intertwined." They also raise the question of whether economic power can achieve goals that are beyond the capabilities of military power. In this respect, I have found it helpful to introduce students to Joseph Nye's concept of "soft power," to which Leffler refers in his article. Soft power raises the question of other means (aside from military or economic power) by which a country can achieve its goals.[13]

It should be evident that up to this point the course reflects a fairly traditional approach to the Cold War as a study of a bilateral conflict between the United States and U.S.S.R. From 1945 to 1949, this is somewhat unavoidable. Most of the Cold War's early conflicts were waged in Europe, where third parties aligned themselves (or were forcibly aligned) with one of the two powers. Unilateral decision making was made more difficult because most European countries were devastated economically after World War II.[14] After

1949, however, this decisively changed, a point Leffler makes implicitly in his essay. Mao's victory in the Chinese Revolution (1949) and the outbreak of the Korean War in 1950 signaled both the globalization of the Cold War and the beginning of an era in which third parties would play greater roles in the conflict.

A good starting point for this is the Korean War. The CIA's initial assessment of the invasion can be used here, with its clear assumption that the Soviet Union was the sole impetus for the invasion.[15] This assumption sets up a straw man of unilateral action, which can be neatly dismantled by turning to other documents that display the complex relationship between the Soviet Union, North Korea, and China. A Soviet diplomat's assessment of the situation on the Korean peninsula in late 1949, which takes into account clear Korean and Chinese interests, illustrates this relationship. The transcript of a meeting between Stalin and North Korean leader Kim Il-Sung, in which Kim pressed the Soviet leader for assistance to reunite the two Koreas, makes the same point.[16] The resulting picture is more complex. Although it is still clear that the U.S.S.R. was actively engaged in starting the war, the Koreans and Chinese nevertheless emerge as autonomous actors in their own rights. Students can debate the extent to which third parties affected the course of the Cold War, and what national interest they sought in doing so.

Studying the Cuban Missile Crisis is another good opportunity to analyze the role of peripheral powers during the Cold War. The full-length Hollywood film *Thirteen Days* (2000) is an excellent illustration of the crisis. The film is a compelling drama that, for the most part, accurately portrays historical events.[17] If time permits, students can read either Robert Kennedy's memoir, *Thirteen Days* (1969), or Max Frankel's *High Noon in the Cold War* (2004).[18]

If the pressure of coverage in the survey course does not afford the luxury of such a detailed examination of the crisis, a briefer approach nevertheless presents an opportunity for spirited classroom debate. To this end, several documents are useful. The minutes of the National Security Council (the famed "ExComm") meeting on October 20, 1962, details the debates over the air strike and blockade options, as does a memorandum written three days earlier by CIA director John McCone.[19] My students tend to be particularly intrigued with the dual responses from Soviet Premier Nikita Khrushchev: the hard-line telegram of October 26 and the more conciliatory letter the following day can be paired, posing the question of how the students think JFK and the ExComm should have responded.[20] Robert McNamara's reminiscences in the award-winning documentary film *The Fog of War* (2000) can also drive the discussion forward.[21] Perhaps most jarring, however, is a letter from Fidel Castro to "Comrade Khrushchev" on October 26 at the height of the crisis. Castro's casual advocacy of nuclear war, "however harsh and terrible [this] solution might be," gives the students insight into the dynamics of a third-party "player" in the crisis. Classroom discussion can revolve around the question of Cuba's role and how it might have pressured the Soviets into an even stronger response than even perhaps Khrushchev intended.[22] Again, the teacher should emphasize a multilateral view of the Cold War during the discussion.

Study of this event also illustrates Leffler's conclusion that "[n]uclear weapons . . . produced paradoxical results." The Cuban Missile Crisis was arguably the most "frozen" part of the Cold War, an event so sobering that both protagonists sought to back away from the nuclear brink.[23] The result was the gradual, if uneven, thaw known as détente. Détente, in turn, laid the basis for the final decade and end to the Cold War. Détente was coupled with further globalization of the Cold War as the superpower rivalry intertwined itself with a bewildering array of political movements, internecine conflicts, covert operations, and wars (of both imperialism and independence) in Asia, Africa, and Central and South America. Some nations and movements sought to manipulate the Cold War to their own advantage, while others deliberately fended it off in what became known as the nonaligned movement.

This international montage affords a dizzying array of choices for the classroom teacher. Instructors can focus on South Africa, where the white minority regime tried to depict the Soviet Union as a threat in its efforts to quash the African National Congress.[24] The complexities of the 1975 Angolan revolution, which intertwined Angola, Portugal, Cuba, the United States, and the U.S.S.R., can be illustrated by examining documents from the U.S. National Security Council, Fidel Castro, one of Castro's ministers, and the Angolan leader Agostinho Neto.[25] But perhaps the best way to get at the role of third-world nations in the Cold War is by examining the Soviet Union's decision to intervene in Afghanistan. Jussie M. Hanhimäki and Odd Arne Westad provide a good selection of documents that include perspectives of the Soviet Politburo, Soviet Premier Brezhnev, NATO, and U.S. National Security adviser Zbigniew Brzezinski. These can be combined with documents from CNN's Web site: a transcript of a telephone conversation between Soviet Premier Kosygin and Afghan President Mohamed Taraki, and a fascinating document by several key Society policymakers, including Yuri Andropov and Andre Grmyko, makes clear the evident difficulties of intervention.[26]

Study of the final decade of the Cold War allows students to analyze its end. By this time, students should be able to discuss intelligently Leffler's conclusion that the United States won the war by conducting it on a number of different fronts: military, diplomatic, and cultural.

But if it was truly a multilateral conflict, then another question should also be engaged: was it a victory for the United States alone, or were other nations at all responsible for the outcome? In this respect, I find John Lewis Gaddis's recent book, *The Cold War: A New History*, to be extremely helpful. The book summarizes a lifetime of scholarship and provides a concise one-volume overview of the subject, appropriate for classroom use at the honors or Advanced Placement level.[27] Gaddis's chapter on the final stages of the Cold War is entitled "Actors," focusing on "leaders who through their challenges to the way things were and their ability to inspire audiences to follow them . . . confronted, neutralized, and overcame the forces that had for so long perpetuated the Cold War. Like all good actors, they brought the play at last to an end."[28] Ronald Reagan is given his due—Gaddis cites his "quiet persuasion, continued assistance to anti-Soviet resistance movements, and his always dramatic speeches."[29] But other participants also contributed to the end of the Cold War. They include Deng Xiaoping, Pope John Paul II, Lech Wałęsa, Mikhail Gorbachev, Václev Havel, Helmut Kohl, and Boris Yeltsin.[30] Teachers who want to address the relative contribution of each leader should assign the final chapters from Gaddis's book, or mine the wealth of document sources available from the period. Excerpts from the negotiations between striking workers in Gdansk, Poland, and officials from the Polish Communist Party illustrate the declining ability of the Soviet Union to compel behavior from its satellite states.[31] Ronald Reagan's belief that the Soviet system could not endure is evident in his 1982 speech to the British parliament.[32] Soviet Politburo debates show just how weak the U.S.S.R. was becoming by the mid-1980s.[33] A vivid description of the opening of Hungary's borders in September 1989 is offered by the British newspaper *Financial Times*.[34] And the drama comes to its end with an account, written by one of his assistants, of Mikhail Gorbachev's final day in his Kremlin office on Christmas Day, 1991.[35]

Leffler's essay offers a concise overview of the various lines of inquiry a classroom teacher might pursue in teaching the Cold War. The complicated interrelationship between military power, diplomacy, ideology, and national culture should serve to help wean high school students from monocausal explanations of historical events. Such complexity, however, presents considerable challenges for the instructor, particularly in the limited time offered in a standard survey course. Regardless of how one chooses to surmount these difficulties, the study of the Cold War can do for students today precisely what it did for Americans who lived through these events: take an insular people, who only gradually and reluctantly became involved in worldwide events, and introduce them to the influence of far-away places on national life.

Annotated Bibliography

CNN's *The Cold War* is an exhaustive (twenty-four-episode) video documentary of the Cold War. As a visual source it is unsurpassed, but its level of detail renders it problematic for classroom use as few teachers will want to spend an entire class period on, say, the Marshall Plan, the impact of *Sputnik,* or the Red Spring of 1968. The accompanying Web site, at <http://www.cnn.com/SPECIALS/cold.war/>, contains a wealth of resources, including an *Educator's Guide,* which correlates the episodes to themes developed by the National Council for History Education. It is easily adapted to testing mandates in particular states. The *Guide* also contains worksheets for evaluating primary sources, maps, and links to other resources, and also has the complete script of each episode.

Gaddis, John Lewis. *The Cold War: A New History.* New York, 2005. A terrific overview by one of the foremost authorities on the Cold War. Suitable for classroom use in a survey course (it has 266 pages of text) as long as you do not want to read much else outside the survey text.

George Washington University, *National Security Archive* [online:] <http://www.gwu.edu/~nsarchiv/>. Though primarily focused on contemporary issues pertaining to national security, the Web site contains a great many resources for Cold War studies.

Hanhimäki, Jussie M. and Odd Arne Westad, eds., *The Cold War: A History in Documents and Eyewitness Accounts* (Oxford, 2003) is a superb collection of more than six hundred pages of documents, including twenty political cartoons, pertaining to the Cold War. An invaluable resource.

Leffler, Melvin. *A Preponderance of Power: National Security, the Truman Administration, and the Cold War.* Stanford, Calif., 1993. Winner of the 1993 Bancroft Prize, this is a superb survey of the early stages of the Cold War through the Truman administration. Leffler produced a brief history of the Cold War, *The Specter of Communism: The United States and the Origins of the Cold War, 1917–1953* (New York, 1994), which I have used to good effect in an AP-level survey course.

United States Department of State has a massive resource, *Foreign Relations of the United States,* available online at <http://www.state.gov/r/pa/ho/frus/>. It consists of more than 350 print volumes digitized into an electronic archive, with pertinent documents drawn from every presidential administration from Lincoln through Nixon.

Woodrow Wilson International Center for Scholars, *Cold War International History Project: Virtual Archive 2.0,* located at <http://www.wilsoncenter.org/index

.cfm?topic_id=1409&fuseaction=topics.home> provides a wealth of documents devoted to studying the Cold War in an international context.

Westad, Odd Arne. *The Global Cold War: Third World Interventions and the Making of Our Times.* Cambridge, 2005. One of the seminal volumes to foment the concept of "Cold War International History" and winner of the 2006 Bancroft Prize. In a densely woven argument, Westad sees the Cold War as a byproduct of nineteenth-century European imperialism, a struggle that laid the basis for today's poor relations between the "pan-European states and other parts of the world" (396).

Notes

1. I am grateful to my colleague at Woodberry Forest, Matt Boesen, for his thoughtful critique of this article. A number of these ideas originated in his classroom. Some of the other teaching strategies in this overview are the product of optimism rather than experience, because I have not "test-driven" all the suggestions offered.

2. Conflict between the two nations can actually be said to have begun with the Bolshevik Revolution in 1917, but the term "the Cold War" is usually reserved for the post–World War II era.

3. For a representative treatment, see James West Davidson et al., *Nation of Nations: A Narrative History of the American Republic,* 5th ed. (1990, 2005), 888–99, 912–20, 933–39, 958–64, 968–72, 1011–21, 1055–58, 1089–90. My own sense is that a rigid chronological framework blurs themes, and that students would benefit greatly if survey textbook authors would organize the post-1945 material thematically, as so many already do for the period between Reconstruction and the Progressive Era.

4. John Lewis Gaddis, *The Cold War: A New History* (New York, 2005), 120.

5. Leffler, however, still sees the heart of the conflict in the superpower struggle. For a view that places more emphasis on the role of third world countries in the struggle, see Odd Arne Westad, *The Global Cold War: Third World Interventions and the Making of Our Times* (Cambridge, Eng., 2005). Westad maintains that "the most important aspects of the Cold War were neither military nor strategic, nor Europe-centered, but connected to political and social development of the Third World" (396). It should therefore be seen in the context of colonialism rather than as a struggle within the Western transatlantic world.

6. The editorial is available in the original issue of *Life* and was reprinted in the *Washington Post,* March 5, 1941, 8. An excerpt is available at Columbia American History Online, <http://caho-test.cc.columbia.edu/ps/10095.html>, accessed July 2007. Luce later elaborated on the argument in his book, *The American Century* (New York, 1941).

7. Drawing up a list of these values is an interesting class exercise in and of itself.

8. A copy is available at the CNN Web site associated with that network's mammoth twenty-four-episode video documentary of the Cold War; see CNN Interactive, "Episode 1: Comrades" [online] at <http://www.cnn.com/SPECIALS/cold.war/

episodes/01/documents/yalta.html. The Web site also has an interactive game, "Take Stalin's Seat at Yalta," which, though somewhat simplistic, can be utilized in getting students to see the Soviet point of view: <www.cnn.com/SPECIALS/cold.war/episodes/01/game>.

9. "Stalin, Roosevelt, and Churchill on the Future of Europe, December 1943" and "British View of Post-war Soviet Aims, March 1945," in Jussie M. Hanhimäki and Odd Arne Westad, *The Cold War: A History in Documents and Eyewitness Accounts* (Oxford, 2003), 26–32.

10. The DBQ is reprinted in *Doing The DBQ—Advanced Placement U.S. History Examination: Teaching and Learning with the Document Based Question* (New York, 2000). My own view is that the documents in the question are tilted somewhat in favor of the revisionist position.

11. Excerpts from the "long telegram" are available at CNN Interactive, "Episode 2: Iron Curtain: 1945–1947" [online] at <http://www.cnn.com/SPECIALS/cold.war/episodes/02/documents/kennan/>, accessed July, 2006. It is also available in its more polished form (attributed to "X"), "The Sources of Soviet Conduct," *Foreign Affairs* (July 1947), available online at <http://www.foreignaffairs.org/19470701faessay25403/x/the-sources-of-soviet-conduct.html>.

12. CNN Interactive, "Episode 2: Iron Curtain: 1945–1947," "Churchill's Iron Curtain Speech," and "Episode 3: Marshall Plan, 1947–1952," "Truman Doctrine," and "Vyshinsky U.N. Address."

13. Joseph S. Nye Jr., *Soft Power: The Means to Success in World Politics* (New York, 2004).

14. This is admittedly simplistic. There is some scholarship that sees U.S. involvement in Europe during this period as "invited" by European nations out of their own desire to contain the Soviet Union. See Geir Lundestad, "How (Not) to Study the Origins of the Cold War," in Odd Arne Westad, ed., *Reviewing the Cold War: Approaches, Interpretations, Theory* (London, 2000), 66. Nonetheless, the superpowers' actions were less constrained by third parties during this period than they would be after 1949.

15. "CIA Analysis of North Korean Invasion," at CNN Interactive, "Episode 5, Korea" [online]: <http://www.cnn.com/SPECIALS/cold.war/episodes/05/documents/cia/>, last accessed August 2006.

16. "Telegram from Tunkin to Soviet Foreign Ministry, in reply to 11 September telegram," Cold War International History Project [online]: <http://www.wilsoncenter.org/index.cfm?topic_id=1409&fuseaction=va2.browse&sort=Collection&item=The%20Korean%20War>, last accessed August 2006; "Stalin Meets Kim Il-Sung, March 1949," in Hanhimäki and Westad, eds., *The Cold War,* 181–83; this document, differently titled "Stalin's Meeting with Kim Il-Sung," is also available at Cold War International History Project [online]: <http://www.wilsoncenter.org/index.cfm?topic_id=1409&fuseaction=va2.browse&sort=Collection&item=The%20Korean%20War>, last accessed August 2006.

17. Much of the script was taken directly from historical transcripts of the events, including the emotional confrontation at the United Nations between U.S. ambassador Adlai Stevenson and Russian envoy Valerian Zorin ("Yes or no—don't wait for the translation—yes or no?"); a copy of the transcript is available in Hanhimäki and Westad, eds., *The Cold War,* 485–87. For a good review of the movie that analyzes both its strengths and inaccuracies, see Philip Brenner, "Turning History On Its Head," The George Washington University, The National Security Archive [online]: <http://www.gwu.edu/~nsarchiv/nsa/cuba_mis_cri/brenner.htm>, last accessed August 2006.

18. Max Frankel, *High Noon in the Cold War: Kennedy, Khrushchev and the Cuban Missile Crisis* (New York, 2004). My colleague Matt Boesen has used both in conjunction with the movie in his survey course.

19. The Avalon Project at Yale Law School, "Foreign Relations of the United States: 1961–1963 Cuban Missile Crisis and Aftermath," document #34 [online]: <http://www.yale.edu/lawweb/avalon/diplomacy/forrel/cuba/cuba036.htm>, last accessed August 2006; "Memorandum by Director of Central Intelligence McCone," October 17, 1962, *Foreign Relations of the United States, 1961–1963, vol. XI, Cuban Missile Crisis and Aftermath* [online]: United States Department of State, <http://www.state.gov/www/about_state/history/frusXI/26_50.html>, last accessed August 2006.

20. Ibid., documents #48 and 61. The letters are also available at <http://www.mtholyoke.edu/acad/intrel/nikita2.htm> and <http://www.mtholyoke.edu/acad/intrel/nikita3.htm>.

21. The film is widely available for purchase. Its official Web site, <http://www.sonyclassics.com/fogofwar/indexFlash.html>, contains lesson plans, samples of the video, rebuttals of negative reviews, and pertinent links.

22. A copy is available online at George Washington University. The National Security Archive [online]: <http://www.gwu.edu/~nsarchiv/nsa/cuba_mis_cri/docs.htm>, last accessed August 2006. Other documents are available in Laurence Chang and Peter Kornbluth, eds., *The Cuban Missile Crisis, 1962: A National Security Archive Documents Reader* (New York, 1999).

23. Melvin Leffler made this point at the Robert Cross Memorial Lecture at the University of Virginia in January 2006.

24. Hanhimäki and Westad, eds., *The Cold War,* 438.

25. The first two are available in Hanhimäki and Westad, eds., *The Cold War,* 518–28, which also contains a cartoon, "Kissinger and Angola," from a British source. The second two may be accessed at CNN Interactive, "Episode 17: Good Guys, Bad Guys," [online] at <http://www.cnn.com/SPECIALS/cold.war/episodes/17/documents/angola/>.

26. Hanhimäki and Westad, eds., *The Cold War,* 544–52; CNN Interactive, "Episode 20: Soldiers of God," [online] at <http://www.cnn.com/SPECIALS/cold.war/episodes/20/>. These documents are supplemented by nearly two dozen others at George Washington University's Web site, The National Security Archive, "Volume

II: Afghanistan: Lessons Learned from the Last War," [online] at <http://www.gwu
.edu/~nsarchiv/NSAEBB/NSAEBB57/soviet.html>, last accessed November 2006.

27. Use of this volume does, however, address in part the dilemma so often raised
by AP teachers, that of what to do after the AP exam in the second week of May.
The College Board's current policy is that no essay question will be exclusively devoted to the post-1980 period, though some components of individual essays and
some multiple-choice questions may address that era. Use of Gaddis's book and its
post-1980 chapters—roughly a quarter of the volume—provides but one example of
the use of monographs that would allow teachers to continue fruitful study of United
States history even after the AP exam.

28. Gaddis, *The Cold War,* 199.

29. Ibid., 235.

30. Ibid., 195–257.

31. Hanhimäki and Westad, eds., *The Cold War,* 568–71.

32. Ibid., 573–75.

33. Ibid., 575–78.

34. Ibid., 600–602.

35. Ibid., 625–27.

CONTRIBUTORS

DAVID ARMITAGE is a professor of history at Harvard University. He is the author of *The Declaration of Independence: A Global History* (2006); *Greater Britain, 1516–1776: Essays in Atlantic History* (2004); and *The Ideological Origins of the British Empire* (2000). He is the editor of *British Political Thought in History, Literature, and Theory* (2006); Grotius's *The Free Sea* (2004); and *Theories of Empire, 1450–1800* (1998); and coeditor of *The British Atlantic World, 1500–1800* (2002), and *Milton and Republicanism* (1995). Armitage is currently working on a study of the foundations of modern international thought and an edition of John Locke's colonial writings.

STEPHEN ARON is professor of history at UCLA and executive director of the Institute for the Study of American West at the Autry National Center. He is the author of *How the West Was Lost: The Transformation of Kentucky from Daniel Boone to Henry Clay* (1996) and coauthor of *Worlds Together, Worlds Apart: A History of the Modern World from the Mongol Empire to the Present* (2002). His latest book is *American Confluence: The Missouri Frontier from Borderland to Border State* (2006).

EDWARD L. AYERS is president of the University of Richmond and formerly the Buckner W. Clay Dean of Arts and Sciences and the Hugh P. Kelly Professor of History at the University of Virginia. He has published extensively on nineteenth-century southern history. His most recent publication is *In the Presence of Mine Enemies: War in the Heart of America, 1859–1863* (2003), which received the Bancroft Prize. An earlier book, *The Promise of the New South* (1992), was a finalist for both the Pulitzer Prize and the National Book

Award. In addition, Ayers is a pioneer in digital media with his prize-winning Internet site, "Valley of the Shadow: Two Communities in the American Civil War," containing original sources related to two towns at either end of the Shenandoah Valley, one in Virginia and the other in Pennsylvania. For more information, visit http://valley.vcdh.virginia.edu.

THOMAS BENDER is University Professor of the Humanities and professor of history at New York University where he also directs its International Center for Advanced Studies. With research interests in cultural and intellectual history, Bender has published most recently *A Nation among Nations: America's Place in World History* (2006), *The Education of Historians for the Twenty-First Century* (2004), and *The Unfinished City: New York and the Metropolitan Idea* (2002). His leadership in the field of transnational and comparative history led to his involvement in the Project on Internationalizing the Study of American History, a joint initiative between the Organization of American Historians and New York University's International Center for Advanced Studies. To learn more about this project, visit http://www.oah.org/pubs/lapietra.

STUART M. BLUMIN is professor of history at Cornell University and director of the Cornell-in-Washington Program. He is the author of *The Emergence of the Middle Class: Social Experience in the American City, 1760–1900* (1989) and (with Glenn C. Altschuler) *Rude Republic: Americans and Their Politics in the Nineteenth Century* (2000). His many articles include "Limits of Political Engagement in Antebellum America: A New Look at the Golden Age of Participatory Democracy" (coauthored with Glenn Altschuler), which appeared in the *Journal of American History* and was awarded the OAH Binkley-Stephenson prize in 1997. His most recent work, *The Encompassing City: Streetscapes in Early Modern Art and Culture*, is forthcoming.

J. D. BOWERS is an assistant professor of American history at Northern Illinois University where he also directs the secondary teacher certification program for history and the social sciences. Bowers previously taught history in Hawaii, Virginia, and Uruguay, and is involved with a Teaching American History grant strengthening the teaching of U.S. history in the Woodstock, DeKalb, Harvard, Belvidere, and Prairie Grove public school districts in Illinois.

ORVILLE VERNON BURTON is University Distinguished Teacher/Scholar, professor of history, African American studies, and sociology at the University of Illinois, Urbana-Champaign. He is also Director, Institute for Computing in Humanities, Arts, and Social Science, and Associate Director for Humanities and Social Sciences at the National Center for Supercomputing Applications. His publications include *In My Father's House Are Many Mansions: Family and Community in Edgefield, South Carolina* (1985; fifth printing in 1998), *"A Gentleman and an Officer": A Social and Military History of James B. Griffin's Civil War* (1996), and two books coedited with Robert C. McMath Jr. on nineteenth-century southern communities. Burton's research and teaching interests include race relations, family, community, politics, religion, and the intersection of humanities and social sciences. His newest book is *The Age of Lincoln* (2007).

LAWRENCE CHARAP is head of the history and social sciences content development group, Advanced Placement Program, at the College Board. Charap received his doctorate in U.S. history from Johns Hopkins University and has taught U.S. and world history at the high school and college levels.

JONATHAN CHU is associate professor of early American history and associate dean of the Graduate College of Education at the University of Massachusetts, Boston. With research interests in American colonial and legal history, Chu currently focuses on the legal and economic impact of the American Revolution on Massachusetts. He is the author of *Neighbors, Friends, or Madmen: The Puritan Adjustment to Quakerism in Seventeenth-Century Massachusetts Bay* (1985).

KATHLEEN DALTON is visiting associate professor of history at Boston University. Author of *Theodore Roosevelt: A Strenuous Life* (2002) and *A Portrait of a School: Coeducation at Andover* (1986), she has spoken widely about Theodore Roosevelt, including appearances on C-SPAN's *Book TV*, the History Channel, the Arts and Entertainment Channel, and public television; her writing has appeared in numerous newspapers. She is currently working on her next book, *The White Lilies and the Iron Boot*, a story of four friends (including Eleanor and Franklin Roosevelt) and their attempts to shape U.S. foreign relations during a dangerous time.

BETTY A. DESSANTS is associate professor of history at Shippensburg University where she specializes in post-1945 U.S. history, particularly Cold War foreign relations and society. She has published in the field of World War II and Cold War intelligence and is coauthor of *The Chicago Handbook for Teachers: A Practical Guide to the College Classroom*.

EDWARD M. (TED) DICKSON is chair of the history department at Providence Day School in Charlotte, North Carolina, a consultant for the College Board, and a reader for the Advanced Placement U.S history examinations. His classroom simulations on historical thinking have been published in the *OAH Magazine of History.* A frequent presenter at both regional and national conferences, he received the 2002 Tachau Teacher of the Year Award from the Organization of American Historians. He also served on the ad hoc OAH/AP Joint Advisory Board on Teaching the U.S. History Survey that guided this project.

KEVIN GAINES is professor of history at the University of Michigan, Ann Arbor, where he also directs the Center for Afroamerican and African Studies. His new book is *American Africans in Ghana: Black Expatriates and the Civil Rights Era* (2006). He is also the author of *Uplifting the Race: Black Leadership, Politics, and Culture during the Twentieth Century* (1996).

FREDERICK W. JORDAN teaches U.S., ancient, and medieval history in the history department, which he also chairs, at Woodberry Forest School in Virginia. A reader and examination leader for the Advanced Placement U.S. history exam, Jordan has a Ph.D. from the University of Notre Dame where he wrote his dissertation on the role of religion in American boarding schools.

MELVYN P. LEFFLER is the Edward Stettinius Professor of American History at the University of Virginia. Currently, he is the Jennings Randolph Fellow at the United States Institute of Peace and holds the Henry Kissinger Chair at the Library of Congress. His book *A Preponderance of Power: National Security, the Truman Administration, and the Cold War* (1993) won the Bancroft, Ferrell, and Hoover prizes. His recent book *For the Soul of Mankind: The United States, the Soviet Union and the Cold War* (2007) examines the history of the Cold War from vantage points in Washington, D.C., and Moscow, the downfall of communism, and how this era influenced U.S. and Soviet policies for decades.

LOUISA BOND MOFFITT teaches history at the Marist School in Atlanta, Georgia. Moffitt is a specialist in and author of curriculum units in Middle East studies. Moffitt earned her bachelor's degree at Emory University and received her doctoral degree from Georgia State University.

PHILIP D. MORGAN is the Sidney and Ruth Lapidus Professor in the American Revolutionary Era at Princeton University. His book *Slave Counterpoint:*

Black Culture in the Eighteenth-Century Chesapeake and Lowcountry (1998) won the Bancroft, Beveridge, and Frederick Douglass prizes. He is coeditor of *Colonial Chesapeake Society* (1988), *Strangers within the Realm: Cultural Margins of the First British Empire* (1991), and *Black Experience and the British Empire* (2004). He is working at the interface of Caribbean and North American history in the early modern era.

MARK A. NOLL is the Francis A. McAnaney Professor of History at the University of Notre Dame. He is the author of *America's God: From Jonathan Edwards to Abraham Lincoln* (2002); *The Rise of Evangelicalism: The Age of Edwards, Whitefield, and the Wesleys* (2003); *Is the Reformation Over? An Evangelical Assessment of Contemporary Roman Catholicism* (2005); and *The Civil War as a Theological Crisis* (2006).

GARY W. REICHARD is executive vice chancellor and chief academic officer at the California State University and has held previous teaching and administrative appointments at the Ohio State University, the University of Delaware, the University of Maryland, Florida Atlantic University, and California State University, Long Beach. A former chair of the OAH Committee on Teaching, he holds a Ph.D. in history from Cornell University and has recently revised and reprinted his book *Politics as Usual: The Age of Truman and Eisenhower* (2004).

DANIEL T. RODGERS is the Henry Charles Lea Professor of History at Princeton University. He is the author of *The Work Ethic in Industrial America* (1978), *Contested Truths: Key Words in American Politics since Independence* (1987), and *Atlantic Crossings: Social Politics in a Progressive Age* (1998), which received the Ellis W. Hawley Prize of the Organization of American Historians and the George Louis Beer Prize of the American Historical Association.

LEILA J. RUPP is a professor of women's studies and associate dean of social sciences at the University of California, Santa Barbara. Her teaching and research focus on sexuality and women's movements. A historian by training, she is coauthor with Verta Taylor of *Drag Queens at the 801 Cabaret* (2003) and *Survival in the Doldrums: The American Women's Rights Movement, 1945 to the 1960s* (1987) and author of *A Desired Past: A Short History of Same-Sex Sexuality in America* (1999), *Worlds of Women: The Making of an International Women's Movement* (1997), and *Mobilizing Women for War: German and American Propaganda, 1939–1945* (1978). She is currently working on a new book, *Sapphistries: A Global History of Love Between Women*.

BRENDA SANTOS received her bachelor's degree from the University of Massachusetts at Amherst and is a graduate of the New York University Graduate School of Education. Currently enrolled in the Ph.D. program at Yale University's Department of History, Santos teaches at Amistad Academy High School in New Haven, Connecticut.

GLORIA SESSO teaches history at Half Hollow Hills High School East in Dix Hills, New York, and is director of social studies in Patchogue-Medford School District. Winner of the inaugural Tachau Teacher of the Year Award from the Organization of American Historians in 1995, Sesso has authored many curriculum units in American history, geography, and social sciences. She is currently president of the Long Island Council for the Social Studies.

CAROLE SHAMMAS is the John R. Hubbard Chair in History at the University of Southern California. Shammas specializes in the socioeconomic history of Britain and English-speaking North America prior to the mid-nineteenth century. She is the author of *A History of Household Government in America* (2002) and *The Pre-Industrial Consumer in England* (1990) and coeditor of *The Creation of the British Atlantic World* (2005).

SUZANNE M. SINKE is an associate professor of history at Florida State University. A specialist in immigration and gender studies in the U.S. context, she teaches a variety of courses in U.S. and comparative social history. She is the author of *Dutch Immigrant Women in the United States, 1880–1920* (2002) and coeditor of *Letters across Borders: The Epistolary Practices of International Migrants* (2006) and *A Century of European Migrations, 1830–1930* (1991). She has published many articles on women and migration.

OMAR VALERIO-JIMENEZ is assistant professor of history at the University of Iowa where he teaches immigration, comparative borderlands, ethnic relations, the American West, and Latina/o history. Valerio-Jimenez received his Ph.D. from the University of California, Los Angeles. His book *Rio Grande Crossings: Identity and Nation in the Mexico-Texas Borderlands, 1749–1890* is forthcoming from Duke University Press.

PENNY M. VON ESCHEN is professor of history and American culture at the University of Michigan. She is the author of *Satchmo Blows Up the World: Jazz Ambassadors Play the Cold War* (2004) and *Race against Empire: Black Americans and Anticolonialism, 1937–1957* (1997). She is currently working on a transnational study of memory and the Cold War.

PATRICK WOLFE is an Australian Research Council research fellow in history at La Trobe University, Australia. He has written, taught, and lectured on race, imperialism, the history of anthropology, and Aboriginal history. He is currently working on a comparative history of the racialization of four colonized populations: Australian Aborigines, African Americans, North American Indians, and Afro-Brazilians.

PINGCHAO ZHU is an associate professor in the history department at the University of Idaho where she specializes in East Asian history, U.S.–China relations, and U.S. diplomatic history. Zhu received her Ph.D. from Miami University (Ohio). Zhu's book *Americans and Chinese at the Korean War Cease-Fire Negotiations, 1950–1953* (2001) examines U.S.–China negotiation strategy during the Korean War armistice talks.

INDEX

The University of Illinois Press
is a founding member of the
Association of American University Presses.

_____

Composed in 10.5/13 Minion Pro
with Frutiger display
by Jim Proefrock
at the University of Illinois Press
Designed by Kelly Gray
Manufactured by Sheridan Books, Inc.

University of Illinois Press
1325 South Oak Street
Champaign, IL 61820-6903
www.press.uillinois.edu